The History of Civilization

Edited by C. K. OGDEN, M.A.

Primitive Italy

Primitive Italy

and the

Beginnings of Roman Imperialism

By

LÉON HOMO

NEW YORK

BARNES & NOBLE, INC.

*Published in the United States of America 1968
by Barnes & Noble, Inc., New York, N.Y.*

*First published in Great Britain in 1927
by Kegan Paul, Trench, Trübner & Co Ltd.*

Printed in Great Britain

FOREWORD

THE MIRACLE OF ROME

*T*HERE *is nothing more remarkable in world history than the concatenation of contingencies that led to Rome's assumption of the leading rôle, different from that of Athens, but no less important. And so we may speak of the miracle of Rome in the sense which we have previously defined—a surprising conjunction of circumstances, an exceptional success.*[1] *A combination of contingencies had created the city—which was to create the Empire, an empire better organized than any that had gone before, equipped with so strong an armament that it would survive as a model when the Empire had itself crumbled to pieces.*

What is known of primitive Italy, the birth of Rome, her growth, the extension of her conquering activity, the gradual assimilation of the peoples of Italy and then of the Mediterranean, is the subject matter of the volumes which open and close the series on Rome (Primitive Italy *and* The Roman Empire). *Three volumes define the nature and action of this Roman genius which has produced such astonishing results so surely—at least in appearance. One, designed to study the work of thought and play, defines what original contribution this genius made or what it owed to Greece in the life of the spirit. Two others reveal it at work perfecting social life. Finally, two volumes, attached to this series, are designed respectively to summarize and trace in the Roman world the economic development of humanity and to introduce the Celts, since it is through their contact with Rome that the latter truly began to play their part in world history. As the reader knows, we have adopted this principle: since historical exposition cannot deal simultaneously with all the varied and unequally significant facts which take place at the same time, we introduce the several countries and peoples at the precise moment when they become active elements in evolution, accelerating or retarding factors of logic.*

[1] *Foreword to A. Jardé's* The Formation of the Greek People.

v

FOREWORD

It is a happy contingency that two peoples existed in the Mediterranean basin endowed with such contrasted gifts as the Greeks and the Romans. The Roman was as practical, prosaic, prudent, and realistic as the Greek was unfettered, mobile, inventive, speculative, and idealistic in spirit. He had a feeling for discipline and a taste for order. He was intellectually timid, but bold and aggressive in the conduct of life. He lacked imagination, but was endowed with a remarkable strength of mind.

Is this character the expression of "race" or of "environment"? Here the reader will see fully verified the theses of our collaborators, Eug. Pittard and L. Febvre. In origin the Romans are an ethnic compost,[1] and this composite "race"—in which the brachycephals seem to have been predominant—was like a crucible in which the most diverse elements continued to be fused. The environment secured certain advantages, but, a land suited for division and regionalism, it presented obstacles: self-interest made use of some and will triumphed over others.[2]

History, far more than anthropology and geography— we observe it more and more—is logic. Contingency furthers or hinders this logic, but it is the principle of intelligibility.

In this volume the reader watches the building, stage by stage, of this empire, one of the vastest that the world has ever seen, and the one which, we repeat, has undoubtedly exercised the most decisive influence on the organization of human societies.

The subject dealt with here has attracted many great spirits, a Machiavelli, a Bossuet, a Montesquieu. But its study is resumed with fresh resources and with all aids with which history is to-day provided by auxiliary sciences— anthropology, archæology, epigraphy, and philology. The fact cannot be over-emphasized that history is gradually being transformed by the convergence of the results of the most diverse disciplines, some of which are, in a sense, militant and wrest from the earth the secrets of the past. The history of Rome had been arranged by the Roman annalists, and a portion of this arrangement had passed

[1] *See especially pp.* 42, 44, *and Pittard, Part II. chap. iv.*
[2] *See pp.* 68, 71, 79, *and* 98.

FOREWORD

into the historical canon, so to speak. Now the reality of her origins is becoming visible stripped of adornments. And in this volume, so accurate and illuminating, the results of long and multiple efforts, hitherto but little known, will replace the legend and will enter the domain of common knowledge.

The lamented Jacques de Morgan has painted his picture of Prehistoric Man in masterly outlines on a vast canvas. In the present volume it is fascinating to watch the details being filled in as far as the early populations of Italy are concerned, as has been or will be done in other domains in some volumes of our first section. The rôle of the Etruscans in particular, that strange people which, side by side with the Hittites and the Ægeans, has been one of the latest and most curious revelations of history, is now clear and distinct. And an arresting spectacle, novel for those who have not followed step by step the works of erudition, is provided by the formation of the city herself—diverse tribes, distinct villages upon the hills, a frontier in the Tiber plain, conflicts and alliances alike inspired by economic interests, a unity in course of creation which becomes unifying.

Unity did not radiate over Greece from any Greek city.[1] Despite the phalanx, Macedon missed Balkanic unity. The civitas romana expanded to embrace the whole world. How was it that Urbs and Orbis ended by coinciding? How was Roman order, the pax romana, established?

For long, failing the designs of Providence, men pinned their faith at least to the designs of the Senate:

Tu regere imperio populos, Romane, memento.

And this idea—the Senate deliberately resolved " to invade every land "—is to-day far from being eliminated. " We are prone to imagine them (the Patres) pursuing step by step, with an unerring and patient ' method,' without letting themselves be distracted from an object once envisaged, the execution of grandiose ' plans ' boldly conceived."[2] One historian has just commenced the assault upon this teleological interpretation with great vivacity. In

[1] See Jardé in The Formation of the Greek People.
[2] M. Holleaux, Rome, la Grèce et les monarchies hellénistiques au IIIe siècle avant J.C., p. 169.

vii

FOREWORD

a work rich in erudition, powerfully built up and thought out, M. Holleaux attempts to prove that everything in Roman policy was just the result of accident, chance, fortune, adventure. " Without precautions, our historians," says M. Holleaux,[1] *" assume at the outset as an axiom that things could not have been different from what they were. At bottom what they declare fated is simply what has happened."* For example, *when the Romans conquered Greece, that was not in the least in virtue of " the invincible attraction exerted upon them at all times by Hellenism, of the instinctive force which urged them towards it, of psychological laws which required that they should become masters of the Greek States and of their long-standing and fixed resolve to subjugate them."[2]* On the contrary, *" it was through an accident and an error of judgment that the* Patres *took the first steps along the path that, leading them further than they ever intended to go, ended in the final establishment of Roman domination over all Hellenism—an ending quite unexpected, and by no means desired by the Senators."[3]*

 M. Holleaux has drawn a psychological portrait of the Patres, *which is striking and contains undeniable truths.[4] He describes " these rich rustics who filled the Senate . . . and whose foreign policy . . . was conditioned by their slowness of mind and poverty of imagination, as well as by the many scruples, the hatred of innovation, the fear of adventure, the timidity in face of the unknown, natural to peasant souls."[5] But as has been justly remarked, the senators were not all at the same time and to an equal degree slow-minded, timid, ignorant of foreign affairs, and indifferent to high policy.[6]*

 " We must picture the Roman neither as a stupid boor nor as a superman."[7] The scientific and complex explanation of imperialism, free from all a priori *ideas and prejudices, is found by our collaborator in the combination of*

---

[1] Op. cit., *p.* 127.   [2] Ibid., *p. iii.*
[3] Ibid., *p.* 334.   [4] Ibid., *pp.* 169-172.
[5] Ibid., *p.* 171.
[6] See A. Jardé, *" L'Histoire de l'Antiquité, méthodes et résultats, à propos d'un livre récent "* (Holleaux) *in the* Revue de Synth. hist., *vol.* xxxv (1923), *pp.* 117-132.
[7] Homo, *p.* 255.

circumstances and the Roman character. We must recognize, and recognize freely, the part played by " intelligences and wills." Some chapters of this book, setting forth in detail within narrow limits of space and time the full complexity of contingencies, only serve to emphasize the directive activity of man, and its rôle, not indeed exclusive but still undeniable, in Rome's history.

Here the reader sees the unification of Italy and the extension of the Empire being accomplished, in default of a comprehensive scheme, through the pursuit of " definite and immediate ends," attainable easily by preventive war waged at the right moment and through the patient solution of problems which forced themselves on the Romans' attention and always led on to others. He will observe in particular the growing importance of economic problems and an increasingly deliberate effort to solve them.

On the other hand, these pages disclose the pressure exerted upon these intelligences and wills by certain historical precedents—for instance, the Etruscan Empire. For there had been an Etruscan Empire, a form which lacked the political organization, the military force, and the judicial equipment to enable it to last, but which Rome was never to forget. " She will grow with her eyes obstinately fixed upon the glorious past which Etruria had once given her and from the religion of memory she will draw one of the primordial elements in her wondrous progress."[1] We find it more difficult to believe in the survival in Rome's memory of a remote European empire—because we do not believe in this empire itself. We consider questionable the idea, so seductively set forth by M. Jullian, and here adopted by M. Homo,[2] that there had been a European State and a European language. It seems to us that there has been here a confusion between the unity of similarity and the unity of organization.[3]

These pages also serve to bring out the suggestive power of military institutions which are at once cause and effect in the formation of a great State. The present volume, with others that have appeared or are to appear in the Evolution of Humanity, *will contribute to the study of that phenomenon*

---

[1] *Homo*, pp. 127-8.   [2] *See p.* 46.
[3] *Cf.* The Earth and Human Evolution, *Foreword.*

so closely connected with imperialism—war.[1] *We have already insisted, in reference to Mesopotamia, for instance, on the fact that, after a certain phase in protohistory, war has been endemic among human groups.*[2] *If Rome gave to the world the benefits of peace, and that for several centuries, it was only after triumphing over other imperialisms, notably the imperialism of Carthage. It was through continuous wars that her qualities, discipline, courage, and tenacity, culminated in successive victories, and that her organizing genius gradually perfected the instrument proper to victory. The massive force of the legion, experience of command, the science of tactics and strategy—when she had at her disposal advantages which a hitherto unequalled military power gave her, she had to go on from defensive to preventive wars, and then to the conquest and exploitation of the whole Mediterranean basin. " From the ability to the will is a short step;" one is drawn on inevitably and imperceptibly. A people whose energy is fired is doomed to ambition. Of this advance, "slow but implacable as a phenomenon of nature,"*[3] *L. Homo gives an account that is a miracle of rigour and lucidity.*

Imperialism, as we have already seen, is deeply rooted in instinct, in the need for fuller being *in men and peoples. This need is satisfied through the egoistic appetite for domination, but it is equally satisfied through solidarity and mutual aid. And often imperialism derives part of its strength from the benefits conferred by the increased solidarity. No empire has been better able to assimilate its conquests than the Roman. L. Homo here defines the happily diversfied forms which Rome's authority knew how to assume in organizing first Italy and then the peoples who composed the greatest Empire. And when this Empire has reached the still barbarous West on the one hand, and the already decadent East on the other, it can be foreseen that her own decadence will be due to the circumstance that Rome has been more attracted by the delights of this*

---

[1] *See* Prehistoric Man, From Tribe to Empire, Mesopotamia *and* Ægean Civilization.

[2] *Introduction to* From Tribe to Empire. *" In primitive Italy stranger and enemy,* hostis *and* peregrinus, *were synonymous terms on the testimony of Cicero and Varro."* Homo, p. 240.

[3] P. 202.

FOREWORD

sumptuous and corrupt East than by the resources of that still virgin West.

The reader will be struck by two seemingly contradictory merits in this volume—scientific caution and power of reconstruction. What a contrast exists between the old-time histories, which seemed definite because they were partly invented, and the history of to-day, full of gaps, studded with notes of interrogation, but capable of perfection! On the origins of Rome " we know little," says L. Homo, " but we are beginning to be well grounded. Beneath its modest mien our progress has been great, and hopes are greater still."[1] The good historian distinguishes between what is known, what is unknown provisionally, and what must in all likelihood remain unknown for ever. He rejects ill-founded hypotheses and paradoxical theses. But he avoids narrow specialism. He makes use of all sources of information. Knowledge of general history and experience of contemporary life help him to interpret the past. It is at bottom humanity which interests him in this or that human group. And so Rome's individuality here appears in the woof of history, linked to the past and the future, weaving in that woof among the contingencies durable creations which answer to the necessities of the people's life, and on which we must insist— political organization and legal organization.

HENRI BERR.

[1] *P.* 22

CONTENTS

CONTENTS

xiv

LIST OF MAPS AND PLANS

PRIMITIVE ITALY
AND THE BEGINNINGS OF ROMAN
IMPERIALISM

INTRODUCTION

SOURCES AND NEGATIONS

THE history of ancient Italy prior to the Punic Wars is overshadowed by one stern fact. Save for some scattered fragments—*rari nantes in gurgite vasto*—rescued by a miracle
from the utter ruin of Western Hellenism, we possess for
this whole period no contemporary documents comparable
to those which reveal to us the history of the various peoples
of the ancient East and even that of preclassical Greece.
The story of the first five centuries of traditional Roman
history only reaches us through the medium of much later
writers, the oldest of whom were contemporaries of Cæsar
and Augustus, such as Livy, Diodorus Siculus, Dionysius of
Halicarnassus, and Trogus Pompeius; the others—Plutarch,
Appian, Dio Cassius—belong to the imperial age. Embodied
in these various works and in secondary abridgments (those
of Florus, Justinian, Eutropius, and Orosius in Latin, of
Zonaras in Greek), this history of primitive Rome presented
and, despite the dark gaps left by the capricious hand of
fate, still presents an imposing structure. Nowhere else in
the world do we meet national history relating the origins
of a people with such a wealth of detail and such a show of
exactitude. But does the quality of the wares offered correspond to their quantity? What is the real value of this
impressive narrative of remote events?

One circumstance cannot fail at once to attract the attention of modern historians, even of the most credulous and
least cautious among them—the substantial number of centuries intervening between the facts of early Roman history
and the composition of the works which are our sole sources

of knowledge of such events. By the seventeenth and eighteenth centuries a Frenchman, Samuel Bochart,[1] and a Dutchman, Perizonius,[2] show evidence of a scepticism interesting for novelty of method and freshness of outlook. In the eighteenth and nineteenth centuries criticism boldly asserts itself against tradition and assumes a systematic form. Four names—those of Beaufort, the gifted author of the *Dissertation on the Uncertainty of the First Five Centuries of Roman History*,[3] Niebuhr,[4] Mommsen,[5] and Ettore Pais— stand out as landmarks of the great stages of this decisive evolution. Th. Mommsen, while throwing overboard the details of traditional history, piously persisted in retaining at least its skeleton, the law of the Twelve Tables and the Consular Fasti, in the foreground. In a work at once powerful and elaborate, M. Ettore Pais[6] does not scruple to cast down these last pillars of the temple. If we believe the learned historian, absolutely nothing is left of the tradition save its ruins.

In scientific circles, more or less loyal to the old Roman legend, the hypercritical method of M. Ettore Pais, which is, in any case, carried to extremes and in more than one place seems quite artificial, has inevitably come as a shock and has provoked a conservative reaction more or less all over Europe.[7] M. Gaetano de Sanctis in particular is the foremost champion of " temperate criticism " in contrast to the " total criticism " of Pais, and has made in his masterly *Storia critica di Roma* a reasoned and reasonable attempt at reconciliation, aiming at preserving in the traditional narrative all that can still be saved without a misplaced excess of credulity.

Defence of the tradition and critical negations, such are the two poles between which the study of primitive Roman

[1] " Geographia sacra," appendix to *Opera omnia*, 2 vols., Leyden, 1675.

[2] *Animadversiones selectæ* (1685).

[3] **LXXXV**.   [4] *Histoire romaine* (1811-1832).

[5] **XV**; **XIV**; **CLXXXIV**; **CLXXXIII**; **CLXXXV**; **CLXXXVI**.

[6] **XXI**; **XX**; **XIX**; **CXCIX**; **CC**; **CCII**.

[7] Notably O. E. Schmidt, in Germany in **L**, 1900, 38-54; in Italy, G. de Sanctis, **XXVI** (1907 *f.*), and in **LV**, 1909, 126-32, 205-14; 1910, 310-19; C. Barbagallo, in **LXIX**, 1919, 85-99, 127-40; G. Ferrero and C. Barbagallo, **V** (1921).

2

history is fated to move and oscillate to-day, however obstinately one thesis or the other be maintained.[1] In such circumstances there can be but one fruitful and reliable method—the critical utilization of the tradition as presented by the great historians of the imperial age. Their works are, we must repeat, posterior by several centuries to the events with which they deal, but we must always bear in mind that intermediate links between the two epochs were not lacking. The methodical reconstitution of these missing links, working backward from the known to the unknown, is the first duty of the historian of ancient Rome.

From the last years of the third century to the end of the Republic very many Roman historians lived and wrote, first in Greek and then in Latin. They constitute the annalistic school, and fórm its natural culmination. But the annalists were contemporary with and participated in the Second Punic War, L. Cincius Alimentus, Cato, Q. Claudius Quadrigarius, Valerius Antias, C. Licinius Macer, and many another are known by name.[2] The great representatives of Roman historiography at the beginning of the Empire—Livy, Dionysius of Halicarnassus, and Diodorus Siculus[3]—will only carry on their work and form its natural culmination. But the annalists were no more contemporary with the primitive period of Roman history which they described than their successors. They too had to work upon older materials which the past put into their hands. What were these materials? So we reach a second stage in our progress into the past.

The material at the disposal of the annalists falls essentially into two groups—(a) extra-Roman material (a literature), and (b) national Roman material (documents). Let us make a few observations on both. The extra-Roman

---

[1] On the sources of primitive Roman history and their use, see especially **CCXIX**.

[2] The fragments of the annalists have been twice edited—H.R.F. (ed. Peter, 1883) and H.R.R. (by the same author, 2nd ed., 1914). On the whole question of the annalists, consult **CXCVIII**; **CCVIII**; **CCXXIV**; H. Peters, in H.R.R. (proleg. iii-ccclxxx); **XX**, I, 52-194; II, 351-58; III, 117-30, 231-68.

[3] The importance of Diodorus as representing the old annalistic school, and, in particular, Fabius Pictor, has often been exaggerated as a result of Mommsen, **CLXXXV**, II, 281-96. In this connection, see the prudent remarks of Ett. Pais, **XX**, I, 118-23, and **IV**, 447-52.

group was represented principally by Greek literature, which had antedated the birth of Roman historical writing by several centuries, and had gradually come to take an interest in the fortunes of Italy as that land emerged from the mists of the remote West into the full light of history. The curtain rises on the new world with the Homeric epos; if the *Iliad* is not yet acquainted with this "Far West" of the Mediterranean, the later *Odyssey* mentions the Sicani and the Siculi of Sicily more than once. In his *Theogony* Hesiod calls the two sons of Ulysses and the enchantress Circe, Agrios and Latinos, chiefs of the Tyrrhenians, mentions the Sacred Isles, and knows of Telegonos, the legendary founder of the Latin Tusculum. Stesichoros, one of the earliest representatives of Greek lyric poetry, in his *Iliupersis*, related the story of the westward voyage of Æneas and follows the hero's wanderings to Cape Miseno. However, at this epoch the Greek world had still but a vague and fragmentary knowledge of the geography of Italy; it was not yet known that Etruria and Latium belonged to the same peninsula, and the existence of a vast western ocean entirely open to navigation still received general credence. About 500 B.C. Hecatæus gave a description of the country for the first time, and half a century later Herodotus mentions the Etruscan port of Argylla and the town of Cortona, although quite incidentally. But in this domain the decisive fact is the birth, at the end of the fifth century, of Western Greek historiography, which naturally was destined to focus the full light of its researches and activity on Sicily and Italy, chiefly South Italy.

In default of the missing works, let us at least mention some names—Hippys of Rhegium, the father of history in the West, who had probably, if only incidentally, touched upon the past or contemporary events in Central Italy; Antiochus of Syracuse (after 424), to whom we are indebted for the earliest reference to Rome which has come down to us; Philistius, likewise a Syracusan, a minister of the two Dionysii, the author of the first general history of Sicily and Italy, wherein the other great traditional peoples of the peninsula, Ligurians and Umbrians, Samnites and Etruscans, appear side by side with the Greeks of the South, who quite naturally monopolized the lion's share of the work. From the Italiote or Siciliote literature of Magna Grecia the historians and geographers of Greece proper—Ephorus, Theopompus, who spoke of the capture of Rome by the Gauls; Aristotle, who, following Hellanicus of Lesbos and Damastes of Sigeum, mentioned the legend of the Trojan connections with Italy; the pseudo-Scymnus of Chios and the pseudo-Scylax, both authors of geographical summaries— were to borrow the vital elements of their data. A little later, Lykos of Rhegium devoted a special book to the campaigns of Alexander the Molossian in Italy. This is the moment when Rome began to interfere in South Italy and came into definite contact with Hellenism. And so, *nolens volens*, Greek historical writing begins to devote ever more space to the newcomer. Callias, the historian of Agathokles, relates in the course of his work the origin of the Roman people; Duris, tyrant and historian of Samos, spoke of the victory of Sentinum, that battle of the nations of pre-Roman Italy; Hieronymus of Kardia, the biographer of Pyrrhus, and Aristoxenes of Tarentum dwelt at length on the history of a country so intimately connected with the catastrophe of Western Hellenism. Finally, a Sicilian from Tauromenium, Timæus (340-250), condensed and, in a sense, codified the remotest traditions of the Italian peninsula in a bulky work which extended from the beginnings to the outbreak of the First Punic War. This history of Timæus, the culmination and synthesis of a cycle of historical evolution, marked a decisive date on the very threshold of the period when the great activity of Roman historiography, itself a typical symbol of the new era, was to begin.

Save for some rare fragments preserved by later historians, like Dionysius of Halicarnassus and Diodorus, this rich and varied Greek historical literature of Italy and Sicily no longer exists. The same remark applies to Etruscan historical writings, the disappearance of which is still more complete. But let us not forget that the Roman annalists possessed both in their integrity and could freely draw therefrom the evidence they needed. Greek historiography and Etruscan historiography, such were the two great sources of extra-Roman origin that the annalists had ready to their hands. But from the point of view of the annalists both were infected with a common redhibitory vice; by definition,

Roman history was not their sole nor even their principal object. They only touched upon it incidentally and by the way. Consequently neither the conception of the annalists nor Roman pride found their due in them. The foreign element may have played an appreciable part in the elaboration of Roman historical writing, but from its very nature its rôle necessarily remained always subordinate and secondary.

Quite different was the fate of the Roman element. Rome already possessed, at the epoch when the annalists took up their task, a long historical past. No doubt national historical writing did not yet exist and Latin literature was scarcely born, but at least a certain number of documents were available—public documents and private documents.

The former themselves fell under two heads, religious documents and political documents. Each religious guild had its private archives in which were preserved archives of various sorts: litanies (*carmina*), such as the hymns of the Salii and Arvales, some fragments of which have come down to us, ritual handbooks (*indigitamenta*), commentaries (*commentarii*), a collection of the decisions of the guild which constituted a body of precedents in case of dispute. Finally, one document stood out among all the rest, the calendar, the composition of which was entrusted to the most august of all the Roman religious guilds, the guild of pontiffs. Originally this calendar had been invested with an essentially, if not exclusively, practical character; the discrimination between lucky and unlucky days, a matter of capital importance from the standpoint of politics, was its essential object. Subsequently a reference to the consuls in charge and a note of the main events of the year were added; thus by a gradual and logical development a history was evolved out of the primitive Roman calendar. This calendar was kept up to date by the chief pontiff on a tablet whitened with chalk (*tabula dealbata*) and set up in the Regia on the Sacred Way. At the end of the year the tablet was replaced by a new one and itself deposited in the pontifical archives. This practice was maintained till the chief pontificate of P. Mucius Scævola (about 123 B.C.), the date when the whole series of tablets was codified in a definite edition—the Great Annals (*Annales Maximi*)—and the traditional usage was discontinued. At the time when the

6

first annalists began to compose the history of primitive Rome the canon was not yet in existence and the pontifical annals were available in the form of a collection of tablets—in the material sense of the word. However tedious and, indeed, repulsive a task delving in such annals might seem, they contained, nevertheless, the substance of a true history, provided, of course, they were studied methodically and intelligently used.

Beside these religious documents stood the political documents. First we must note some marked deficiencies which resulted in an exceptional restriction of the number of such. The Romans of the Republic knew no equivalent for our *Gazette* nor any Hansard reports of meetings of the popular assemblies or of the Senate; the publication of such at a late date was due to Cæsar's initiative. But, in default of such regular periodical publications, there still existed official documents of diverse nature—treaties, laws, decrees of the Senate, lists of magistrates. The ancient authors make express mention of a number of such documents in dealing with the first centuries of Roman history: the treaty of alliance, concluded in the days of Servius Tullius, between Rome and the Latin cities, which was piously preserved in classical times in the temple of Aventine Diana engraved on a bronze tablet; the treaty of one of the Tarquins—it is uncertain which—with Gabii inscribed on a leather shield in the sanctuary of Semo Sancus on the Quirinal; the first treaty between Rome and Carthage, cited by Polybius[1] and attributed by him to the first year of the Republic; the treaty made by Spurius Cassius with the Latins (493), visible in the first half of the last century of the Republic on a bronze column in the Comitium; the law relating to the Capitoline nail in the temple of the Capitoline Triad; the lex Acilia on the allotment of the Aventine; the treaty between Rome and Ardea; the celebrated law of the Twelve Tables, and a few others besides. Other documents of general interest were preserved in the archives of the several colleges of magistrates, censors, consuls, or quæstors; such included collections of formulæ and decisions (*commentarii*), or statistical documents of various kinds, such as the census tablets (*tabulæ censoriæ*), at once lists of returns and survey plans.

---

[1] Pol., III, 22-23.

INTRODUCTION

Let us mention, in conclusion, the *libri lintei* of the temple of Juno Moneta on the Arx, where lists of magistrates, and especially the most important of all, that of the consuls, were to be read; they were written on linen.

Finally, private documents were in existence. Each of the great Roman families (the Claudii, the Fabii, the Cornelii, the Valerii, and the rest) possessed its great domestic archives handed down from generation to generation in the *tablinum* of the house. These family papers were very varied in nature—genealogies, the *stemma* of the family from a comparatively remote epoch; eulogies (*elogia*) engraved or painted beneath the ancestors' busts, describing their political careers and their great deeds; funeral orations (*laudationes funebres*), solemn panegyrics pronounced at the burial of the dead, and the collection of which constituted a complete history of the whole family. Tradition also speaks of lamentations (*næniæ*) pronounced by professional mourners (*præficæ*), who had their fixed place in the funeral procession, and of banqueting songs devoted to the glory of the ancestors. The latter are celebrated as having inspired Niebuhr with his famous theory of primitive Roman epos, to-day quite properly consigned to the shades of oblivion.

Such are the many and varied elements, written or oral, available to the annalists on the Roman side. The critic is at once confronted by two problems—how far back did such material reach? what was its value as evidence?

At least, in the case of the written documents an indisputable *terminus post quem* exists—the introduction of writing at Rome. On this point, in default of absolute chronological accuracy, we can at least arrive at a satisfactory approximation. The comparative study of the alphabets proves beyond possibility of doubt that the Latin alphabet is not derived from the Etruscan, a discovery which, while seeming merely negative, is none the less of first-rate importance; this alphabet must have been introduced into Rome before the beginning of the Etruscan conquest—that is, before the end of the seventh century B.C. It is derived directly from the Chalcidian alphabet, and came by way of Cumæ, the advance post of Hellenic civilization in Central Italy. The chronological canon of antiquity placed the foundation of Cumæ in the middle of the eleventh century B.C.

No; the archæological discoveries at the site, evidence of a decisive character, show that this event could not be placed before the end of the ninth or the first years of the eighth century, and it is to some such date that the colonization of the city must undoubtedly be assigned. The Etruscans, on the other hand, found the Chalcido-Cumæan alphabet already in use at Rome before the end of the seventh century. Accordingly, the introduction of that alphabet dates back either to the end of the eighth century or the first half of the seventh, the first possibility being infinitely the more likely. Nevertheless, we do not possess any written documents from Rome or Latium older than the end of the seventh or the beginning of the sixth century, to which period the Duenos vase and the Præneste fibula may be assigned.

But in the case of writing, as with any other advance, a distinction must be drawn between the invention and the diffusion. Inventions of whatever kind require a relatively considerable time before they come into general use; one of the two most venerable known Latin inscriptions, that on the Præneste fibula, comprises only four words. In point of fact, writing remained a very rare practice till well on in the sixth century, and its use was limited to peculiarly significant documents of religious character, brief dedications to the gods, or of political importance, such as international treaties, laws, lists of magistrates. The first written document of any considerable length was the law of the Twelve Tables from the middle of the fifth century, and this fact invests it with exceptional importance in the history of primitive Rome. It is only after this decisive date that the use of writing becomes general and was adopted also for private purposes. So there cannot have been much in the way of written documents before the fifth century, and the presence at Rome some centuries later of documents—or alleged documents—ascribed to this remote epoch in itself proves nothing in respect of the vital question of their authenticity. The analogy of the apocryphal documents which swarmed in the history of primitive Greece—or, to come closer to our own days, of the innumerable charters forged in the Middle Ages—is not calculated to appease scruples or dissipate distrust. The archives of the magistrates could not, by definition, begin before the creation of the office; in the case of the consuls at the beginning of the Republic, in that of the censors in the middle of the fifth century. The pontifical annals, the essential historical basis of the annalistic histories, were only kept regularly from a comparatively late date. Cicero affords us some precise information on this subject; the earliest eclipse of the sun entered in these annals was, he says, that mentioned by the poet Ennius in the year 403 B.C. He adds that this eclipse was taken as a point of reference by the pontiffs and that all future eclipses were calculated from this one. Consequently the oldest pontifical tablets preserved in the historical epoch went back no farther than the end of the fifth or perhaps even the beginning of the fourth century.

A further question, not the least important, is raised by these remote documents—that of their historical value. Documents anterior to the fourth century were not and could not be numerous for the conclusive reasons which we have just given. A further accidental circumstance intervened to augment this regrettable quantitative and qualitative paucity; this was the burning of Rome by the Gauls in 390. That catastrophe exercised a determining influence on the genesis and transmission of the national tradition. It introduced an irreparable break of continuity, the importance of which the Roman historians, who suffered so seriously therefrom, did not fail to emphasize. No doubt all was not lost—Livy[1] expressly says, *pleræque interiere*—but there were losses, and substantial ones. The damage was not merely quantitive; what was far worse, it affected the quality of the material. Efforts were made to replace as far as possible the destroyed documents; after the departure of the Gauls, side by side with the rebuilding of the city, went feverish activity in restoring the archives, but we are justified in remaining sceptical as to the real value of some at least of the documents thus revived. One definite fact reported by Plutarch is symptomatic. In a passage of his *Life of Numa* the biographer tells us of a certain Paulus Claudius[2]—perhaps the annalist Claudius Quadrigarius—the author of

[1] Liv., VI, 1, 3.
[2] Plut., *Num.*, 1 (=H.R.F., p. 108; H.R.R., p. 178, 1). On the person's identity, see H.R.R., pp. ccxxxviii-ix.

a chronology (ἔλεγχος χρόνων), who had taken as his starting-point, not the origin of Rome in the traditional style, but the capture of the city by the Gauls, and to justify this unwonted procedure against the assaults of critics, affirmed as an article of faith :

> " During the sack of Rome by the Gauls the ancient registers perished, and the deeds which are exhibited to-day are forgeries, the work of toadies of certain persons who wished at all costs to trace back their lineage to the first Romans and to find a place among the most illustrious families."

Not everybody at Rome, therefore, blindly accepted the elucubrations of official history, and among the annalists themselves *l'enfant terrible* made himself heard, as Claudius' phrase shows.

The pontifical annals, the recording of which had only just begun, were not seriously affected by the fire and their reconstruction offered no formidable difficulties. To documents subsequent to 390, this fundamental ground for suspicion naturally does not apply, but, nevertheless, their quality was not always beyond reproach and their authenticity gave rise to more than a legitimate doubt. Official chronology seems for a long time to have rested, not on the Consular Fasti, as in the classical epoch, but on the rough reckoning by the Capitoline nails. Hence it may be inferred that for the earliest times—for the greater part, if not the whole, of the fifth century—no official list of the Consular or dictatorial Fasti was in existence at Rome, and that this list in the form in which it has come down to us must have been drawn up later with the aid of public documents and, in default of such, of family archives. Such a procedure, as will be readily understood, opened the door to a host of errors, not all of which were unintentional. The same remark applies to the Triumphal Fasti, an annalistic composition which, for all that it was engraved on stone, often offers no better guarantees of authenticity than the other.

As for the private documents, the ancient authors themselves have taken care to tell us what should be thought of them :

> " It is not easy," writes Livy,[1] in reference to the events of 322 B.C., " to choose one fact in preference to another, one author

---

[1] Liv., VIII, 40, 4-5.

11

in preference to another author. I am convinced that the tradition of the past has been altered through funeral eulogies and false inscriptions on busts, because each family wants to claim for itself all the glory of exploits and magistracies by the aid of lies and subterfuges. Hence arises the confusion in the deeds of each individual and in the public documents of history. From this period not a single author is left whose testimony is reliable enough for one to build upon it." And Cicero says:[1] "The funeral orations have filled our history with lies. In them are related facts which never happened, imaginary triumphs, consulates, the numbers of which have been inflated, forged genealogies, forged adoptions into plebeian families, making out that men of obscure family were born in illustrious families of the same name, as if I were to declare myself the descendant of M. Tullius, who was a patrician, and was consul with Serv. Sulpicius ten years after the expulsion of the kings."

Who speak thus? Paradox hunters? Far from it. Professional sceptics? Even less. These are the words of Cicero, of Livy, the stoutest protagonists, the most ardent champions of the national tradition. Such testimony in the mouth of such men acquires added weight and constitutes the most damning indictment of the documents to which it refers.

In the second half of the fourth century B.C. Rome became a great Italian power. She came into contact with the Greek world, waiting to take her place there as mistress. The Greeks had a brilliant past and gloried in it. Rome, with the natural feeling of an upstart intensified by the unexpectedness of her fortune, could not bear to leave them even this platonic satisfaction and retrospective superiority. She, too, had a long past, but what did she find there? Rare or doubtful documents, a few legends, generally only annihilation's waste! It was, then, inspired by imperious patriotism and guided by the aims of national policy that she began to construct her history. Was it a process of deliberate and systematic falsification? No; such a description would not be accurate. Roman tradition is not purposely deceitful, but only by necessity and for lack of better things. Rome had forgotten her past history as a whole, and had no authentic materials at her disposal to allow her to revive it with certitude. The work of reconstruction was prolonged over three centuries, and did not end till the last

---

[1] Cic., *Brut.*, 16, 62.

days of the Republic and the beginning of the Empire. The responsibility for it has often been laid at the door of the annalists alone. In reality the elaboration of the history of primitive Rome had begun before their entry upon the scene and was to be continued when they had left it. As authors or systematizers, they no doubt played a prominent part, but it is only fair to remember that they were not the first, nor the last, nor the sole agents.

History includes two essential elements—the framework furnished by chronology, and the historic plot produced by the facts. The constructive activity that resulted in the traditional history of Rome was applied to both.

Originally, Rome had possessed no official era, and so no solid starting-point for an exact and coherent chronology. The would-be historian of the first centuries of the Republic was faced with two discordant chronologies—that of the Consular Fasti, which began with the expulsion of the kings, *post reges exactos;* and that of the Capitoline nails, the origin and motive of which was the dedication of the temple of the Capitoline Triad. In dealing with the regal period, *ab urbe condita,* he no longer had any framework at all. And so Roman chronology as a whole is the result of a long, artificial, and complicated process of elaboration, the only possible method since, in spite of all, a certain number of concrete historical facts existed and could not be eliminated, but must, for good or ill, find a place in the official reckoning. Thanks to a long series of adaptations, expedients, and—let us be frank—tricks, Rome at last found herself in possession of a chronology from the Trojan War to the classical period all the more complete and harmonious because her chronographers had taken care to make it so. This chronology, which received its finishing touches by the end of the Republic, was to be accepted as gospel truth by the historians of the Empire through whom it has been transmitted to us.[1]

At the same time as the chronological framework was being drawn up, the plot to fill it was being elaborated. The task would seem especially arid for the period preceding the

[1] On the very delicate and complex problem of Roman chronology during the first centuries of the Republic, see especially **CLXXXIII**; **CLXXIV**; **CLV**; **CCXXV** and the bibliography, pp. 1-18.

capture of Rome by the Gauls; rare and often doubtful documents dealing with the rise of the Republic, vague traditions concerning the regal epoch, fragmentary or incidental data offered by the literature of Magna Grecia and Etruria, such was the meagre and discouraging inventory that the history of the first centuries of Rome had to offer. The documentary material, which was too often lacking, was drawn from various sources. First came the legends. The Romans, an observant and coldly rational people, were not gifted with imagination, and it is probable in view of the hopeless aridity of their primitive religion that, left to themselves, they would not have made much progress in this direction. But no upstart—least of all Rome, one of the most extraordinary upstarts in history—has ever been at a loss for genealogists or heralds to provide coats-of-arms; the Greeks[1] applied to the invention and presentation of the legends of ancient Rome those qualities of ingenuity and practical tact so characteristic of their national genius. Hellenic Italy, with Livius Andronicus and Ennius, played a leading part in this respect. And so, to take a concrete example, we can watch the emergence and gradual embellishment of the legend of Roman origins. Hellanicus of Lesbos and Damastes of Sigeum (second half of the fifth century B.C.) already knew of the kinship with Troy. When, on the morrow of the revolution of 509, the Romans set up on the Capitol the bronze she-wolf,[2] haughty symbol of their nationality, they seem to have been still unacquainted with the legend of the twins which was destined to enjoy such a brilliant career in the future. The story of the seven kings took shape at the end of the fourth century, the Trojan kinship appears in Aristotle, and at the beginning of the third century, Romulus and Remus already figure in the historical work of Callias of Syracuse. In 296 the brothers Ogulnii set up a second bronze she-wolf on the Capitol, but this time with the addition of the twins, who hereafter remained classical. About 239, Justinian tells us,[3] the Senate granted

---

[1] On the predominant rôle of the Greeks in the formation of the legends of primitive Rome, see W. Schur in **LVI**, 1920, 137-52; G. Siegwart, *ibid.*, 1921, 16-32; **XX**, I, 231-62.

[2] Petersen, in **LVI**, 1908, 440-56; 1909, 29-47.

[3] Just., **XXVIII**, 1, 5.

its protection to the Acarnanians, harassed by the Ætolians, because they alone among the Greeks had held aloof from the war upon the Trojans, the ancestors of the Roman people. A few years later the poet Nævius, the forerunner of Virgil, brought Æneas to Carthage, and Ennius made Romulus the Trojan hero's grandson.[1] The legend of the origin of Rome in its essential features—the Trojan ancestry, the rôle of Æneas, the she-wolf and the twins, the seven kings—took shape, therefore, at the end of the fourth and the beginning of the third centuries—that is to say, at the same time as Rome became a great power in Italy and won the hegemony in the peninsula. This cannot be a fortuitous coincidence nor an accidental parallelism.

Now for the second element—the falsification of public or private documents. Documents, as we have seen, were rarities for the first century of the Republic, exceptional or even non-existent for the regal period. This regrettable lacuna was remedied by the fabrication of apocryphal documents. The alleged regal laws furnish a typical example of this procedure. At the end of the Republic a whole body of laws existed which tradition attributed to the regal period and which were codified in a collection, the *Jus Papirianum*. That the collection was due to a certain Papirius was unanimously agreed, but opinions were divided as to his identity. Some referred him to the reign of the Tarquins, others to the first years of the Republic, immediately after the expulsion of the kings. In reality, the documents in question were not laws but very ancient religious and ritual prescriptions, not all of them necessarily forgeries, but codified at a late date—no doubt during the third century before our era. The forgeries extended also to private documents, and it may be easily imagined what a large field was opened to the families' ingenuity in this domain exempt from public scrutiny. Livy[2] and Cicero,[3] in the two typical passages quoted above, give us a suggestive summary of the means employed—the systematic exaggeration of the number of triumphs or magistracies with which ancestors had been rewarded (*falsi triumphi*, *plures consulatus*), the multiplication of their exploits (*multa scripta sunt in eis quæ facta*

---

[1] J. Mesk, in **LXXX**, 1914, 1-35.   [2] Liv., VIII, 40, 4-5.
[3] Cic., *Brutus*, 16, 62.

INTRODUCTION

non sunt), and false *elogia* inscribed on their busts (*falsi imaginum tituli*). Such pious falsehoods did not lie within the reach of all families; they, at least, presupposed the existence of some ancestors who had participated in some degree in the government of the State. For the benefit of others, especially of the plebians who were newcomers to office and all the more anxious in consequence to gild their escutcheons retrospectively, false genealogies (*genera falsa*) were manufactured and fictitious links with patrician families of the same name were established under the guise of *transitiones ad plebem*.

The explanation of the present provided further material of capital importance for the reconstruction of the past; topography, political and religious institutions, and linguistics were systematically laid under contribution, and each provided their stone for the great edifice of national history. The ancient monuments—remains of fortifications, the stairs of Cacus, the Mundus of the Palatine, old temples (Saturn, Jubiter Stator, Vesta) or altars (Saturn, Ops) in the Forum, the Mamertine prison, the Pons Sublicius, and many others— gave rise to a swarm of topographical theories in which, as might be expected, legend simply revelled. The same method was applied to contemporary institutions on the plausible pretexts of seeking their origins in the past; the reigns of Romulus and Numa, in the concrete form which tradition has given them, are the product of such research. Language was treated in like fashion; the philologists commented on the vocabulary till they were out of breath and hunted for etymologies. Varro's work, especially the surviving part of his treatise on the Latin language (*de lingua latina*), is peculiarly instructive in this connection. To pad out her history, the legends and cults of the ancient cities of Latium, Lavinium, Alba, Tusculum, and others were annexed to Rome without scruple. Finally, the legends and institutions of Greece were available, a rich mine from which the annalists drew largely to fill up the gaps in national tradition: Servius Tullius will borrow many traits from Solon; Spurius Cassius and Spurius Mælius will be indebted for the brightest parts of their stories to memories of Greek tyranny.

And this is not all; distortion was added to invention. Numerous events of the present were projected into the past, which thus appeared fashioned in the image of the present. Hence arose the characteristic anticipations or repetitions (duplications or triplications) of facts. The meaning of history was twisted or, at least, modified. Sometimes the account of early events was altered to suit national pride; the traditions relating to the accession of the Tarquins, the double capture of Rome by Porsenna and by the Gauls are typical illustrations. Sometimes the rôle of Rome was arbitrarily magnified in cases where, in point of fact, far from taking the lead in the general history of Italy, she had obviously been merely imitative, as in the cases of the struggle against the Alban hegemony and of the anti-Etruscan reaction in Latium at the end of the regal period.

Some numerical data cast a very curious light upon this work of historical construction. On the testimony of Dionysius of Halicarnassus, the early annalists had treated the first centuries of Rome in a very summary fashion, but soon, with the extension of literary education and the new taste for rhetoric, the Roman public demanded something more than the dry epitomes of a Fabius Pictor or a Cincius Alimentus; it wanted long narratives, minute descriptions, striking scenes, and plenty of brilliant speeches. And so the annalistic works quickly expanded out of all proportion. Cn. Gellius described the rape of the Sabine women, although one of the first events of Roman history, in the second book of his Annals, and the treaty between Romulus and Tatius in the third. The whole work occupied ninety-seven volumes, and the Annals of Valerius Antias filled seventy-five. Hence such writers describe the past the more luxuriantly and circumstantially the farther they are removed from it, a seemingly paradoxical fact that appears only logical when we envisage the exact conditions under which early Roman history was elaborated.

Let us conclude with two remarks, both of prime importance. The composition of early Roman history lasted a very long time; it was being carried on for three centuries and was only finished on the threshold of the Empire. In this prolific line of annalists the latest were not the least important. The later annalism, that of the first half of the last century of the Republic, represented, above all, by the names of Valerius Antias and Licinius Macer, exaggerated yet more the defects of the school—diffuseness, political tendencies, neglect of criticism, literary pretensions of dubious taste, impudent falsifications. We can only speak by hearsay of these annalists, but the work of Dionysius of Halicarnassus, directly inspired by them, allows us to judge both of the ideal aimed at and the result attained.

This initial remark brings us to a second. The concept of history in the modern sense of that word, as a disinterested and objective science, was never fully grasped by the Romans —at least, under the Republic. They saw in history a national work, a school of citizenship and an instrument of government. So this general character of Roman historical writing involved serious consequences. The annalists concentrated their attention upon the history of Rome; events in the rest of Italy, *a fortiori* international questions, interested them only in so far as such referred to this particular object. To embellish and enrich Rome's history they did not scruple to borrow from other peoples and, in case of need, they did not hesitate to violate historical truth. Finally, the annalists' work reflects contemporary political conflicts; Rome's past, as they pretend to evoke it, too often appears as a weapon in the hand of factions, a platform from which politicians may declaim.

And now the time has come to conclude. Any impartial inquiry devoted to the history of the first centuries of Rome necessarily leads to a degree, and a very large degree, of scepticism. Livy, the most enthusiastic partisan of Roman tradition, felt himself compelled to disburden his conscience as an historian in the preface to his work.[1]

> " These accounts of the period which preceded the foundation of Rome, a period which we know rather through poetic legends than from indisputable historical monuments, I will neither affirm nor improve. It is one of the privileges of antiquity to mingle the divine and the human and to add lustre to the origins of cities by the intervention of deities. If there be any people which is justified in deifying its origins and referring them to the gods, the military glory of the Roman people is such that all nations will admit its claims to descent from Mars through Romulus as readily as its domination. None of these legends, however they be regarded, to whatever judgment they be submitted, will I call into question."

---

[1] Livy, I. preface, 6-8.

SOURCES AND NEGATIONS

And it is not only this remote period that the great historian has in mind in thus making his profession of faith. The obscurity of the first centuries of national history, right down to the last years of the fourth century B.C., remains one of his favourite themes :[1]

> "I have set forth," he writes, after describing the Gaulish invasion, "in five books the history of the Romans from the foundation of the city of Rome to the capture of the same city by the Gauls, first under the kings, then under the consuls and dictators, the decemvirs, and the consular tribunes, their wars abroad, and their disputes at home. It is an obscure story, both because of its extreme antiquity like an object scarcely visible owing to its great distance, and because of the inadequacy and extreme rarity in those same epochs of writing, the sole faithful guardian of the memory of past deeds, and, finally, owing to the almost complete destruction of the pontifical commentaries and of other public and private documents in the burning of the city."[2] Further on, in reference to the conflicting traditions about Lake Curtius, he remarks: "I would have spared no pains if any way could have led to the truth, but to-day we must cling to the traditions, since the antiquity of the fact does not allow of its authenticity being established."[3]

Such texts, which might be multiplied,[4] are thoroughly characteristic and incidentally prove that the celebrated credulity, currently attributed to Livy, comes very near having existed only in the imaginations of certain moderns infinitely more credulous and enamoured of tradition than he. Nevertheless, that we may give such declarations the weight they deserve, let us not forget that at the close of the Republic tradition had acquired the prestige of an official dogma and a national creed; to disbelieve it was, in the eyes of public opinion, an affront to the State and almost treason. In such circumstances, Livy's scepticism is a minimum which it is not for us moderns to reduce. Let us not be in practice more royalist than the king—I mean, more Roman than Livy. The historical truth is—and it cannot be repeated too often—that at the moment when, having become the greatest power in Italy, Rome determined to

[1] Livy., VIII, 40, 4-5, under date 322.
[2] *Ibid.*, VI, 1, 1-3.   [3] *Ibid.*, VII, 6, 6.
[4] Note, for instance, the scepticism mingled with a certain irony with which Livy (II, 10, 11-12) recalls the exploits of Horatius Cocles or speaks of the alleged naval battle of Fidenæ in 426 (IV, 34, 6-7).

write her national history, she realized that she had un-learned it and that the authentic documents rescued from the wreck did not suffice for its reconstruction. Materials for the reconstruction were no doubt available, to some extent, either in Greek or Etruscan historical writings or in the written tradition, public and private, at Rome itself. But, they remained rare and were, in addition, often of dubious authenticity. Oral tradition had likewise preserved, at the cost of serious alterations, some memory of some of the most prominent events of the past. The annalists have trans-mitted these various materials to us, drowned in a confused hotchpotch of legends, forgeries, distortions, and errors. The picture of early Roman history as it is presented in the writers of the imperial age, therefore, appears as the result of long artificial labours, a collective synthesis on which the great corporations of the State, the several classes in society, three centuries of political conflicts, and six generations of annalists have left their mark.

The facts exist, dazzling proofs against which it would be futile and rather childish to revolt. A chronology, artificial for the regal áge or a rough approximation for the early Republican period, scattered and often distorted authentic data, a mantle of historical appearance, but only of appearance, prudishly draped over the fantasies of legend or the hollows of the void—that is the aspect under which we must figure to ourselves the history of Rome prior to the catastrophe of 390. We have, indeed, a general canvas on which the outlines—the barest outlines—are authentic; detailed history worthy of credence we lack and will always lack as far as it is humanly possible to prophesy. But at least, and here we reach solid ground again, we shall be able to increase, albeit to a limited extent, the number of known facts and scientifically established data with the aid of the auxiliary sciences. The study of legends and institu-tions, the history of religions, philology, toponymy, Etruscan research and, as far as the earliest periods are concerned, anthropology each have their contributions to make to the task, but in the heart of this necessary work of reconstruc-tion, the place of honour is incontestably due to archæology— prehistoric and protohistoric on the one hand, and historic on the other. Under the name of palæoethnology a regular science of prehistory has been elaborated in Italy; for half a century it has been expending tremendous energy and amassing a vast body of material; the museums of Italy—the Prehistoric Museum at Rome, the Museums of Turin, Milan, Verona, Parma, Modena, Bologna, Este, Florence, Ancona, Palermo, and many others—to-day shelter the varied collections it has assembled. Among the many representatives of this brilliant school of palæoethnology, let us mention— honour where honour is due—L. Pigorini, one of the founders of the *Bollettino di Paletnologia italiana* (1875), G. Chierici and G. A. Collini (Neolithic and especially Chalcolithic periods), E. Brizio and G. Ghirardini (Iron Age and Villanova culture), and P. Orsi (pre- and protohistoric Sicily).

At Rome itself, not to mention Etruria and the rest of the peninsula, archæology has advanced from triumph to triumph in the last twenty-five years. The discovery of the necropolis under the Sacred Way in 1902-3, and the excavations on the Palatine in 1907 have confronted us abruptly with a pre-Romulan Rome hitherto unsuspected; the proto-historic cemeteries of the Quirinal and the Esquiline, explored since 1877, and the exhumation of the black stone, and the archaic cippus in the Forum in 1899 have provided invaluable sidelights on the synœcism of the Tarquins; let us recall, in conclusion, the debt the early history of writing owes to a discovery like that of the Duenos vase on the Quirinal. The scientific examination of the metropolitan soil still has more than one surprise in store. Yet it is proper to call attention to the exceptional obstacles—repeated disturbances, the presence of later buildings, the frequent impossibility of excavating the oldest strata—presented to the archæologist's spade by the site of a town that has grown into a great modern city and the capital of contemporary Italy. These are local difficulties, especially at Rome itself, but the suburban regions remain, generally still virgin soil, and from them the science of origins is entitled to expect much. The exploration of the Alban cemeteries, the discovery of the Præneste fibula, the sensational unearthing of the Veii statues in 1916 which cast such a flood of light on Etruscan art and civilization in the sixth and fifth centuries B.C., and the finds at Monte Mario in 1921 prove that it is not a question of vague hopes but of reasonable possibilities on the

INTRODUCTION

way to realization. No doubt archæology by herself cannot replace the missing historical tradition, but at least the problem of the origins of Rome will find solid ground and an indisputable basis. No doubt we know little, but we are beginning to be well grounded. Beneath its modest mien our progress has been great and hopes are greater still.

A pauper before the beginning of the Republic, still oppressed with poverty in the fifth century B.C., Roman history begins to come into the light with the Gaulish invasion. In the fourth century the ground is already more sure. Through the formation of Italian unity, Rome enters the circle of great Mediterranean powers; the Greek historical writers of Sicily and Italy devote more and more attention to the deeds and exploits of the great upstart of Latium. But if the master lines begin to stand out, forgeries, distortions, and errors still abound. The wars with Samnium and Pyrrhus have much of the element of the historical novel about them, and even in the midst of the First Punic War legendary episodes like that of Regulus will still see the light of day. It is only with the Second Punic War that contemporary evidence becomes plentiful, that we enter at length into the full historic epoch, and that the long " uncertainty " of the first centuries of Rome—to use the significant expression of Beaufort—closes in a flood of light.

BOOK I

THE PEOPLES AND CITIES OF EARLY ITALY

CHAPTER I

ORIGINS AND INVASIONS

I

THE FIRST CIVILIZATIONS

APART from a respectable list of misdeeds, the Roman annalists bear the responsibility for two false ideas which they have launched in the domain of ancient history, and which modern science has not yet succeeded in altogether eliminating. The first is that we possess the early history of Rome in an authentic and detailed form; a glance at the first books of Livy, or, better still, of Dionysius of Halicar-

Bibliography.—In view of the complexity of the subject and the multiplicity of questions involved, the bibliography must be given separately for each paragraph of this chapter.

Principal Works and Articles. — (a) *Stone Age* (Palæolithic, Neolithic, and Chalcolithic Periods): **XIII**, 1-156; **XXIII**, 21-296; **XVI**, I, 29-54, 191-97, 560-74, 613-32 (B. pls., 1-43, 36, 114-17, 128-29); L. Pigorini, in **XLII**, 1893, 162-68; B. P. Colini, *id.*, 1906, 117-81; 1907, 100 *ff.*, 193 *ff.*; G. Chierici, *id.*, 1884, 133-64; 1885, 138 *ff.*

(b) *Bronze Age:* **XVI**, I, 29-230, 575-602 (B. pls. 1-42, 118-23), **XIII**, 143-228; **XXIII**, 296-491; L. Pigorini, in **LVIII**, VIII, 1882-1883, 265-318; *id.*, in **LXIII**, I, 1892, 121-54; *id.*, **LVIII**, I, 1876, I, 1876-1877, 295 *ff.*; A. Mosso, in **LXIII**, XVIII, 1907, 573-690; Q. Quagliati, in **LXV**, 1900, 345-53, 411-64; Q. Quagliati and D. Ridola, in **LXIII**, XVI, 1906, 5-166; **CLXXV**.

(c) *Iron Age:* **XVI**, 251-308, 333-458, 653-90, 695-730, 783 *ff.* (B. pls., 46-59, 66-99, 135-41, 143-50, 167 *ff*, 254-58); **XIII**, 287-340; T. E. Peet, in **LXX**, 1910², 378-400; L. Joulin, in **LXX**, 1914¹, 67-73; **CXL**, 33-87, 127-59, 179-311.

(d) *Etruscan Civilization:* **XVI**, 779-1024 (B. pls., 166-253, 259-354, 375-83); O. Montelius, " Preclassical Chronology in Greece and Italy," in **LII**, 1897, 261 *ff.*, and **CLXXXVII**; **CLXXII**; **CXXIX**; **CXXV**; **CXL**, 88-126, 179-311, 312-458 ; **CCXXXIV**; **CCXVI**; G. Körte, in **XXII**, *s.v.* " Etrusker," 730-70, and for the latest excavations at Marsigliana d'Albogna and Populonia, A. Minto's two works, **CLXXXI** and **CLXXXII**.

(e) *Greek Civilization:* **CLIX**, 265-71; **CCXVIII**, 57-118; **CXXXV**.

23

nassus, suffices to reveal this rather bold claim. The second misconception is that Rome played a preponderant part in Latium almost from her infancy, and quite early assumed the rôle of directing power in Italy. The effect of these naïve conceptions, both equally false, is to distort completely the history of early Italy, and it is essential at the outset to relegate both to the kingdom of errors whose frontiers they never should have crossed. In point of fact the first centuries of Rome are very little known; we have said so above, and we shall often have occasion to reiterate it in the sequel.

On the other hand, Rome only very slowly won her place in the limelight of history. Italian palæoethnology, in re-action against the impenitent nationalism of the annalistic tradition, has emphasized this point, and that is one of its great merits. The formal starting-point of the annalists—the appearance of Rome in an Italy which was already old, populated with various ethnic layers, and exposed to complex civilizing influences—is to-day revealed as a culmination—we might almost say with a touch of paradox, as a conclusion. Till the end of the fourth century B.C. Rome did not guide the destinies of Italy, but the great facts of Italian evolu-tion—the Etruscan conquest, the Sabellian advance, and the Gaulish invasion—explained and conditioned early Roman history. During this long period Rome kept her place—a very modest one—in the general history of Italy until the day when the formation of the first Italian unity reversed their mutual rôles and entrusted to the city on the Tiber the destiny of all Italy. It took two centuries of furious combat for Rome to become the political centre of Italy. By forgetting that, the Roman annalists are guilty of a monstrous error of perspective which has not only to be entered in the charge-sheet against them, but has to be corrected and readjusted, a far more delicate task.

The history of ancient Italy only begins to be written with the arrival of the Greek colonists and the consequent introduction of the alphabet. On their arrival the Greeks collected and handed down a certain number of oral tradi-tions concerning Italy's past; still the artificial elucubra-tions of relatively recent origin with which historical writing of the classical age enriched this original kernel are to be regarded with suspicion. The monuments of prehistory and the data of archæology, on the other hand, provide valuable indications, contemporary and certain, relating to the remote origins and gradual development of Italic civilization. We may also appeal to the ethnological study of the peoples whom we find installed on the soil of Italy at the opening of the historic period and that of their several languages in so far as these sciences have penetrated, only a little way as yet, into their mysteries. And all these diverse and complicated materials will allow us at least to sketch the main outlines of the settlement of primitive Italy and the first stages of its civilization if we cannot fill in the details.

In Italy, as in the rest of Europe, history, or rather prehistory, opens with the Palæolithic period; man has left the traces of his presence and activity in the diverse regions of the peninsula, especially from the Acheulean and Mousterian epochs.[1] A complete enumeration of the sites would be tedious and useless. Let us confine ourselves to mentioning the great Palæolithic stations and the chief centres of finds : in Liguria, the Ligurian caves explored since 1850, notably those of Balzi Rossi and delle Fate; in the Po Valley, the stations of Rivoli and Breonio (Veronese foothills) and of Traversetolo (Province of Parma); in Emilia, Goccianello, near Imola; in Umbria, S. Egidio, Busco, and Petrignano; in the Abruzzi, Maiella (Chieti); on Mount Gargano; in the Lipari Islands; and, finally, in Sicily (Provinces of Palermo and Trapani).[2] It was an epoch of ultra-rudimentary culture in which man struggled with the beasts for food and shelter. His livelihood was gained by hunting, fishing, and the collection of wild fruits. He dwelt in caves, like the Ligurian and Sicilian caverns, but probably he was already able to build rough huts. He flaked stone to provide him with the decisive factors in his pre-eminence, tools (knives and chisels) and weapons (hand-axes, arrow-heads, lances, stilettos). He worked horn and bone and, no doubt, wood and leather as well, although all trace of these has naturally disappeared. Though his clothing was scanty (furs and skins), he possessed the feeling and the taste for adornment, gratified by shells and animals'

[1] **XIII**, 1-21; **XXIII**, 21-35.

[2] For the prehistory and protohistory of Latium, see Chapter III, pp. 67-75 below.

teeth, worn as ear-rings or threaded on a string for necklaces. His ideas of social life were presumably still limited by the family. The funeral rite in vogue was inhumation, probably not connected with any precise religious ideas.[1] Let us remember the immense gaps in this nascent civilization; agriculture, the domestication of animals, even the coarsest pottery, were still unknown. Such is the general picture presented by the oldest and longest of the several ages of humanity in Italy as in other European countries.

Many millennia pass away, and the Old Stone Age gives place to the New, and polished replaces chipped stone.[2] This second era of Italy's prehistory has left abundant and widespread vestiges on the soil of the peninsula: in Piedmont, the great station of Alba (Province of Cuneo); in Liguria, the grottoes of Pollera and Arene Candide in addition to those of Balzi Rossi mentioned above; in the Po Valley, the numerous finds from the Provinces of Placentia, Cremona, Brescia, and Mantua; in Tuscany (caves in the Apuan Alps), in Umbria, in Picenum (grottoes of Salomone and St. Angelo), in the Vibrata Valley, on the Island of Pianosa (natural and artificial grottoes), in Basilicata (Matera), in Apulia (Molfetta), and in Sicily [notably the caves of Puleri and Geraci, Villafrati (Province of Palermo), la Seggia, la Scorosa, Molinari, Due Paperi, and Stentinello (Province of Syracuse)]. An already developed civilization is represented by more complex and varied remains: cave-dwellings, flint workshops (for instance, near Imola, at Chianti, in Tuscany, and on the Island of Elba), numerous hut-foundations in the Vibrata Valley (Picenum), weapons (arrow and lance-heads, daggers, and polished sling-stones), and tools (axes, hammers, knives, saws, and fishing tackle). Man's life has grown richer, and new domains have been opened to his activity. Neolithic man is no longer, like his ancestors of the previous epoch, merely a hunter and fisher; he has domesticated animals and breeds them. Sometimes he continues to dwell in caves, but the use of the hut tends to become general. The remains from the Vibrata Valley reveal it in the form of a round or oval hut, excavated deep in the soil with a pit for the hearth in the centre, a type which will remain classical in ancient Italy,

---

[1] **XIII**, 20; **XXIII**, 165.   [2] **XIII**, 3-68; **XXIII**, 36-184.

and of which the cabin of the Roman Campania appears even to-day as the remote survival. The implements of Palæolithic times have been perfected and the introduction of polishing has endowed them with a hitherto unknown efficiency. Man has now at his disposal a veritable armoury of weapons for striking (axes, lances, stilettos, knives, and daggers) and throwing (sling-stones, arrows, and javelins), and implements (axes, picks, hatchets, saws, shovels, and scrapers); an invention of immense practical import was the sewing-needle with an eyelet. Industry has developed and has put forth new branches; Neolithic men can sew clothes, clay has yielded up its secrets, and dark-faced or black pottery, already adorned with some zigzag incisions, makes its modest début. Inhumation remains the rule; caves are often adapted for use as sepulchres, like those of la Pollera, in Liguria, but often, too, trenches are cut in the bare earth (for instance, at Collecchio, Province of Parma; Alatri, Province of Rome; Corona de' Coppa, Province of Campo Basso; Casone, Province of Caserte, and Taranto).[1] In the inhumation of his dead, man observes definite rites, the skeleton is placed in the trench in a contracted position and accompanied by a funerary furniture, of which arms, objects of apparel, and vases constitute the typical elements. Finally, social life has been materially widened; men live grouped in villages. A large central hut surrounded by smaller ones is the plan of the Neolithic settlement as preserved in the typical hut-foundations of Alba, in Piedmont, and in those of the Vibrata Valley. The pre-Hellenic East is already beginning to exercise its civilizing influence; as a result of her privileged geographical situation at the point of contact between the basins of the Mediterranean, Sicily in the Neolithic Age, Orsi's Sicanian period, takes up that function of mediator which is to become more prominent in the next phase; the pottery gives evidence of this since it indisputably exhibits the influence of the pre-Minoan art of Crete.[2]

The end of this period, already so fruitful in achievements in all domains, is marked by a step forward of capital importance—the appearance of metal, at first in the form of copper and gold. The remains of this period, termed

---

[1] **XXIII**, 36-37, 88-111, 113-22.   [2] **XXIII**, 138-43; **CXXXIX**, 222.

Chalcolithic (the *periodo eneolitico* of Italian archæologists),[1] which is really only a subdivision of the Neolithic, are found scattered throughout the whole of Italy: the Po Valley (especially the necropolis of Remedello di Sotto, in the Province of Brescia), Lombardy (pile-dwellings on Lakes Maggiore, Varese, Como, and Iseo), Tuscany (grotto of Castello, north of Pisa, Buca delle Fate, near Livurna, and Monte Bradoni, not far from Volterra), Umbria (Poggio Aquilone), and Sicily (especially the cave of San Lazaro and the cemetery of Castelluccio, in the Province of Syracuse). How did this first introduction of metal into Italy come about? Through the immigration of a civilizing people? Perhaps, but perhaps without an ethnic upheaval by simple commercial infiltration; or perhaps—and this seems most probable—by both methods. Copper was known in Egypt by the fifth millennium, and in Cyprus by the beginning of the fourth, and had therefore been long in common use in the East. The decisive part was this time played by Sicily, which had been already in relations with pre-Minoan Crete in Neolithic times, as noted above. This view by no means excludes the possibility that a second current, this time Continental and emanating from Central Europe, may have simultaneously introduced the new metal into North Italy.[2]

In any case, it is an indisputable fact that Italy made the acquaintance of copper in the second half of the third millennium before Christ. An invention, however important, never results in an immediate transformation of the pre-existing civilization as if by the touch of a magician's wand; Neolithic Italy was not exempt from the operation of this general law. Metal, copper and gold alike, is at first rare and a mere imported commodity and so remains for a long time an article of luxury for ornament or the toilet. Then man discovers its pliability and malleability, practical advantages both for tools and weapons which were foreign to stone. He uses it for the manufacture of axes and daggers. The discovery and increasing exploitation of local copper-lodes offers him the means of extending production in this direction. But, in spite of such advances, stone long pre-

---

[1] **XIII**, 69-142; **XXIII**, 185-296.
[2] On the various copper routes, see **XXIII**, 278-88.

serves its traditional pre-eminence; in the Chalcolithic cemetery of Remedello, as in the artificial grottoes of Sicily, stone axes, arrow-heads, and daggers remain the rule while metal arms are still the exception.

In addition to this characteristic feature, the appearance of metal, the Chalcolithic epoch is marked by another innovation no less fruitful, the introduction of agriculture. Man in Palæolithic times had been essentially a hunter and fisher, in the Neolithic period he had practised stock-breeding; Chalcolithic man remained a hunter, a fisher, and a pastoralist like his predecessors—*natura non facit saltus*—but he has been involved in a revolution of boundless consequences; the earth has revealed her food-giving qualities. Agriculture has been born; the Chalcolithic inhabitant of Italy knows how to cultivate wheat and bake bread. The age of hunters gives place to the era of cultivators. Hitherto the guest, rather than the master, of the peninsula, the Italian now proceeds to take full possession of his country and to embark upon its systematic exploitation. In Tuscany, in Latium, in Campania, along the shores of the Adriatic and the Ionian Sea, the marshes are being dried up and the forest retreats before the blows of the metal axe. Precursors of the Etruscans, Greeks, and Romans, the Chalcolithic peoples were the pioneers in clearing ancient Italy. A third feature remains no less important than the foregoing. The Cretan-Oriental influence, already noticeable in Sicily in Neolithic times, becomes more marked during the Chalcolithic period, Orsi's First Siculan period, which corresponds to the Early Minoan age in the Ægean. Its effect is distinctly visible in the Sicilian pottery from the standpoint of colour, form, and decoration alike.[1] The appearance of metal, the introduction of agriculture, and the growing influence of the Orient are then the fundamental characteristics of the Chalcolithic period in Italy which attained their full expression in the first centuries of the second millennium B.C.

In the course of the same millennium, approximately between 1800 and 1600 B.C., Italy entered upon the second age of metal, the Bronze Age.[2] Product of a technical inven-

---

[1] **XXIII**, 284-88.
[2] **XIII**, 143-228; **XXIII**, 296-491; **XVI**, 29-230 (B. pls., 1-42).

tion, the alloy of copper and tin, bronze, which is harder than copper, appears simultaneously at the two extremities of the Italic world. In Sicily we meet it in Orsi's Second Siculan period in the form of ornaments (decorated plaques) or luxury implements (knives, notably those of olive-leaf shape); in the North, in the Valleys of the Po and the Adige, it is associated with the civilization of the Terremare and the Venetian lake-dwellings, the most momentous stage and critical point in the evolution of early Italian civilization. The Terremare[1] are ancient villages built on piles, not on lakes, like the pile-structures of Lombardy and Venetia, but on dry land. They are met at once on both banks of the Po, on the right bank below Placentia, and on the left bank from Cremona to the line of the Panaro twelve miles west of Bologna, but they are particularly numerous in Emilia, especially in the Provinces of Parma, Reggio, and Modena. The general study of them began in 1860, but two, those of Castione dei Marchesi and Castellazzo, both in the Province of Parma, have been described in detail in particularly full monographs; a series of more recent discoveries has confirmed and supplemented the results thus obtained.

The idea of a pile-village must naturally have arisen in a region and at a period in which the watercourses of the Po Valley, draining the Alps and the Apennines, had not yet been banked or rectified, and in which the constant danger of flood haunted the minds of the country's inhabitants as an obsession.

A wooden platform, resting upon piles and covered with a layer of clay or gravel, formed the artificial ground for the cluster of dwellings; it varied in area according to the number of persons it had to accommodate, but regularly assumed the form of a trapeze, always orientated in the same direction. Two streets, intersecting at right angles, the one running north and south, the other east and west, the remote prototypes of the cardo and decumanus of the classical Roman camp, divided the settlement in four. Other secondary streets linked up these great arteries, and by their intersection delimited blocks in which were dispersed the dwellings, modest round huts built of straw, wattle, or mud. The whole aggregate was surrounded with

[1] **XIII**, 156-215: **XXIII**, 331-71,

an earth rampart and, outside that, with a moat filled with water. Refuse of all sorts, thrown out by the villagers or

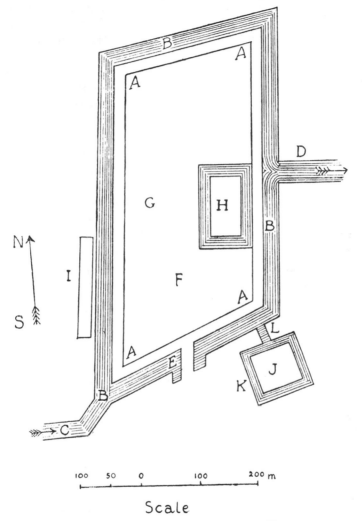

Fig. 1.—The Terramara of Castellazzio di Fontanellato.

A, Rampart; B, Moat; C, In-flow channel; D, Out-flow channel; E, Bridge; F, G, Streets and Dwellings; H, Terraced mound; I, J, Cemeteries; K, Moat; L, Bridge.

accidentally falling between the piles, eventually produced mounds three or four metres high, a record of the highest value for the study of the terremaricoli and their civilization,

The inhabitants of the Terremare, a numerous and flourishing people judging by the remains they have left, mark a stage of culture much higher than that of the Neolithic Age.[1] While hunters and fishers like their predecessors in Italy, they were primarily an agricultural people. In the glades of the vast Padane forest, which had been partly cleared, they cultivated edible and useful plants (wheat, beans, vines, fruit-trees, and flax) and pastured their flocks and herds (cattle, swine, sheep, barnyard animals). They carried on a textile industry (weaving for clothes and the plaiting of twine), wood-working (axe-hafts, baskets of withies, spades, knives, chisels, polishers, dishes, basins, ladles, straight or curved staves, and bows), bone-working and horn-working (needles, knives, hammers, chisels, combs, hair-pins, and spindle-whorls), and a ceramic industry (pottery, unbaked or baked at the open fire, and distinguished especially by a crescent-shaped projection on the handle and its decoration (lines, furrows, or " kicks "). Finally, a bronze industry characterized this new civilization. Bronze was used for arms (axes, daggers, knives, arrowheads, and swords) and implements (razors, sickles, blades, tweezers, hair-pins, and combs), and, finally, for ornaments (little wheels, pendants, and violin-bow fibulæ). The metal was cast in a mould, but technique was still primitive. The dead had Terremare of their own, analogous to those of the living, forming isolated cemeteries; there are two, for instance, at Castellazzo reached by a bridge. The funerary rite is cremation, which seems to have made its appearance in Italy during the Chalcolithic epoch in the lake-dwellings of Lombardy, and appears universal in the Terremare culture. The corpses were burned and the ashes deposited in urns or ossuaries of terra-cotta. Civilization has not yet reached the social stage of city life, which the peninsula will not attain for many centuries still, but the circle of the original family has been extended; the people of the Terremare already are acquainted with the life of a clan.

To the same period belong the latest group of the North Italian lake-dwellings,[2] those on the Venetian lakes, Garda, Fimon, and Arqua; the most celebrated and best studied

[1] **XIII**, 167-99; **XXIII**, 343-71.
[2] **XIII**, 199-207; **XXIII**, 296-330; **XVI**, 55-80 (B. pls., 5-10).

is that of Peschiera, on the southern shore of the Lake of Garda. Civilization there on the whole presents very similar characters to that of the Terremare, but, if there be analogies between them, the two are not identical. The Terremare of the Po Valley and the Venetian lake-villages constitute two contemporary groups, no doubt closely related, but which, in view of their respective peculiarities, could only be confused by an arbitrary abstraction. In the rest of the peninsula likewise the Bronze Age civilization is represented by numerous finds; confining ourselves to the chief, let us just mention those of Chiavichetto, Castellaccio, Fiastri, Romei, De Morta, Bologna, Prevosta, Bertarina, and Toscanella in Eastern Emilia; Le Conelle and Offida in the Marche; Battifolle and Monte Merano in Tuscany; Nicolucci, Pertosa, and Zachito in Campania; Felci in the Island of Capri; Matera and Timmari in Basilicata; Taranto, where, isolated in the heel of Italy, a Terramara of northern type has been found, and the discoveries in Sicily, where Orsi's Second Siculan period was developing by then. As a general rule, the population lived grouped in villages; among others we may mention those of Chiavichetto, Castellaccio, Le Conelle, Offida and Caldare, and Cannatello in Sicily.[1] In contrast to the builders of the Terremare and the lake-dwellings who cremated their dead, Bronze Age man in the rest of Italy and in Sicily remained faithful to the traditional practice of inhumation. The Terramara, near Taranto, and the cremation necropolis of Timmari, in this respect, constitute two exceptions of supreme interest to the historian.

Two ages of metal, the Copper Age (roughly from 2000 to between 1800 and 1600 B.C.) and the Bronze Age (from between 1800 and 1600 B.C.), have succeeded one another in Italy. Towards the end of the second millennium[2] a new

---

[1] For the very important excavations of A. Mosso at Caldare and Cannatello, see **LXIII**, XVIII, 573-690; **XXIII**, 450-53.

[2] In conformity with his general system of long chronology, O. Montelius puts the beginning of the Iron Age about 1100 B.C.; Déchelette (**CXX**, II, 534 ff., and in **LXX**, 1913, 128) brings it down to about 1000; A. Grenier, in **CLX**, 12, reduced this date till the eighth century, but now, in the light of the subsequently discovered cemetery, "fuori porta San Vitale," at Bologna (**LXX**, 1914¹, 321-31), declares for the ninth or even the tenth century (id., p. 326). Déchelette's date remains the most acceptable.

metal, iron, the future sovereign of historical times, makes its appearance and spreads very rapidly right to the extremities of the peninsula. With the introduction of iron a new age opens; prehistory gives way to protohistory. During the First Iron Age in Italy, several distinct and specific regional groups have been distinguished: the Golasecca group south of Lakes Maggiore and Como, an Atestine group in Venetia, with its centre round Este, a Villanovan group in the region of Bologna,[1] a Tuscan group (Vetulonia, Corneto, Bisenzio), a Latian group, the Novilara group on the Adriatic slopes of the Apennines from Pesaro to Sangro, a Campanian group (Cumæ, Suessuela, and the graves of the Sarno Valley), a South Italian group (Torre Mordillo, Crichi, Locri),[2] and a Sicilian group, Orsi's Third Siculan period (the cemetery of Finocchito). The necropolis of Villanova, five miles from Bologna, yields the most complete and typical picture of this civilization, although it would be incorrect to use this term for Italy as a whole, or even for all North Italy. The remains of habitations and, above all, the tombs with their abundant furniture provide for our purpose the most important remains of this period. The graves take the form of pits, and the funerary rite remains cremation as in the Terremare culture; the ashes are deposited in an ossuary in the form of two truncated cones united at the base, the biconical urn typical of the Villanova period, and closed with a lid. Mingled with the ashes are found some fragments of ornaments (fibulæ, pins, collars, and bracelets) left from the funeral apparel burned with the corpse. Further, the cinerary urn contains the funeral furniture, the dead man's table-ware (saucers, plates, drinking-cups, and small receptacles with or without handles) with the viaticum with which he could not dispense beyond the grave. The usual decoration is geometrical, and consists in incised designs, straight lines, sometimes combined with small concentric circles, above all, in the form of the meander or the swastika. The Villanova civilization appears further

---

[1] For Bologna and the surrounding region the fundamental source is Grenier's book, **CXL**. For the subsequent discovery of the cemetery "fuori porta San Vitale," see G. Ghirardini, "Note to the R. Accademia delle Science dell'Instituto di Bologna," June 26, 1913, and A. Grenier, in **LXX**, 1914[1], 320-31.

[2] For P. Orsi's excavations at Locri, see below, p. 61, note 1.

as an epoch of brilliant metallurgy. The metal in most common use remains bronze, which continues to provide the majority of the weapons (axes and daggers), implements (razors, knives, bits, and harness pieces), and objects of apparel (bracelets, pendants, fibulæ, and pins). Iron has made its appearance, but man only gradually acquires familiarity with its use in the course of the three periods—Benacci I, Benacci II, and Arnoaldi—into which the Villanova Age has been subdivided. A rare and precious metal, as copper and then bronze had once been—it will only become abundant and so generally used after the sixth century—iron is at first reserved for adornment; small luxury objects and little fibulæ are made of it. Then, in consequence of the discovery of the mineral deposits in continental Etruria and on Elba, its use becomes general; it is utilized for the manufacture of arms, tools, and horse gear. In this respect the substitution of the new metal for bronze remains gradual, and the latter is never completely ousted during the First Iron Age. In conclusion, let us note a renewal of influences from the East towards the end of the period. These, emanating first from Cyprus, then from Phœnicia and European Greece, are expressed, especially in the eighth century, in the diffusion of the pottery of the Italo-Geometric style throughout the peninsula.

In Venetia, on the other hand, from the Po delta to Istria, a peculiar civilization develops. These two cultures, Villanovan and Venetic, are paralled in time and show, at least at first, many common traits, but from the second Benacci period peculiarities become manifest and divergences are intensified. Though the funeral rite remains the same in both domains, the Villanova ossuary yields place in the cemeteries of Venetia to the bronze situla decorated with geometric designs or with rows of animals. This civilization was centred in the region of Este, and attained its fullest development there.[1] One final remark : in the matter of burial rites Italy was no more a unity in the first Iron Age than in the Bronze Age. The people of the five northern groups — those of Golasecca, Este, Villanova,

---

[1] **XVI**, 273-308 (B. pls., 50-59), and for the bibliography, 279-82; **CXL**, 183.

Tuscany, and Latium—practised cremation; those of the four southern groups—Novilara, Campania, South Italy, and Sicily—on the contrary, inhumed their dead. Survivals? Foreign influence? Probably both.

The long prehistory of Italy closes at last with the appearance in the peninsula of two forms of culture, far superior to those that had gone before—Etruscan civilization and Hellenic civilization. Each only attains its apogee in the historical epoch, but in their origins and first manifestations both belong still to the primitive period. The great Etruscan civilization[1] begins with the eighth century, especially under the influence of the Greek colonies to the south. Its two distinguishing characteristics in this first phase are the city walls and the chamber-tombs. Many remains of the stone city walls survive in Etruria;[2] Pyrgi, Cosa, Saturnia, Populonia, Volaterræ, Rusellæ, Fæsulæ, Volsinii, Clusium, Arretium, Cortona, and Falerii are the chief examples of this work. But though all are inspired by one and the same principle from the architectural standpoint, divergences in its application and peculiarities in technique are numerous. We find polygonal masonry with little stones filling up the interstices (Pyrgi, Cosa, Populonia), quadrangular blocks of varying dimensions (Populonia), regular squared work (Volterræ, Rusellæ) and *opus quadratum* with the blocks arranged lengthwise and crosswise in alternate courses (Fæsulæ, Volsinii, Clusium, Arretium, Cortona, Falerii). Such diverse styles of construction do not belong to the same period, and have been taken as the basis for attempts at chronological classification, all the details in which are still far from being absolutely established. The oldest of these fortifications go back, in all probability, to the end of the eighth or the beginning of the seventh century B.C., but the greater number date from a substantially later time (the sixth century at the earliest). The same variety is observed in the structure of the chamber-tombs.[3] The oldest, that of the Warrior (Corneto), seems to belong at the latest to the end of the eighth century;

---

[1] See above, p. 23.

[2] **XIII**, 373-85; G. Körte, in **XXII**, *s.v.* "Etrusker," 749-50.

[3] **XIII**, 352-53; **XVI**, 779-1024 (B. pls., 166-249); L. Joulin, in **LXX**, 1914[1], 93.

the Regulini-Galassi tomb at Cære seems difficult to date owing to the disturbance caused by successive burials, but the earliest elements may go back to the same date as the Warrior's Tomb.[1] The rich and varied funeral furniture reflects strong Oriental influence either in the guise of direct imports (Egyptian, Phœnician, Assyrian, Cypriote, and Greek) or of native articles suggested by and modelled on Eastern types.[2] The last trait of this Etruscan civilization at its beginnings was the introduction of writing, dated at latest to the end of the eighth or beginning of the seventh century B.C. Inscriptions are met already in the circle graves (Tomba del Duce at Vetulonia) and in the oldest chamber-tombs (Regulini-Galassi tomb at Cære). The alphabet used is the Chalcidian, introduced through the colony of Cumæ, later to be modified slightly by the Etruscan scribes.[3] The mention of Cumæ, the vanguard and sentinel of the Hellenic world in Central Italy, brings us to the latest in date of the civilizations of the peninsula before the full historical epoch, the Greek.

With the introduction of Greek civilization into South Italy, the historian finds himself for the first time on firm ground. The process of colonization began with the foundation of Cumæ[4] (end of the ninth or beginning of the eighth century B.C.) and was continued, at first on the coasts of Sicily and then in South Italy, during the latter half of the eighth and the whole of the seventh centuries. The immigrants from Hellas brought with them the contemporary culture of the motherland, from the political aspect, the city state and the institutions derived there-

---

[1] On the chronological question, see **XVI**, 821, 906; O. Montelius, **CLXXXVII**; *id.*, in **LII**, 1897, 265; W. Helbig, "Cenni sopra l'arte fenicia," in **XXXII**, 1876, 234-44, and 1877, 407-10; G. Karo, in **XLII**, 1898, 145; **CLXXII**, 115-17; G. Körte, in **XXII**, *s.v.*, "Etrusker," 743-44; **XIII**, 449-67; **CCIX**, 64.

[2] U. Kahrstedt, in **LVI**, 1912, 461; L. Joulin, in **LXX**, 1914[1], 67-68, 73.

[3] On the subject of the various Etruscan alphabets—those of Regulini-Galassi at Cære, of Formello at Veii, and of Marsiliana at Albegna—and the complicated problems raised thereby, see Bréal, "Inscriptions du vase Chigi," in **LVII**, 1882, 203-6; F. Lenormant, "L'alphabet grec du vase Chigi," *ib.*, 302-8; Th. Mommsen, in **XLI**, 95; J. Anziani, "Le vase Galassi," in **CLXXVIII**, 17-30; **CLXXXI**; and A. Grenier's summary in **LXX**, 1922, 368 *ff.*

[4] **CXXXV**, 213 *ff.*

from, from the standpoint of material culture, architecture and sculpture in stone, city walls, the technique of decoration, and the alphabet. They remained in close and continuous relations with their compatriots across the seas, which made them the natural intermediaries between the centres of civilization in the East and the barbarism of the West. And so the newcomers played the part of initiators of progress to their adoptive country either directly or through the agency of Etruria. The effect of their political, intellectual, and artistic activity is apparent even during the period of settlement in the eighth century, and becomes more marked and reaches its full vigour in the seventh.[1]

Chipped stone, polished stone, the Copper, Bronze, and Iron Ages, the Terremare and Villanova periods, Etruscan and Greek colonizations, such are the great phases of civilization in primitive Italy. A second question now arises : Who are the actors who have occupied the stage during this long succession of centuries ? To what peoples, to what races, are we to attribute these various grades of civilization ? Let us begin with an essential word of caution. Any human advance in a given country may be due to three causes— local discovery, the immigration of a new people, or the pacific infiltration of a superior culture from without. To which of these causes are we to ascribe the advances of the Neolithic Age, the introduction of metal in its three varieties of copper, bronze, and iron, the development of the pottery, the rite of cremation; in a word, the decisive changes which took place in the general advance of Italic civilization ? As far as we can judge, the first of the possible causes, local invention, seems to have played only a subordinate part in Italy. The other two are left—immigrations of peoples or mere civilizing influences without ethnic renewal. Both theories find their votaries and their supporters. Some writers on prehistory incline on principle to the explanation in terms of migration ;[2] the transition from the age of chipped stone to that of polished stone, the introduction of copper, bronze, and iron, the appearance of cremation would be

---

[1] **CLIX**, 212-9. On the substitution of Hellenic for Phœnico-Oriental influence, see U. Kahrstedt, in **LVI**, 1912, 461, and E. Gabrici, in **LXIII**, XXII, 1913, 365-439.

[2] *E.g.*, **XIII**, 103-13, 143-48, 207-11, 217-28, 302-11.

explained by the intrusion of fresh peoples into Italy. So, for instance, the Neolithic civilization in the peninsula would originate in an immigration from Africa,[1] the builders of the lake-dwellings of Lombardy would have brought with them the rite of cremation, the inhabitants of the Terremare would have introduced bronze,[2] and later on the Umbrians would be the bearers of iron.[3] This theory rests on a solid basis, the analogy with the beginning of the historical era when the development of Hellenic and Oriental civilization in Italy appears indisputably connected with a double immigration of peoples, the Etruscan and the Greek. It cannot be doubted that it contains a large measure of truth, but still it should not be taken as of absolutely universal and exclusive application. This first remark leads us to a second, yet more important and necessary. From the concrete data of prehistory and protohistory arbitrary, or, at least, hazardous, conclusions of an ethnographic or historical character have frequently been drawn—the Italian school of palæoethnology has not always avoided this defect. Documents of this nature, although valuable in revealing " states of civilization," cannot restore to us a history lost for ever any more than they can enable us with certainty to follow the track of peoples or retrace their different migrations on the map. The same remark applies to anthropology or philology. If hypothesis must occupy a prominent place in a field where literary tradition is too often lacking, caution at least should be the rule, unless we wish to see our conclusions running away with our premises.

The second cause, civilizing infiltration, may and must also claim its legitimate place in the sun. It is in this guise that we conceive the influence of the East—Cyprus and Crete —on the Neolithic civilization of Sicily during the pre-Minoan epoch, and that of the Ægean world on Sicily and the Italian shore of the Ionian Sea in the Bronze Age.[4] Of the same nature, too, must have been the influence of Greece on the evolution of the Villanova culture[5] in the First Iron

---

[1] **XXIII**, 165 *ff.*

[2] L. Pigorini, in **XLII**, 1903, 200-3; **XXIII**, 493 *ff.*

[3] On the Umbrians, see below, p. 50.

[4] **XXIII**, 123-43, 200-23, 280-88, 490-91, 510-15; T. E. Peet, in **LXX**, 1910², 379 and 390; **CXXXIX**, 254-59.

[5] T. E. Peet, in **LXX**, 1910², 398 and 400.

Age, and that of Phœnicia at the genesis of Etruscan art as it is revealed in the oldest chamber-tombs, and, finally, that of Hellenic Italy on the later development of Etruscan civilization, attested chiefly by the introduction of the Chalcidian alphabet.[1] To the civilizing current come by sea from the east must be added the action of Central Europe, exercised by land ways, which played its part—often, as, for example, in the Iron and Bronze Ages, a decisive part— in the evolution of the diverse civilizations of the peninsula.[2] Popular immigration, peaceful penetration; in reality, both factors have been at work equally and sometimes even concurrently. The ground thus cleared of this preliminary question, we reach the essential problem : Who, as far as we can recognize them, were the peoples of primitive Italy ?

II

THE GREAT INVADING PEOPLES

Here, again, the only logical method is to proceed from the known to the unknown. Three main sources of information are at our disposal—the ethnological map of historical Italy, the literary traditions, and anthropology.

On the eve of unification under Rome's hegemony

Bibliography.—Texts: (*a*) Siculi and Ligures: Dionysius of Halicarnassus, I, 9, 1-40, 3; Thucydides, VI, 2; Strabo, VII, 3, 7 (p. 300 C); Festus, *s.v.* " Sacrani " (pp. 424-25).

(*b*) Umbrians: Herodotus, IV, 49; Dionysius of Halicarnassus I, 10, 13, 18, 19, 20, 26; II, 49; Strabo, V, 1, 10 (p. 216 C); Florus, I, 12; Pliny, *Hist. Nat.*, III, 38-138; Scylax (G.G.M., I, pp. 24-25).

(*c*) Veneti: Herodotus, I, 196, 1.

(*d*) Iapyges: Hecatæus, frag. 54 (F.H.G., I, p. 4); Strabo, IV, 6, 10 (p. 207 C); VII, 5, 2 (p. 313 C); Pliny, *Hist. Nat.*, III, 139.

(*e*) Chaones: Aristotle, *Politics*, VII, 9, 3 (p. 247 Imm); Strabo, VI, 1, 4 (p. 255 C); VI, 1, 4 (p. 264 C); XIV, 2, 10 (p. 654 C).

(*f*) Liburnes: Polybius, III, 10, 2; Pliny, *Hist. Nat.*, III, 110.

*Principal Works and Articles.—***XX**, I 316 *ff.;* **XXVI**, I, 50-116, **XVIII**; **XIII**, 113-228, 287-340; **XXIII**, 166-77, 479-87, 492 *f.;* **LXXXIV**; **CLII**; **CX**; **CXX**, II, 1 *ff.;* **CXCII**, III, 173-193; **XI**, I, 110 *ff.;* **CXXVI**, 151-56, 180-88, 196-97; C. Julian, in **LXXII**, 1916, 263-79; 1917, 125-33;

---

[1] U. Kahrstedt, in **LVI**, 1912, 461 *f.*

[2] **CCXVII**, I, 452; **XXIII**, 283, 504-10; T. E. Peet, in **LXX**, 1910², 394-96, 399.

(at the end of the fourth century B.C.) the racial map of historical Italy looked very complicated.[1] Let us cast a glance over the land from north to south, noting on our way the essential features. In the north, Celts, the Gauls, occupied the whole plain of the Po, with the exception of western Piedmont, and spread along the Adriatic coast as far as Ancona. The modern Venetia, from the Mincio and Lago di Garda on the west to the Adige and Po in the south, was the domain of the Veneti. The Ligures inhabited the mountainous arc to the west, the Alps, from the Rhône to the Mediterranean and the Apennines, down to the sources of the Arno. Tuscany and the western part of Umbria were in the hands of the Etruscans. The Central and Southern Apennines, the great spine of Italy, formed the domain of Italic peoples divided into two main branches, the Umbro-Sabellians and the Latins. The Umbro-Sabellians themselves fell into two distinct groups: the Umbrians held eastern Umbria, coming right down to the Adriatic coast, where they came in contact with the Gauls; the Sabellians dwelt to the south of the foregoing and were themselves divided into numerous branches; the Sabines occupied the highest part of the Central Apennines, the valleys of the Aternus (Aterno) and of the Nar (Nera); along the Adriatic, between the Æsis and the Truentus, dwelt the Picentines; the Vestini and Marrucini occupied the territories to the north and south of the Aternus respectively; the Frentani lived between the Sagrus (Sangro) and the Frento (Fortore); the Marsi around the Fucine Lake; the Pæligni in the middle valley of the Aternus; and, finally, farther south, the Samnites, Lucanians, and Bruttians, the most powerful of all. The Samnites, settled between the sources of the

CXLVII; CCXVII, I, 407 ff.; CXL, 183 and n. 7, 389 ff., 473-509; CCIX, 20-21, 57, 78; CCII, I, 31-60.

It is well to eliminate from Italian prehistory the Pelasgians (LXXXIV, I, 74-128; CXXVI, 116-24; CCIX, 43-61), and the Aborigines (CXXVI, 188-89; CCIX, 84 and 125l), who do not represent specific peoples in ancient historical tradition, but whose names are applied in a loose way to the prehistoric populations as a whole, in contrast to the well-known peoples of the historic epoch (J. L. Myres, " A History of the Pelasgian Theory," in LIII, 1907, 170-225.

[1] On this point, see especially XVIII, XCII.

Vulturnus and the Sagrus on the north and the Silarus (Sele) to the south, were themselves an aggregate of four tribes— the Caraceni (Upper Sagrus), the Pentrini (east of the middle Vulturnus), the Caudini (district of Benevento), and the Hirpini round the springs of the Aifidus (Ofanto) and the Calor (Calore); the Lucanians dwelt south of the Silarus in the modern Basilicata; and, lastly, the Bruttians in Calabria. The second branch of the Italici, the Latins, occupied the Latin plain to the east and south of the Lower Tiber, between the Apennines, the Alban Hills, and the sea. One of their branches, the Falisci, had advanced like a wedge into Southern Etruria. Belonging to the same Italic family and intermediate between its two branches, the Æqui (Upper Anio), the Hernici (Valley of the Trerus, the modern Sacco), and no doubt also the Volsci (settled from the coast of the Tyrrhenian Sea south of the Alban Hills to the Liris), linked the Latins to the Sabellian peoples of the Central Apennines. In Campania dwelt the Oscans, or Opici, and in their immediate vicinity to the north-east their near relatives, the Aurunci, or Ausones. The extreme south of Italy was held by the Iapyges, who were divided into three tribes—the Daunians (Northern Apulia), the Messapians (Central Apulia), and the Peucetians (Peninsula of Otranto). Along the coast of Italy, south of the Bay of Naples, the Greek colonies were strung out, divisible into four distinct groups according to the homes of their founders—Chalcidian (Cumæ, Dicæarchia, Naples, Rhegium), Dorian (Tarentum), Achæan (Croton, Metapontum), and Ionian (Elea, Thurii).

Let us recapitulate the general features of the picture. Pre-Roman Italy represents a world, a chaos of nationalities, a mosaic of different peoples, to which only the map of the Balkans or the Caucasus can to-day offer us a parallel. Political unity is non-existent; the Italian unity, momentarily attempted by the Etruscans in the latter half of the seventh and at the beginning of the sixth century B.C., will only be achieved by the Romans in the course of the fourth. Ethnic unity has not been reached; on the soil of the peninsula numerous peoples jostle one another—Ligurians, Gauls, Veneti, Etruscans, Italici, Oscans, Iapyges, and Greeks are mutually perfect strangers. Linguistic unity is far off; the Ligurian, Gaulish, Venetian, Etruscan, Iapygian, and Greek tongues have no elements in common. The Italici themselves, not to mention innumerable dialectic differences, speak three languages—Umbrian, Oscan, and Latin—which are quite distinct, although sprung from one common stem;[1] in opposition to the third the first two, however, constitute a well-defined linguistic group—Osco-Umbrian.

Finally, as the consequence and expressions of its political, ethnic, and linguistic division, the Italian peninsula still lacks a name to denote it as a whole. The word Italy[2]—in Oscan, Viteliú or Vitelliú—which was destined for such an exceptionally brilliant career, is, even in the fifth century, still only a local appellation, the name given to the southern part of Bruttium, the modern Calabria. Its denotation will expand step by step with the advance of political unity, and the peninsula will only finally win its name after achieving national unity under the ægis of Rome.

The historical schools of Sicily and Magna Grecia, the first to arise on Italian soil, had collected and handed down certain oral traditions about the distant past of these peoples. The writers of Greece proper began to take an interest in Italian affairs from the fifth century, and the dense fog shrouding the west was gradually dissipated before their eyes. Herodotus[3] and Aristotle[4] tell us about the

---

[1] On the languages and dialects as a whole, in addition to **CLXXVII**, 43-46; **CLXXXVI**; **XCIX**; **CXVI**, and **CCXIV**, see the excellent reviews by W. Schwering and M. Bacherler, in **LI**, 176 (1916-1918), 1-127, and by M. Bacherler, ib., 184 (1920), 140-97. Umbrian is known almost exclusively from the Eugubine Tables, a sacrificial ritual anterior to the Christian era. We possess numerous inscriptions from Samnium, Lucania, and Bruttium written in Oscan, the domain of which embraced all South Italy, with the exception of the Iapygian and Greek territories. With Oscan are connected the several dialects spoken by the tribes of the Central Apennines—Sabini, Marsi, Pæligni, Marrucini, Vestini, Hernici, Æqui, Prætuttii. The position of the Volscians is doubtful (for linguistic kinship with Umbrian, **CXL**, 474,; with Latin, **XXV**, 5). Faliscan appears to be closely related to Latin.

[2] On the etymology of the word—a generic name belonging to an Italian tribe, the Vitali, or a simple allusion to the cattle-breeding, which formed one of the staple industries of the country—which is still disputed, consult **XVIII**, I, 58 ff.; **C**, n. 79a and § 138; B. Niese, in **XLVI**, 1885, 243, a¹; **CXLVIII**; G. Tropea, in **LXXVI**, I (1895-1896), 120-49; and H. Philipp, in **XXII** (3rd suppl.), s.v. " Italia " 1246-50

[3] Hdt., I, 94.

Arist., Pol., III, 5. 10 (p. 90 Imm), VII, 9, 3 (p. 247).

Etruscans and, as was natural, Magna Grecia occupied a prominent place in the literature of the mother-country. This literary activity was of very unequal value, but it had faithfully recorded a number of local traditions, and for this reason undoubtedly represents an authority of the first rank. On the other hand, the complete unification of Italy was only accomplished after the Social War and, in fact, at the foundation of the Empire. Accordingly the peoples of Italy, even in classical times, for long enjoyed, if not independence, at least autonomy, and so national traditions were kept alive till late. The writers of the end of the Republic and of the Imperial Age, and Dionysius of Halicarnassus[1] and Strabo,[2] more than the rest, have preserved their echoes. In this collection of traditions legend, no doubt, occupies all too large a space, and its rôle only grows more dominant the farther the reader penetrates into the past. But good grain is not wanting amongst the chaff. Our most accurate information on the early history of the Greeks in South Italy, of the Gauls in Gallia Cisalpina, of the Ligurians, of the Etruscans, and of the Siculi, is derived from these sources.[3]

Finally, for the origins of life in Italy, when literary tradition itself plunges into a world of fantasy and fiction, one thread alone remains to guide us—anthropology. The great periods of prehistory—the Palæolithic, Neolithic, Copper, and Bronze Ages—have all made their contributions to this science. We may, for instance, cite for the Palæolithic and Neolithic periods the skulls from the Ligurian caves, and for the Copper Age those of the cemeteries of Remedello di Sotto, Sgurgola, and Cantalupo Mandela (Latium), and the Sicilian grottoes. The skulls have been studied and measured according to the exact methods of craniometry; as elsewhere they have been divided into brachycephalic and dolichocephalic. But with their ethnographic and historical interpretation difficulties begin. In addition to the scantiness of the available evidence, anthropological theories are still too fluid and unstable for the historian to be able to adopt their conclusions with an easy

---

[1] Dion., especially I, 9-90.
[2] Strabo, notably the books dealing with Italy (V-VI).
[3] **XX**, I, 35 *ff.*

mind. Such data allow of the formation of hypotheses; it cannot be said that they furnish certain knowledge.[1]

The oldest people of which tradition has preserved any memory in Italy were the Ligurians. It is generally agreed that they were one of the oldest peoples of Western Europe. The Siculi, stated by Dionysius of Halicarnassus,[2] who is here, no doubt, following Antiochos of Syracuse, to have been the oldest inhabitants of Latium, apparently belonged to the same family. There was no lack of theories about the origin of the Ligures; Cato[3] and a tradition recorded by Strabo[4] derived them from Greece, others assigned them other homes. In point of fact, nothing was known on the subject, and Dionysius of Halicarnassus naïvely admits it.[5] In truth, the Ligurians seem to have been neither a people nor a race. They represented a social and political condition, the culture of the Neolithic Age, resulting from a long evolution in which ethnic elements, very disparate in origin and nature, had been gradually fused.

In default of literary sources, only anthropology, philology, and archæology could afford any accurate information about the remote past of this Ligurian world. A famous theory[6] ascribes the population of Italy to a race of dolichocephals come from Eastern Africa at the end of the Palæolithic Age; this race would have peopled prehistoric Egypt and then, bifurcating into two streams, would have spread, on the one hand, to Syria and Asia Minor, on the other, to the peninsulas and islands of the Mediterranean and so to Gaul. This is pure speculation, and is contradicted by more than one scientifically established fact. To limit ourselves to Italy, the skulls appear much mixed by the Neolithic period and attest the fusion of diverse peoples. On the genesis of these diverse elements, anthropology has so far taught us nothing more than the fact of their diversity.

Philology and archæology have shown themselves more fruitful. They allow us, if not always to retrace with certi-

---

[1] **LXX**, 1912², 192; 1918¹, 195; **XX**, I, 325-26; **CCIX**, 71-73.

[2] Dion., I, 16, 19-22; **LXXXIV**, I, 308-29; **XIII**, 127-37; **CXXVI**, 190-93; **XXIII**, 480-83.

[3] Cato, quoted by Dion., I, 11.

[4] Str., IV, 2 (p. 202 C).   [5] Dion., I, 10-11.

[6] **CCXXIII**; **XIII**, 107-13; **XXIII**, 165-77, 483-84.

tude, at least to catch a glimpse of the general outlines of Italian history in the earliest stages of its evolution. The racial history of primitive Italy is indissolubly bound up with the general history of Europe. It is connected therewith as the part to the whole, as the branch to the trunk. It is essential, therefore, to define in a few words the main features of this remote past of Europe.

Before 2000 B.C. there existed in Northern Europe, especially in the basin of the Baltic and in Scandinavia, a vast aggregation of tribes whose origin and past is unknown. It is these who gave birth to the world, long designated by the name Indo-European, a word which it is to-day the tendency—and that a right one—to replace by European. These tribes led the life of agriculturalists, they spoke a common language,[1] and enjoyed the Neolithic civilization. The time came when for various causes, but, above all, under the pressure of increasing population, a migratory movement began among them. We see them in quest of new territories setting out on a southward march, a slow and laborious progress, interrupted by frequent halts and long pauses. We know nothing definite as to the exact route they followed, but we can at least perceive the general features of this collective migration. Germany, the British Isles, France, Spain, and Italy were submerged thereby. Thus in Central and Western Europe a " European " State was founded,[2] and in its bosom a fusion soon took place between the immigrants, a minority, and the mass of the pre-existing population.

Accordingly the new State did not, strictly speaking, possess an ethnic unity any more than our modern States, and consequently nothing justifies us in speaking of an Indo-European or even of a European race. The State's unity was essentially of a political and moral order. It enjoyed a common civilization,[3] as did the Hellenistic or the modern Arab world, and the conquerors had everywhere imposed upon their subjects their own special language—European—the venerable ancestor of the family of languages which custom has designated Indo-European. This European

---

[1] **CLXXVII**, 54-56, 338 *ff.*; **CLII**, I, 82 *ff.*, 231 *ff.*
[2] C. Julian, in **LXXII**, 1917, 125 *ff.*; **CLXI**, 64 *ff.*; **CLXXVII**, 360-76.
[3] C. Julian, in **LXXII**, 1917, 126-28; **CLXI**, 76-78; **CLXXVII**, 376.

State was apparently the first of the great unitary organizations that our continent has known. Italy, save perhaps for the southern extremity of the peninsula, formed an integral part of it. The isles of the Western Mediterranean—Corsica, Sardinia, and Sicily—if they had not been completely annexed by conquest, had, in any case, not been untouched by the new order.

This stage of political and social life corresponds to the Neolithic period in Italy. If this be historical truth, and the main outlines of the picture seem correct, one cardinal problem will incidentally be automatically solved. Controversy has long raged over the question whether the Ligurian tongue, of which we possess a few scattered fragments, did or did not belong to the Indo-European family. On the view just sketched the answer could only be in the affirmative.[1] The Neolithic peoples of Italy are accordingly identified with the Ligurians, themselves, from the political standpoint, a constituent element of the vast European Empire of the West.

Towards the end of the Neolithic period, in the first half of the second millennium B.C., the European Empire broke up, apparently owing to internal causes.[2] New movements of peoples began which entailed substantial alterations of territorial frontiers. Philology, toponymy, and archæology provide some general indications as to these complex events. The languages sprung from the original European fall into two main geographical groups: Italic, Celtic, Germanic, Albanian, and Greek constitute the western group; Balto-Slavonic, Armenian, and Indo-Iranian the eastern.[3] In the first group Italic, the language of the Italici, the ancestral idiom from which Umbrian, Oscan, and Latin subsequently sprang, is revealed by grammar and vocabulary to be most closely allied to Celtic. This circumstance suggests that, after the disruption of the European unity, when other tribes had been dispersed in different directions, the Celts and Italici remained for a relatively long period in immediate contact and continued to speak the same language.[4] This

[1] C. Julian, in **LXXII**, 1916, 270; **CLXI**, 79-80.
[2] **CLXXVII**, 376 *ff.*   [3] **CLXXVI**, 33; **CLXXVII**, 30, 43-45.
[4] C. Julian, in **LXXII**, 1916, 263-276; *id.*, 1917, 123-33; **CLXI**, 80-81; **CXLI**, 34-35; **CLXXVI**, 12, 33; **CLXXVII**, 43.

fact, inferred by philology, may be translated into geographical terms with the aid of archæology.

Between 2000 and 1500 B.C. two new civilizations made their appearance simultaneously in Central Europe—the Aunjetitz (Unetice) civilization, with its centre in Bohemia and Silesia, and the so-called barrow-culture in Western Germany, between the North Sea, the Lake of Constance, the Moselle, and Thuringia.[1] Now, the study of these two cultures reveals a number of peculiarities. In the first place, their appearance was simultaneous and corresponded to the movements of peoples accompanying the disruption of the European political unity. Secondly, they exhibit a certain undeniable affinity. Finally, they both present striking analogies with well-known stages of later civilization—the barrow-culture with that of the Celts, the Aunjetitz culture with the Italic. Such are the facts. The consequences seem quite plain. On the ruins of the European unity an Italo-Celtic community, with its centre in Central Europe (Hungary, Bohemia, Bosnia, and Austria), was formed in the Bronze Age.[2] Its idiom, Italo-Celtic, sprung from the original European, gave rise through divergence to the two tongues, Italic and Celtic.[3] It is this community that finally, through successive migrations, came to furnish Italy with the second constituent element of her population, the Italici.

Towards the end of the Chalcolithic period the Italo-Celtic community began to expand southward. A first band of invaders, coming no doubt from Switzerland, crossed the Central Alps and built the lake-dwellings of Lombardy, especially those on Lake Varese.[4] It was, undoubtedly, this band that brought to Italy the rite of cremation hitherto unknown in the peninsula. Then, after the middle of the second millennium B.C., the body of the future Italici in their turn began to move and descended upon Italy by way of

[1] CXLI, 33-34.

[2] C. Julian, in LXXII, 1916, 263-76; id., 1917, 123-33; XXIII, 509-10; CLXXVII, 376.

[3] C. Julian, in LXXII, 1916, 263; CLXXVI, 33; CLXXVII, 43; CLXI, 94 ff.

[4] L. Pigorini, in XLII, 1903, 200-2; XIII, 151-56; XXIII, 494, 510; T. E. Peet, in LXX, 1910², 378-79.

the passes over the Eastern Alps, the Carnic Alps, and no doubt also by the Brenner.[1]

And now comes the first problem : Is there any direct relation between the arrival of the Italici in the peninsula and the erection of the Terremare in the Po Valley ? The construction of the Terremare has been attributed in turn by modern writers to various peoples—Ligurians, Etruscans, even Celts. L. Pigorini[2] has shown that they were the work of the Italici, and his theory remains convincing and decisive despite the attacks it has provoked. The peoples of the Terremare are in truth the Italici, and their long sojourn in the Po Valley represents the first stage on their march across the peninsula. The objects discovered in the Terremare accordingly give us exact information about the life of the newcomers and the form of civilization that they brought with them from Central Europe—bronze, village life, the rite of cremation replacing the inhumation practised during the Ligurian epoch, certain special customs, such as the regular orientation of settlements and, we may add without exaggerating the value of inferential evidence as some do, certain habits of order and discipline in social life. If the Italici, as may legitimately be supposed, introduced bronze into Italy, their civilizing influence in this respect did not extend to Sicily or even to the south of the peninsula, where Ægean inspiration seems infinitely more probable.[3]

The Italici did not enter Italy all in one block. Their immigration took the form of partial movements and successive waves.[4] History preserves the memory of those " sacred springs " at which the younger generations, sprouts budded-off from a common stem, set out in quest of adventures and to win fresh lands.[5] About this traditional process which persisted into the historical era, philology and archæology can supply definite information. Among the Italic dialects there is one, Umbrian, in which the points of contact with

---

[1] **XXIII**, 323, 503; T. E. Peet, in **LXX**, 1910[2], 379.

[2] L. Pigorini, in **XLII**, 1903, 202-3; **OXLVII**, 41 *ff.*; **XXIII**, 494-95. With this theory is contrasted especially that of E. Brizio (**XCVIII**, xlii *ff.*), who denies the Italic origin of the Terremare, and attributes them and the lake-dwellings of Northern Italy to the old Neolithic population (*cf.* **XXIII**, 496-510).

[3] **XXIII**, 427-30, 490-91.   [4] **XIII**, 207-11, 217-28.

[5] Str., V, 12 (p. 250 C); Pliny, *Hist. Nat.*, III, 110; **XX**, 338-41.

Celtic seem to be peculiarly numerous and close. The logical explanation of this fact is to be sought in the persistence of a language spoken in common by the Celts and the future Umbrians at a date when the other Italic tribes, Latins and Sabellians, had already been dispersed.[1] The Umbrians were accordingly the last to reach Italy. On the other hand, there exist particularly striking relations between the culture of the Terremare and the pristine Latin civilization of later days. A long series of typical signs, notably the presence of the crescent handle on the vases, has marked the trail of the Italici from the Po Valley to Latium.[2] As ancestors of the future Latins, the inhabitants of the Terremare represent the first column and vanguard of the great invasion.

Remaining long behind, the Sabellians and Umbrians in their turn took the road in two successive waves. First came the Sabellians—Marsi, Frentani, Vestini, Marrucini, Samnites, and Lucanians—who occupied the whole of the Central Apennines, the acropolis of the Abruzzi, whence the two last-named tribes would push on farther south. They were followed about 1000 B.C. by the Umbrians. The latter, finding the rest of the peninsula already in the hands of their confrères, halted in Northern Italy—Tuscany, where the name of the River Ombrone has preserved their memory and Umbria as far as the frontiers of Picenum and the Po Valley. Chronologically, the Umbrian invasion is to be placed near the end of the second millennium, and consequently synchronized with the opening of the Iron Age. History remembers the Umbrians as a great people. Dionysius of Halicarnassus[3] tells us that they occupied a vast territory, possessed a large population, and traced their ancestry to remote times. Herodotus[4] says more precisely that they extended to the northern boundaries of Italy, and adds that the Rivers Alpis and Carpis, the Drave and the Save, rose in the country im-

---

[1] Consult especially **CCXXXIII**.

[2] L. Pigorini, in **XLII**, 1900, 21 *ff.;* **XIII**, 228-85; **XXIII**, 424, 495-96; T. E. Peet, in **LXX**, 1910[2], 386-87. But Pigorini exaggerates the range of the terramaricoli from the north when he explains by their immigration into South Italy the Terramara of Taranto and the necropolis of Timmari. South Italy, as a whole (F. v. Duhn, in **LXVIII**, 1913, 472-98, and A. Grenier, in **LXX**, 1914[1], 328), seems in reality to have been beyond the range of their migrations.

[3] Dion., I, 19, 1; II, 49; *cf.,* Flor., I, 12.   [4] Hdt., IV, 49, 3.

mediately adjoining that of the Umbrians. Finally, it was in the shelter of the Umbrian Empire, the most powerful State in Italy at the beginning of the first millennium B.C., that the Villanovan civilization flourished and attained its apogee.[1]

Umbrian conquest, appearance of iron in Italy, Villanovan civilization—it must be asked whether the synchronism of these three phenomena can be considered a pure coincidence. It would, on the contrary, be tempting to regard the Umbrians as the people who introduced iron into Italy, or, at least, North Italy; the possession of iron would explain at once the hegemony of the Umbrians and the development of the Villanova culture upon their territory.[2] This theory of the Umbrian origin of iron, plausible though it may appear, must not entice us too far. If it may be admitted that the iron-using civilization as it developed in North Italy is rooted in Central Europe;[3] the supposition is not excluded, at least in the case of South Italy, that iron-working came by way of the Mediterranean. Iron was in use in the eastern basin of that sea at least from the last centuries of the second millennium B.C. There is every likelihood that its use, as previously that of copper and perhaps of bronze, early reached South Italy by way of Sicily.[4] Geographically Italy is situated at the confluence of two distinct civilizing currents, the continental and the maritime currents; the phenomenon recurs too often in her history for it to cause us any surprise at this remote epoch.

The Italic immigration, of which the advent of the Umbrians marks the close, entailed two consequences : the Ligurian population, the oldest stratum of the peninsula's population, had been either driven out, some like the Siculi to Sicily, others into the Alps and Apennines, or subjugated to the conquerors, not without exerting a profound influence on the social, religious, economic, and domestic life of their masters ; secondly, the Ligurian unity of the Stone Age gave place to an Italic unity in which bronze and iron represent

[1] **CXL**, 505-9.

[2] **XCVIII**, xcii; **XIII**, 302 *ff.*; **XXIII**, 498-99; **CXL**, 505 *ff.*; A. Grenier, in **LXX**, 1914[1], 331.

[3] A. Grenier, in **LXX**, 1914[1], 395-96; T. E. Peet, in **LXX**, 1910[2], 395.

[4] **CXCI**, 129; T. E. Peet, *l.c.*, 395.

two successive cultural phases. This new balance of power was not destined to last long; towards the end of the second millennium Italy became the scene of fresh invasions, and an influx of new peoples quickly came to complicate still further the political and racial map of the peninsula.

As at earlier periods, the transformations of Italy at the end of the second millennium and the beginning of the first were only consequences and repercussions of wider events; their causes must be sought without in the two regions which exerted a decisive influence on the course of Italian prehistory, Central Europe and the eastern basin of the Mediterranean. At this moment a peculiarly intense ferment was active among the peoples of the Danube Valley. The second band of Hellenic tribes, the Dorians, invaded the Balkan Peninsula, driving before them the Illyrian tribes. The latter retreated westward along the Valleys of the Drave and the Save into the Alpine regions.[1] The Umbrians were thus cut off from their base in Central Europe, while the Illyrian nations, following on their tracks, hurled two of their tribes on to Italian soil. These came to settle there permanently—the Veneti in the north and the Iapyges in the south.

Herodotus[2] expressly states that the Veneti were an Illyrian people, and archæology confirms his statement. In fact, close relations subsist between their civilization and that of the Illyrian regions. Coming by land along the Adriatic coasts and doubtless also across the Julian Alps, the Veneti settled in the old Ligurian territory between Istria and the Po delta in the region which still bears their name to-day. The contemporary culture of the full Villanova period, distinguished by the bronze situla ornamented with geometric designs or zones of animals, was their creation. However, they do not seem to have brought it with them ready made, but rather to have borrowed it from Emilia, marking it with their own stamp and modifying it considerably.[3] Later, the Veneti began to absorb fresh influences —Greek influence in the seventh century B.C., and Etruscan

[1] **CLIX**, 97-98; **CXXXIX**, 67-68.
[2] Hdt., I, 196, 1.
[3] G. Ghirardini, in **LXIII**, II, 161-252; VII, 5-200; **X**, 5-222; **XXVI**, I, 155.

influence from the end of the sixth after the permanent installation of the Etruscans in the Po Valley.[1]

The Iapygians, whom we find at the classical period established in the south-east of Italy from Mount Gargano to the Iapygian promontory, were likewise an Illyrian people. The ancient authors thus describe them. The study of names gives support to their testimony; in Northern Illyria we meet a tribe of Iapodes, and similar personal and topographical names. Finally, the surviving inscriptions betray, as in the case of Venetic, a close kinship with Illyrian. The Iapygian invasion came by land along the Adriatic, perhaps in conjunction with the Venetic; possibly, too, other analogous elements subsequently came by sea across the Straits of Otranto to reinforce the original nucleus. Later on, the Iapygians were to come into conflict with the Greek colonies in South Italy, particularly with Tarentum. After a very fierce struggle they were driven back into the interior, and Tarentine civilization exerted a deep and lasting influence upon them.[2]

The Veneti and Iapyges were the two chief Illyrian nations in Italy, but there were others, such as the Chaonians on the Gulf of Otranto, and no doubt also the Liburni of Truentum on the coast of Picenum, since in each case homonymous tribes are mentioned on the Balkan coasts of the Adriatic. Both had probably come by sea. The ancient historians further assigned an Illyrian origin to the Pæligni in the Central Apennines[3] and to the Volsci. In each case the theory may have been based on local traditions, but remains to be proved. On the whole, the Veneti and Iapyges only played a secondary part in the political life of primitive Italy. The position of the Etruscans is very different.

---

[1] **CXL**, 377-85, 401-14.   [2] Hdt., VII, 170, 3.
[3] Fest., art. " Peligni," p. 248, **XCI**, 38-39.

III

THE ETRUSCANS

The Etruscans, the greatest people of pre-Roman Italy, also constitute its most puzzling enigma. In connection with them three fundamental problems confront us—their origin, the date of their arrival in Italy, their language. Piles of theories and controversies have been built up around these three points; what is the state of the question to-day?

Let us begin with their origin. The ancients already express contradictory views on this subject. According to Herodotus,[1] the Etruscans came by sea from Lydia under the leadership of Atys and his son Tyrsenos. Hence the name Tyrseni. However, this Oriental theory gave rise in antiquity to several variants: a historian of the Alexandrian age, Anticlides,[2] adds to the Etruscans the Pelasgians of Imbros and Lemnos, while Hellanicus of Mytelene[3] mentions only Pelasgians. Dionysius of Halicarnassus,[4] on the contrary, expresses a view in complete opposition to the Oriental theory. In the Etruscans of Italy he sees not immigrants from Asia Minor, but an authochthonous people ($\epsilon\pi\iota\chi\omega\rho\iota\omega\nu\ \tau\grave{o}\ \check{\epsilon}\theta\nu\sigma$). Antiquity in a general way adopted the former thesis; it is the classical tradition of Greek historical schools, represented by Timæus, Strabo, Diodorus, Plutarch, and Appian, in addition to Herodotus; it is the Roman tradition found in Cicero, Livy, Pliny the Elder, Tacitus, and poets of the Augustan age such as Virgil, Horace, and Ovid.[5] It is, finally and most significantly, the genuine Etruscan tradition. At the beginning of the Empire the Etruscans officially recognized the inhabitants of Sardes, the capital of ancient Lydia, as their racial kinsmen.[6] On

Bibliography.—Texts: Hdt., I, 94; Dionysius of Halicarnassus, I, 28; Livy, I, 25; V, 33, 7-8.

Principal Works.—**XIII**, 341-468; **XX**, I, 345-361; **XXVI**, I, 117-55: **XVIII**; **XII**, II, 500-3; **CXXVI**, 128-37; **CCIX**, 61-67, and the several works mentioned above in the bibliography to § 1.

[1] Hdt., I, 94.

[2] Quoted by Strabo, V, 2, 4 (p. 221 C) (=F.H.G. at the end of the edition of Arrian, p. 151, n. 21).

[3] Quoted by Dionysius, I, 28 (=F.H.G.. I, p. 45, 1).

[4] Dion., I, 30.   [5] **XIII**, 347-48.   [6] Tac., *Ann.*, IV, 55.

the contrary, the theory of Dionysius of Halicarnassus appears as an isolated exception.

In modern times a theory of N. Fréret's, revived and systematized by Niebuhr, derived the Etruscans from Central Europe. Since then the historians have been divided into two camps—the partisans of the Oriental thesis in the one, those of the continental in the other, while some have oscillated from one to the other.[1] It must be acknowledged that the Oriental theory rests on numerous and substantial arguments. It received the almost unanimous support of ancient tradition and the official adhesion of the Etruscans themselves. Moreover, all that the ancients tell us of the religious, civil, social, and domestic institutions of Etruria and of its civilization as a whole, notably augury, music, dress, and nomenclature[2] (omitting elements legitimately to be referred to later influences), indisputably concurs in its support. The Etruscans' peculiar aptitude for a seafaring life and their long-continued practice of piracy are scarcely compatible with the theory of a continental origin. Finally, the great mass of the archæological evidence points unambiguously in the same direction; while resemblances to the body of Italic civilization remain rare or non-existent, Etruscan architecture, sculpture, painting, and decoration betray an undeniably Oriental character.

In the course of the last few years the East has yielded fresh material for a solution of the problem. Egyptian documents mention the Tursha, evidently the Tyrscni or Etruscans, among the Peoples of the Sea who invaded Egypt under the Nineteenth and Twentieth Dynasties (thirteenth century B.C.). On Lemnos[3] a double inscription has been discovered which, if not written in Etruscan, appears at least to have been composed in a very closely related tongue. These are two complementary presumptions in favour of the

---

[1] Among the modern champions of the Oriental theory, we may mention: S. Reinach, preface to **XIII**, pp. vi-vii, and in **XXXIII**, 1897, 215-23; **LXXXIV**, 74-168; G. Körte, in **XXII**, *s.v.* "Etrusker," 731 *ff.*; P. O. Schjott, *Die Herkunft der Etrusker* (1910); C. F. Lehmann-Haupt, in **CXXXVI**, III, 102-3; **CLI**; **CXXVI**, 129-30; **CCIX**, 61 *ff.*; **XX**, I, 345-53; A. Cuny, in **LXXIII**, 1923, 97. Among the supporters of the continental theory, **CXC**, II, 309; **CXLVII**, 100; W. Helbig, in **XXXII**, 1884, 108 *ff.*; **CLXXII**, 9-30; J. Beloch, in **CXXXVI**, III, 204-9; **XXVI**, I, 126 *ff.*

[2] **CLI**, and A. Kannengiesser, in **LVI**, 1911, 26-47.

See p. 59, note 4 below.

Oriental hypothesis, two landwarks for the reconstruction of the Etruscans' Odyssey.

In the face of all these facts, old and new, the Oriental origin of the Etruscans can now scarcely be called in question. They came, if not from Lydia, as Herodotus maintains, at least from northern Asia Minor. In this connection Anticlides' version of the story which associates their migration with the Pelasgians of Imbros and Lemnos deserves particular attention. We must undoubtedly expect the final solution of the problem of Etruscan origins from future discoveries in Asia Minor between the Mediterranean shore and the Caucasian region.

The date of the Etruscans' arrival in Italy is as hotly debated as their origin. What did the people concerned think and say on the topic themselves? The Etruscans possessed a scientific chronology, the essential principles of which have been recorded in Roman tradition.[1] The life of the Etruscan nation was destined to last ten centuries, and the tenth century was reputed to have begun on the very day of Cæsar's funeral.[2] The duration of the Etruscan century was not strictly limited to a hundred years; the fifth contained 123 years, the sixth and seventh 119 each. But in round numbers this chronology led to the last years of the second millennium B.C. It was then, according to Etruscan national tradition, at the end of the eleventh century that the Etruscans set foot in Italy and founded their first settlements.

Of course, Etruscan chronology has provoked many objections in modern times and has been made the victim of attempts at substantial abridgments. Etruria, like Egypt, boasts to-day its long chronology,[3] the traditional one, and its short—perhaps over-short—chronology—the quite artificial product of modern speculation.[4] To believe the advocates of the short chronology, the Etruscans had inflated the

---

[1] Varro, quoted by Censorinus, de Die Natali, 17, 6.

[2] Serv., ad Æn., IX, 47.

[3] Represented particularly by O. Montelius, **XVI**, 821, 906; id., in **LII**, 1897, 254 ff., and **CLXXXVII**.

[4] W. Helbig, in **XXXII**, 1876, 234-44, and 1877, 407-10; G. Karo, "Cenni sulla cronologia preclassica nell'Italia centrale," in **XLII**, 1898, 145 ff.; **CLXII**, 115-17; G. Körte, in **XXII**, s.v. "Etrusker," 743-44; **CCIX**, 64.

span of their national history by three or four centuries. The first four Etruscan centuries would be purely conventional, and consequently the Etruscan immigration would be put, at earliest, in the eighth, perhaps even in the seventh century B.C. The casting vote in this debate lies with the auxiliary sciences of archæology and philology.

The first factor in the solution of the problem is the date of the Etruscan chamber-tombs. On this point no agreement has been reached by modern authorities, and the two rival chronologies encounter us again. Some push back the oldest tombs (*tomba del Guerriero*) right into the tenth century, the tombs of Regulini Galassi, Bernardini, and del Duce being assigned to the ninth. The others bring these dates down to the end of the sixth century. The historical truth would seem to lie between these two extremes : the oldest Etruscan tombs appear to belong to the second half of the eighth century. But their architecture and the character of the grave goods presuppose a long preparatory period of growth and evolution. A second factor in the establishment of the chronology is provided by the alphabet. The Etruscans received their alphabet from Cumæ after landing in Italy; accordingly, they did not bring it with them. Now, the alphabet made its appearance in the region of the Ægean towards the end of the tenth or the beginning of the ninth century. Hence it follows that the migration of the Etruscans must be placed before this date.

There is, finally, an argument from the onomasticon which is no less weighty. By the beginning of the sixth century the Etruscan inscriptions reveal a mixture between two systems of names, one Greek, the other Italic. This fact necessarily implies an already prolonged sojourn, lasting certainly several centuries, of the Etruscan people on the soil of Italy. The long chronology, therefore, is the right one; the Etruscans reached Italy at the end of the eleventh century or, at latest, during the first years of the tenth.

The linguistic question remains—one of the most thorny problems that antiquity has bequeathed to us. The Etruscan people, Dionysius of Halicarnassus[1] had already remarked, and he was not alone, resemble no other known people either in language or in customs. To-day, despite the innumerable

---

[1] Dion., I, 30.

patient researches of the last fifty years, Etruscan still remain as profound a mystery as ever. The reason is easily understood. We possess numerous Etruscan inscriptions,[1] some quite long, like the terra-cotta of Capua, the cippus of Perusia, the lead of Magliano, and, best of all, the Agram mummy wrappings.[2] But we still lack bilingual inscriptions of any length—Etruscan has not yet found its Rosetta Stone. On the other hand, no language nor dialect at present known is derived from the ancient Etruscan language. But failing a complete solution, we are at least beginning to discern the direction in which it is to be sought.

One question, a preliminary question, presents itself at once. Does Etruscan belong to the great family of languages termed Indo-European or no?[3] The partisans of an affirmative reply, despite countless attempts, have never succeeded in proving their thesis. One preliminary fact seems to-day fully established: Etruscan is not an Indo-European language.[4]

For the actual decipherment, Etruscology has employed two methods simultaneously: the combinatory method—guesswork would be more correct—which professes to appeal solely to the Etruscan and bilingual texts for its solution of the problem, and the comparative or pseudo-comparative method—the method of specious resemblances, it has been called[5]—which aims at deciphering Etruscan by means of comparisons with some other known language or group of

[1] Collected in the C.I.E. of C. Pauli, O. A. Danielsson, G. Herbig, and A. Torp.

[2] J. Krall, in **XLV**, 1892; **CLXX**; G. Herbig, in **XXVIII**, 1911.

[3] For the affirmative (Etruscan Indo-European), **CXVII**; **CXXII**; **CII**; **CI**, and the numerous publications of E. Lattes, particularly in **LXXIV**, 1913, 515-28; 1914, 464-76; **LIX**, 1914, 139-242, and last in **LXXVII**, 1919[1], 228-94, suppl. 71-78; 1919[2], 392-405, and suppl. 121-36.

For the negative (Etruscan not Indo-European), M. Bréal, in **LXXI**, 1874, 321-23; 1876, 81; **CCXXVII**; **CXXI**; **CCV**; **CXVI**; **CCXXVIII**; **CCXXIX**; F. Skutsch, in **XXII**, *s.v.* "Etrusker," 770-806; **CLXIII**; G. Karo, in **LXI**, 1908, 65-74; E. Littmann, in *Sardis*, VI, 82; A. Cuny, in **LXXII**, 1923, 97-112.

On the general position of the question, see W. Deecke's review in **LI**, vol. 87, 1897, 1-125; F. Skutsch, *l.c.*, A. Kannengiesser, in **LVI**, 1908, 252-62; G. Herbig, in **LI**, vol. 140, 1908, 79-145; Th. Lenschau, *ibid.*, vol. 179 (1916-1918), 131-36, and A. Cuny, *l.c.*

[4] A. Meillet, in **XXXIX**, 1918, 303-4, and **CLXVII**, 43.

[5] R. Gauthiot, in **LV**, 164-75.

languages. The first method has yielded but meagre results.[1]
A certain number of words have been guessed with a greater
or less degree of probability, but attempts at a translation
of longer texts[2] have landed the translator in a jungle of
arbitrary and baseless speculations. The second method,
more ambitious and quicker as well, provided it succeeds,
has in reality yielded no positive results. The attempts at
comparison with the Finno-Ugrian languages in particular
have led to a cul-de-sac.[3]

The Etruscan question would, therefore, have remained
on the brink of death had not the discovery of fresh evidence
in the last few years opened up anew alluring vistas. First
came the double inscription from Lemnos[4] written, if not
in Etruscan, at least in a pre-Hellenic language closely allied
thereto. That was followed by the discovery of Lydian
inscriptions, including a substantial Lydo-Aramæan bilingual.[5] From it it is supposed to be possible to deduce
numerous and far-reaching resemblances between Lydian and
Etruscan. These striking facts, recalling the ancient tradition of the Oriental origin of the Etruscans, seem at length
to guide researches into a right channel after so many arbitrary and desultory efforts.[6] The Etruscan tongue seems
really to be related to the pre-Hellenic languages of Asia
Minor. Apart from the possible discovery of a long bilingual inscription in Etruria, there is every reason to expect
that it will be the Orient that will some day provide the key
to the mystery of Etruscan speech.

---

[1] See especially the list drawn up by E. Lattes—who, however,
exaggerates the results established—in **LXXIV**, 1913, 515-28; 1914, 464-
76; *cf.* G. Herbig, " Zum heutigen Stand der etruskischen Frage," in
XXIX, 1907, Nos. 92, 129-32, and 93, 139-42; and, lastly, E. Lattes, in
LXXVII, 1919, *l.c.*

[2] *E.g.*, in the case of the Agram wrappings, E. Lattes, in **LXIX**,
1919, 69-84; 1921, 3-14; 30-37, 256-67.

[3] **XCVII** (kinship with Berber); **CXI**, and, in favour of the Finno-
Ugrian hypothesis, **CLXXIII** (*cf.* I. Taylor, already in 1874, in **XXXV**,
7). On **CLXXIII**, see also R. Gauthiot's review in **LV**, 1914, 163-75.

[4] I.G., XII, viii, 1, and the facsimile on p. 8; G. Cousin and F. Dürr-
bach, in **XXXVIII**, 1886, 1-6; **CCVI** (2nd ed), 146 *ff.*; M. Bréal, in **LX**,
1892, 323; **CCXXX**; E. Nachmanson, in **LXI**, 1908, 47 *ff.*; G. Karo, *ib.*,
65-74; A. Cuny, in **LXXII**, 1908, 276-78; **XIII**, 400-2.

[5] A. Cuny, in **LXXII**, 1920, 259-72; *id.*, 1922, 1-27; *id.*, 1923, 98 *ff.*

[6] **CLXIII**; A. Cuny, in **LXXII**, 1923, 97-112.

PEOPLES AND CITIES OF EARLY ITALY

Accordingly, in the present state of our knowledge, this is how the journeys of the Etruscan people and their installation in Italy may be reconstructed: The Etruscans, the Tyrsenoi of the Greeks and the Tursha of the Egyptian documents, in the thirteenth and twelfth centuries B.C. were one of the pre-Hellenic peoples of the Ægean basin; they inhabited Lemnos, the adjoining islands, and some points on the coasts of Europe or Asia. They were a maritime folk and lived by piracy. Towards the end of the second millennium (1200-1000) B.C. came the Dorian invasion, which was to play a decisive part in the history not only of the Balkan Peninsula but also of the whole Mediterranean basin. In their southward progress the Dorians drove out towards the islands the earlier Greek peoples, Æolians and Ionians. The repercussion of this movement extended to the Tyrseni; under the pressure of the newcomers they had at least partially to evacuate their territories. They emigrated by sea, evidently in small bands as a natural corollary of the maritime exodus. After pursuing for a while their wonted life of piracy they ended by travelling westwards, and landed on the coasts of Central Italy.

What was their landing-place? Herodotus[1] apparently brings them to the western coast, the Tuscan shore; according to Hellanicus of Mitylene,[2] on the contrary, they landed on the Adriatic coast at the mouth of the Po, near Spina, abandoned their boats, and, crossing the peninsula, ultimately settled in Etruria. There is no need to hesitate in choosing between these two theories; the centre of Etruscan expansion must be sought in the west, in the coastal zone of Tuscany.[3] The metropolis, and no doubt the oldest of the twelve Etruscan cities, Tarquinii, which bears the name of the great Etruscan eponym Tarchun, stands close to the Tyrrhenian Sea. The land of Tuscany, at that time in the hands of the Umbrians, was in enjoyment of the Villanova culture. The new arrivals brought with them arts and equipment superior to those of the natives, but, having come by sea and from afar, like the Norman bands in the Middle Ages, they necessarily only arrived in small numbers. That

[1] Hdt., I, 94.
[2] Quoted by Dion., l.c.; **CCXV**, II, 297-99; **XIII**, 439-49.
[3] **XX**, I, 353; II, 395-96.

is the best explanation of the slowness of their conquest. We possess no details. Pliny[1] tells us that the Etruscans took three hundred *oppida* from the Umbrians, but this figure refers also to the subsequent expansion of the Etruscans into the Po Valley. Silius Italicus[2] and Servius[3] record a tradition relating to the foundation of Bologna in which we may perhaps recognize a reminiscence of the first Etruscan conquest.

The vital points are the general course of Etruscan penetration and its ultimate result. Starting from the shores of Tuscany, the conquest spread gradually inland, driving the Umbrian tribes back step by step into the Apennines. The Etruscan cities of the Tyrrhenian region (Tarquinii, Cære, Vetulonia, and Vulci) are the oldest, the urban centres in the Tiber Valley (Clusium, Perusia) and Cortona and Arretium on the Upper Arno mark a later stage. Originally divided up among autonomous communities, each ruled by a king or *lucumon*,[4] Etruria was later organized as a federation of twelve cities,[5] probably (we have no official list) Arretium, Cære, Clusium, Cortona, Perusia, Populonia, Rusellæ, Tarquinii, Vetulonia, Vulci, Volaterræ, and Volsinii.[6] But we are in complete darkness as to the date when this federation was established and as to the conditions under which it was constituted. The Etruscan people has vanished, taking its secret with it. Its history has perished and in all probability will never be resurrected.

The activity of the Etruscans was essentially a conquest. But their achievement was, at the same time, a work of fusion, assimilation, and improvement. Like the Normans in England or the Europeans in America, the intruders were only a minority, a ruling class, but, thanks to the superiority of their equipment and the spell of their civilization, they ended by assimilating the natives. The latter furnished the vast Italic battalions that, guided by Etruscan squadrons, poured forth in the seventh and sixth centuries to conquer

---

[1] Plin., *Hist. Nat.*, III, 112-13; **CXL**, 62-67.
[2] Sil. Ital., VIII, 599.　　　　　　[3] Serv., *ad Æn.*, X, 198.
[4] **XXVI**, I, 152-53; **XX**, II, 397-99.
[5] **XX**, II, 399; **XXVI**, I, 434-36.
[6] List drawn up by E. Bormann, in **XXXIV**, 1887, 103 *ff.; cf.* also **XVIII**, I, 435, n. 3; **XX**, II, 399-400.

the peninsula.[1]   Finally, the Etruscans were talented engineers and builders.   They transformed the conquered land, thanks to a thorough and systematic plan of public works : forests were cleared, marshes drained, rivers regulated, aqueducts and sewers built, harbours deepened. Under their inspiration agriculture, industry, and trade flourished luxuriantly.   Even before the seventh century Etruria was in touch with the great centres of Mediterranean civilization—Greece, Sicily, Phœnicia, and Carthage—and began to assume her function as leader of progress in Central Italy—a function she was destined to retain and which constituted her true originality.

IV

THE GREEKS

The great movement of Greek colonization, which for South Italy and Sicily was destined to promote a complete revolution in civilization, began at the opening of the eighth century B.C.   What peoples did the Greek emigrants find in their adopted homes ?   Sicily was occupied by the Siculi and Sicani, to whom must be added some trading posts founded by the Phœnicians in the west of the island.   Italy was inhabited by the Italici from Campania to the Ionian Sea, and by the Illyrian nation of the Iapyges from Mount Gargano to the Gulf of Tarentum.   In the course of a couple of centuries the Greeks won for themselves a place in the sun, subjugating or driving into the interior the old masters of the soil.   There was, however, one exception ; the Phœnician colonies in Sicily, backed by Carthage, were able to hold their own.

The movement began with the Chalcidian colonization. The Chalcidians from Eubœa, venturing upon the coasts of the Tyrrhenian Sea, despite the jealous rivalry of the Etrus-

Bibliography.—*Texts:* Thucydides, VI, 3, 5; Eusebius, *Chronicle*, II, pp. 61, 78-88, 83-93 (ed. Schœne).

Principal Works.—**III**, I, 364-440; **XXVI**, I, 312-28 (particularly for the chronology I, note 1, on p. 316); **XXI**, I, 1-334; **CCII**, II, 1-26; **XVIII**; **CLIX**, 212-222.

---

[1] Dion., VII, 3; **CCIX**, 65-67.

cans, came and founded Cumæ, north of the Bay of Naples, traditionally held to be the oldest of the Greek colonies in the West.[1] According to Eusebius' chronology[2] this event occurred about 1050 B.C., an untenable date, constituting a case of historical anticipation to which the early history of Italy offers many parallels. On this point, the archæological evidence is explicit; the native tombs, anterior to the foundation of the Greek colony, come down at least to the second half of the ninth century B.C.[3] Under such circumstances, Cumæ cannot have been founded before the end of the ninth or the beginning of the eighth century; even so, it antedated the beginning of Greek colonization of Sicily by half a century or more.[4]

In the introductory section of the sixth book of his history, Thucydides,[5] probably here following Antiochus of Syracuse, gives some chronological data. By combining these we reach the following foundation-dates for the Greek colonies in Sicily: Naxos, 734-33 B.C.; Syracuse, 733-32; Leontini, Catana, and Megara, 727-26; Gela, 688-87; Acræ, 663-62; Casmenæ, 643-42; Selinus, 627-26; Camarina, 598-97; Agrigentum, 580-79. The earlier dates, however, do not appear to be invested with absolute certainty and should perhaps be reduced by a few years, as in the case of Cumæ, though on a smaller scale. The earliest colonies would then fall late in the eighth century, a dating which is confirmed by the archæological discoveries.[6] In Sicily, as at Cumæ, the Chalcidians took the lead in the colonizing movement; they were soon followed by the Dorian founders of Syracuse. On the continent in South Italy the process of colonization followed a parallel course. Eusebius has preserved a series of dates referring to it: Metapontum and Pandosia, 773-72; Sybaris and Croton, 708-07; Tarentum, 705-04; Locri, 673-72; Lipara, 627-26. The antiquity of Metapontum and

---

[1] Str., V, 4 (p. 243 C); **XXI**, I, 156-64.

[2] Eus., *Chron., epit. syr.*, ad ann. Abr. 965 (=1052 B.C.); Hier., ad ann. Abr. 967 (=1050 B.C.), ed. Schœne, II, p. 61. Although defended by Montelius (**CLXXXVII**), this date is rightly rejected by **CXLVI**, 430-34; **LXXXVII**, 435-37; **XXI**, I, 162.

[3] G. Pellegrini, in **LXIII**, XIII (1903), 207, n. 2; E. Gabrici, in **LXIII**, XXII, 1913, 212.

[4] E. Gabrici, *l.c.*, 439-47.   [5] Thuc., VI, 3, 5.

[6] P. Orsi, in **LXV**, 1895, 109 *ff.*

Pandosia looks rather exaggerated; in point of fact, the colonization of Sicily and that of South Italy must have been practically contemporaneous. The Chalcidians founded Rhegium; the Achæans Croton, Sybaris, Siris, and Metapontum; the Locrians Locri; and the Dorians from Laconia Tarentum. Then the Greek colonies in Italy themselves began to send off branches. Locri founded Medma and Hipponium; Croton Terina, Scilletium, Caulonia, and Pandosia; Sybaris Laos, Scidros, and Posidinia; and Siris Pyxus. Thus Greek cities multiplied from Cumæ to Tarentum on the southern shore of the Tyrrhenian Sea and along the Ionian Sea. The Italian shore of the Adriatic on the whole remained untouched by their activity.

The occupation of the coast was not accomplished without a struggle. The peoples whom the Greek settlers encountered were rude but brave and warlike.[1] They had, however, to yield before the material and moral superiority of the newcomers. Some were reduced to servitude and Hellenized; the rest were expelled from the coasts and driven into the interior. Through agriculture and trade by sea with the mother-country, the East, Carthage, and Etruria, and by land with the neighbouring peoples of Italy, the Greek colonies quickly became powerful and rich; the opulence of Sybaris soon became proverbial. Intellectual and artistic development attained its apogee in the sixth century. Locri could boast of the lyric poet Stesichorus, Rhegium of Ibycos and Hippys, the oldest of the Greek historians of Italy. Velia became a prominent centre of philosophical speculation under Xenophanes, Parmenides, and Zeno.[2] Croton and Metapontum came to form chief centres of Pythagoreanism. Radiations from this brilliant civilization soon reached the hinterland; directly or indirectly all the peoples of Italy came to receive their alphabets from the Greeks. The Italici in Central Italy and the Iapyges learned their letters in the school of Tarentum, the Oscans of Central

---

[1] On this, see especially the important excavations of P. Orsi at Locri in 1889, 1890, 1908, and 1919 (cf. P. Orsi, "Appunti di protostoria et storia locrese," in **LXXXVIII**, 155-68), and W. A. Oldfather's summary in **LXVII**, 1912, 321-31.

[2] **XXVI**, I, 322-24; **CXIX**, II, 339-46, 516-32, 543-51, 586; **CXIII**, 113-14, 162-66, 334, 426-27; **CLIX**, 261-71; **CCXVIII**, 57-118.

Italy in those of Cumæ and Naples. The first cities of Apulia, Arpi and Canusium, were built in imitation of the

FIG. 2.—PRE-ROMAN ITALY IN THE MIDDLE OF THE SEVENTH CENTURY B.C.

Greek towns, and even in Etruria Hellenic influence reached its maximum strength only in the seventh century.[1]

By the middle of the seventh century B.C. all the peoples of classical Italy were already on the stage, with the sole

[1] **CLXXV**; U. Kahrstedt, in **LVI**, 1912, 461.

exception of the Gauls. The latter crossed the Alps only two and a half centuries later, but, with this exception, the ethnic map of Italy already exhibited all its essential colours, and the two great foçi of civilization which exerted a decisive influence on ancient Italy, Etruria in the centre and Magna Grecia in the south, had already begun to radiate their light.

The time is come for a last backward glance over the past of Italy and for its recapitulation in a few words. From the first beginnings of her history, thanks to her exceptional situation in the centre of the Mediterranean basin, thanks also to the charm of her climate and the fertility of her soil, Italy appears as a centre of attraction to men and things and as a potent crucible for the fusions of races and cultures. Immigrants from the north and the south—Gauls and Italici on the one hand, Etruscans, Illyrians, and Greeks on the other—civilizing impulses from Central Europe and the Ægean, life-giving streams from north and east met, clashed, or fused there. By the eighth century the period of adolescence was over, and the great revolution represented by the introduction of the alphabet through the Greeks heralded the new era. With his biting irony, Cato[1] said of the Ligurians : *inliterati mendacesque sunt et vera minus meminere*. Apart from the accusation of falsehood, this remark might justly be applied to all the peoples of primitive Italy. The alphabet marks the end of this age-long impotence. Italic prehistory draws to a close and history takes the stage.

[1] Cato, quoted by Serv., *ad Æn.*, XI, 715 (=H.R.R., p. 64, fr. 31).

CHAPTER II

PRIMITIVE LATIUM AND THE BEGINNINGS OF ROME

I

PRIMITIVE LATIUM

STRICTLY speaking, the history of Latium, as of the rest of Italy, only begins with the colonization of Magna Grecia in the eighth and seventh centuries B.C. For the earlier period, apart from a few scattered survivals in the domain of institutions, we are forced to rely on the fragmentary data of prehistory and protohistory and a limited number of traditions which are, in any case, more legendary than scientific. In early times, Latium was no spoilt child of Nature. The low-lying portions of the country, covered with water within the limits of mortal memory as far as the first foothills, formed a vast swamp fed by the violent periodical floods of the Tiber.[1] Consequently, this lower Latium was not inhabited

Bibliography.—Texts: Livy, I, 1-34 (*cf.* Florus, I, 1; Eutropius, I, 1-5; Orosius, II, 4, 1-11; Dionysius of Halicarnassus, I-III, 45; Diodorus, V-VIII (fragments); Dio Cassius, I-II (fragments, *cf.* Zonaras, VIII, 1-7); Plutarch, *Romulus, Numa, Roman Questions;* Appian, *Basilic.,* frag. 1-7; Cicero, *de Repub.,* II, 1-19; Justinian, XLIII, 1-3, 3; Varro, *de Ling. Lat.,* V, 48; VII, 28; Strabo, V, 3, 4 (p. 230 C); Pliny, *Hist. Nat.,* III, 56, 69-70; Tacitus, *Annals,* XII, 24; Festus, *s.v.* " Sacrani " (pp. 424-25), " Septimontio and Septimontium " (pp. 458-59, 474, 476); Servius, *ad Æn,* I, 6, VI, 783.

Inscriptions.—Triumphal fasti (C.I.L., I², p. 168).

*Principal Works and Articles.—***CCXIII**; **XIII**, 2-7, 24-27, 226-85; **XXIII**, 32, 116, 176, 193, 269, 273, 396-99, 424, 480-81, 484, 496-98; **XVI**, B. pls., 355-70; **XX**, I, 366-377, 381 *ff.;* **XXVI**, I, 171-223, 344-96; **CXL**, 47-56; **CCIX**, 87-231, 235 *ff;* **XVIII**, *passim,* **VIII**; **IX**; **CXII**; P. Graff-under, in **XXII**, *s.v.* " Rom," 1011-21; L. Mariani, in **XL**, 1896, 5-60; G. Pinza, *ib.,* 1898, 53-301; *id.,* 1900, 147-219; A. Grenier, in **LVII**, 1905, 293-328; E. Kornemann, " Urbs et Polis " in **LVI**, 1905, 72-92; U. Kahr-stedt, in **LVI**, 1912, 461, 219-473; A. Rosenberg, in **XLVII**, 1919, 113-42; **XIX**, IV, 78-91; M. Gelzer, in **XXII**, *s.v.* " Latium," 943-51; the maps of W. Gell and A. Nibby (**CCXXXVIII**), and A. Verri (**CCXXXIX**).

[1] **XVIII**, I, 254-263; **CCXIII**, 8-13; L. Mariani, in **XL**, 1896, 54 *ff.;* **CXII**, 47 *ff.,* and the geological map of the Roman Campagna by A. Verri, **CCXXXIX**.

till a relatively late epoch and long remained marshy and pestilential. Volcanic activity, the centres of which were the Ciminian Mount on the north and the Alban Hills on the south, raged for a long time. The significance of these two natural phenomena, malaria and volcanic eruption, for the early history of Latium can scarcely be exaggerated. Let us add that the Latin plain, bounded by the sea on the west, by the Tiber on the north, by the Apennines on the east, and by the Alban Hills on the south, formed an ideal setting for a continental State, a geographical potentiality that the human factor in the guise of Rome undertook to realize in the most brilliant manner.

When did man appear in Latium? For Palæolithic occupation there is no certain evidence. A few fragments—remains of animals or tools, found notably in the gravels of the Tiber and its tributary the Anio (Ponte Molle, Acqua-traversa, Tor di Quino, Ponte Mammolo, Ponte Salaro, Caprini, below Monticelli, near Tivoli), and other discoveries made near Porto d'Anzio and Palestrina—appear to belong to that age, but two reservations are necessary: some of these objects may well belong only to the Neolithic Age, during which the manufacture of older types of implement continued; others, embedded in diluvial deposits and carried by water, were not *in situ*. So there is room for doubt.

For the Neolithic period, on the contrary, the discoveries at Monticelli, Palestrina (implements, hut foundations), Grotta Ferrata (graves), and Farnesina (Monte Mario) certainly attest the presence of man in the lower valleys of the Anio and Tiber by this epoch. To the Neolithic and Chalcolithic periods belong the graves of Monticelli near Tivoli, Sgurgola, and Cantalupo-Mandela (the first on the slopes of Monti Lepini, the second on the Sabine Hills), and the cemetery of Viterbo.[1] The funerary rite, as the skeletons found in position show, was inhumation; the grave goods include coarse clay vases, weapons (axes and arrow-heads) of flint, and, finally, at Sgurgola, a copper awl of the most archaic type.

If the full Bronze Age has yielded only sporadic finds in Latium,[2] the end of the period—the epoch of transition from

---

[1] **CCXIII**, 17-33; **XIII**, 25-27; **XXIII**, 193-94, 248-49; **XVI**, 613-25 (B. pl., 128). [2] **XXIII**, 396.

bronze to iron—is very well represented. To it belong the finds from Tolfa and Allumiere, near Civita Vecchia, of Ardea, south of Rome, and, above all, the important cemeteries on the Alban Hills (Marino, Castel Gandolfo, and Grotta Ferrata), and at Rome itself on the Esquiline and the Sacred Way.[1] This civilization has been called Latian, since its area lies within the very boundaries of Latium, the Etruscan frontier on the north, Palombara Sabina on the east, and Velletri on the south. It was distinguished by the practice of cremation; the tombs were pits; the ashes were enclosed in a clay ossuary in the shape of a hut-urn representing the habitation of the living, and were accompanied by a relatively complete funeral furniture of vases for offerings; the sepulchre was closed by a heavy slab, sometimes rough, sometimes already trimmed. The rite of inhumation is also encountered, but only exceptionally. But the most striking feature of this Latian civilization at the dawn of the Iron Age is its close and unmistakable affinity with that of the Terramare in the Po Valley. Fibulæ of a very special type and the crescent handle on the vases which recurs in the Alban cemeteries, in the oldest village on the Germal, on the Palatine, and as far as Ardea,[2] testify to this affinity. In all probability some tribe, the remote ancestors of the Latins of historic times, the vanguard of the great Italic migration, came from the Po Valley about the middle of the second millennium B.C. to settle in the vicinity of the Alban Hills.[3] There the invaders found older peoples, the Neolithic men of prehistory, the Ligurians of tradition, whose survival is betrayed by the sporadic instances of inhumation and with whom the newcomers ultimately mingled. Ligurians and Italici, inhumationists and cremationists, represent the two constituent elements, the two primordial cells from which were to grow the primitive

---

[1] **CCXIII**, 34-39, 324 *ff.*; **XIII**, 229-31; T. E. Peet, in **LXX**, 1910[2], 381-82. For the Alban cemeteries, in particular **XXXII**, 1867, 5-72; 1871, 239-79; **XLI**, 1878, 7-10; **LXV**, 1902, 135-98; G. Pinza, in **XL**, 1900, 147-219; **CCXIII**, 350 *ff.*; **XVI**, II, 653-90 (B. pls., 135-41); **XIII**, 242-44. For Rome, see pp. 80 *f.* below.

[2] L. Pigorini, in **XLII**, 1900, 21 *ff.*; *id.*, 1903, 204-6; **XIII**, 230-31; T. E. Peet, in **LXX**, 1910[2], 386-87.

[3] L. Pigorini, in **LXII**, 1900, 21 *ff.*; **XIII**, 229-85; **XXIII**, 496; I. dall'-Osso, in **LXVI**, 1924[2], 339-40.

Latins, the Prisco-Latini, the most remote ancestors of the Roman people.

In addition to the two characteristics we have just mentioned, geographical limitation and close relations with the Terremare, Latian civilization exhibits a third—an extraordinary stability. In the course of the succeeding Iron Age, while the brilliant Villanova civilization was spreading north of the Tiber, Latin culture underwent very little development and enrichment. No doubt the Villanova civilization, which radiated even to Campania, did not fail to affect Latium—the contrary would be more surprising. Villanovan influence is seen in the material from Latium itself and from the Faliscan territory (Monte Merano, Monte Sant'Angelo, and Narce), but it seems to have been far less intense in this region than elsewhere. The biconical vase of Villanova type is very rare and did not succeed in supplanting the traditional Latian hut-urn, which remained in vogue for the future. Villanovan influence is betrayed principally in the accessory pottery both in its form (jugs, cups with vertical handles, little amphoræ in the shape of a bladder), and in its decoration (geometric ornamentation, particularly with meander motives). In Latium the Villanovan civilization did not choke the older Latin culture any more than the Umbrians, its great representatives, crossed the Tiber or occupied the Latian plain permanently.

In the first centuries of her history Latium knew no cities. Varro[1] recalls the time

" when men lived in huts and cabins and knew not the meaning of a wall or a gate."

This phase of social life when men still live scattered in villages was that of primitive Latium. It was the normal mode of life throughout Italy at the same period.[2] And we see it lingering on into classical times in regions which had not been directly exposed to the influence of Greek or Etruscan urban life, such as the Sabine and Samnite territories at the moment of the Roman conquest and among the peoples of the Central Apennines (Pælignians, Vestini, Marsi, and Marrucini), even under Augustus, according to

[1] Varr., *de Re Rust.*, III, 1, 1-3.
[2] E. Kornemann, in **LVI**, 1905, 78-88; **CXL**, 47 *ff*.

Strabo.[1] The country was divided into territorial units or *pagi*; part of the population lived utterly scattered in the country, the rest congregated in refuge-villages (*vici, oppida*) whither men and beasts fled together for safety in time of peril. These are the conditions of life which are found much later among the Germans and which Cæsar met in Britain on crossing the Channel.[2]

These villages of refuge were very numerous; in speaking of the Umbrians, Pliny[3] mentions three hundred *oppida* taken by the Etruscans. The Latin *oppida*, in conformity with their purpose, were normally erected on an elevation, a deeply rooted custom never to be forgotten in Latium. The Latin towns of historical times—Tibur, Præneste, Tusculum, Aricia, Velitræ, Lanuvium, Collatia, and Ardea—generally conformed to this ancient rule. Even to-day the centres of habitation still avoid the plain and take refuge on the hills; they take the form of terraced villages on the first slopes of the mountains, the Sabine or Alban Hills, such as Palestrina, Frascati, Grotta Ferrata, Albano, or Rocca di Papa, or scattered outposts perched on a series of hummocks on the edge of the plain, like Monterondo, Zagorolo, Mentana, and others. No doubt the Roman Campagna at the epoch of the Prisco-Latini was not the dreary waste that it is to-day; it possessed a population, if not dense—there has been a tendency towards such exaggerations[4]—at least quite appreciable, but that population already obeyed the general laws of distribution which are operative even to-day. It shunned the plains and sought out the heights.

This plan of settlement was conditioned by two fundamental considerations. The first of these, of a geographical nature and accordingly essentially permanent, may be seen at work under our very eyes; it was hygienic. The Roman Campagna is unhealthy and badly drained, the waters run off slowly, malaria is endemic. In such a realm of fever the heights constitute oases of salubrity; *saluberrimi colles* are the words which Livy puts in the mouth of Camillus in speak-

---

[1] Str., V, 4, 2 (p. 241 G). [2] Cæs. *Bell. Gall.*, V, 21, 3.

[3] Plin., *Hist. Nat.*, III, 113.

[4] For instance, in T. Frank, **XXX**, 1919, 267-76, and **CXXXVII**, 8-9. On this point, E. Pais, **XX**, I, 623-26, strikes the right note, see the Carta di Dintorni di Roma, by W. Gell and A. Nibby (**CCXXXV**).

ing of the hills of Rome.[1] The other reason, essentially historical, was supplied by the special conditions of political and social life in those days. The inhabitants of primitive Latium loved war and pillage; still in a pastoral stage, they lived, not as sedentary cultivators, but as half-nomad herdsmen.[2] Now, cattle is a particularly mobile and precarious form of wealth, and intertribal raids are of constant occurrence; so people resolved to plan the most unassailable refuges possible, and to ensure the necessary security the heights were quite naturally selected.

We should mark this ancient distinction between the high land and the flat country, the *montes* and the *pagi;* we shall encounter it again at Rome, and even in the classical age it will remain one of the essential characteristics of local topography. Accordingly, in this ancient Latium there was no genuine city life. Alba itself, which ultimately became the religious metropolis of the whole region, formed only a very modest centre from the material standpoint. The dispersal of the Alban cemeteries, scattered over an area of two square miles, from Grotta Ferrata to Castel Gondolfo, seems in reality to reflect a similar distribution of the dwellings of the living.[3] The idea of a city, an *urbs*, did not reach Latium till the second half of the seventh century with the Etruscan conquest.

The political unit was not yet the city, but the horde. In a famous passage, the Elder Pliny[4] gives a list of such hordes, or what he took for such, which were later members of the Alban league, but had disappeared by the beginning of the Empire.

But this list frankly does not profess to exhaust the primitive Latin nations. Neither Gabii, nor Bovillæ, nor Labici, nor Ardea, nor Lavinium, nor Aricia, nor Tusculum figure in it, though they participated in the Feriæ Latinæ at the classical period.[5] We shall come very close to the truth

---

[1] Liv., V, 54, 4; *cf.* Cic., *de Rep.*, II, 6.

[2] Varr., *de Re Rust.*, II, 4; A. Grenier, in **LVII**, 1905, 323.

[3] G. Pinza, in **XL**, 1900, 219.

[4] Plin., *Hist. Nat.*, III, 69-70 (ed. E. Detlefsen, in the *Quellen und Forschungen zur alten Geschichte und Geographie*, of W. Sieglin, Heft IX, Berlin, 1904). For a commentary, consult primarily **XVIII**, II, 555-60. and A. Rosenberg, in **XLVII**, 1919, 122-42.

[5] **XXVII**, I, 378-81; A. Rosenberg, in **XLVII**, 1919, 114-22.

if we estimate the minimum number of such primitive Latin peoples at about forty in round numbers. This figure, very substantial for a territory the superficial area of which scarcely exceeds 750 square miles, or an average of 20 square miles per unit—suffices to prove that Pliny's *populi* were not truly peoples, but rather hordes or tribes. The Alban Hills constituted at once their centre and their acropolis. A network of outposts, defences advanced to the very frontiers of the Latin world—Ardea and Lavinium in the direction of the coast, Collatia and Antemnæ towards the Anio, and Ficana and the Palatine colony, the cradle of the future Rome, towards the Tiber—watched over the neighbouring peoples and guaranteed the inviolability of the natural frontiers of Latium.

At a later epoch, Latium advanced from the stage of dispersion to that of federation. Under the pressure of military necessities and also of economic needs, a new idea, the notion of the league, was conceived by the Prisco-Latini. Its application to Rome in the form of the Septimontium was only a particular case of this general phenomenon. But the realization of the federal idea in Latium was only accomplished through a series of stages. First, partial local federations were constituted—as, for example, that of Lavinium.[1] These primitive federal groupings were not only numerous, they were extraordinarily unstable both in extent and in respect to their constituent elements. The constitution or dissolution of such unions of hordes was the sport of military events or economic necessities. After a long series of troubles and intestine conflicts, the geography of Latium, after centuries of instability and fluidity, began to become fixed with the formation of the Alban league at some date, not precisely determinable, but prior to the formation of the Roman Septimontium (end of the eighth or beginning of the seventh century B.C.). The whole body of the Latin peoples, or at least the great majority of them—forty in round numbers[2]—united round the Alban Mount in an exclusive federation, in

[1] **XX**, I, 372; C. Julian, in **IV**, *s.v.* " Feriæ latinæ," p. 1067.
[2] Forty-seven, according to de Sanctis, **XXVI**, I, pp. 378-80; only thirty-six according to A. Rosenberg (**XLVII**, 1919, 146), who, moreover, refers the formation of the league to the fourth century B.C. (*ib.*, pp. 114 *ff.*).

which the older local leagues were absorbed or obliterated. Federated on an essentially religious basis, the members of the league made their federal headquarters the shrine of Latial Jupiter on Monte Cavo, the highest peak in the Alban Hills. There was no capital in the material sense; Alba itself was only a group of hamlets or, at best, of small fenced villages. And so, in the absence of a city or a people strong enough to exercise a genuine and durable hegemony, the

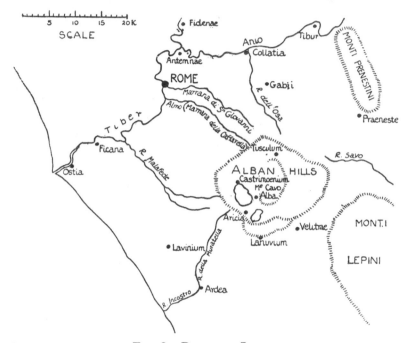

FIG. 3.—PRIMITIVE LATIUM.

federal union of the Latins remained always loose and precarious. Rome, the daughter of Latium and the image of her institutions, presented an analogous aspect in her early days.

Involved in the wider life of the Mediterranean through her front on the Tyrrhenian seaboard, midway between the two chief foci of culture in primitive Italy—Etruria and Magna Grecia—Latium began to emerge from her isolation and open her doors to foreign influence[1] even before the seventh cen-

[1] **CCXIII**, 569 *ff.*; **XX**, I, 368-69; U. Kahrstedt, in **LVI**, 1912, 467-68.

tury. The wood of her forests, the wool of her hardy flocks, and the plenteous fruits of her still virgin soil attracted the mariners of Carthage, Etruria, and, above all, of Greece. Commercial relations were established between foreigners and natives. The first rudiments of a superior culture pene-trated the country with the merchants, and soon the cults of Magna Grecia—Leucothea, Artemis Phaselis, Juno Argiva, and Aphrodite—were officially recognized at Satricum on the Volscian side, and even in the heart of Latium at Lavinium and Aricia.

But this Greek influence hardly extended beyond the coastal zone. In the eighth century B.C., the Prisco-Latini of the hinterland were still only poor, half-nomad shepherds, living a rude life and still observing often ferocious customs, if we may judge from the typical survival of the *rex nemoren-sis*, "the king of Nemi." They were acquainted neither with writing nor, probably, with the agriculture in which they were to be instructed by the Etruscans. That is the geo-graphical, political, and social environment in which Rome was born and grew up for centuries. In the light of these positive facts, her history, stripped of the veil of legend, will now appear more solid and distinct.

II

The First Roman Villages of Rome

The account of the foundation of Rome, as we have it enshrined in the histories of Livy, Dionysius of Halicar-nassus, or Plutarch, or hymned by the poets of the Imperial Age—like Virgil, Ovid, and Propertius—belongs to the domain of legend. Two, and only two, of the traditional statements may be accepted: the Palatine does, in con-formity with tradition,[1] really represent the original nucleus of the city; and, on the other hand, the first settlers to occupy the hill did come from the Alba. Despite its

---

[1] Despite the unsuccessful attempt of H. Degering, in **XXXVII**, 1903, 1645, to rob it of this prerogative; of the recent paper by I. dall'Osso, "l'Urbs Quadrata sul Palatino e la vera Roma sul Tevere," **LXVI**, 1924², 338-58. On the Palatine, see the two maps by Lanciani in his *Forma Urbis Romæ* (**CCXL**), and of the *Scuola d'applicazione per gli ingegneri* (**CCXLI**).

apparent coherence and specious accuracy, the tradition makes only a very meagre contribution to the history of Rome in the pre-Etruscan period, and even this is all too often utilizable only with caution. It is to modern archæological discoveries, particularly the excavations on the Palatine in 1907[1] and in the cemeteries of the Esquiline, the Quirinal, and the Sacred Way, that we must look for detailed and authoritative information.[2]

At the very outset one question arises : Had Roman soil been inhabited prior to the colonization of the Palatine? Covered with marshes, in the midst of which only a chain of densely wooded hills rose like an archipelago, periodically inundated by the Tiber floods, and continually exposed to the ravages of fever, the environment of the future Rome had nothing to attract man or to induce him to reside there.[3] The Palæolithic and early Neolithic Ages have left no vestige of human element there;[4] the polished stone axes found on Roman soil have either been brought thither by the waters or discovered in cemeteries of later date. In fact, the earliest inhabitants of Rome were the Neolithic Ligurians, and Roman tradition tells us of the foundation of a Ligurian village on the Aventine prior to the advent of the colonists from Alba.[5] The very name of the Aventine, for which the ancient authors invented a host of fantastic and puerile etymologies, appears to be Ligurian in origin. These early occupants of the Aventine bore the name of *Casci* (Helmets), and perhaps we may recognize in Cacus, Hercules' ill-starred rival, just the eponymous hero of this ancient community.[6] This poor hamlet of hunters and herdsmen was destined to fall before the attacks of its neighbours, the Latins of the Septimontium, and eventually to disappear, the victim of a superior race and a better equipped culture.

The first trace of colonization which archæology has detected on the soil of Rome is the village of the Germal, on

[1] For the bibliography, see p. 77, n. 2.
[2] **CCXIII**, 43-314; **IX**, 35-36, 115-16; on the necropolis on the Sacred Way, see Boni's official reports, cited on p. 80 below.
[3] Livy, V, 54, 9, "Cum in his locis nihil præter silvas paludesque esset"; **XX**, I, 621-47; L. Mariani, in **XL**, 1896, 54-56.
[4] **CCXIII**, 8-16.
[5] **CLXXX**, 27-33; **CCIX**, 287-88.
[6] **CCIX**, 288.

the western part of the Palatine.[1] The excavations of 1907
resulted in revelations which are decisive on this point.[2]
They brought to light elliptical or quadrangular hut-foundations, remains of fortifications, pits designed to supply the
population with water from the subsoil, and a necropolis
consisting of two series of tombs—the older in the form of
pits (tenth century B.C.), and the later trenches (eighth to
seventh centuries). The fragments of pottery of Villanova
type found in place allow the settlement to be precisely
dated; they go back to the tenth century and prove that by
this remote age the colony of the Germal was in existence
upon the Palatine.[3] The tradition of the annalists placed the
foundation of Rome in the middle of the eighth century, but
it preserved also the memory of a pre-Romulean colony on
the Palatine, allegedly of Arcadian origin and connected
with the name of the legendary Evander. It is fascinating
to see the excavations of the Palatine confirming its testimony, at least, from the chronological point of view[4]—and
this is not the only case in which prehistory has come to the
aid of the tottering tradition.

This date of the tenth century B.C. represents a fact of
the highest importance for the history of Roman origins.
We thus possess two sure footholds—the presence of an
Alban colony on the Germal and the minimum date of its
foundation. Why was this site selected, and why was it
occupied just then? The excavations on the Palatine raise
these two primary questions, and now we must attempt to
answer them.

We are immediately struck by one coincidence—the tenth
century was the time when the Etruscans, having landed a
few years previously on the shores of the Tyrrhenian Sea,

---

[1] Fest., *s.v.* "Septimontium et Septimontio," pp. 458, 459, 474, 476;
CCXIII, 785-89; **IX**, 4.

[2] See the four official reports by D. Vaglieri, in **LXV**, 1907, 185-205,
264-82, 444-59, 529-42, and, for the controversy with L. Pigorini, **LXIX**,
1907, 669-80; 1908, 201-10; 1909, 249-62; P. Graffunder, in **XXII**, *s.v.*
"Rom," pp. 1014-16; **IX**, 35.

[3] **IX**, 4, 3.

[4] *Cf.* Montelius, as early as 1899, in "Roma prima di Romolo e
Remo," in **LXIX**, 1899, 196, and **XVI**, 643. He is, however, in loyalty
to his system of long chronology, guilty of an exaggeration in pushing
back *at least* to the twelfth century the first foundation of Rome.

were advancing to conquer the interior.[1] From the summit
of their citadel on the Alban Hills the Latins watched with
anxious eyes the progress of the invasion. They saw the
Etruscans approaching the Tiber, the northern frontier and
natural bulwark of the Latin country. To guard the Latin
bank and keep a watch over the opposite shore were
obviously the first defensive measures to take, and the
archæological discoveries show us that the inhabitants of
Latium actually took these precautions. On the sector,
twenty miles long, from the junction of the Anio to the mouth
of the Tiber one point inevitably attracted the special attention of the defenders, that, namely, where the presence of an
islet—the Tiberine Island of later days—reduced the risks
and perils of a crossing to a minimum.[2] Opposite the islet
on the left bank a series of hills, with faces worn steep by
erosion, formed a suitable observation-post and an invaluable
defensive position in case of need. It was there, facing the
possible point for a hostile crossing, that Latium must establish
her outpost; the presence of an Alban colony on the Germal
by the tenth century shows that the step was taken. Already,
no doubt, the shepherds of the Alban Hills, following their
flocks in obedience to the inexorable laws of transhumance,[3]
had often descended the valleys of the Marrana and the
Almo and pitched their tents on the summit of the Palatine—
a temporary sojourn which was to become permanent.

Struck by the exceptional fortune of Rome, the writers
of the later Republic and the early Empire speculated much
as to its original causes. Cicero[4] in his treatise *On the
Republic*, and Livy[5] in the speech which he puts into the
mouth of Camillus when the dictator was trying to induce
his fellow-citizens not to abandon the city after its sack by
the Gauls, enumerate with pride the exceptional advantages
of Rome's situation. Moderns in their retrospective quest
for causes have displayed an even more astonishing perspica-
city. Both are, we must remember, being wise after the
event, and we may be sure that the humble founders of the

---

[1] See p. 61 above.   [2] **XCI**, 3 *ff.*
[3] I. Guidi, in **XL**, 1881, 65-68; **XX**, I, 607, on the part played by the
periodical transference of flocks from summer to winter pastures in the
beginning of Roman history, see A. Grenier, in **LVI**, 1905, 323 *ff.*
[4] Cic., *de Rep.*, II, 5-6.   [5] Liv., V, 54, 4-5.

colony on the Germal did not aim so high. The rôle of the Tiber in the economic life of Central Italy, vital during the classical period, could not be invoked in the same way to explain progress at the time of Rome's remote origins without a flagrant anachronism. The natural declivity of the hills and the healthy oasis they offered in a tract infested with malaria were no doubt taken into account, but only as secondary and subordinate factors. If Rome's greatness rested on undeniable geographical advantages, it was also— and I would say chiefly—based on intelligence and will. The first serious colonization of the soil of Rome was inspired by essentially military and strategic considerations. Rome was created to mount guard, like a vigilant sentinel, over the frontier of the Latin world, just like Lavinium and Ardea towards the coast and Collatia on the borders of Sabine territory. In claiming the god Mars as ancestor, this nation of soldiers was only decking with legendary trappings an undeniable historical truth. This sacred mission, as it justifies her existence, helps to explain Rome's subsequent progress.

For a guard-post, to be which was the supreme reason for the new colony's existence, none of the Roman hills offered more favourable conditions than the Palatine. It fulfilled the ideal of a mountain spur that the Prisco-Latini demanded for their *oppida*;[1] the steepness of its slopes and the presence of marshes spreading like a natural moat all round its foot endowed it with the maximum of defensive strength; the isthmus of the Velia permanently ensured the safety of communications with the interior;[2] water was available in plenty at the foot of the hill, its height placed it beyond the reach of fever. Thus it combined all the strategic, topographical, and hygienic conditions that could be desired. Only the Aventine could apparently have compared with it, but the Aventine was already occupied by the old Ligurian village, and, for the moment, to oust that was out of the question.

The crest of the Palatine presents two distinct peaks—the Germal on the west and the Palatual (or Palatuar, a less likely form) on the east, separated by an appreciable saddle which was artificially filled up at the end of the Republic

---

[1] O. Richter, in **XXXII**, 1884, 90-107; **CCXIII**, 517, fig. 160.
[2] IX, 1.

and in the first century of the Empire.[1] It was on the Germal, and on the portion of it overlooking the depression of the Velabrum, that the little colony from Alba, sent like a forlorn hope to guard the Tiber in the face of the menacing Etruscans, came to be established. Under the name of Roma Quadrata, a geometrical plan that the Prisco-Latini had apparently affected in the construction of their *oppida*, Roman tradition has preserved the memory of this original settlement.

In the light of the excavations of 1907, this village appears as a centre of a very limited area and very rude culture. Scarcely any artificial preparation of the land had been made. A rampart of earth and clay, possibly reinforced with a palissade, constituted its fortifications. Round or elliptical huts, which had left their impression in the earth, served as dwellings for the living. The dead reposed in pit-graves, which in the next phase were to give place to trench-graves.[2]

This colony on the Germal, traceable on the summit of the Palatine from the tenth century B.C., was not left for long in isolation on Roman soil. A little later a second village was established on the western peak of the Esquiline, the Fagutal;[3] the tombs under the Sacred Way, discovered during the excavations of 1902-1903, represent its necropolis.[4] Still later, in the seventh century, we find analogous villages established on neighbouring heights—on the Palatual, the second peak of the Palatine, on the Quirinal and its annex the Viminal, on the Querquetul or Querquetual (the whole or part of the Cælian), and on the Velia.[5] The dates of the settlements on the Quirinal, the Oppian, and the Cispian are fixed by the objects found in their respective cemeteries;[6] for the rest, we can only say that their foundation antedates the formation of the league of the Septimontium during the eighth century.[7] Thus by that time a crown of at least seven villages encircled the old colony on the Germal.

[1] **IX**, I, 19; **CCXIII**, 785-86.   [2] See p. 77 above, and **IX**, 35.
[3] Fest., *loc. cit.;* **CCXIII**, 782-83.
[4] See before all else the official reports of G. Boni, in **LXV**, 1902, 96-111; 1903, 123-70, 375-427; 1905, 145-93; 1906, 5-54, 253-294; 1911, 157-90; **CLVIII**, 199-205; **CCXIII**, 273-314; **IX**, 115-16.
[5] Fest., *loc. cit.;* **CCXII**, 776-91; **IX**, 4.
[6] **CCXIII**, 43-248 (Esquiline necropolis), 248-64 (Quirinal necropolis).
[7] Fest., *s.v.* " Septimontio et Septimontium," pp. 458-59, 474, 476.

First there was on the Palatine itself the village of the Palatual, the remains of which are still covered by the later buildings of the Imperial Palace; its necropolis, probably situated in the valley separating the Palatine from the Cælian, has not been identified. The same remarks apply to the two villages on the Velia and the Querquetu(a)l; beyond their names and their approximate sites we know nothing about them. Modern archæological researches have thrown fuller light on the topography of the four others— the Quirinal-Viminal, the Cispian, the Oppian, and the Fagutal. The extension of the Quirinal and the Viminal is indicated by the boundaries of their cemeteries; they occupied the whole southern part of the two hills bearing their names.[1] Of the two great mountain spurs jutting out westward from the Esquiline, the northernmost bore the village of the Cispian;[2] the more southerly was larger, and was divided between the two villages of the Oppian[3] on the east and the Fagutal on the west. The names of these hills have been suggested by pastoral life[4] (Pales, the goddess of flocks), or the forest vegetation which clothed their soil (Querquetu(a)l, Oak Hill; Fagutal, Beechy Hill; Viminal, Willow Hill). And pastures and forests were the determining facts of nascent Roman life.

From an ethnological and chronological point of view these villages are distinguished by two characteristics. In origin and population, as the archæological discoveries show,[5] they were Latin villages with the exception of the Quirinal and its extension, the Viminal, which were in possession of a Sabine colony. Apart from the Germal, the original occupation of which dates back, as we saw, to the tenth century at latest, and the Fagutal, which was settled a little later, none of these villages seems to be older than the eighth century B.C. Hence, omitting the old Neolithic village of Ligurians on the Aventine, the Germal appears in reality to be the oldest colony established on Roman soil. Only later did the neighbouring villages come to grow up beside it.

---

[1] **CCXIII**, 776-82.　　[2] **CCXIII**, 784-85.　　[3] **CCXIII**, 782-84.

[4] On the pastoral and semi-nomadic life of the first Romans, see Livy, I, 4, 8; II, 1, 4; Varr., *de Re Rust.*, II, 1, 9; Plin., *Hist. Nat.*, XVIII, 11; L. Mariani, in **XL**, 1896, 44 *ff.*; A. Grenier, in **LVII**, 1905, 323-28.

[5] **CCIX**, 18, 289-91; IX, 4.

In considering the causes of this gradual peopling, we must distinguish between the Latin villages (Palatual, Cispian, Oppian, Fagutal, Querquetu(a)l, and Velia) and the Sabine colony on the Quirinal-Viminal. The Latin villages

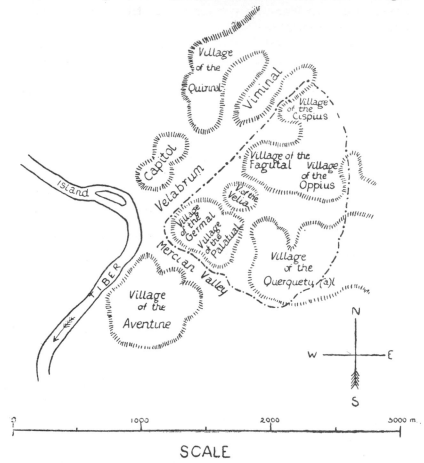

SCALE

FIG. 4.—THE HISTORICAL GROWTH OF THE CITY OF ROME.

ᴧ̄ᴧ̄ᴧ̄. —.—.—.—. Boundaries of the Septimontium.

appear clustered along the route to the hinterland, which for the Germal represented the link with its metropolis, Alba, and its pastures. Two of these villages figure in Pliny's list[1] as members of the future Alban league. By origins, affinities, and political or economic interests, these Latin villages con-

[1] Plin., *Hist. Nat.*, III, 69-70.

stitute a homogeneous and coherent group; their population even at this epoch apparently bore a special name, Quirites, an appellation which was to be overshadowed by the term Romans as a result of the Etruscan conquest, but would never disappear completely from official titles and formulæ even in the classical period.

The case of the Quirinal is quite another matter. The date of its colonization, about two centuries later than that of the Germal, reveals that here military considerations were not the governing factor, and that is not surprising. The Etruscan peril must necessarily appear less grave and pressing to the Sabine mountaineers than to the inhabitants of Latium. The decisive factor must have been economic. An important centre of trade had grown up at this point of contact on the Tiber, where the outposts of the Latin and the Etruscan peoples had been confronting one another for two centuries. Through it passed the main road from the interior, notably the salt route, the future Via Salaria, the main artery of the Quirinal and the way of access to the Sabine lands. The Sabines recognized that at this vital junction they, too, had their economic interests to safeguard and their views to express. The colony on the Quirinal was to be a watch-post to insure them the means to that end. Thereafter Latins, Etruscans, and Sabines found themselves in constant contact, face to face, and it is not irrelevant to observe that this meeting-place of the great peoples of Central Italy was two centuries later to assume the immortal name of Rome.

As outposts of the Latin and Sabine worlds, the Roman villages faithfully reflected their political life and stage of culture.[1] They were, before all else, fortified centres like the other *oppida* of Latium, in which defence was the first consideration. This preoccupation found expression in the first place by the choice of the sites, not isolated hills, but mountainous spurs connected with the rest of the country only by a neck that could easily be defended in case of need.[2] This type of settlement, constantly repeated in Latium, was re-

---

[1] *Cf.* the results of the recent excavations on the Hill of S. Agata, north of Monte Mario, which have laid bare the ruins of a village of the Latial period; I. M. Palmarini, in **LXVI**, 1922², 253-58; I. dall' Osso, *ibid.*, 1923⁴, 353-56, and 1924², 343.   [2] **CCXIII**, 514-18.

produced in several copies on the hills of Rome—the Palatine, Quirinal, Viminal, Cispian, Oppian, Fagutal, and Querquetu(a)l. The natural strength of the site was enhanced by artificial works. The steepness of the slopes was emphasized, and in more vulnerable spots, notably on the connecting neck, an embankment, sometimes surmounted by a palisade, was heaped up and a trench was dug to hinder access. At least one memorial of such primitive fortifications was visible at Rome at the end of the Republic; Varro mentions the earthen wall of the Carinæ (*murus terreus Carinarum*), no doubt a relic of the ancient defences of the Fagutal.[1]

The size of the Roman villages was proportionate to the available land; those in the centre were necessarily only small (maximum figures are 17 acres for the Germal, the same for the Palatual, 15 for the Fagutal, and 7 for the Velia); those on the circumference could spread more widely (the Oppian about 37 acres and the Quirinal about 100). But the village did not take up all the available space, and as a general rule the portion actually inhabited occupied only a fraction of the fortified area. Groves were not uncommon; in the classical period some still survived on the Esquiline, the Janiculum, and elsewhere, and the names of the hills— Fagutal, Viminal, and Querquetu(a)l are suggestive. Moreover, each family plot ordinarily included two kinds of extension; a yard for cattle and a vegetable garden (*heredium*) to supply family needs were normally attached to each dwelling.[2] And so the population in such circumstances could not exceed insignificant figures; a few hundred inhabitants in the smaller hamlets, rather more in the larger communities like the Quirinal, a couple of thousand as the total, such would be the modest returns of a census of the Roman world in the first two centuries of her momentous career.

The house,[3] the type of which has been preserved, thanks to the foundations of circular or elliptical huts on the Germal, and the cinerary urns from the cemeteries, and also the pious conservativism of tradition, as in the case of the Temple of Vesta on the Sacred Way,[4] was the cabin, or

---

[1] Varr., *de Lingua Lat.*, V, 48; **CCXIII**, 783-84.
[2] **CCXIII**, 483-90; G. Pinza, in **XL**, 1898, 100.
[3] **CCXIII**, 467-92; G. Pinza, in **XL**, 1898, 95 *ff.*; **CXII**, 107 *ff.*
[4] **X**, *s.v.* "Templum Vestæ "; **IX**, 26.

tugurium, with walls of rushes and straw supported by a wooden frame and plastered inside and out with a facing of clay. Originally curvilinear in outline, it tends towards a rectangular form the nearer we come to the Etruscan period. Each village boasted of its citadel, or *arx*, at once a fort and a religious centre, where the chief shrine of the community was erected—that of the triad, Jupiter, Juno, and Minerva on the Capitol of the Quirinal, the *Capitolium vetus*.[1]

Stone has not yet appeared in architecture, even for the gods' temples; for that we must await the Etruscan conquest. Furniture was poor, as is natural among a pastoral folk.[2] The excavations on the Palatine and the cemeteries on the Sacred Way, the Quirinal, and the Esquiline—pre-Romulean cremation graves in the form of circular pits (ninth to eighth centuries)—have given us some idea of what it was like: the pottery was locally made, rough and rudely fashioned of coarse, unlevigated clay, the material being plentifully supplied by the tufa of the subsoil. Gold and silver were rare, bronze was employed for the manufacture of weapons (lance-heads and sword blades), tools (razors), and articles of apparel (fibulæ). Iron was already used for weapons, implements, or fibulæ, but only sparingly, for we are still in the First Iron Age. A few substances were imported, notably amber, which occurs in the form of little discs decorating the bows of fibulæ or strung together as necklaces. The Roman villagers at the time of dispersion seem to have been still unacquainted with writing; the earliest Roman evidence for the use of letters; the Duenos vase found in the Quirinal, belongs at the earliest to the Etruscan period (end of the seventh and beginning of the sixth centuries).[3]

In conclusion let us summarize the general features of Roman life at the time when the era of dispersion was drawing to a close. The villages of the Roman hills, outposts of the Latin and Sabine peoples, perched upon the heights while the slopes and hollows formed the sites for their cemeteries, were small groups of herdsmen, isolated among their woods and marshes, without much intercourse with their

[1] **CCXIII**, 592-514.

[2] On the civilization of the Roman villages of the First Iron Age as a whole, see especially **CCXIII**, 519-705.

[3] See p. 98 below.

neighbours and almost cut off from life-giving impulses from without. Their inhabitants, with only the rudiments of political and social organization, lived a poor, hard, and comfortless life. We have reached the Iron Age, but that metal still remains rare and its use is restricted. Their paucity in resources corresponded to the moderation of the people's needs. But already the preparations for a significant revolution were in train. In this Central Italy, where the Etruscan peril was daily increasing, an idea was born, that of federation, remote forerunner and imperfect embryo of the future unity. From Latium it spread to the Roman villages, or, at least, to such as were Latin in origin. The period of autonomy draws to a close, and the federal system appears on Roman soil in the guise of the league of the seven hills—the Septimontium.

III

THE LEAGUE OF THE SEVEN HILLS

The very existence of the league of the seven hills[1] has often been called in question,[2] but wrongly so-in our opinion. A jurisconsult of the time of Augustus, Antistius Labeo, quoted by Festus, attests its historical reality and gives a detailed list of its constituents.[3] This is, it has been objected, an isolated and valueless document. Were that true, the fact would not suffice to cancel his evidence, but better proof still is at hand—the topographical tradition represented by Antistius Labeo recurs in Servius[4] and in Lydus.[5] Finally, an inscription of the Republican period, mentioning the *magistri et flamines montani montis Oppi*, affords convincing proof—at least, as far as the Oppian is concerned.[6]

Two additional considerations should be borne in mind. Rome, an integral part of Latium, quite naturally reflects

[1] **CXXXVIII**, I, 161-244; **X**, *s.v.* "Septimontium," p. 129, and plan I; **VIII**, *ibid.*, 517-18; **CXCIX**, 234-38; **XX**, I, 636-37; **IX**, 4.

[2] **CCXIII**, 754-62; P. Graffunder, in **XXII**, *s.v.* "Rom," pp. 1018-21; E. Kornemann, in **LVI**, 1905, 87, n. 4.

[3] Fest., *s.v.* "Septimontio et Septimontium," pp. 458-59, 474, 476.

[4] Serv., *ad Æn.*, VI, 783.   [5] Lyd., *de Mens.*, 118.

[6] C.I.L., VI, 32455.

her political organization and evolution. The formation of leagues on Latin territory must ultimately involve a like result in the case of the Roman villages. The birth of the league of the seven hills is, accordingly, only a particular case of a general phenomenon. On the other hand, at Rome itself tradition tells us of a previous synœcism of the Albans on the Palatine and the Sabines on the Capitol under their two kings, Romulus and Titus Tatius.[1] It is possible that this first experiment in amalgamation represents a genuine historical fact, but, if so, the experiment was but ephemeral. From the topographical point of view, the Capitol belongs to the Quirinal, and without the inclusion of the latter hill— occupied as we saw by a Sabine colony—the union between the Capitol and the Palatine could but be precarious. Furthermore, the marshy depression of the Velabrum, by making permanent relations between the two hills difficult or impracticable, tended towards the same result. And so the Capitol, excluded from the community of the seven hills, was not destined to enter the city till the morrow of the Etruscan conquest and simultaneously with the Quirinal— a striking coincidence.

The league of the seven hills, as defined by the text of Antistius Labeo, included the Germal, the Palatual, the Velia, the Fagutal, the Cispius, the Oppius, and a part of the Querquetu(a)l (Cælian) under the name of Sucusa.[2] Such was the result. Can we ascertain the process which led to the new formation? The passage from dispersion to federation was not the work of a day; it presupposes a comparatively long evolution, in which archæology and a study of topography allow us to discern two phases—a Palatine phase and a Septimontial phase.

Roman tradition preserves the memory of a time when the Palatine constituted a political unit. The passage of Tacitus[3] describing the Pomerium of the Palatine affords conclusive proof of this. The section can refer neither to the primitive *Roma quadrata* nor to the subsequent period of Etruscan unification. It refers to the Septimontium phase and throws some light on the process of evolution. The

---

[1] **CXXXVIII**, I, 244-368; **CCIX**, 294 *ff*.

[2] **CCXXXVII**, I, 19; **CXCIX**, 234-38; **XX**, I, 636-37; IX, 4.

[3] Tac., *Ann.*, XII, 24.

discovery of the Palatine Mundus,[1] a round domed chamber cut in the tufa, unearthed under the tablinum of the Flavian palace, comes to confirm the historian's testimony. In fact, this mundus, situated at the geometrical centre of the Palatine, presupposes at least a relative unity on the hill. On the other hand, in the league of the seven hills the Palatine does not figure in its unified form, but under the name of the two crests forming it—the Germal and Palatual. Its political unity under such circumstances can only have been of a federal nature.[2]

The guiding considerations in this union are easily grasped. There was no lack of causes of friction and conflict between the two adjacent villages of the Germal and the Palatual. In the first place, both were close neighbours in space, unseparated by any marshy depression, an exceptional position on Roman soil. Economic causes contributed to produce the same result, and in this connection the question of pastures was particularly delicate. The Palatine was almost entirely surrounded by a continuous chain of marshes—the Forum, the Velabrum, the Vallis Murcia, and the valley between the Cælian and the Palatine; a single route led to the pastures of the hinterland. This ran across the central depression of the Palatine to the Porta Mugonia—the gate of lowing herds, as it was suggestively called—and then followed the Velia neck. This route served the two villages of the Palatine in common, and an enforced partnership of this kind all the world over engenders manifold disputes. For a pastoral society like that of primitive Rome it was a question of life or death.

We do not know the full course of the conflict nor its fortunes, but we can at least discern its final outcome—an alliance between the two villages concerned in the form of a Palatine federation. This union was too loose to impair the autonomy of its constituent elements or to entail, as far as we can judge, the construction of a common fortification wall. Recent discoveries and operations still in progress have, in fact, shown that the remains of walls built of tufa blocks, traditionally attributed to the primitive period of

[1] L. A. Constans, in **XLIV**, 1914, 109-11; **IX**, 46-47.
[2] S. B. Plattner, in **XLIII**, 1906, 69 *ff.*; J. B. Carter, in **XXXI**, 1908, 175; **XXVI**, I, 185-86; **IX**, 4.

Roman history, do not as a whole go back beyond the Gaulish invasion, and so date, at the earliest, from the first half of the fourth century B.C.[1]

The next and final stage on the way to the federal system was the formation of the Septimontium, the league of the seven hills. How did the transition from the Palatine phase to this final consummation come about? The Palatine indubitably played a decisive part in this enlargement of the federation, and the reason for this is very plain. In addition to the advantages of its geographical situation and its traditional prestige, the Palatine now enjoyed the political power that the federation of its two parts ensured. The logical consequence was that the federation of the Roman villages would be effected primarily, if not exclusively, to the advantage of the Palatine, the most favoured of the hills both politically and geographically. On this occasion again, then, for the second time in its history, the Palatine, thanks to the exceptional advantages it enjoyed, was called upon to play the dominant part in the evolution of the city.

The course of the process was no doubt less simple and rapid than might be thought. On this point we have but one guide, topography, but it is a very valuable guide indeed. The Palatine, we must again recall, was surrounded on four sides by low depressions always marshy and regularly submerged at the time of the Tiber flood; it possessed only one easy and permanent link with the outside world, the Velia neck.[2] The road along the Velia, the main route to the pastures and the sole *tratturo* for ancient Roman transhumance, had, as we saw, already come to the forefront in the formation of the Palatine federation. Now, beyond the Porta Mugonia this route was doubly barred, first by the village of the Velia and beyond that by the three villages on the Esquiline—those of the Fagutal, the Oppian, and the Cispian. Since the peoples of the Palatine were vitally interested in keeping this road open, a conflict with the neighbouring villages must sooner or later break out, and no doubt it soon did.

The fact that the village of the Velia and that on the Querquetu(a)l[3] were members of the Alban federation must

---

[1] **CCXIII**, 788-89; **CXCIX**, 233; **IX**, 57.　　　　　[2] **IX**, 1.
[3] Plin., *Hist. Nat.*, III, 69-70; **CCXIII**, 786-87, 790.

make the clash more bitter. Nevertheless, the Palatine, better equipped for the combat both geographically and politically, finally triumphed. The Velia and the three villages on the Esquiline united with the Palatine villages to form a permanent league; to them were added, either originally, or, as seems more probable rather later, the village of the Querquetu(a)l under the name of Sucusa as a seventh member. The federation of the seven hills thus assumed its final shape; it united the two villages on the Palatine (the Germal and the Palatual), that on the Velia, the three on the Esquiline (Fagutal, Oppius, and Cispius), and the village on the Cælian.[1] The Velia constituted its geographical centre until it became also its religious centre with the erection of the Temple of the Penates.

This league of the seven *montes* was still only partial; it excluded three of the traditional hills, the annexation of which was needed to complete the formation of historical Rome. The Quirinal, with its geographical annex, the Viminal, the outpost of the Sabine world, continued to live its independent life; the Capitol and the Aventine, facing the Tiber and protected by their isolation, remained outside the new federation. Synœcism was the order of the day, but to bring it to a successful conclusion the tenacious will and the iron hand of the Etruscan tyrants were needed.

The date of the formation of the Septimontium can be at least approximately fixed. No doubt it had been a tedious process, preceded and accompanied by battles between the adjacent villages. It was finished by the second half of the seventh century, at the time of the Etruscan conquest, and, since the league had lasted for an appreciable time, it is reasonable to assume that by the beginning of the seventh century at latest—perhaps even by the end of the eighth— the federation of the seven hills at Rome had assumed its final form.

After formation comes organization. The first peculiarity we notice is that the Septimontium did not constitute one city in the material and unitary sense of that word. Without geographical unity no unity as a city is possible. Now, owing to the depressions and marshes separating them, intercommunication between the several villages was always

[1] **IX**, 4.

difficult and precarious. No road linked up the several communities on the seven *montes*, and even in classical times the statutory exclusion of vehicles on the day of the traditional festival of the Septimontium was a reminder of a long past age. The Septimontium constituted a league and, according to the Latin plan of those days, an essentially religious league.[1] In such circumstances, the league's members must, and in fact did, preserve a large degree of autonomy; within each village the political and social structure would remain unchanged.

This federated community did not build a common wall for its defence, whatever may have been stated in the past; it did not yet even bear the name of Rome. Its official title was the Septimontium, the name of a federation of the Latin type, and not of a city—a political conception which was still alien to the soil of Latium. Here we touch on a very delicate question—that of political organization, on which we shall have more to say in a later volume in the Evolution of Humanity.[2] Referring to pre-Etruscan Rome and so to a period which obviously corresponds to the stage of the Septimontium, tradition tells us of a political system, the three tribes of Ramnes, Tities, and Luceres and thirty curies, and of organs of government, a king, comitia, and a Senate. If tradition speak the truth, this centralized organization might have been contemporary with the formation of the league or represent a subsequent phase of its evolution. What is to be thought of this? Such constitutional questions are not of a kind that can be solved by topographical studies or archæological discoveries.

However, it seems that this alleged unified constitution is nothing but a pure anachronism. Perhaps some executive or legislative organ common to all the members of the league did exist; the fact is that we do not know, and unless we pin our faith blindly to the tradition which, as we have seen, does not deserve such confidence, we are left in the realm of pure speculation. Provisionally, at least, then, the safest course is to stick to the facts. Prior to the Etruscan conquest

[1] Fest., *loc. cit.*; **CCXXXVI**, 335 rem. 2, and 372; J. B. Carter, in **XXXI**, 1908, p. 175 and note 2.

[2] *Roman Political Institutions: the Republic and Cæsarism*, by L. Homo.

there was no urban unity nor even any city at Rome.[1] We therefore believe ourselves justified in concluding that the creation of a central authority and the establishment of a common system of social divisions were, like so many other institutions, the work of the Etruscans. Conceived in the primitive form of a mere federation of villages, the Septimontium doubtless remained faithful to its original notion down to its disappearance.

Furthermore, tradition attributes to the pre-Etruscan period of the regal age military exploits described with a wealth of detail compatible with their high importance and leading to the conquest of the environs of Rome. The subjugation of Antemnæ, Cænina, and Crustumerium under Romulus is depicted as the corollary of the conflict provoked by the melodramatic rape of the Sabine women; the destruction of Alba is presented as the consequence of the combat between the Horatii and the Curiatii and the treachery of the Alban dictator, Mettus Fufetius, in the reign of Tullius Hostilius; we hear of the conquest of Politorium, Tellena, Ficana, and Medullia, and the extension of the Roman sphere of influence to the coast through the colonization of Ostia in the days of Ancus Martius. What is the value of these assertions? Can this conquest of the environs of Rome in the form given it by tradition be regarded as an historical fact, or should we reject it *en bloc* with the rubbish of legend? Let us examine the facts.

The topography of the area, in so far as we can identify the several localities, furnishes one method of checking the account. The site of Antemnæ on the right bank of the Anio, opposite its junction with the Tiber four miles from the Palatine, is known, and important archæological discoveries have been made there.[2] The position of Cænina is still uncertain, but it should doubtless be sought in the same region on the left bank of the Anio, but further upstream, between the Via Nomentana and the Via Tiburtina at approximately the same distance from Rome as Antemnæ. Crustumerium lies on the left bank of the Tiber, north of

[1] K. J. Neumann, in **XXIV**, 361-64; P. Graffunder, in **XXII**, *s.v.* " Rom," p. 1024.

[2] **LXV**, 1882, 115; 1883, 16-17; 1887, 64 *ff.*; **CLXVIII**, 111-14; **XVIII**, II, 544.

Fidenæ, eighteen miles from Rome. Alba in the centre of the massif of the Alban Hills was seventeen miles away from Rome. Ficana (near the present tenuta of Dragoncello) lay on the left bank of the Tiber at the eleventh milestone on the Via Ostiensis. Politorium and Tellena lay in the same region and Medulla on the right bank of the Anio, but their sites cannot to-day be precisely located.[1] Finally, the colonization of Ostia presupposes that by this epoch the zone subject to Rome extended right to the shores of the Tyrrhenian Sea.

Confining ourselves to localities actually identified, these results would assign to pre-Etruscan Rome a minimum territory of twelve and a half miles radius, on the left bank of the Tiber, at least. Are they tenable? In the first place, they involve material impossibilities. Rome would have conquered Crustumerium and Alba, and reached the Mediterranean coasts without having been able even to annex even the Quirinal or the Capitoline. The subjugation of Antemnæ, lying on the line of communication between the Sabine colony on the Quirinal and the rest of the Sabine country, could not, practically speaking, have preceded the annexation of the Quirinal itself. The same sort of argument applies to Crustumerium; it lies to the north of Fidenæ, which, according to the tradition itself, was not finally conquered till the Etruscan period.[2] Finally, some accurate data allow us to plot the actual limits of the original territory of Rome. On the north it did not extend beyond Antemnæ, four miles from the Palatine; to the south-east, in the direction of Alba, it reached as far as the Fossæ Cluiliæ, fifteen miles away, up the Tiber, on the left bank, sixteen miles along the Via Laurentina, and fifteen miles along the Via Campana on the right bank.[3]

In these circumstances, what remains of the traditional data? In all, three facts, and only three, may be retained as far as the pre-Etruscan period is concerned—the annexation of the Aventine, the fall of Alba, and the colonization of Ostia.

One disputed point of a military and economic kind affected the relations between the Aventine and the federa-

[1] On these several places, consult **XVIII**, II, 561-63, 582-84.
[2] Liv., I, 38, 4; Dion., III, 49, 50.   [3] **XX**, I, 605, n. 2.

tion of the seven hills; this was the right of access to the Tiber. Once the Aventine colony was annexed by the Roman villages,[1] their hold on the river was consolidated and extended. However, the hill did not enter the league on a footing of equality with its original members; it became conquered territory, *ager publicus*,[2] a rural district or *pagus*[3] —a state of inferiority which was maintained for the future, even when it had lost all meaning. Forest and pasture land, the common property and domain of the community of the seven hills, it was exploited by and for the profit of the latter. Cicero, Livy, and Dionysius of Halicarnassus tell us that Ancus Martius planted there the conquered inhabitants of Politorium, Tellena, and Medullia, and Dionysius adds the population of all the cities that this king captured.[4] The story, if founded in fact, has certainly been greatly exaggerated by these various texts; the settlement of too large a conquered population upon the Aventine would have entailed more embarrassments than advantages for Rome, but a colonization on a small scale remains quite conceivable.[5]

In the sphere of foreign policy, the most important event of the period was undeniably the fall of Alba, an event which involved far-reaching consequences for the history of Rome and Latium. From the historical standpoint the fact could only be questioned by an excess of misplaced scepticism,[6] but it is none the less true that the traditional account is far from accurate. We are here confronted with one of those cases of systematic distortion which too often disfigure the pages of the Roman annalists. Livy[7] and Dionysius of Halicarnassus[8] depict this episode as a simple duel between Rome and Alba; after her victory Rome, having borne the labour alone, alone reaped its fruits. She transplanted the body of the inhabitants of the conquered city to her own territory and claimed to succeed her rival as the metropolis of Latium.[9]

On this point, as in all analogous cases, we should discount the exaggeration due to Rome's national pride and

---

[1] **CLXXX**, 26 *ff.*; **CCIX**, 287-88. [2] Dion., X, 31.
[3] *Pagus Aventinensis*, C.I.L., XIV, 2105. [4] Dion., III, 43.
[5] **CLXXXV**, 36-41.
[6] **XX**, I, 613-14; **XXVI**, I, 385-86. [7] Liv., I, 22-30, 3.
[8] Dion., III, 2-31. [9] Liv., I, 52, 2-3.

view the general history of Latium from a loftier angle. The Latins, like all the Italic peoples, cherished for centuries the passion for local autonomy, which we find asserting itself most energetically after the expulsion of the Etruscan dynasty, after the capture of Rome by the Gauls, and, for the last time, after the intervention in Campania. The centrifugal movements which we observe in the historical period rousing the Latins against Rome had been directed against Alba in an analogous manner in the preceding period. Unstable and loose though Alba's hegemony may have been, it none the less seemed burdensome to the members of the league, who were extraordinarily jealous of their independence. This state of mind ultimately provoked an anti-Alban reaction, which led to the disruption of the league and then to the fall of Alba herself.

In one particular instance we can grasp the genesis of the phenomenon. The Velia and the Querquetu(a)l[1] were members of the Alban league; we have seen them desert it to enter the new federation of the Septimontium. The movement did not stop at this preliminary phase; it culminated in the capture and destruction of Alba, a feat of the Latins, and not, as tradition maintained, of the Romans alone. But if Rome was not alone in compassing this result, it is none the less true that she played a part in the struggle. The Germal, as an Alban colony, was inextricably bound up in the life of Latium, and the accession of two members of the Alban federation (the Velia and the Querquetu(a)l) to the league of the Septimontium testifies to the connection linking these two epoch-making events—the formation of the league of the seven hills and the dissolution of the Alban federation.

Hence Rome contributed to the destruction of Alba, but her intervention had not been isolated and had been limited in proportion to her means. In point of fact, and despite Rome's claim to succeed to the inheritance of her old metropolis, the fall of Alba inaugurated a period of chaos and anarchy in Latium, which cleared the way for the Etruscan invaders and facilitated their advance. The real heirs of Alba and the chief beneficiaries by her fall were not the Romans but the Etruscans.

The question of the colonization of Ostia remains to be

---

[1] Plin., *Hist. Nat.*, III, 69-70.

considered. According to the traditional history, Ostia, the oldest of the Roman colonies, would have been founded by King Ancus Marcius.[1] In this bare and unqualified form, the claim is inadmissible; the excavations at Ostia have shown that the colonization of this town in the full sense of the word did not antedate the fourth century B.C.[2] Must we then convict the tradition of falsehood, or error, or of simple distortion? Some precise data, both historical and archæological, suggest that here, as in the case of Alba, the second alternative is the right one.[3] It may very probably be conceded that a village was already in existence on the site of Ostia, even before the Etruscan conquest of Latium.[4] The creation of this village to watch over the entrance to the Tiber would have then been the reply of Latium to the growing danger from the Etruscans. Rome would here, too, have taken her part in the common work, but it is inconceivable that she had taken the lead, still more that she had a monopoly of it.

In the domain of culture,[5] too, this period of the Septimontium, corresponding to the end of the First and beginning of the Second Iron Age, was marked by notable advances. The cemeteries on the Sacred Way, the Quirinal, and the Esquiline, and various finds in Latium and the adjacent region are our primary sources of information on this topic. For dwellings the rectangular type tends to replace the circular plan, and the change becomes more marked the nearer we approach the sixth century. The proofs of this statement are provided by the discoveries in the Faliscan country to the north, and at Conca, the ancient Satricum, south of Latium. The foundations of the Faliscan houses generally affect a rectangular or square form; those of Conca are round, elliptical, or rarely square. They are hollowed out in the ground and have yielded abundant relics (portable terra-cotta stoves, mill-stones, various vases, implements, spindle-whorls, and fibulæ) which give us an exact idea of

---

[1] Liv., I, 39, 9; Dion., III, 44; so also **CCIII**, 36 *ff*.

[2] **XX**, I, 470; **CCXXXI**, 2 *ff.;* **CVIII**, 14-35.

[3] T. Frank, in **XLIII**, 1919, 314-16.

[4] **XXVI**, I, 383-84; T. Frank, in **XLIII**, 1919, 316, n. 1; *cf.* **CCIII**, 24-31, who wrongly assumes an Etruscan settlement. On the question of pre-Roman Ostia, see **CVIII**, 36 *ff*.

[5] **CCXIII**, 519-654.

the Latin huts of the Second Iron Age. At this time stone structures, even for public buildings, were still probably unknown; they were to appear in Latium in the succeeding period with the Etruscan domination.

The ceramic industry has been improved through the more general use of the wheel on the one hand, and through the invention of new forms on the other. The first vases with geometric patterns combined with zoomorphic motives (aquatic birds, etc.) of Protocorinthian fabric or perhaps also Chalcidian and Argive, appear in cemeteries of the First Iron Age, but their greatest diffusion in Latium is reached only in the next phase. They are found principally in the graves on the Esquiline and the Romulean tombs in the cemetery of the Sacred Way in the form of scyphi, pitchers, cups, lecythi, and other perfume vases. At first pure imports, these products of Greek workshops soon inspired local imitations. The Italo-geometric vases copy both the shapes (scyphi, œnochoæ, olpæ, dishes, and arbylli) and the decoration (linear patterns of horizontal or meander ribbons) of the Greek originals, but are at once distinguishable by the coarseness of the material and the crudity of the workmanship.

Commerce was developing, and the rôle of the Greek world, Magna Grecia and old Greece alike, was assuming substantial proportions. Here again the bulk of the evidence is furnished by the archaic cemeteries on Roman soil; apart from the Greek vases noted above, the imports consist principally of glass paste or enamel beads, spindlewhorls, figurines in a sort of fayence, and glass paste scarabs. In the industrial sphere the use of iron was becoming general, and through the adoption of new processes metallurgy freed itself from the shackles of the Bronze Age tradition. Let us note in conclusion an innovation of incalculable importance—the introduction of writing,[1] or, to be precise, the Chalcidian alphabet through Cumæ.[2] The Præneste fibula and the Duenos vase, the two oldest documents from Rome and Latium on which this alphabet appears already in use, are dated to the last years of the seventh or the beginning of

[1] Mariani, in **XL**, 1896, 23 *ff.*; **CCXIII**, 643-54.
[2] And not through the Etruscan alphabet, as has recently been suggested by **CXLIII**.

the sixth century.[1] The approximate date of the introduction of the alphabet into Latium may be fixed at the eighth or the beginning of the seventh century—*i.e.*, it was contemporary with the federal phase at Rome.

Towards the middle of the seventh century, at the moment when the great Etruscan expansion was to begin, Latin civilization on Roman soil still remained rudimentary and poverty-stricken despite the advances noted above.[2] The poor Roman villages, lost on the banks of the Tiber and sunk in their marshes, still only experienced foreign influence to a very slight degree. The currents of trade passed them by, and a few miles from the brilliant cities of southern Etruria—like Tarquinii, Veii, and Cære—the inhabitants of the Palatine, Esquiline, and Quirinal continued to live as savages and primitives, whatever a partial tradition may say. In any case, struggling against thankless nature and protected by their very isolation from the temptations of the outside world, these first Romans, a rude people of herdsmen always on duty, learned from daily experience the force of discipline and the value of effort. They still lacked the political structures and the material means that only a superior civilization could supply. The Etruscans were at hand to reveal these.

[1] Præneste fibula, C.I.L., I², 2; **CCXIII**, 644, 649-50; **CXLV**, II, p. 260, n. 1572. Duenos vase, C.I.L., I², 4; **CCXIII**, 643, 647-49; **CCIX**, 80, 301. For a full bibliography, see C.I.L., I², 2 and 4, and the summaries by W. Schwering and M. Bacherler, in **LI**, vol. 176, 1916-1918, 83-92, and by M. Bacherler, *ibid.*, vol. 184, 1920, 175-87.

[2] L. Mariani, in **XL**, 1896, 36-47; **CCXIII**, 519-69.

CHAPTER III

THE ETRUSCAN EMPIRE

I

The Etruscan Expansion and the First Experiment in Italian Unity

"Almost the whole of Italy (*pæne omnis Italia*)," wrote Cato, "belonged to the Etruscans," and Livy says:

> "Before the establishment of Roman power the Etruscans had extended their dominions far over land and sea. The very names of the two seas, the upper and the lower, which girdle Italy like an island, attest the power of this people; the Italic peoples had called the one the Etruscan Sea from the common name of the nation, and the other the Adriatic Sea from the name of Adria, an Etruscan colony; the Greeks name them the Tyrrhenian and Adriatic Seas."

Cato[1] with some exaggeration and Livy more accurately[2] both allude to a well-founded historical fact of cardinal

Bibliography.—Texts: Livy, I, 34-II, 13; IV, 37, 1; V, 33, 7 and 10; XXXIII, 37, 3; XXXVII, 57, 8; XXXIX, 55, 8 (*cf.* Florus, I, 1, 2-4; Eutropius, I, 6-8; Orosius, II, 4, 11-15); Dionysius of Halicarnassus, III, 45-V, 36; VII, 3-4; Dio Cassius, II-IV (fragments, *cf.* Zonaras, VII, 8-12); Plutarch, *Valerius Publicola;* Polybius, II, 17; VI, 55; Cato (fragments, H.R.F., p. 45, frag. 12; p. 53, frag. 58; p. 53, frags. 62 and 69); Varro, *de Ling. Lat.*, V, 843; Appian, *Basil.*, frags. 8-10; Strabo, V, 4, 3 (p. 242 C); Cicero, *de Repub.*, 20-31; Velleius Paterculus, I, 7, 3-4; Pliny, *Hist. Nat.*, III, 61, 70, 112-13, 115, 120, 130; XIV, 88; XXXVI, 104; *de Viris Illustribus*, 6-13; Servius, *ad Æn.*, I, 422; X, 198; XII, 603.

Inscriptions.—Fasti triumphales (C.I.L., I, p. 168); C.I.L., I², 3 (Præneste fibula), 3 (Duenos vase); XIII, 1668 (Claudius' oration to the Senate); C.I.E.

*Principal Works.—***XX**, I, 353-61; II, 3 *ff.;* **XXVI**, I, 429-58; **XII**, II, 701-10, 806-14; **CXCIX**, 128-67, 185-203; **CCII**, II, 277-93; **CXL**, 54-55, 88-126, 160-205, 312-458, 469-509; **CCIX**, 65-67, 264-311; **CCXIII**; **CCXXII**, with the classification of place names by regions by K. F. Schmidt, in **XXXVII**, 1906, 1581-93, 1614-21, 1647-57; 1907, 157-60, 189; P. Graffunder, in **LVI**, 1911, 83-123; *id.*, in **XXII**, *s.v.* "Rom," 1021-26; **X**; **VIII**; **IX**; **CCXVI**; **CCXXXIV**; **CVI**, I, intr., vii-x.

---

[1] Cato, quoted by Serv., *ad Æn.*, XII, 567 (H.R.F., p. 53, frag. 52; H.R.R., p. 73, frag. 62).

[2] Liv., V, 33, 7-8; *cf.* I, 2, 5.

importance, the existence of a vast Etruscan empire in pre-Roman Italy. And Greek historians, too, have preserved a detailed recollection of it. Dionysius of Halicarnassus writes :

> " There was a time when the Latins, the Umbrians, the Ausoni, and many others were called Etruscans by the Greeks. . . . Many historians have even held that Rome was an Etruscan city." [1]

At the beginning of the seventh century B.C., with the gradual occupation of Etruria proper and a considerable part of Umbria, the Etruscan nation was reaching its natural frontiers in Central Italy—the Apennines on the north and east, the Tyrrhenian Sea on the west, and the Tiber on the south. The work of fusion between victors and vanquished was in course of completion ; the emigrant Etruscan bands had created a nation. But soon the expansion of the population and the increase of its prosperity produced their usual effects. On their own territory the Etruscans found themselves cramped for room, and the next two centuries witnessed a brilliant age of expansion for this race. What form did the movement take ? Doubtless it was not inspired by the central authority, but in all probability the initiative was taken by the several Etruscan cities acting independently. Etruscanized racial elements, including Ligures and Umbrians, freely participated in it, and Dionysius of Halicarnassus in describing the Etruscans' attack upon Cumæ in 524 notes the presence of Umbrians, Daunians, and many other barbarians in their army.[2] The expansion took place at once by land and sea, and followed three directions—southward, westward, and northward. Let us trace these in chronological order.

The southward expansion appears to be the earliest and to have started from the Etruscan cities of the maritime zone—Tarquinii, Cære, and perhaps also Vetulonia. In their southward march the Etruscans began by conquering Latium, a preliminary stage to which we shall return later. Then through the lands of the Rutuli, the Volsci, and the Aurunci, where ancient tradition preserves the memory of their passage, they reached Campania, attracted by the exceptional richness of its wheat-fields and pastures, and established themselves firmly. The permanent occupation of Campania

---

[1] Dion., I, 29.   [2] Dion., VII, 3; **CCII**, II, 279 *ff*.

brought the Etruscans into contact with the Hellenic world, the northern outpost of which was the town of Cumæ, the first link in the chain of Greek colonies that dotted the whole coast-line of Magna Grecia.

The historical tradition, here represented by Polybius[1] and Strabo,[2] and a multitude of data derived from other sources—topography, archæology, numismatics, and philology—categorically attest the durable settlement of the Etruscans in Campania. They are found at Capua, Nola, Herculaneum, and Pompeii; coastwise they advanced along the Gulf of Salerno, where they founded the colony of Marcina, and pushed on to the River Silarus, which was henceforth to be their frontier against the Greeks of Posidonia. The Greek colonies of Naples and Cumæ in Campania were thereby reduced to a state of subservience until they could be directly attacked. The Etruscan conquest of Campania was going on till the end of the sixth century, when it suffered a check under the walls of Cumæ that foreshadowed its final retreat.[3] This Etruscan conquest of Campania exercised a profound influence on the cultural development of pre-Roman Italy. For the first time the Etruscans became the immediate neighbours of the Greeks, the Chalcidians of Cumæ and the Achæans of Posidonia. Political, commercial, intellectual, and artistic relations between the two peoples were intensified; the cemeteries of Cære and Vetulonia in Etruria and of Præneste on the borders of Latium have brilliantly illustrated this fact.

At the end of the seventh century and the beginning of the sixth[4] the colonizing offensive of the Greeks in the western basin of the Mediterranean was still in full swing. The movement, begun in the last years of the eighth century, had continued throughout the seventh both in Sicily and in Magna Grecia. Ionians from Samos and Phocæa had made their way as far as the land of Tartessos in Southern Spain. At the beginning of the sixth century the Phocæans founded Massalia (Marseilles), which was to become, side by side with Syracuse, the great political and commercial centre of

---

[1] Pol., II, 17, 1.   [2] Str., V, 4, 3 (p. 242 C).
[3] Dion., VII, 3-4.
[4] On the maritime expansion of the Etruscans in the sixth century B.C., **XX**, I, 357-61.

western Hellenism. Its colonies—Monæcus (Monaco), Nicæa (Nice), Antipolis (Antibes), Athenopolis (Saint-Tropez), Olbia (Saint Pierre d'Almanarre, near Hyères), Tauroeis (Sanary or Saint Cyr), Citharista (La Ciotat), Agathe (Agde), Rhodanusia (perhaps opposite Arles), Rhode (Rosas), and Emporia (Ampurias)—would cover the coast of Southern Gaul and Northern Spain in the course of the fifth century.[1] Finally, Hellenism attacked Corsica. In 560 B.C. the Phocæans from Ionia came and founded the colony of Alalia on the west coast of the island.[2]

So a triple offensive had culminated in Magna Grecia, the colonies on the Ligurian coasts, and those on the islands. It aimed at the encirclement of Etruria. The Etruscans resolved at all costs to break this circle which threatened to stifle them. The alliance with Carthage, the great idea and corner-stone of Etruscan policy from the sixth century onwards, was to furnish the means to this end. The rivalry between the Semites of Phœnicia and the Greeks had constituted the dominant fact of Mediterranean life for a thousand years. The Phœnicians had been forced step by step to yield to their rivals in the Eastern Mediterranean; as practical people, they had sought compensations for their losses in the west, and had colonized in turn the coasts of Western Sicily, Southern Spain, and Northern Africa.

But, encouraged by their past successes, the Greeks were not slow to venture on to these remote coasts. The misfortunes of Phœnicia in the sixth century supervened conveniently to smooth the path of Hellenism towards the realization of these ambitions. The vulnerable point of the Phœnician peoples had always lain on land, and the great Oriental monarchies had for centuries been a permanent menace to them. Phœnicia had already suffered severely from invasions by Egyptians and Assyrians; the formation of the Babylonian Empire dealt it its death-blow. In 574 B.C. Tyre succumbed to the attacks of Nebuchadrezzar; Phœnician independence, the nurse of such a brilliant past, was henceforth but a memory. However remote, however foreign to the destinies of the Western world this catastrophe may appear, its repercussions none the less affected directly and vitally the history of primitive Italy.

[1] **XI**, I, 396-402; **CXV**, 21.   [2] Hdt., I, 165, 1.

THE ETRUSCAN EMPIRE

The Phœnician colonies in the west, abandoned to themselves owing to the collapse of their mother-country, had no choice but to turn to Carthage; for she was the most prosperous among them and so the best fitted to ensure the defence of their national patrimony.[1] As heir of Phœnicia, Carthage raised her standard and revived her programme, but now, for the first time, gave it the support of all the resources of a great military power. That was a new fact which involved incalculable consequences for the Western Mediterranean. In the sixth century, however, Carthage's greatness was only in its infancy. The Phœnician colonies, in complete confusion, were still hesitating between the old protector and the new. The Greeks, always quick to seize an opportunity, took advantage of this unique occasion to hasten their advance and drive home their successes. Driven from Ionia by the Persian conquest in 545 B.C., the Phocæans came to join their compatriots in the trading-posts of the west and to reinforce with their contingents the man-power of Western Hellenism.

The Etruscans had already had a quarrel to pick with the Greeks about the Lipari Islands, and the dispute had not terminated to their liking. No doubt they cherished no particular affection for the Semites of Africa, foreigners and competitors, but sound policy always recommends recourse to the most interested party. The common danger united the Etruscans and the Carthaginians in a close alliance against the Western Greeks, for the moment, especially against the Phocæans of Marseilles and Ionia.[2] The Western Mediterranean was divided into two distinct spheres of influence. Corsica fell to the Etruscans, Sardinia to the Carthaginians.

The results of this political and commercial pact were soon made manifest. The combined fleets of Etruria and Carthage met the Phocæan fleet in the Battle of Alalia, the first of the great naval contests for the hegemony of the Western Mediterranean to be recorded in history.[3] The Phocæans were victorious, but they suffered such serious losses that they dare not renew the contest, evacuated

[1] **CLXXIX**, I, 142 *ff.*; **VII**, I, 419.
[2] **XX**, I, 357-69; **VII**, I, 425.
[3] Hdt., I, 166; **I**, I, 380; **XXVI**, I, 335.

Corsica, and went and founded the city of Velia (Elea) on the coasts of Magna Grecia (about 535).[1] The Etrusco-Carthaginian alliance, so speedily crowned with complete success, did not remain a mere political expedient or a temporary device. Both nations, having had proofs of its efficacy, hastened to strengthen its provisions and adapt them gradually to the development of the situation created by the victory. Thus through an enlargement of the original provisions, Campania came to be added to the Etruscan sphere of influence, while Sicily and Spain were assigned to Carthage. The relations between the two countries could only become closer as time went on. Aristotle was to be able to write in his *Politics* that

> " Etruscans and Carthaginians form one single city."[2]

In this form his assertion is doubtless an exaggeration, but it is explained and justified by the unity of action that these two irreconcilable foes of Hellenism had made an axiom of their foreign policy.

As far as Italy was concerned two results followed. In the first place Hellenism sustained a check. On the coasts of the Tyrrhenian Sea, north of the Gulf of Naples, there existed a certain number of Greek, and especially Phocæan, trading-posts, such as Amunclæ, near Fundi, in the land of the Aurunci;[3] Satricum on the Volscian coast; and Pisa on the northern frontier of Etruria.[4] All were smitten down and vanished. Henceforth the line of the Vulturno will form a frontier which Hellenism may not pass.[5] Furthermore, even in Southern Italy no new colonies were established with the sole exception of Dicæarchia (Pozzuoli), founded in 528 B.C. by a band of Samian emigrants.

Secondly, the field was left open for Etruscan expansion. Thanks to the guarantees offered by the alliance with Carthage, Etruria consolidated her hold on Campania and Latium. She developed her maritime power on the Tyrrhenian Sea, undertook the exploitation of Corsica, whence she drew supplies of resin, wax, honey, timber, and slaves, and, finally, she launched out upon the conquest of Southern Italy,

---

[1] Hdt., I, 167, 4-5.
[2] Arist., *Pol.*, III, 5, 10-11 (p. 90 Imm).   [3] **CCII**, II, 295-307.
[4] *id.*, 331 *ff.*   [5] **XX**, 359-60.

whither we shall shortly follow her. In every respect the Carthaginian alliance may properly be termed the pivot of Etruscan foreign policy. It rendered possible the first experiment in Italian unity, and for this reason deserves a place of honour in the history of primitive Italy.

The Etruscan expansion northwards came later; it may be assigned to the last third of the sixth century B.C.[1] The Etruscans had already conquered Latium and Campania, chased the Greeks from the north of the Tyrrhenian Sea, and laid hands on the coast of Corsica, while their northern frontier had remained unchanged. The southward expansion had been, as we saw, the work of the coastal Etruscans; the northward expansion was due to the Etruscans of the interior reinforced for the moment by a solid contingent of Umbrians. The invasion seems to have followed the passes over the Tuscan Apennines that debouch upon Bologna; at least, that may be inferred from two well established facts. After the conquest Bologna became the capital of Etruria Padana; and, secondly, the Reno Valley constituted the regular line of communication between the Etruscans of the mother-country and those in Northern Italy.

At the time of the invaders' arrival the Po Valley was in the hands of the Umbrians, who had several centuries previously driven the old Ligurian population to take refuge in the borderland of the Alps and the Apennines. The Umbrians had to submit to the newcomers, and the Etruscans made themselves masters of the plain of the Po, where they maintained their hold for a century. What was the limit of their dominion? Apart from a few scattered texts[2] two accessory sources of information come to our aid—philology, especially the study of place-names, and archæology, with the Etruscan objects and inscriptions that it unearths.[3] From these it may be deduced that along the Adriatic the zone of Etruscan occupation extended from the Po delta to

---

[1] **XX**, I, 352-53; **CXL**, 187-98, 459 ff.

[2] Liv., V, 33, 7; XXXIII, 37, 3; XXXVII, 57, 7-8; Corn. Nep., quoted by Plin., *Hist. Nat.*, III, 125; *id.*, III, 120; Serv., *ad Æn.*, X, 198.

[3] **XX**, I, 353; for the place-names, see especially the epoch-making work of W. Schulze (**CCXXII**), with the classification by regions of K. F. Schmidt, in **XXXVII** (for further details, see the bibliography on p. 99 above).

the heights of Pessaro on the south, and that it included the whole Po Valley save for the foot-hills of Piedmont. On the whole, its frontiers extended right up to the foot of the

FIG. 5.—THE ETRUSCAN EMPIRE AND MAGNA GRECIA (SEVENTH TO FIFTH CENTURIES B.C.).

mountains. The Ligurians in the Alps and the Apennines and the Veneti beyond the Adige were to retain their independence.

The Etruscan conquest of Northern Italy was carried out under conditions closely analogous to those under which

Etruria proper and Western Umbria had been subdued. In both cases the Etruscans represented only a tiny minority in comparison with the subject populations; they must, accordingly, have followed the same plan of action in each case. Too few to scatter themselves abroad with impunity, they remained concentrated in cities which they established at the chief strategic points and which thus constituted garrison towns in the midst of the vanquished. Melpum, Verona, and Mantua acted as guard-posts at the mouth of the Alpine passes; Placentia and Cremona watched the fords of the Po; Parma, Modena, and Bologna marked stages on the future Via Æmilia; and Pisaurum, Ariminum, Ravenna, Adria, and Spina were strung out as sentinels along the Adriatic coasts. This system of occupation, in which the city formed the keystone and the primordial cell, was as sagacious as it was economical.

On the indigenous races, which he neither stifled nor exterminated but complacently dominated, the Etruscan bestowed two boons—his political institutions and his culture. The former were characterized by city life and the federal system. In Campania, apart from the Hellenic seaboard, in the Po Valley and, as we have already seen, in Latium, political life had not yet outgrown the stage of the horde and the tribe. The framework of Etruscan political life, on the contrary, was the city. And so both for military reasons and on account of their social habits, the Etruscans appear as great founders of cities and authors of new synœcisms.[1]

As far as the cities of Latium are concerned, Roman tradition notes this fact expressly and speaks of city foundations of Etruscan type (*etrusco ritu*).[2] In the newly conquered territories, where the political situation and exigencies were analogous, the Etruscans went to work in the same way; archæology and philology supply convincing proofs of this. In Campania we see the Etruscan conquerors founding a whole series of towns—Capua, the general plan of which as revealed by the ruins conforms to the normal rules of Etruscan town-planning, Nola, Marcina on the Gulf of Salerno, and Pompeii, shown by its ruins to have been rebuilt in limestone and in accordance with a regular plan.

[1] **XX**, I, 353; **CXL**, 54-55.
[2] Varr., *de Ling. Lat.*, V, 143.

To the north a similar work was accomplished in the Po Valley, and here recent discoveries are particularly illuminating. Felsina, the metropolis of the province and the Etruscans' base of operations for their northward advance, was founded by the Etruscans in the immediate vicinity, if not actually on the site, of Villanovan Bologna.

Another Etruscan foundation is that city lying seventeen miles south of Bologna in the Valley of the Reno, in the neighbourhood of the modern Marzabotto. The name of this ancient town remains a mystery, but we can at least appreciate the importance of this centre as a station on the great fortified Pistoia-Felsina route, which connected Etruria with its conquests in the Po Valley. Its ruins constitute one of the most precious documents for the history of Etruscan civilization.[1] Other cities—the names of which disclose, or seem to disclose, a similar origin—are not wanting; we may cite Cremona, Acerræ, Volturnia, Placentia, Parma, and Modena in the Po Valley, and Ravenna, Cæsena, and Ariminun on the Adriatic coastlands. Even to-day Northern Italy, with its dense network of urban centres, such as Milan and Mantua at the foot of the Alps, Piacenza and Cremona on the Po, and Parma, Modena, Bologna, and Ariminum strung out along the slopes of the Apennines, in its master lines preserves the plan given it by the Etruscans. Normally, when older centres of any size were already in existence, the Etruscan city was established close to them and not substituted for them. The two capitals of Etruria in the Po Valley and Etruria in Campania, Felsina and Capua, are typical illustrations of the procedure adopted.

In addition to the city system, the Etruscans introduced into the conquered country the second feature of their political life, federation, in the form of the dodecarchy, or federation of twelve cities, that had already been elaborated in Etruria proper. The new Etruria on the Po had its dodecarchy. We possess no list of the twelve cities of Etruria of the North, but we at least learn from Pliny that Felsina was its capital.[2] Mantua was certainly a member, and as to the rest we may suggest the various cities of the Po Valley (Melpum, Placentia, Cremona, Parma, and

---

[1] Brizio, in **LXIII**, I, 249-426; **CXL**, 99-122.
[2] Plin., *Hist. Nat.*, III, 115; **CXL**, 187.

Modena), and also the Etruscan cities on the Adriatic sea-board, Adria, Ravenna, Spina, Ariminum, and perhaps also Pisaurum.[1] In Campania there was an analogous dode-carchy; Capua probably stood at its head, and Nola, Hercu-laneum, and Pompeii must have been its chief members.

From the eighth century B.C. Etruria, under the inspira-tion first of Oriental and then of Greek influences, had become the great focus of culture in Central Italy. Apart from the Greek colonies in the south, no people could com-pare with the Etruscans in culture or prosperity. This brilliant civilization the Etruscans then proceeded to intro-duce into the conquered lands. Let us recall its main features. In the first place, the Etruscans used stone archi-tecture, while all round them, owing to the many forests, wood was in general use, as it was to remain at Rome for a long time. Here, again, we must rely upon archæology for our information. We have seen that the Etruscans had rebuilt Pompeii in stone, but the most vivid and conclusive evidence comes from Marzabotto, the nameless city of the Reno Valley, the " Etruscan Pompeii."[2]

The city was built on a natural terrace, the Misano of to-day, protected on three sides by the course of the river. It was laid out in accordance with a regular plan, the straight streets dividing the houses into regular blocks. The houses, of which only the foundations in dry masonry survive, were built of brick or adobe. The extant remains reveal the Etruscan house as an aggregate of small rooms grouped around a central court connected with the street by a corridor, with a second story of wood and a flat roof. Round the town ran a fortification wall, of which only the east gate, formed of courses of huge blocks, remains. On a higher terrace of more limited area above the city proper—the Misanello—rose the acropolis, protected by a stone rampart. It contained the Mundus, the religious centre of the community, and three shrines, one with a single cella, the other two with three cellæ, in conformity with the normal

---

[1] Consult especially **CCXXII**, 163, 207, 219, 567-68, 572-73, 578; **CXL**, 188-98.

[2] **CXL**, 98-122; **XVI**, 495-520 (B. pls., 107-110); **CXCVII**, 593 *ff.*; **CLXXII**, 287 *ff.*; G. Patroni, in **LXIX**, 1902, 467-507; C. Schuchhardt, in **LXXVIII**, 1914, 277-302.

Etruscan rule exemplified at Rome in the famous temple of the Capitoline Triad. Beside the city of the living lay the dwellings of the dead. Both inhumation and cremation were practised simultaneously, but the former rite preponderated greatly. A rich furniture accompanied the skeletons.

Among the Etruscans engineering did not lag behind architecture. In the Po Valley, still clothed with forests and marshes and traversed by irregular and torrential streams, the conquerors found ample scope for their national skill and highly developed science. They drained the marshes, laid the axe to the root of the forest trees, and regulated the course of the rivers by dykes and channels,[1] and finally undertook the improvement of the land. The Romans in antiquity and the Lombards in the Middle Ages were inspired by their example and carried on their work.

Finally, in the industrial and commercial sphere the establishment of Etruscan domination represented to the conquered lands an immense advance and a brilliant expansion, at least, in comparison with their former state.[2] Black-figured and red-figured pottery (great craters, kelebes, amphoræ, œnochoæ, cups, and bowls), cast, engraved, or repoussé-work, bronze ware (situlæ, handled jugs, footed cistæ, pateræ, forks, ladles), on which the geometric ornament of the preceding age was supplemented by a rich repertoire of figural motives of Etruscan type, perfumevases, gold and silver jewellery, bone and ivory plaques, mostly Greek or Etruscan imports, bear witness to a refined, aristocratic, and luxurious civilization.[3] At the end of the sixth century Northern Italy had still been in the Villanova period of culture in which primitive means fulfilled primitive needs. The Etruscans widened this narrow horizon roughly and violently at the point of the sword. The discoveries in the Etruscan region of the Po Valley and the Apennines disclose the full significance of the conquest and illustrate its immediate results. They also define and illuminate the history of Latium during the Etruscan period despite the traditional legends and falsifications.

[1] Plin., *Hist. Nat.*, III, 120.
[2] **CXL**, 88-126, 160-178, 312-458.
[3] C. Julian, in **LXX**, 1914[1], 93-94; **CXL**, 312-458.

THE ETRUSCAN EMPIRE

II

THE ETRUSCANS IN LATIUM

On their way to Campania the Etruscans conquered Latium and remained its masters for a century and a half (from the middle of the seventh century B.C. to the last years of the sixth).[1] The traditional narrative[2] has systematically misrepresented this intervention in order to rob it of its character of a conquest, and so gives us scarcely any help to an understanding of the history of this vital incident. However, a few scattered hints allow us at least to catch a glimpse of the historical truth. The family of the Tarquins in the person of its head, Tarquin the Elder, had come from Tarquinii; Tarquin the Proud, when finally defeated, retired to Cære. The mention of Tarquinii and Cære leads us to that maritime region which had been the cradle of Etruscan power and civilization. Thence, and not from the interior, the great expansive movement towards the south had started. Central Etruria only came to the rescue after the fall of the Tarquins' dynasty in the person of Porsenna, the *lars* of Clusium. The natural route for the invasion by Etruscans of the coast was through the corridor between the sea and the last slopes of the Tuscan Apennines, the modern Maremme road, and came out directly on the lower reaches of the Tiber between Rome and the sea. No doubt the Etruscans on their southward march did approach Latium from this quarter.

We have other landmarks. A passage in Cato informs us that the Volscian country had fallen into the hands of the Etruscans.[3] Appian applies the name Tyrrhenoi to the Rutuli,[4] and an old tradition in which we may recognize an

[1] This account has been confirmed archæologically by the recent excavations by I. dall'Osso at the Hill of S. Agata, north of Monte Mario, where an Etruscan settlement was superimposed upon an old native village of the Latial epoch. I. M. Palmarini, " Le scoperte archeologiche del Prof. Innocenzo dall'Osso a Monte Mario," in **LXVI**, 1922², 253-59; I. dall'Osso, " Una nuova visione di Roma primitiva," *ibid.*, 1923⁴, 356 *ff.*; *id.*, " L'Urbs Quadrata sul Palatino e la vera Roma sul Tevere "; *ibid.*, 1924², 346-54.

[2] Livy, I, 34-II, 15; Dion., III, 46-V, 36; **XX**, I, 353 and 794.

[3] Cato, quoted by Serv., *ad Æn.*, XI, 567 (=H.R.F., p. 53, frag. 62).

[4] App., *Bas.*, 1.

anticipation of subsequent events makes the lord of Cære, Mazentius, an ally of their king.[1] In Tarquinii and Cære we have their starting-points, with the Rutuli and Volsci as their terminus. The Etruscan invasion followed the coastal route, and the invaders, after forcing the crossing of the Tiber low down stream, took possession of Latium as a whole; we find them there at Tusculum, Velitræ, and Rome.

The Etruscans' work in Latium, as in all the regions of Italy where they set foot as conquerors, was the result of two factors. The one they found awaiting them, the other they brought with them. In the former it is essential to distinguish between political life and state of civilization. Politically Latium had not yet attained the urban phase; the future Rome, a particular expression of a general situation, was still only in the federal stage of the Septimontium. Latium as a whole was a restless sea of autonomous hordes and ephemeral leagues. The age of large scale agriculture had not yet begun; pastoralism, with its nomadic, or, at least, semi-nomadic, habits, was still the rule. We are in the age of the Latial culture of the seventh century, as revealed by the various Roman burial-places on the Quirinal, the Esquiline, and the Sacred Way.

What, then, was the Etruscans' contribution? As far as the political system they established throughout Latium is concerned, the answer is easy; we simply do not know. Rome had had a series of Etruscan kings; probably the rest of Latium was ruled by similar dynasties. But though we know no details, we can at least grasp the general result. In Latium the Etruscans were inspired with the same spirit and accomplished the same political and cultural task, as in the other regions of Italy subject to their sway, first Campania and then the Po Valley.

In the first place, they founded cities and promoted synœcism; through their agency the peoples of Latium passed from the tribal to the city stage of culture. Prior to the Etruscan domination Latium had been a mosaic of tribes, grouped in manifold unstable and shifting confederacies, as Pliny[2] reminds us. By the departure of the

---

[1] Cato, quoted by Macr., *Sat.*, III, 5, 10 (=H.R.F., p. 59, frag. 12); Varro, quoted by Plin., *Hist. Nat.*, XIV, 88.

[2] Plin., *Hist. Nat.*, III, 69-70.

invaders at the end of the sixth century, the political geography of the district had been entirely transformed; the tribes had amalgamated and concentrated to form cities. Cato has left us a list of the towns which constituted the Latin league of succession States at the beginning of the Republic: Tusculum, Aricia, Lanuvium, Laurentum, Cora, Tibur, Pometia, and Ardea.[1] The names of Tusculum and Velitræ betray patently their Etruscan ancestry.[2] The introduction into Latium of the idea of *urbs* and the establishment of a number of Latin towns as centres of population, such was the Estruscans' lasting and decisive achievement in Latium from the political standpoint.

The Etruscan engineers inaugurated the improvement of the Roman Campagna by a scientific system of irrigation and drainage works. Agriculture gradually took the place of pastoral life. The peoples finally settled down and the great Latin battalions which were to create Italian unity under Rome and for Rome began to spring from the ground.[3] Stone replaced wattle and daub in domestic architecture and earthworks in fortifications. At the touch and under the pressure of a higher civilization Latium, subjected to a systematic exploitation which developed its natural economic potentialities beyond all expectations, underwent a complete revolution in culture. But it is at Rome, which had now become the Etruscans' base of operations and fortress in the Latin country, that the full significance of this revolution was to be revealed and its full effects made manifest.

III

ETRUSCAN ROME

The existence of Etruscan kings at Rome during the latter part of the seventh and during the sixth century seems an indisputable fact. Tradition gives us the names of three Etruscan kings—Tarquin the Elder, Servius Tullius, and Tarquin the Proud. These names are Romanized forms;

---

[1] Cato, quoted by Priscian, I, pp. 129 and 137, ed. H. Keil (=H.R.F., p. 52, frag. 58; H.R.R., p. 72, frag. 58).

[2] **CCXXII**, 542, 567.

[3] T. Frank, in **XXX**, 1919, 267 *ff.*, and **CXXXII**, 8 *ff*.

the Etruscan equivalents are Mastarna in the case of Servius Tullius and Tarchu for the two Tarquins. The two Tarquins have sometimes[1] been taken for conventional duplications of one and the same person. But it may be pointed out that for a span of a century and a half three sovereigns do not look like an exaggerated figure; instead of omitting one it would be more logical to admit that there might—or shall we say, must ?—have been others.

A famous painting from Vulci,[2] brought to light in 1857, portrays Servius Tullius and Tarquin of Rome, calling them both by their Etruscan names, Mastarna and Tarchu,[3] the latter being qualified by his prænomen and city of government—Cneve Tarchu Rumach. This document, which is not older than the fourth century, obviously would not be enough by itself to prove the historicity of the actors it depicts, but it at least shows that the Etruscan and Roman traditions agreed in a general way on this point and that is an argument by no means to be despised. The first kings of Rome lose themselves in a cloud of legend, and their very existence is open to question. The Etruscan kings, on the contrary, are thoroughly historical personages. With their appearance we emerge from the domain of legend to walk, gingerly at first, on the solid ground of history.

The canonical tradition makes these three Etruscan kings —Tarquin the Elder, Servius Tullius, and Tarquin the Proud —members of the same dynasty and related by blood (Tarquin the Proud, the son of Tarquin the Elder) or marriage (Servius Tullius son-in-law of Tarquin the Elder, Tarquin the Proud son-in-law of Servius Tullius). That is a mere product of simplification with no counterpart in reality. The Etruscan tradition is more reliable because less partial, and gives an entirely different version of the story. It represents Masterna as a bandit chief who had seized the Cælian at the head of a troop of adventurers and ousted Tarquin the Elder by force of arms.[4] Furthermore, upon the fall of the Etruscan dynasty under Tarquin the Proud,

[1] *E.g.*, **XX**, I, 519-21.

[2] **CCXXXII**, I, 45-52 (pls., XXI-XXX); **CXXXVI**; G. Körte, in **XLIX**, 1897, 57 *ff.*; F. Munzer, in **LXXIV**, 1898, 596-620; E. Petersen, in **XLIX**, 1899, 43-49; G. de Sanctis, in **LVI**, 1902, 96-104; **XX**, 510-18.

[3] **CXCIX**, 128-51.   [4] C.I.L., XIII, 1668.

the tradition mentions a counter offensive by the Etruscans under Porsenna, the *lars* of Clusium.

Strengthened by Umbrian reinforcements, they descended the Tiber Valley and laid siege to Rome. Horatius Cocles, Mucius Scævola, and Clælius, heroes of romance who had risen to the emergency, must be banished from history to join the Sabine women, Lucretia and Virginia, in the limbo of legend. The truth is—and Pliny,[1] Tacitus,[2] and Plutarch[3] are our authorities—that Rome succumbed and Porsenna proceeded systematically to disarm its inhabitants. The Wall of Servius Tullius was dismantled and the use of iron, except for agricultural operations, was forbidden to the population. The excavations on the Palatine in 1907 have completely and dramatically confirmed these isolated data; in the course of the contest a fierce fire wasted the Germal and the charred débris have thickly covered, as with a shroud, the ruins of the older colony.[4]

These facts are conclusive. Etruscan domination at Rome did not take the form of a single, continuous and firmly established dynasty. A series of Etruscan chiefs, the Tarchu, Mastarna, and Porsenna, comparable to the sixteenth century condottieri, and representing successive waves of invasion, had in turn usurped the throne without being able to perpetuate their sway or found genuine dynasties.

As masters of Latium, the Etruscans had sought to secure an uncontested and lasting hold upon it. To attain this aim they must, before all else, establish a solid grip on the Tiber ford and on Rome, which was the key thereto. The strategic position was thus inverted by the Etruscan conquest. Latin Rome had been for centuries the outpost of Latium against the Etruscans; Etruscan Rome was to be Etruria's base in the Latin country and the buttress of her sway south of the Tiber. The conquest of Campania, at the end of the seventh and the beginning of the sixth century B.C., would still further increase the military and political importance of Rome. Thanks to her exceptional situation

---

[1] Plin., *Hist. Nat.*, XXXIV, 139.
[2] Tac., *Hist.*, III, 72.
[3] Plut., *Rom. ques.*, 18.
[4] **LXV**, 1907, 450, 457; **IX**, 35-36.

she became the keystone of the whole Etruscan Empire, and for the first time enjoyed a foretaste of her glorious career as capital of a unified Italy.

Accordingly, after the Etruscan conquest, and just because of that conquest, the old community of the Septimontium found itself called upon to play a leading part in Central Italy geographically, politically, and strategically. The result of the Etruscan conquest was far-reaching and complex; we may distinguish five principle aspects according as it affected the city, political life, military organization, economics, and culture. We will cast a fleeting glance at all five.

The Septimontium, as we have seen, had not been a genuine city, but rather a loose federation of poor hamlets scattered upon the several hills of Rome, separated by marshy tracts, and lacking all real cohesion. The Etruscan invaders had brought with them the concept of the city, *urbs*, that had been strange to the old inhabitants of the Roman *montes* and *pagi*.[1] This city type the Etruscans reproduced upon Roman soil as elsewhere. They founded the city of Rome *etrusco ritu*,[2] according to their traditional rules and with their traditional rites, just as in the past they had founded the cities of Tuscany and in the near future they were to found the new cities of Campania and the Po Valley. This material creation of the city of Rome was not accomplished by a stroke of the wand nor in a day; it advanced step by step with the power of the Etruscan kings, and might indeed serve as a measure of their progress. During the first stage, before 600 B.C., as the archæological study of the cemeteries on the Esquiline and the Sacred Way proves,[3] the old Septimontium gave place to a new Rome, which included the Palatine, the Esquiline, the Velia, the Cælian, and their annex, the Aventine, but still excluded the Capitol and the Sabine colony on the Quirinal and Viminal. This city needed a name; that the Estruscans

[1] E. Kornemann, in **LVI**, 1905, 88-91; **CXL**, 47 *ff*.

[2] Varr., *de Ling. Lat.*, V, 143; **XX**, I, 646, and note 5; I. dall'Osso, in **LXVI**, 1923[6], 367-68; 1924[2], 353-54.

[3] The Etruscan etymology of the name Rome (**CCXXII**, 579-82; *cf.* Graffunder, in **XXII**, *s.v.* "Rom," p. 1024, and E. Kornemann, **LVI**, 1921, 204, n. 4) is far from proven.

supplied, and the name Rome, the city of the river,[1] or the " Rumon," as the Prisco-Latini used to call it,[2] then made its début on the stage of history. Later on, in the course of the sixth century, as a second stage, Rome annexed the Sabine colony on the Quirinal and the Capitol. The old necropolis on the Sacred Way went out of use, and the Forum, formally opened, set out on its future career.

The unity of the city was accordingly established. A series of measures was taken to supplement and cement it. Materially a great programme of public works was inaugurated. The swampy depressions were drained by a system of conduits, in which the *Cloaca Maxima*, originally open but vaulted over under the Republic, represented the main artery, and which transformed the valleys from obstacles into natural ways of communication and intercourse. The unified city was enclosed in a vast circuit of fortifications of the Etruscan type, the Wall of Servius Tullius, to secure the safety of the Etruscan princes from attacks from outside. Other measures were of a moral nature. The old villages must be weaned from their ingrained traditions and local customs by giving the new Rome that principle of unity without which the ancients could not imagine a national life—a common cult. The Capitol, the citadel of the fortified town, became also its religious centre with the erection of the Temple of the Capitoline Triad, the symbol of Rome's greatness, destined to endure as long as she.[3]

Politically, the Etruscans were the first to give Rome a centralized government. As they had founded the city of Rome, so they created the Roman State.[4] Here, too, several stages may be distinguished. The first step was the whole work of political unification, traditionally attributed to Romulus, the city's founder, which, in fact, was first accomplished under the Etruscan kings. The three primitive tribes, Ramnes or Ramnenses, Tities or Titienses, and Luceres, which, in tradition, represented the amalgamation

---

[1] W. Corrssen, **LXXXII**, X, 1861, 18 *ff.*, and **CXVIII**, I², 279, 364, 536; I. Guidi, in **XL**, 1881, 69-70; **XXVI**, I, 190, and n. 1; **XX**, I, 635, n. 3.

[2] Serv., *ad Æn.*, VIII, 63, 90.

[3] **VIII**, *s.v.*, 583-84; **IX**, 173.

[4] We shall have occasion to return to this subject in our book on *Roman Institutions*.

of three different racial elements—Latin, Sabine, and Etruscan—were in reality simply the territorial and administrative divisions applied to unified Rome by the conquerors in the first phases of the synœcism. The Ramnes correspond to the Palatine region, the Tities and Luceres to the Cælian and Esquiline, but in the case of the latter the identification must stop there. The thirty curies, likewise territorial divisions, were merely subdivisions, the several quarters of the three urban regions.

The second stage saw the new Rome expand and the power of the Etruscan kings consolidated. The war with the Sabine colony ended with the defeat and annexation of the latter. For it a fourth region was created, and that involved the transition from the system of the three old tribes to that of the four so-called Servian tribes—Suburan, Palatine, Esquiline, and Colline—which would remain the official division of the city to the Imperial Age.

On the other hand, during the Etruscan period numerous classes of citizens, particularly merchants and artisans, who had been unknown in the primitive town, came and settled at Rome. They took up their abodes chiefly in the hollows which the great drainage works of the Tarquins had opened up to settlement; such was the case with the Velabrum, the main street of which took and kept for the future the suggestive name of " Street of the Etruscans," Vicus Tuscus.[1] Thereafter two groups of people found themselves permanently juxtaposed on Roman soil; on the one hand stood the old population of the seven hills, on the other the newly incorporated people of the Quirinal and the settlers who had established themselves at Rome voluntarily. The first represents the patricians and their clients; the second the mass of the plebs. Both were enrolled in the same regional classes, the urban tribes, the same classes as survived in historic Rome.

Etruscan Rome appears as a great military force, the attraction of which must have been felt over a wide range. To this period and to it alone are to be assigned those distant conquests of Crustumerium and similar villages which we saw were inconceivable in the previous period. Tradition expressly attributes to the Etruscan kings certain

---

[1] **VIII**, *s.v.*, 60; **IX**, 317-18; I. dall'Osso, in **LXVI**, 1924, 354-55.

conquests belonging to the same class. Collatia (Castell'-Lunghezza), at the junction of the Anio and the Osa ten

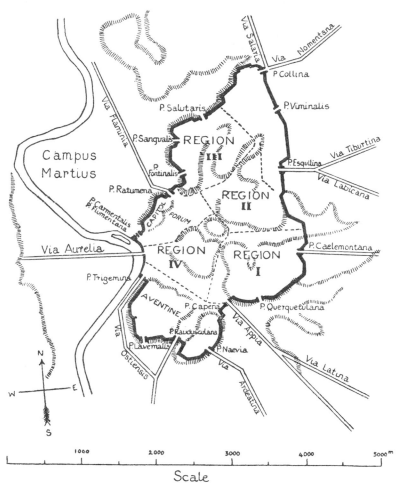

FIG. 6.—THE SYNŒCISM OF ROME. THE CITY, THE FOUR REGIONS,
AND THE WALL OF SERVIUS TULLIUS.

————— Wall of Servius Tullius.
- - - - - - Boundaries of the Four Regions.

miles from Rome, Nomentum (Mentana), Ficulea, Corniculum, Cameria, and Ameriola, the sites of which have not been identified, but all situated in the neighbourhood of the

119

Via Nomentana, north of the Anio and Apiolæ, of which we know nothing, were subdued under them.

Etruscan Rome did not confine her activities to conquests in the immediate vicinity. Taking advantage of the state of chronic anarchy into which the disappearance of Alba had plunged Latium, she successfully asserted her title to the hegemony of the Latin peoples and gave it the form of a federation. A Temple of Diana on the Aventine, dedicated, we are told, by Servius Tullius, replaced the old religious centre of the Alban Mount and consecrated the new political situation.[1] Under the Etruscans Rome became the commercial capital of Latium and the great outlet for the Etruscan countries. Industries grew up there, merchants and craftsmen came to settle there in large numbers, the Tiber became a commercial highway and, thanks to the Etruscan conquest, for the first time realized the economic potentialities that Nature had bestowed upon it.

Finally, the Etruscan domination at Rome, as elsewhere, was the signal for a brilliant spurt in civilization.[2] Tradition has preserved the memory of the monumental works executed by the dynasty of the Tarquins. Even in the Imperial Age the *Cloaca Maxima*, the collecting sewer of Rome, and the enormous substructures supporting the Temple of the Capitoline Triad excited universal wonder.[3] On this point we are not reduced to reliance upon the word of the ancients. The extant remains and modern discoveries supply a startling confirmation of their assertions.[4] In the domain of architecture we may mention, in addition to the foundations of the Capitol,[5] the Wall of Servius Tullius, or, rather, the parts of it which genuinely go back to the regal period, and the two cisterns on the Palatine—one of the seventh, the other of the sixth century. As illustration of the decoration of the epoch we may point to the fragments of terra-cotta yielded up in large masses by the soil of Rome which attest most strikingly the transformation of the external aspect of the city. We have tiles painted with

---

[1] Liv., I, 45, 52; Dion., III, 54; IV, 25-26, 48; **CCXXVI**, I, 383-84; **VIII**, *s.v.*, 559; **IX**, 308.

[2] **CVI**, I, vii-x. [3] Plin., *Hist. Nat.*, XXXVI, 104.

[4] **CCXIII**, 496-514.

[5] **CCXIII**, 499-500; **CXXIII**, 12 and pl. II, fig. 2; **X**, 20; **IX**, 173-76.

meander ornaments from the ancient Temple of Capitoline Jove; two antefixes, one from a temple on the Arx, the other from a shrine on the Esquiline near the modern church of San Antonio;[1] ornamental fragments from one or more temples on the Palatine, and other remains.

The contemporary development of art in Etruria proper offers interesting points of comparison in this respect. Let us just refer for painting to the tombs of " dei Tori " at Corneto (first half of the sixth century), " degli Auguri," " del Pulcinella," " degli Iscrizioni " (middle of the sixth century), " del Barone," " delle Bighe," " dei Leopardi," and " dell Orco " (the last three from the end of the sixth century);[2] while sculpture may be illustrated by the recent discoveries at Veii, which lay, it must be remembered, only ten miles from Rome.[3] Roman tradition mentions the Etruscan terra-cotta statues which adorned the Temple of the Capitoline Triad; the Apollo and other statues from Veii afford a complete and vivid illustration of this statement.

It is well established that the Etruscan period represented an era of greatness for Rome, but in points of detail the tradition in its usual manner exaggerates and distorts the true facts. Let us take two specific examples. Traditional history enumerates a number of wars against the Sabines, the Æqui, the Volsci, and the Etruscans, waged under the leadership of the Etruscan kings.[4] If we believe it, the military force of Rome made itself felt far beyond the borders of Latium on the northern frontier of Etruria, in the valley of the Sacco, and as far as Terracina on the southern coast. Part of this list is doubtless due to later fabrications, but, as a whole, it more probably represents a mere distortion of the truth. These events, outside the political and military horizon of the Rome of those days, may well be episodes in the great Etruscan conquest, but cannot be the direct and unaided feats of the Etruscan kings of Rome. Rome may doubtless have participated in these exploits, but not alone, nor, in all probability, as leader.

---

[1] **CCXIII**, 496-511, 508-14, 746-53, 787-88; **IX**, 6-9, 35-36.
[2] **CCXVI**, 9-28, 30-32, 49-51.
[3] G. G. Giglioli, in **LXV**, 1919, 13-37.
[4] Livy, I, 36-38, 4, 53-56, 4; Dion., III, 55-66; IV, 49-54; **XX**, I, 477, 530-31.

In this case, the tradition has enriched national history with a mass of deeds which it has not scrupled to magnify and misrepresent on patriotic grounds.

The great public works executed at Rome by the Etruscan dynasty of the Tarquins furnish our second example. Tradition attributed to the Etruscan kings two of the mightiest and most imposing structures of ancient Rome— the *Cloaca Maxima* and the Wall of Servius Tullius. In each case the actual study of the monuments leads to decisive results. In its present form the *Cloaca Maxima* dates from the beginning of the Empire, and the network of Roman sewers as a whole does not go back beyond the Republican Age. What Tarquin the Elder constructed was not the main collecting sewer of the classical period, but just an open channel in which the waters flowed. Tradition ascribed to Servius Tullius the fortifications of Rome as they appeared in the last centuries of the Republic. Now, an examination of the architecture and the specific facts which it reveals— the frequent use of the " foot " of twenty-nine centimetres in cutting the stone blocks, the employment of mortar for bonding, and the discovery of later graves right inside the limits of the fortified area—prove up to the hilt the falsity of that opinion. As a whole, the wall which under the Republic passed for that of Servius Tullius really dated from the second third of the fourth century B.C., and was not anterior to the capture of Rome by the Gauls.[1] But archæological researches have likewise demonstrated that certain portions of the wall are substantially older, and may with much probability be regarded as works of the Etruscan dynasty.[2] The Etruscans had then, in fact, girt Rome with a wall, but this wall as a whole was not that which the Romans of the Republic had before their eyes. Thus, on this point, the tradition was not guilty of fabrication but, as in the case of the *Cloaca Maxima*, of distortion. If such a procedure is not exactly praiseworthy, history, at least, is more easily able to find her proper material through it.

[1] **CCXIII**, 746-53; **IX**, 6-8.

P. Graffunder, in **LVI**, 1911, 83 *ff*., and his conclusion, p. 123; **T.** Frank, in **XXXI**, 1918, 181-88.

THE ETRUSCAN EMPIRE

IV

THE LATIN REACTION AND THE COLLAPSE OF ETRUSCAN DOMINATION

Etruscan domination in Latium lasted approximately for a century and a half. Then it foundered in a violent and sudden catastrophe which traditional history designates the Revolution of 509.[1]   What can we discover about this event?

The classical narrative as a whole, and not merely the episode of Lucretia, smacks of legend. Four essential features deserve attention. According to tradition, the movement for emancipation originated at Rome, and Rome by herself was able to bring it to a successful termination. In a word, Rome, and Rome alone, expelled her Etruscan kings. The revolt was not a national insurrection against foreign masters, but merely a political reaction against rulers who had become tyrants. When the revolution had succeeded at Rome, the Latins declared for the Tarquins and took arms against Rome to restore them to power. Finally, Porsenna, hastening to the rescue, abandoned the capture of Rome and retreated after making an honourable peace with the city. What can we say of this tradition?

We have already seen that the last statement referring to the part played by Porsenna was contrary to historical truth. Let us for the moment pass over the first point, the part taken by Rome in the movement for liberation, to which we shall have to return later. The political, as opposed to national, aspect given to the revolution is plainly the logical corollary of the whole tendency of the tradition to disguise the Etruscan conquest under the mask of usurpation by individuals. Such a thesis obviously left no room for a national reaction. But the rôle of the Latins in the affair cannot fail to provoke surprise. We are a trifle astonished to see those Latins, who had been conquered and grievously oppressed by the Tarquins, rush to arms to restore them to the throne they had just lost. The tradition of the Revolution of 509 and Porsenna's counter-offensive as transmitted

[1] Liv., I, 56-II, 15; Dion., IV, 64-V, 36.

by Livy[1] and Dionysius of Halicarnassus[2] is therefore nothing but a tissue of fictions, contradictions, and errors.[3]

However, certain specific data enable us, if not to reconstruct the whole truth—a task which had better be renounced without more ado—at least to cast a little light on this tract of darkness and chaos. In the first place, since their occupation of Campania, the Etruscans had been at grips with the Greeks, represented especially by the colony of Cumæ. They attempted a decisive effort to seize the rival city, but the men of Cumæ, under the able generalship of Aristodemus, repulsed them.[4] Greek chronology referred this event to the year 524 B.C.; we content ourselves with this bare statement, lest we become the dupes of a chronology which has only the appearance of precision till the end of the sixth century.

The second step in the conflict was for the Greeks to initiate a counter-offensive. As good strategists, they wished to take full advantage of the Etruscan reverse and to lose no time in so doing. Aristodemus put himself at the head of operations, for his victories opened his way to the tyranny. The chief danger for the Etruscans in the south was the length and precarious nature of their line of communication with the mother-country. Latium, and particularly the Tiber ford, constituted their strategic centre and consequently the vulnerable point in their dominions. To rob them of Latium, to cut them off from Etruria, their natural base, and so to reduce them to using the difficult and inadequate maritime route if they tried to maintain their hold upon Campania, was the logical plan for the Greeks, and they proceeded to act upon it. Now, in Latium the ground was prepared for such an operation. Oppressed by the Etruscans, the Latins were impatient of the yoke of their hereditary foes, whom they had so long watched and kept at bay beyond the moat of the Tiber. An alliance was made and a plan of action elaborated. Latium gave the signal when an insurrection broke out. The Greeks of Cumæ under Aristodemus hastened to support them, and a battle

---

[1] Liv., I, 56-II, 15.   [2] Dion., IV, 64-V, 36.
[3] **CXCIX**, 152-67, 185-203; **XX**, I, 536-53; II, 89-123.
[4] Dion., VII, 3-4. On Aristodemus in general, see Livy, II, 34, 4; Dion., VII, 2-11; Diod., VII, frag. 10.

was fought near Aricia, in which the Etruscans were worsted.[1]

No doubt the Battle of Aricia was only one of the many episodes which must have marked the Latin revolt and preluded the expulsion of the Etruscans.[2] But the two vital facts, the Latin revolt and the intervention of the Greeks, were none the less connected, and decided the subsequent course of events. Let us note that there is no reference to the Romans in the whole story, a remark that is not without significance. If they had had any appreciable share in the victory, annalistic tradition—so jealous of national honour, even at the cost of historical truth—would not have failed to boast of it. One conclusion, therefore, seems inevitable : if the Romans are not mentioned, it is for the very simple reason that at the moment of the battle Rome was still in the hands of the Etruscan kings, and the expulsion of the latter, far from being the result of a purely Roman movement, was in reality the consequence of a Latin reaction from which Rome apparently at first stood aloof. The victorious revolt in Latium then caused a repercussion in the guise of an outburst of national sentiment, the dynasty of the Tarquins could not maintain its position and had to retire into exile.

Tradition distorts, in the interests of Rome, the true character of the Revolution of 509, just as it had that of the fall of Alba previously. Whatever it may say, Rome did not take the lead in the movement of emancipation. She did no more than follow in it, and nothing proves that she did that spontaneously. The very site of the battle of Aricia, twelve miles south of the Tiber, gives cause for reflection. At that time the Etruscans had not yet been driven across the river; they were still holding Rome, the bridge-head, and the key to the ford, and we may be sure that they only evacuated her at the last extremity. Possibly we should also recognize at this crucial moment a diversion

[1] Liv., II, 14, 5-9; Dion., V, 36; **XXVI**, I, 450-52.

[2] Another episode may be inferred from the recent discoveries on the hill of S. Agata, north of Monte Mario, where it is evident that the Etruscan necropolis had been systematically desecrated at the time of the Latin reaction. The fact that none of the ceramic remains unearthed date back beyond the end of the sixth century confirms, in a general way, the traditional chronology. I. M. Palmarini, in **LXVI**, 1922[2], 256-58.

caused by the Sabine mountaineers, who, by threatening the Etruscans' flank, may have precipitated their departure.[1]

We are justified in doubting whether Rome rallied voluntarily to the national cause even after the Latin victory, for two reasons. As the creation of the Etruscans and the base of their power in Latium, Rome was allied to their cause by self-interest as much as by compulsion. To her the Etruscan rule represented political and military hegemony and economic prosperity; merchants, industrialists, and artisans, the whole new population which had come to settle in the city in the train of the Etruscan dynasts, constituted a faction with a stake in the country which was far from negligible and which stood for the maintenance of the régime to which its prosperity and security were due. There was, therefore, no lack of Etruscan sympathizers at Rome, and we may be sure that, if they bowed to circumstances, they only did so under compulsion.

Furthermore, even after the catastrophe, all the Etruscans were not systematically expelled from Rome; for a time, at least, even members of the Tarquins' family were to be found there. An inference pointing in the same direction may be drawn from the conduct of the Latins. On the morrow of the Revolution of 509 the Latins made war upon Rome. Why? Because, voluntarily or no, she remained morally attached to the defeated cause, the cause of the foreigners, and because, rid of the Etruscans, she none the less claimed their inheritance. That is the awkward fact that Roman tradition was endeavouring to disguise when it attributed the initiative in the revolution to Rome, and transmuted the Latins, the first agents of rebellion, into obstinate champions of the Tarquins.

The general course of events may therefore be reconstructed as follows. A Latin rising broke out which received the support of the Greeks of Cumæ. The Etruscans were defeated at Aricia. The movement quickly spread; it reached Rome, and the Etruscan monarchy succumbed. How did the last phase develop? Tradition sets forth the respective attitudes of the two sections of the populace at

---

[1] But it is not correct to attribute the fall of the Etruscan dynasty at Rome to the Sabines alone, and that in the fifth century, as E. Pais does in **XX**, I, 801; IV, 247; and **XIX**, I, 347 *ff*. (*cf.* also **LXXXVIII**, 93 *ff*.).

Rome, the patricians and the plebs. The former represent the old Roman tradition, hostile to the autocratic system of the Tarquins, and the embodiment of the agricultural interests, whose hostility had been aroused by the economic policy of the Etruscans. They accordingly took the lead in the revolt. It was the patricians who resented the injury done to Lucretia, raised the army, and after the victory presided over the organization of the Republican government. The plebians in the meanwhile, exhausted by military service and wearied by forced labour, remained passive and left the nobles to act. This account of the events really seems to correspond to the reality. In any case, it accurately reflects the general situation and the respective attitudes of the two parties on the morrow of the expulsion of the kings.

The fall of Etruscan domination in Latium closes one era and opens another. A decisive step, pregnant with far-reaching consequences for Italy and mankind as a whole, had been taken. Cut into two sections, Etruria proper and its extension to the Po Valley on the one hand, and Etrurian Campania on the other, the Etruscan Empire was broken. The first experiment in Italian unity had failed. Italy was not fated to become Etruscan. But, on the other hand, in ebbing from Latium after an occupation of a century and a half, the Etruscan flood left behind it a thoroughly rejuvenated and transformed country. The stern hand of the invaders had substituted the phase of city life for the earlier stages of tribe and federation. The old Prisco-Latin hordes have laid aside the garb of primitive barbarism to clothe themselves in the full panoply of civilization.

Etruria had made a people of sedentary peasants out of the semi-nomadic pastoral folk they had found, and with this change had marked it out for its future greatness. Henceforth a new city stands on the banks of the Tiber, the finest creation of the Etruscans—Rome. Fate had decided that the unity of Italy should be postponed for two centuries, and that it should not be the work of Etruria, but of Rome. But, at least, it was Etruria that had forged the engine of this unification and equipped it for its glorious function. She was the first to make Rome a great power, and, among a conservative people like the Romans, this memory was never to be effaced. In the midst of all the troubles which followed during the first century of the Republican era and which more than once endangered even her national unity, Rome would never forget. She would grow up with her eyes resolutely fixed upon that glorious past which Etruria had once given her, and from the religion of memory she would draw one of the vital elements of her wondrous expansion.

The Etruscan Empire fell, not through a want of intelligence or idealism in its founders, but through lack of means; they had not been able to endow it with the political organization, the military force, nor the judicial apparatus without which permanent success must remain a vain dream. The antagonism of the Hellenic element and the reaction of the native races, of which the revolt in Latium was the first symptom, dealt it a mortal blow. The Gaulish invasions and the progress of Rome were to do the rest. But, though Rome was the first to bring Italian unity to fruition, though she could claim the title of mother of the Latin peoples, let us not forget that Etruria could justly claim the name of grandmother. To ignore that would be a misapprehension of history aggravated by its ingratitude.

BOOK II
ROME'S HOUR AND THE FIRST ITALIAN UNITY

CHAPTER I

THE ROMAN MIDDLE AGES AND THE ARMED VIGIL OF THE FIFTH CENTURY

I

ROME AND ITALIAN UNITY

FOR the first time in history Rome created Italian unity, and this unification, her political masterpiece, was the foundation of her extraordinary greatness, owing to the effective means of action it placed in her hands. At the beginning of the sixth century, when the Roman people, rid of the Etruscan domination, were taking their first painful steps in national policy, nothing seemed to foreshadow for Italy such a brilliant future as a unified State.

Geographically, Italy appears in the heart of the Mediterranean world as a perfect example of a land of regionalism and division. Her natural conformation is peculiar; the striking disproportion between her length and her breadth has always rendered communications between the peoples of the north and those of the south difficult; and, finally, the

Bibliography.—*Texts:* Livy, II, 16-V, 31 (*cf.* Florus, I, 5-6; Eutropius, I, 9-20; Orosius, II, 5; III, 12-13, 19); Dionysius of Halicarnassus, V, 37-XI, XII-XIII (frags.); Diodorus, XI-XIV; Dio Cassius, IV-VI (frags.; *cf.* Zonaras, VII, 12-22); Plutarch, *Valerius Publicola, Coriolanus, Camillus;* Appian, *Basil.,* frags. 12-13; *Italic.,* frags.; Strabo, V, 4, 2 (p. 240 C); V, 4, 12 (p. 250 C); VI, 1, 4 (pp. 254-55 C); Antiochus, in F.H.G., I, p. 183, frag., 13; Scylax, in G.G.M., I, 19-20; Polyænus, II, 10, 2, 5; Cicero, *de Republica*, II, 31-37 (down to the Decemvirs); Valerius Maximus, II, 4, 5; Servius, *ad Æn.*, VII, 706; *de Viris Illustribus*, 13-23 and 25.

Inscriptions.—*Fasti consulares* (C.I.L., I, pp. 98-119); *Fasti triumphales*, particularly years 504, 475, 459, 458, 449, 443 (*id.*, pp. 98-119); C.I.L., I², 1 (archaic cippus from the Forum).

Principal Works.—**XX**, II, 13 *ff.;* **XXVI**, II, 1-155; **CCII**, I, 61-132, 133-77; II, 123-34; **CCIX**, 267 *ff.;* A. Rosenberg, in **XLVII**, 1919, 113-73; 1920, 337-63; **XIX**, IV, 92 *ff.;* **XXV**, 8-11; **V**, 26-59.

peninsula falls into a plurality of diverse and contrasted natural provinces : Piedmont, the Po plain, Venetia, and Liguria in the north; Tuscany, Umbria, Latium and the Abruzzi in the centre; and Campania, Basilicata, and Apulia, the littoral of the Tyrrhenian and Ionian Seas, in the south.

During the thousands of years, in the course of which the racial aspect of Italy had been established, man had further emphasized nature's work and as it were deliberately aggravated the obstacles he would have to surmount on his laborious way towards unity. The most diverse races hailing from the opposite points of the compass jostled one another on Italian soil. The old Neolithic substratum of Ligurians had been overlaid by a whole heap of invading peoples. Italici had descended from the north in the successive waves of Latins, Sabellians, and Umbrians; the Veneti and Iapygians had come from Central Europe along the Illyrian seaboard; Etruscans and Greeks were strangers from the shores of the Eastern Mediterranean, come by sea from Asia Minor and Greece respectively. The list is not yet complete; it will be enlarged by a fresh element, the Gauls. After a long period of confusion and conflict a territorial equilibrium was ultimately established for good or ill. Liguria and the Western Alpine valleys fell to the Ligures; the Etruscans kept Etruria proper, part of Umbria, and the Po Valley; the Veneti, the Umbrians, and the Latins held the respective countries which still bear their names. The Sabellians occupied the Central Apennines, Samnium, and Lucania, and the Iapyges Apulia. Finally, the Greeks had colonized the coasts of the peninsula south of the Bay of Naples and on the shores of the Ionian Sea.

The same division and heterogeneity reigned in the linguistic domain. In the fifth century B.C. a dozen languages were current in Italy — Ligurian, Etruscan, Venetian, Messapian, Greek, and soon also Celtic, besides the two great languages sprung from primitive Italic, Latin and Osco-Umbrian respectively. The first six had nothing in common with one another or with the last two. Even within the Italic family Latin and Osco-Umbrian represent not mere dialects, but two distinct languages, and are each divided in their turn into a multiplicity of separate dialects.

Despite dialectic peculiarities, Greek remained a single language and a Greek could make himself understood throughout the whole Hellenic world. To this Italy offered no parallel. Even within the domain of the Italic languages a Latin, an Oscan, and an Umbrian could not understand one another; the plight of Etruscans, Ligurians, Veneti, Iapygians, or Greeks was, of course, still worse. Thus Italy was a kaleidoscope of races and a mosaic of languages, to which a parallel could be found to-day only in the Caucasus or Eastern Europe.

Finally, as the logical and concrete result of her extreme division, Italy did not possess even that minimum of unity that is represented by a common appellation. The name Italy, the Viteliu of the Oscans, originally only denoted an obscure canton in Calabria, buried in the extreme south of the peninsula. Only the Roman conquest will carry it as a symbol and an ensign to the Apennines, and then to the Alps.[1] German unity and the second Italian unity, the resurrection of a brilliant past, were, above all else, the works of collective will and enthusiasm. Ancient Italy lacked any such inspiration. At the moment there was no community of State nor of race nor of language; there was no memory of national life in the past; neither geography nor history afforded any support or basis for the idea of unity.

Nevertheless, a humble city of Latium succeeded in three centuries of conflicts and struggles in achieving this unity of Italy; through her the idea of unity proceeded slowly and painfully to shake off the trammels of secular particularism, to which the peninsula seemed condemned for ever. That is not to say that the city of the Tiber had from the start

---

[1] On the gradual extension of the word Italy between the fifth century B.C. and the beginning of the Empire from the Straits of Messina to the Sinus Scylaceus (Gulf of Squillace) on the east and to the Sinus Terinæus (Bay of Sant'Eufemia) on the west about 500, to the whole of Bruttium from the River Laus (Laino) on the west and Metapontium on the east to the Gulf of Tarentum about the middle of the fifth century, to the Gulf of Pæstum about 350, then to the northern frontier of Campania, to the whole Italic federation in the peninsula as far as the Arno and the Æsis, later to the Rubicon after the end of the war with Philip, and finally to the geographical Italy after the conquest of Cisalpine Gaul, see especially H. Philipp, in **XXII** (suppl. III) *s.v.* " Italia," 1246-50.

a programme of unification nor the faintest suspicion of the glorious future that should be hers. Far-sighted conceptions and bold speculations were not to be expected from the Roman, a timid, cautious, unimaginative spirit.

Nevertheless, by the beginning of the fifth century, the issue no longer appeared quite unprejudiced. In Italy, and at Rome no doubt more than elsewhere, men cherished the fresh memory of that great Etruscan Empire, first embryo of Italian unity that had succeeded for an instant in holding under its sway the whole country from the Alps to the Gulf of Salerno. Rome was never destined to forget that she had held a brilliant place in the heart of this empire, and that she had been indebted to the Etruscan dynasty for the first rays in her halo of glory, the hegemony over Latium. In fact, even in the throes of the trials that beset her unsparingly in the fifth and early fourth century she would loyally preserve this memory of the past, and her eyes would be turned towards this period of greatness while she pursued with her customary tenacity the most immediate of her aims, the re-establishment of the Roman hegemony in Latium. Among this nation of realists the task of unification never presented itself with the rigidity of a theoretical idea and a systematic plan, but always in the urgent form of immediate problems involving ever wider and wider issues, the solutions of which were always dictated simply and solely by the needs and possibilities of the moment.

The first form of the programme and its first stage was the unification of Latium (fifth and first half of the fourth century B.C.). Rome desired to revive for her own profit the hegemony in Latium which she had lost through the expulsion of her Etruscan kings. In addition to memories of the past, economic needs, provoked by the growth of the population, urged her imperiously in this direction. After a century and a half of fruitless attempts, experience at length revealed to her the sole means of attaining her object, the encirclement of Latium. The occupation of Campania was to answer to this strategic plan. In 338 B.C. the object was attained; Rome had finally brought about the unity of the Latin country by her own unaided forces and for her sole advantage.

The entry of Campania into the sphere of Roman policy

marked the opening of the war against the Sabellians, a duel to the death which was to be prolonged for more than half a century. Through its inevitable repercussions it involved the entry upon the scene of the great peoples of Central and Northern Italy, the Etruscans, Umbrians, and Gauls. Hence in its development the problem assumed a new shape; the issue now was the unification of Central Italy, the second stage on the road leading to Italian unity, which would be traversed in the first years of the third century.

The third stage now opened out ahead. The conflict with the Sabellians had, by the very fluctuations of its fortunes, brought the Roman armies to the shores of the Adriatic and into contact with the Magna Grecia. From the experience already gained, the idea of Italian unity was inevitably suggested, but it was still limited by the frontiers of peninsular Italy. With the defeat of Pyrrhus and the fall of Tarentum (272 B.C.) Roman policy attained this new objective.

One stage remained to be travelled, the conquest of continental Italy and the entry of the plains of the Po and the Adige, as well as of the Ligurian seaboard, into the Italian federation. The achievement of this work of unification was postponed for half a century longer, and it needed the stern lessons of the Gaulish tumults and the Punic wars to demonstrate its urgency. Rome created Italian unity by blood and iron. By curbing beneath her equal yoke the diverse peoples who shared the soil of the peninsula, she gave Italy the unity of a State. To pass from the unity of a State to the unity of a nation, and by the triumph of Latin to community of language, and to make the whole of Italy the Romano-Latin nation she became, required two more centuries. Fashioned by the Republic, Italian unity would only come to full fruition under the Empire.

II

The Crisis in the Roman State in the Fifth Century

The activity of the Etruscan kings at Rome had had a double aspect. At home they had founded the city of Rome and created the Roman State. Abroad the Etruscans had made Rome the basis of their sway in Latium, and in virtue of this position the city had exercised a veritable hegemony within the Latin country. The expulsion of the Tarquins imperilled the work of the Etruscan dynasty in both its aspects. The Revolution of 509 marks the beginning of a violent crisis both external and internal, a sort of medieval era for Rome; after several narrow escapes, it took the city more than a century to recover from it.

Internally the work of centralization, accomplished by the Etruscans, was endangered in its entirety. Not only Rome's power, but her very national unity was on the brink of destruction in the turmoil. In the first place Rome lost one of the most potent bonds of her unity in the Wall of Servius Tullius. The conqueror, Porsenna, had systematically dismantled the fortifications, and a century and a half would pass before Rome would be in a position to restore them. Rome tended to relapse into a mere federation of villages grouped round a common citadel such as she had been in the pre-Etruscan period.

In this connection the excavations on the Palatine in 1907 have brought to light interesting details. They show that the fragments of walls, long attributed to the regal period, cannot, in fact, go back beyond the first half of the fourth century, and must be later than the Gaulish invasion.[1] In 390 B.C. the Gauls occupied the whole of the city, including the Palatine, without striking a blow, and only the Capitol was in a position to offer any resistance. On the departure of the enemy, the citizens' first care was to put the Palatine at least in a position to resist in the event of a second attack. The remains of walls still in place on the west slope of the hill along the Velabrum are survivals of the fortifications erected at this juncture.[2] The isolation of the several hills from a defensive standpoint was only ended some twenty years later with the construction of a new wall, the so-called Wall of Servius Tullius, belonging to the Republican period.

At the same time as her material unification, Rome's political unity, too, seemed threatened, and the old local factions, momentarily curbed by the Etruscan dynasts' iron hand, once more raised their heads. The two essential com-

[1] **IX**, 35. [2] **IX**, 35 and 37.

ponents of the Tarquins' town, patricians and plebeians, now faced one another without any central power capable of restraining them, still less of conciliating them. Now, the opposition between patricians and plebs was more than the conflict of two parties, or, to use the classic term, of two orders. In the fifth century Rome also took on the aspect of a very sharp local division. The patriciate as a whole, the patricians and their clients, represented the old population of the Septimontium. The body of the plebs, on the other hand, was the population of the new quarters, the Quirinal, the Viminal, the Aventine, and the Velabrum.

This vital fact explains why the conflict between the two orders so easily took a local turn. We shall have occasion to return to this question in our book on *Roman Political Institutions* in this series. Here let us content ourselves with recalling those incidents, so suggestive from the geographical standpoint, of the retreat of the plebs to the Sacred Mount and the secession to the Aventine. It would, in any case, be a mistake to overestimate the importance of this topographical and political dislocation. It has been stated[1] that the city had then been divided into two rival federations : the patrician federation would have held the *montes*, the Septimontium, on the north; the plebian, the *colles*, the Quirinal and Viminal, on the south. Each would have possessed its own political organs—the two consuls and the Senate in the case of the former; the *comitia tributa* and the tribunes in the case of the latter. No. As we have seen, the Septimontium corresponded to an earlier stage in the history of the city of Rome. On the other hand, the domain of the plebs included, besides the *colles*, the low-lying quarters of the city, such as the Velabrum and the Aventine. There had been no complete disruption, but, at least, serious threats of disruption had not been wanting, and it was to prevent this mortal peril that the whole internal policy of the Republican Government was directed for nearly a century and a half.

The plan was a return to the centralized régime such as had been set up by the Etruscan dynasty, but in the actual state of the parties and in the absence of a central power strong enough to carry it through, the only remedy left was

[1] **CCIX**. 306-7.

that invariably adopted by weak Governments, a policy of compromise. The great acts of Roman internal policy during the fifth and the first third of the fourth century, the Laws of the Twelve Tables, the Valerio-Horatian laws, the final organization of the system of classes and centuries, the appointment of military tribunes with consular power, and the Licinian laws, had no other aim nor intention.[1] Final remedies they did not provide; they were mere expedients of an enlightened opportunism, but at least they succeeded in preserving the unity of the Roman State and safeguarding its possibilities for the future at the cost of mutual concessions.

III

THE DESCENT OF THE MOUNTAINEERS

Abroad, the departure of the Etruscans had completely upset the balance of power in Latium. To the Latins the Revolution of 509 represented the end of the Romano-Etruscan hegemony. And so all Latium rose to assert its independence, and the majority of the Latin cities, Tusculum, Aricia, Lanuvium, Cora, Tibur, Pometia, and Ardea (but note, among others, the absence of the powerful Præneste, which only joined the league subsequently) had hastened to form an independent league with an autonomous organization and a federal centre at the Spring of Ferentina on Arician territory.[2] Rome, on the other hand, intended not to renounce, but to maintain the policy of the Etruscan hegemony, but now without the Etruscans and for her own sole benefit. The Latin and the Roman programmes were, accordingly, diametrically opposed and irreconcilable. The decision must be referred to the arbitrament of arms.

Reduced to her own territory by the defection of her former allies and with her very independence threatened, Rome at first ran a very grave risk. She was saved by the Battle of Lake Regillus, an historical event which tradition has drowned beneath a sea of legends. Its result was a

---

[1] **II**, 68-95; **CCIX**, 272 ff.

[2] Cato, quoted by Priscus, IV, p. 129 (=H.R.F., p. 52, frag. 58; H.R.R., p. 72, frag. 58); cf. Fest., p. 128; **XXVI**, II, 90-93; **CCXXVI**, I, 303-6; A. Rosenberg, in **XLVII**, 1919, 143.

victory, or, better, a half-victory, which allowed Rome, if not to recover her former position, at least to re-establish equitable and permanent relations with the Latin peoples by a peace of compromise. The terrible danger with which the Revolution of 509 had threatened her was thus surmounted, but though she had saved her independence by a supreme effort, hard times and stern trials were still in store for her.

Throughout the whole of the fifth century Rome lived and moved in the narrow arena of Latium. Her political horizon was bounded by the mountains, the Apennines and the Alban Hills, that rose upon the distant sky-line. She was still far from guiding the history of Central Italy. Lacking power to direct, she was fain to follow. Her history, the importance of which tradition has persistently tried to magnify, not scrupling in case of need to distort its nature, was merely that of a little town of Latium, constantly at war with her neighbours, in which the general events of Italian history were mirrored. Two great facts dominated the history of Italy in the fifth century—the Sabellian thrust and the decline of Etruria. These facts were to determine the history of Rome and Latium in the same period. They were the underlying causes, everything else their repercussion or reflection.

At the end of the sixth and the beginning of the fifth century the Sabellian world[1] became the prey of an intense ferment. The highland no longer sufficed to support their prolific peoples, who cast envious eyes on the rich and fertile plains that opened at their feet. The movement started in the Central Apennines. Preceded by the emblems of the tribe, wolf, bull, or boar, the bands of the " Sacred Spring " set out to conquer new territory, and joined battle with the former masters of the soil.

In the north the Sabines crossed the Tiber, occupied the Faliscan plain, came into contact with the Etruscans, and pushed on as far as Mount Cimanus. Further south the Sabellians, brushing aside the Hernici who barred their way, came out into the valley of the Liris. On the Adriatic slopes the Picentines, descending from the mountain, drove the

[1] On the many Sabellian invasions in the fifth century as a whole, consult **XX**, II, 385-86; IV, 243-52: **XIX**, I, 347 *ff*.

Umbrians from the seaboard and installed themselves in their places. In Southern Italy the phenomenon was on a larger scale and still more irresistible. The Sabellians invaded Apulia and forced the Iapyges into the Peninsula of Otranto. The recoil of the invasion was felt at Tarentum; in 473 B.C. the Iapyges inflicted a memorable defeat upon that city.[1] The Lucanians, a branch of the Samnite stock, overflowed into Southern Italy, south of the Silarus, and came to threaten the Greek colonies on the Ionian Sea.

Finally, the Bruttians, south of the foregoing, formed the vanguard of the great migration of mountaineers. Throughout the whole of Southern and Central Italy the migrants were streaming down upon the plains and the coasts. From Ravenna in the north-east, to the borders of the forest of Sila and the Sallentine plain, the Sabellians, swooping down from their citadel in the Abruzzi, appeared and ultimately took root. The older inhabitants, expelled or subdued, had to bow before the invaders; new States were founded. During the fifth century the political and the ethnographic maps of Italy were alike redrawn. The Sabellian peoples, young and overflowing with vigour, everywhere advanced. In the meanwhile Etruria, exhausted by her conquests and the resultant dispersion of her forces and mortally wounded by the loss of Latium, was now reduced to the defensive, a position from which she was not destined to extricate herself.

The Sabellian thrust and the decline of Etruria, these two dominant features of Italian history in the fifth century, also supply the key to the political and military evolution of Rome during the same epoch. The Sabellian invasion must and did react upon the inhabitants of the mountain fringe that encircled Latium, the Sabines, Æqui, and Volsci. A Sabine conquest of Rome[2] at the end of the sixth or the beginning of the fifth century has been suggested, but that is a pure hypothesis, the proof of which remains to be given. On the other hand, a multitude of warlike encounters between the Sabines and the Romans forms a part of our historical heritage. At the classical period several great families at Rome were proud to recall their Sabine lineage.

[1] Hdt., VII, 170; Diod., XI, 1-5; **XX**, IV, 244-45.
[2] On the Sabines, **XVIII**, I, 593; II, 453-80; **XX**, I, 801; II, 417; **XIX**, I, 349.

Such were the Valerii of Eretum, the Postumii, and the Claudii of Regillum. Tradition itself, and in respect of this definite statement we have no reasons for doubt, had preserved the memory that Attius Clausus, the head of the gens Claudia, had come to settle at Rome with his whole clan, and his clients to the number of five thousand persons. This immigration of a Sabine tribe is only a typical case, which probably was not isolated. Peaceable or violent, or probably both, the Sabine infiltration played an important part in the political history of Rome, and even in the formation of the Roman people.

South of the Sabines in the massif of the present Mounts Ruffi and Prenestini, in the Apennine foothills bounded on the north by the Anio Valley, on the south by the territory of Præneste, and on the west by the Latin plain, lived the people of the Æqui.[1] Even in antiquity opinions were divided as to their origin. Some regarded them as a fragment of the old Ligurian folk driven into the Apennines by a later invasion. Others, with more probability, saw in them a branch of the great family of the Italici. In any case, they inhabited a poor country and lived a rough and savage life. Cattle-breeding supplemented in case of need by brigandage formed their staple occupation. During the fifth century the thrust of the Sabellians, transmitted by their neighbours, the Hernici, frequently hurled the Æqui on to the plain. Tusculum, Aricia, and Lanuvium suffered much from their incursions, and Rome itself was not safe from their periodical raids.

Finally, adjoining the Æquian country, lived the Volsci, who occupied the bastion of the Monti Lepini.[2] The sterility of their territory naturally drove them into the plains to the side, the valleys of the Trerus (Tolero or Sacco) and of the Liris (Liri-Garigliano) on the east, and the Pontine region on the west, for here were agricultural resources that offered a tempting bait to a poor and prolific people. On the east their successes were but meagre. The powerful city of Præneste watched over them from her eyrie and held them at bay. But in the direction of the coasts, where the collapse of the Etruscans had left the land defenceless, their efforts

---

[1] **XVIII**, I, 514-15; II, 457-63; **XX**, II, 418; **XCII**. *s.v.*, p. 21.
[2] **XVIII**. I. 518-19; II. 667-78; **XX**. II, 421; **XCII**, *s.v.*, p. 823.

were more amply rewarded. They captured Velitræ, the key to the plain, subdued the Aurunci, who peopled the region, and through the pass of Privernum and the valley of the Amasenus proceeded to occupy Terracina, changing its name to Anxur.

As a result of this victorious advance the Æqui now constituted a powerful State. The whole seaboard from the plain of Anxur on the south to the vicinity of Ardea on the north recognized their sway. On the slopes of the Monti Lepini they possessed a bulwark of strong cities, Ecetra, Cora, Norba, and Setia. Having made themselves masters of the coast, these mountaineers soon had a navy. Antium became their chief port, and the commerce of the Tyrrhenian Sea, subjected to regular exactions by their fleet, was soon paying them a tithe of its earnings.

IV

THE DEFENSIVE WARS

Accordingly the whole circumference of Latium from the Sabine country on the north to Terracina on the south was swept by a tumultuous flood of mountain folk swept along voluntarily or under compulsion in the great thrust of the Sabellian tribes.[1] Reduced to taking the defensive for the whole of the fifth century, Rome found herself continually at grips with these warlike and tenacious invaders. She was embroiled in exhausting and inglorious contests, in which her existence was daily at stake. Yet by one of those just compensations, of which history is not always prodigal, she was to forge in the furnace of these trials the implements of her future greatness.

With the Sabines[2] hostilities were incessant for more than fifty years. The Anio front, especially the district round Eretum, some eighteen miles from Rome, was the battlefield. The Triumphal Fasti, the detailed testimony of which is only admissible as a list of events, record Roman victories in 504 and 475 B.C. In 460, in view of the internal

[1] **XX**, II, 128-61, 302-18, 404-26.
[2] Liv., II, 16 *ff.*; Dion., V, 37 *ff.*; Plut., *Val. Publ.*, 20-23; *Fast. tr.*, years 504, 475, 449.

troubles which paralysed Rome, the Sabines risked a bold attack; one of their captains, Appius Herdonius, laid hands on the Capitol without, however, being able to hold the position. A new war is mentioned in 449, and then silence falls. A conquest of Rome by the Sabines in the middle of the fifth century has been suggested as an explanation.[1] We cannot accept that hypothesis. Let us merely say that,

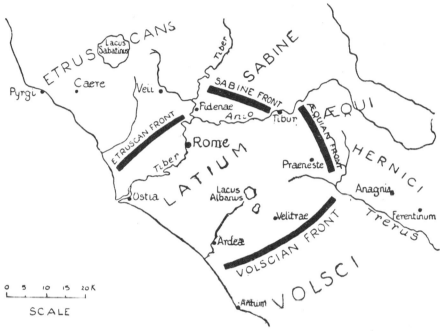

FIG. 7.—ROME'S POLITICAL AND MILITARY HORIZON IN THE FIFTH CENTURY B.C.

wearied of these sterile conflicts, the Romans and Sabines resolved to conclude a lasting truce. In any case, we hear nothing of hostilities between the two peoples for a century and a half.

With tedious prolixity and a disturbing wealth of detail tradition recounts the endless wars that Rome had to wage with the Ædui during the first years of the fifth century.[2] Let us content ourselves with recalling their two chief

---

[1] See p. 126, note 1 above.
[2] Livy, II, 58 *ff.*; Dion., VI, 34 *ff.*; *Fast. tr.*, years 462, 459, 458.

episodes. In 462 B.C. an Æquian and Volscian army forced its way right to the gates of Rome, and in the campaign of 458 the check sustained by the consul, L. Minucius Augurinus, was avenged with interest by the success of the celebrated L. Quinctius Cincinnatus. The Volsci,[1] for their part, pursuing northward their victorious drive, invaded Latium, and in 491 B.C., on Livy's chronology, a Volscian army under the exiled Coriolanus came to threaten Rome. In 485 the Volsci were beaten in several engagements, and were finally driven back to their own territory.

Sabines, Æqui, and Volsci were not the only foes Rome had to face in the fifth century. Apart from the contingency of an Etruscan counter-offensive, always possible, she had to reckon with the permanent hostility of her powerful neighbour, the city of Veii. The main question at issue between the two peoples was that of free access to the sea, a matter of life and death for Veii. As an inland city the latter could only communicate with the littoral of the Tyrrhenian Sea by way of the Tiber. And so freedom of navigation on the river and the control of the right bank, the Ripa Veientana, as the Romans called it, were the guiding considerations in her relations with Rome. The Etruscan city could rely for the support of her political and economic claims on her neighbour, Fidenæ, whose position and interests were analogous.

Tradition had mentioned a first war between Rome and Veii even under the kings.[2] Romulus would have stripped Veii of the salt-deposits of the Tiber mouth and her possessions on the right bank opposite Rome (the *Septem Pagi*). Under the Republic the conflict which was destined to last for over a century broke out inevitably immediately after the Revolution of 509. In the maze of legends which obscures the story of the capture of Rome by Porsenna, one specific fact deserves attention. Porsenna despoiled the defeated Romans of the right bank of the Tiber, the region of the *Septem Pagi*, and restored it to the Etruscans.[3]

Of course, on the departure of Porsenna the Romans' most urgent task was to reclaim the disputed strip, and

---

[1] Livy, II, 38 *ff.*; Dion., VI, 3 *ff.*; *Fast. tr.*, years 462, 459, 443.
[2] Liv., I, 15, 5; Dion., II, 54-55.
[3] Liv., II, 13, 7; 15, 7; Dion., V, 36, 65.

hostilities soon broke out. Tradition mentions a first war, lasting from 482 to 474 B.C. A Roman army, composed of the members of the gens Fabia and its clients, took up a position on the Cremera, a small tributary of the Tiber on the right bank, in order to cut the natural line of communications between Veii and Fidenæ, and so to strike a mortal blow at the former. After some successes their venture took a turn for the worse; the troop of the Fabii was annihilated and the men of Veii with their usual astuteness took advantage of their success to occupy the Janiculum. They were soon expelled, but Rome was exhausted and had to sign a peace dictated by her victorious rival. Veii kept the right bank of the Tiber (474).

At the expiration of the truce war raged afresh for thirteen years (438-425). Fidenæ rose against Rome and returned to the alliance with Veii. The king of the latter town, Tolumnius, was slain in single combat by the military tribune, A. Cornelius Cossus, who won the *spolia optima* on this occasion for the second time. The dictator, A. Servilius Priscus, recapture Fidenæ in 435. A new revolt broke out in 426, once more supported by Veii. The Romans again succeeded in reducing the rebel town, and Veii, threatened herself, had to agree to a twenty years' truce (425). The two prizes of the contest, Fidenæ and the monopoly of navigation on the Tiber, remained in the hands of Rome. The reverse of 474 was avenged.

The details as presented in tradition seem open to suspicion, both chronologically and even in respect of their historical content, and it would be rash to swallow them all with closed eyes. But at least the general characteristics of the savage campaigns of the fifth century can be disentangled. In the first place battle was joined on several fronts (Etruscan on the north, Sabine on the north-east, Æquian on the east, and Volscian on the south) at once. This simultaneity is explained by the geographical position of Rome at the centre of a wide plain washed all round by the hostile flood.

Secondly, the wars were continuous. The striking definition given by the historian Florus of the Æqui and the Volsci, " the implacable and daily foes of the Romans,"[1] is

[1] Flor., I, 5, 11-12.

equally applicable to all the other enemies whom Rome then had to face.[1]

Thirdly, these campaigns had a peculiar character. They were just a series of surprises and raids among neighbouring peoples for whom war was the normal state.[2] Every spring the Romans and their enemies took the field. They set out to pillage their adversary's territory, *ire prædatum*,[3] as it was technically termed, and to burn his crops. Then they returned home with rich booty or empty hands according to the fortune of war, and abandoned hostilities, to recommence operations next season. The object in view was always a surprise. Hence men lived a life of continual alertness, of which the annalists, for once truly echoing the past, have seen fit to leave us a graphic and picturesque description.[4] The battles were most often fought in the vicinity of Rome, sometimes in the very suburbs. The campaigns on the Middle Anio, on the Algide, or in the district of Labici are represented as distant expeditions and exceptional enterprises.[5] The objectives, the forces, the equipment, and the distances were all alike on a mean scale in fifth century Rome.[6] Let us take care to discount the optical illusion which falsifies the whole tradition of the Roman school of history, and from which even moderns find a difficulty at times in emancipating their minds.

Immediately after the Revolution of 509, therefore, Rome found herself surrounded with a circle of foes, but though she was in an even more perilous plight than her neighbours in virtue of her position as a frontier town, she was not the only one thus situated, and was to find in this circumstance one of the mainstays of her safety. Etruscans and mountaineers were equally a danger to all the cities of Latium. On the other hand, the men of Veii, the Æqui, and the Volsci had each their own foes to contend against; the first were embroiled with the town of Cære, the two last with the Hernici. Roman diplomacy had, therefore, solid footholds to work from and real opportunities if it knew how to use

---

[1] *Cf. Flor.*, I, 6, 1, on the men of Veii "*assidui et anniversarii hostes.*"

[2] Livy, II-IV, *passim;* Flor., I, 5, 11, 5 *ff.;* **XX**, I, 677-79.

[3] Livy, I, 54, 2; III, 60, 4.

[4] Dion., IX, 56, 68; XI, 3.   [5] Flor., I, 5, 11, 5 *ff.*

[6] *Cf.* Livy's passage on the naval battle of Fidenæ, IV, 34, 6-7.

them. History shows that she did not fail in her heavy task. From the political and military chaos of the fifth and early fourth centuries, three diplomatic achievements of the highest rank stand out clearly, the Latin alliance, the alliance with the Hernici, and that with Cære.

Defeated at the Battle of Lake Regillus, the Latins had signed a peace with Rome. On the whole, they had attained their object; the revival of Roman hegemony, as bequeathed by the Etruscans, had been avoided. On the morrow of her half-victory Rome had had to renounce her claims and, constrained to adjust them to her diminished means, to accept a peace of compromise. The mutual interests of the contracting parties conferred upon this peace the character of a close and permanent friendship. Despite their dissensions Romans and Latins needed one another, both militarily and economically, and knew it.

Their enemies were the same, Etruscans, Sabines, Æqui, and Volsci. All the forces of Latium, including Rome, were none too many to withstand the attempts at revenge of the one or of conquest of the others. Economically[1] Latium, in the fifth century, was, as a result of the Etruscans' activity, an overpopulated region, and her resources, limited by the nature of the soil, no longer sufficed for the support of her numerous population. She needed fresh lands to colonize, and she meant to get those lands at the expense of less densely congested populations. The urgency of their danger as much as the sharpness of their land-hunger prompted the adversaries of yesterday to salutary reflections. The concrete outcome was the Treaty of Spurius Cassius, which tradition assigned to the year 493 B.C. (to keep within the limits of prudence, let us say some years after the expulsion of the kings[2]), and the text of which has come down to us through Dionysius of Halicarnassus.[3]

The authenticity of this document has often been questioned,[4] but on an impartial examination of the facts it remains perfectly credible. The Treaty of Spurius Cassius was

---

[1] **CXXXII**, 51 *ff.*   [2] Liv., II, 33, 4; Dion., VI, 95.

[3] Dion., VI, 95; Fest., *s.v.* " Nancitor," p. 166.

[4] **XX**, II, 144-45; L. Hartmann, in **LXXX**, 1912, 265-69; W. Soltau, *ibid.*, 1913, 258-66; **CCXXVI**, I, 276-317; A. Rosenberg, in **XLVII**, 1919, 173; 1920, 337-63. On the contrary, on behalf of its authenticity, see **XXVI**, II, 96-98, and M. Gelzer, in **XXII**, *s.v.* " Latium," pp. 962-63.

engraved on a bronze column set up in the Comitium, and Cicero declares that he had seen it there in his youth—that is, at the beginning of the last century of the Republic.[1] This has been stigmatized as an error on his part. Nevertheless, arguments of that nature must not be abused. Cicero was neither an ignoramus nor a fool, and his personal testimony deserves some consideration even from those who refuse to recognize it as decisive.

On the other hand, the provisions of the treaty accord perfectly, both with the mutual positions of Rome and Latium on the morrow of the Revolution of 509, and with the well-established facts of the sequel. After the fall of Etruscan sway Rome had tried to recover the hegemony in Latium on her own account. She failed, she recognized at once the autonomy and the federation of the Latin cities, and was content with a position of strict equality over against the League. This state of affairs necessarily involved conditions of perfect parity and reciprocity between the contracting parties and must find concrete expression from a legal standpoint in a *fœdus æquum*. That is just what the Treaty of Spurius Cassius provides, and that is why the translation of it left by Dionysius of Halicarnassus is, at least, in its general outlines, perfectly credible. It is only to be deplored that only the first four articles and the conclusion and the fifth paragraph all by itself have come down to us. At the same time we find that the Romans and Latins did meet together at the Ferentina Spring, near Aricia, and choose in common and on a footing of absolute equality a commander-in-chief to direct their operations, and continued to do so down to the middle of the fourth century.[2]

So the alliance between Rome and the Latin League was based upon the principle of strict equality between the two parties. The League preserved its independence and its full sovereignty. As in the period of secession, its centre remained at the spring of *Dea Ferentina*, in the vicinity of Aricia, and it was thither that the Roman statesmen repaired, in case of need, to maintain contact with their allies and to ensure the indispensable community of action. In the

---

[1] Cic., *Pro Balbo*, 23, 53.

[2] Cincius, quoted by Festus, *s.v.* " Prætor," p. 276; A. Rosenberg, in **XLVII**, 1919, 147.

foundation of Latin colonies both peoples took an equal share of the burdens and rewards.

United by a common danger and allied in a single task, Rome and the League supported one another solidly and divided functions. In conformity with deeply rooted tradition, the duty of guarding the Tiber against the Etruscans, and especially against Veii, fell to Rome. It was left to her Latin allies to cover the rear against the mountain peoples. Two main routes of invasion opened upon the Latin plain, the Valley of the Anio on the north, and the Valley of the Sacco on the south. Tibur barred the first, Præneste the second. The necessity of this association was from the start so obviously fundamental that the Treaty of Spurius Cassius was maintained intact till 338 B.C. Then Rome succeeded in replacing the system of equality by her own hegemony for the first time by force of arms.

But though each party found her interests consulted in this pact, it was undeniably Rome that derived the most substantial benefits therefrom. She was allied to Latium, but not amalgamated with her; her rear was covered by her allies while her movements in the direction of Etruria and towards the sea along the Tiber were left free. And so she inaugurated an individual policy, the fruits of which she would reap alone. On the border of Latium she would grow until the traditional balance of power was finally upset; then Latium would find her master, and under the ægis of Rome would achieve unity.

The alliance with the Hernici, the second of the great diplomatic achievements of fifth-century Rome, was inspired at once by a political idea and a strategic necessity. The Hernici[1] occupied the region between the Liris and the Trerus (Sacco). They formed a confederation, the chief cities in which were Anagina, Capitulum, Ferentinum, Aletrium, and Verulæ. Their position at the rear of the Æqui and the Volsci gave this nation an exceptional importance in the eyes of Romans and Latins, and predestined them to the part of allies in the rear, of which history gives so many examples in all countries and at all times.

Rome had already had a quarrel to pick with them, and

[1] **XVIII**, I, 515; II, 647-56; **XCII**, *s.v.*, pp. 364-65; A. Rosenberg, in **XLVII**, 1919, 163.

tradition mentions a victory under the date 487. Roman diplomacy, with a breadth of vision which does it credit, recognized what advantages it could derive from these rude mountaineers. In 486, according to tradition, the Hernici were admitted into the Roman-Latin alliance on a footing of complete equality with both the original parties, and the articles of the Treaty of Spurius Cassius were simply extended to embrace them.[1] Henceforth in the task of common defence the Hernici had their allotted part, that which nature indicated—namely, to engage their turbulent mountain neighbours in the rear. Two of their cities, Ferentinum and Verulæ, the nation's great sentinels, were to mount guard over the mountain fastnesses of the Æqui and the Volscian country with the corridor of the Liris respectively. The Hernici remained loyal to the pact of alliance till the morrow of Rome's capture by the Gauls, when they joined the Latin revolt against Rome.

Finally, in Etruria, Veii's claim to the right bank of the Tiber and a permanent access to the sea aroused the jealousy of another Etruscan city, Cære, the modern Cervetri. Hence the policies of Rome and of Cære coincided in a mutual hostility to Veii. Identity of economic interests, overriding ties of race, resulted in the conclusion of an alliance between Rome and Cære; Veii, cut off from the coast and blocked inland, must resign herself to being the victim of its results.[2] In her relations with Etruria the alliance with Cære was to fulfil for Rome the same function as did the alliances with the Latins and the Hernici in her relations with the mountaineers of the south and east.

V

The Roman Counter-Offensive

The alliances with the Latins, the Hernici, and Cære were therefore the three vital articles in the Roman diplomatic creed of the fifth century. Diplomacy had paved the way; it remained for arms to do the rest. This rough medieval

---

[1] Livy, II, 41, 1; Dion., VIII, 68-70; **XX**, II, 420-21.
[2] Livy, V, 40, 10; Str., V, 2, 3 (p. 220 C).

epoch of Roman history, this long armed vigil, a stern school for Roman diplomacy and strategy, was destined ultimately to bear fruit. A people that does not succumb in such a crisis—and not all are so fortunate—is left ennobled by the struggle and tempered to endure fresh trials. In the last years of the fifth century B.C. the heroic phase of the struggle for existence terminated. Rome proceeded to a counter-attack on all fronts. On the Æquian front Labici was conquered in 418 B.C., Bola in 415, and finally Vitellia, and as a result of the victorious campaigns of 397 to 392 the land of the Æqui was definitely annexed. On the Volscian front Rome's great offensive opened at the end of the century. Anxur (Terracina) was taken by the military tribune, N. Fabius Ambustus, in 406, and as a result of a fresh Volscian attack the Latin colony of Circei was founded in 393.

On the Etruscan front hostilities with Veii broke out again in 405. The war was waged pitilessly, and, according to Roman tradition, lasted ten years (406-396 B.C.). Rome, always cautious, did not embark upon the contest till two preliminary guarantees of success seemed to be in her hands: she had secured a cover against the Volsci, allowing her to concentrate her forces in the north without excessive risk, and, on the other hand, the first stragglers of the Gaulish invasions in the Po Valley created an imperious diversion to distract the attention of Etruria and leave Veii a defenceless prey to the desperate assault of the Roman army. Rome recognized that the favourable moment was come. The time for her traditional defensive policy was past; her object now was the conquest of Veii and, if fortune favoured her arms, of all Southern Etruria. Both geographically and racially this region of Veii, Falerii, Capena, Sutrium, and Nepete was sharply differentiated from the rest of Etruria. It was separated from the latter by the natural frontiers of the Cimanian and Sabatine mountains, and the purely Etruscan element was there neither so numerous nor so compact as in the rest of the country. These two exceptional circumstances were favourable to the success of the enterprise.

The traditional narrative of the war with Veii still borders upon the domain of myth:[1] the siege lasts ten years, like the

---

[1] For a critique, see **XX**, II, 309-18, 435-40.

Trojan War, a coincidence too striking to be accidental. Prodigies are multiplied and the gods do not disdain to enter the arena. But, keeping to the sober truth, two facts may be regarded as certain: the siege of Veii was the first operation on a large scale that the Romans had attempted since the fall of the Etruscan dynasty, and, on the other hand, she had only been able to bring it to successful termination at the cost of many sacrifices and prolonged efforts. Having willed the end, Rome had had to create the military and financial means for its achievement. Under the circumstances the traditional plan of summer campaigns was evidently ineffectual and out of date; the troops must be kept continuously in the field. The Roman cavalry, composed of *equites equo publico*, constituted a ridiculously inadequate force; the duty of military service as a knight was extended to the whole first census class. The introduction of military pay compensated the citizens for the exceptional sacrifices of continuous duty that the State demanded of them.

Despite all precautions the course adopted by Rome was fraught with many risks and perils. Would Etruria allow Veii to perish without coming to her aid? Would she make such a confession of supreme and helpless impotence in the eyes of the whole Italian world? At the annual Etruscan assembly at Fanum Voltumnæ, two cities of Southern Etruria, Falerii and Capena,[1] no less threatened than Veii herself by the Roman army's advance, vehemently urged the Etruscan federation not to shirk its duty. Their efforts were fruitless, and the cities of Southern Etruria were thrown back upon their own resources.

Thanks to her strong position, Veii had the means of offering a prolonged resistance, and she did not fail to do so. But deplorable intestine divisions within the ranks of her own citizens weakened her; through fear of the democratic faction the aristocracy showed itself sympathetic to the Romans. A diversion engineered by the men of Capena and the Faliscans failed, and in 396 B.C. the Roman army, under the celebrated M. Furius Camillus, at last succeeded in taking the city. It was pillaged and systematically wrecked. With the fall of Veii the whole of Southern

---

[1] Livy, V. 7, 12-13.

Etruria was lost; it was a debacle. Capena, Falerii, Sutrium, and Nepete succumbed.

When the Roman armies were already at her doors, Central Etruria began to bestir herself—too late. Volsinii, the Etruscans' holy city, was in its turn defeated and forced to conclude peace. Her allies, the citizens of Sappina, soon followed her example. In 387 four new tribes—Tromentina, Arnensis, Stellatina, and Sabatina—were organized on the conquered territory. By the annexation of Southern Etruria Rome secured two ends: she acquired a rich and fertile country, the wheat land that her overflowing population needed; and, secondly, she obtained the line of the Cimanian and Sabatine hills, a solid defensive bulwark which gave her the best of natural frontiers to the north. Her internal and external revival was now accomplished. Her strategic position was consolidated, her economic resources were augmented. For the first time since the expulsion of the Etruscan kings the clouds began to lift from her political and military horizon.

By the beginning of the fourth century two results of the highest importance had been achieved—Latin and Roman victories. By the Latin victory the thrust of the Sabine mountaineers towards the plain of Latium had been checked. The Sabines had been reduced to the defensive, the land of the Æqui occupied, and the Volsci driven back. Old Latium expanded territorially by the foundation of the Latin colonies of Velitræ, Signia, Norba, Ardea, Antium, and Circei, new Latin cantons added to the League. The triple alliance of Romans, Latins, and Hernici had become one of the first powers in Italy, and had fully attained its aims. After its long trials it is just that it should also have enjoyed the rewards of honour.[1]

The Roman victory was more complex. Rome had survived the terrible crisis which supervened upon the fall of the Etruscan dynasty. On the margin of the Latin alliance she had sketched her own individual policy in the north. The conquest of Southern Etruria and of Fidenæ represented the brilliant consummation of the latter. At the beginning of the Republic Rome covered less than 390 square miles; in the early years of the fourth century her area exceeded 800

---

[1] A. Rosenberg, in **XLVII**, 1919, 171-72, 191.

square miles.[1] These figures are instructive; a comparison of them suffices to measure the immense territorial advance accomplished. Hemmed in and jealously watched by her neighbours in Latium, Rome had finally created an extensive and fertile domain for herself where her hands were free and where her allies could not interfere. She had become the dominant State in Central Italy, and this new position was expressed in the international field by two definite steps : on the morrow of the capture of Veii Rome despatched an offering to Delphi, and she signed a pact of friendship with the pirates of Lipari.

Theoretically Rome's position in relation to her allies remained unaltered, and the legal equality which was the very foundation of the triple alliance was still unimpaired. In practice Rome's conquests in the north had disturbed the balance, and the effects of this disturbance were soon felt. From the beginning of the fourth century Rome claimed the first place even in the heart of Latium, and aimed at replacing the policy of the federation by her own. Doubtless her aim was not fully attained, and much time must elapse before she could claim to guide the destinies of Latium, and *a fortiori* the general policy of the peninsula. But at least by her energy and skill she had surmounted the terrible crisis of the fifth century. " Aide toi, et le ciel t'aidera." Rome had helped herself, and she deserved the help of heaven. In the sequel heaven was to be represented by the great events of Italian history during the fourth century.

[1] **LXXXIX**, 69 *ff.*; **XXVI**, II, 103-4, 153.

CHAPTER II

THE RETREAT OF ETRURIA, THE DECLINE OF HELLENISM, AND THE GAULISH INVASIONS

I

THE RETREAT OF ETRURIA

THE general evolution of the Italian peninsula in the fourth century B.C. was governed by three fundamental facts : the retreat of Etruria, the decline of Hellenism, and the Gaulish invasions. These events, which in magnitude and scope overflow the framework of the Roman annalistic tradition to an exceptional degree, exerted by themselves, and still more by their interaction, a decisive influence upon the destinies of Rome, and they alone render her extraordinary fortune intelligible.

The decay of Etruria was no new phenomenon. It was a process which developed, and an evolution which gathered speed. The defeat before Cumæ and the loss of Latium at the end of the sixth century, the first acts of the drama, resulted in a great change in the international situation in Italy and elsewhere. The decay of Etruria was accelerated in the fifth century and soon became irremediable. External and internal causes combined to bring about this result—the reaction of the long-subdued native races, re-

Bibliography.—*Texts:* Livy, V, 32-VII, 28 (*cf.* Florus, I, 7-8; Eutropius, I, 20-II, 6; Orosius, II, 19; III, 3-7); Polybius, I, 6; II, 18, 22, 39, 5-7; Dionysius of Halicarnassus, XIII-XV (frags.); Diodorus, XIV-XVI; Dio Cassius, VII (frags., *cf.* Zonaras, VII, 23-25); Plutarch, *Camillus;* Appian, *Celtic.*, frag. 1; Antiochus, in F.H.G., I. p. 183, frag. 12; Aristoxenes, *id.*, II, p. 291, frag. 90; Timæus, *id.*, I, p. 218, frag. 99; Strabo, V, 1, 4 (p. 212 C); V, 2, 8 (p. 226 C); V, 4, 2 (p. 241 C); V, 4, 7 (p. 246 C); V, 4, 9 (p. 248 C); VI, 1, 13 (p. 263 C); VI, 1, 1 (p. 252 C); VI, 1, 2 (p. 253 C); VI, 1, 14 (p. 264 C); VI, 3, 4 (p. 280 C); Justinian, XX, 5; XXVIII, 2, 6-7; Velleius Paterculus, I, 4, 2; Pliny, *Hist. Nat.*, III, 133; Scylax, in G.G.M., I, pp. 24-26; *Ined. Vatic.*, III; *de Viris Illustribus*, 23-24.

Inscriptions.—*Fasti consulares* (C.I.L., I², pp. 120-28); *Fasti triumphales*, especially years 360, 358, 357, 356, 354, 350, 346 (*id.*, p. 17).

Principal Works.—**XX**, III, 3-323, 377-81; IV, 251-69, 271-74; **XXVI**, II, 156-290; **XXV**, 8-15; **CCII**, II, 162-76, 201-19, 221-25, 351-61; **CXL**, 99, 322-24, 452-56; **CXLI**, 64-76.

peated attacks from neighbouring peoples, political and social decay, the disappearance of the military spirit and moral relaxation. In the final collapse of the Etruscan Empire at the end of the fifth century and in the first half of the fourth, we may distinguish three main episodes: the loss of Campania, the loss of the Po Valley, and, finally, the loss of Southern Etruria. In discussing the Roman conquest, we have already referred to the last. Let us proceed to describe the others.

The Etruscans' defeat before Cumæ had broken their offensive, materially weakened their position in Campania, and given fresh impetus to victorious Hellenism. Then the revolt of Latium had supervened, and we have seen what a prominent part the general of Cumæ's forces, Aristodemus, who later became tyrant of the city, had played in that incident. With the loss of Latium the line of communications by land with the mother-country was severed for ever; only the sea route was left to the Etruscans. The Campanian Greeks plotted to rob them of the control of this route, too, and favoured by the general march of events in the Western Mediterranean they were soon successful.

Etruria had made the alliance with Carthage the first principle of her foreign policy. Her fate was therefore bound up with that of Carthage. Now, the beginning of the fifth century marked an eclipse for the Semites of Africa. Allied with the Persians in their crusade against Hellenism, Carthage was involved in their disaster. Defeated by the Greeks of Sicily at Himera (480 B.C.), she was forced to draw in her horns and to remain a prudent spectator of Sicilian and Italian affairs for the next sixty years. Syracusan imperialism took advantage of its victory to launch out on the conquest of the Tyrrhenian Sea, where the Etruscans, deprived of the help of Carthage, were now left to face the buffets of triumphant Hellenism alone.

The general situation counselled prudence to the Etruscans of Campania. But Aristodemus had just died. The moment seemed opportune for an attempt at revenge, and so, resolved not to let the occasion slip, the Etruscans repeated the attack upon Cumæ, which half a century earlier had turned out so ill. Cumæ, in these straits, appealed for aid against the traditional enemies of Hellenism to Syracuse, now at the zenith of her power. Hiero sent ships, and other Greek cities followed his example. In a memorable battle fought off Cumæ, the confederate fleet won a complete victory (474 B.C.). This event was celebrated throughout the Greek world as a triumph for Hellenism, and Pindar has immortalized its memory in one of his Pythian odes.[1]

The defeat at Cumæ wrecked Etruria's mastery of the sea, and was thus a terrible blow to the Etruscans in Campania. Henceforth, isolated from their mother-country and surrounded by a sea of enemies, Greeks on the coast and Sabellians in the interior, the only prospect for them was apparently to fall fighting or to be merged for ever in the mass of the natives. But though strong enough to defend their national independence, the Greek colonies in Campania did not command sufficient man-power to reduce the inland Etruscans. Thanks to this favourable circumstance the latter succeeded in maintaining themselves for half a century longer. It was then that the third band of marauders, the Apennine Sabellians or Samnites, was to appear.

Towards the middle of the fourth century, favoured by the intestine disputes in the Campanian towns, where the rival factions did not hesitate in an emergency to invoke the aid of foreigners, the Sabellian tribes redoubled their pressure. Soon these intruders came to put an end to the secular rivalry of the two racial elements by subjecting both to their own impartial yoke.[2] Capua fell in 424 on Livy's[3] chronology, in 438 on that of Diodorus,[4] a divergence to which too much importance should not be attached in view of the quite approximate nature of all such early dates. After the submission of the interior the turn of the coast came soon. A few years after Capua, Cumæ and Dicæarchia also succumbed. Save for Naples, Capreæ, and Anaria, where the Greeks kept their hold, the whole Campanian region from the Gulf of Cumæ to the Gulf of Salerno became Sabellian.[5]

---

[1] Pind., *Pyth.*, I; Diod., XI, 51, 2-3; Str:, V, 4, 9 (p. 248 C); *cf.* Hiero's dedicatory inscription at Olympia (C.I.G., 16; I.G.A., 510, and D̄itt., *Syll³*, 35 for the bibliography).

[2] **XX**, II, 369; **XXVI**, II, 188-89.

[3] Livy, IV, 37, 1-2.   [4] Diod., XII, 31.

[5] Livy, IV, 44, 12; Diod., XII, 76; Vell., I, 4, 2; Str., VI, 1, 1, 2 (p. 253 C). According to Livy, *l.c.*, the fall of Cumæ took place in 420 B.C.; **XXVI**, II, 188.

THE FIRST ITALIAN UNITY

The victorious Samnite tribes installed in Campania did not organize any unitary government, but, in conformity with their ancestral habits, parcelled out the land among a number of separate federations. The Campanian League in the centre was the most important, and comprised the capital, Capua, and the cities of Calatia, Atella, Casilinum, Puteoli, Cumæ, Suessola, and Acerræ, and perhaps also Nola and Abella. Further north the Sidicini were grouped round Teanum, the south was held by the federation of the Nucerini, with its capital at Nuceria Alfaterna, and embracing the towns on the southern shores of the Bay of Naples, Herculaneum, Pompeii, Stabiæ, and Surrentum. Among these diverse leagues among which they were dispersed, the last remnants of the Etruscan nation gradually lost their identity, and eventually vanished utterly.

The loss of the Po Valley[1] is a particular episode in the great Celtic invasion, which we shall discuss below. Here we shall just indicate the essential facts in so far as they affect or explain the collapse of the Etruscan Empire itself. At the end of the fifth century B.C. the Gauls crossed the Alps and emerged in North Italy. The first event definitely established is the fall of Melpum, the outworks of the defence and the capital of the Etruscan domain north of the Po. A fragment of Cornelius Nepos, quoted by Pliny the Elder, informs us that the city fell on the same day and in the same year as Veii.[2] If this synchronism, too exact not to excite suspicion, should not perhaps be taken literally, it at least indicates a general contemporaneity of the two events which there is no reason to question. According to the annalistic tradition the sack of Veii took place in 396 B.C. Hence we may safely conclude that Melpum fell either in the last years of the fifth century or in the first years of the fourth. On the capture of the city the invaders proceeded to occupy the Transpadane plain systematically. The Salassi settled in the Aosta Valley, the Leponti at the foot of the Simplon, and round Lake Maggiore, the Taurini, and Libici in Piedmont, near the junction between the Po and the Dora Riparia, and in the region of the Vercelli respec-

---

[1] **CXL**, 322-24, 452-56; **XX**, III. 293-98.
[2] Plin., *Hist. Nat.*, III, 125.

tively, the Levi, the Insubres, and the Cenomani in Lombardy between the Sesia and the Adige.

South of the Po the Etruscans offered a more energetic and more stubborn resistance. The region included many rich and powerful towns, and reinforcements from Etruria were more easily able to intervene. The Gauls took half a century in conquering this region, and only advanced step by step. The funerary stelæ of Bologna,[1] which depict Etruscans and Gauls in combat, afford invaluable contemporary evidence of the stubborn resistance offered by the Etruscans of Bologna to the Celtic invaders.

It is again archæology that yields the most precise data on the chronology and the phases of this conquest. The series of imported Greek vases is especially helpful. The latest vessels of this category found in the cemeteries of Felsina had been manufactured at Athens about 370 B.C. Allowing an interval of at least twenty years before their burial, we are led to the conclusion that Felsina, the Etruscan capital on the Po, held out till somewhere near the middle of the fourth century.[2] A study of the ruins of Marzabotto, where stray skeletons, traces of fire, and Etruscan and Gaulish arms scattered about the ground recall to life the last scene of the capture of the town by storm, leads to similar chronological conclusions.[3]

Finally, Adriatic Etruria, as logic required, was the last to succumb. In this connection we possess an exact chronological datum. The pseudo-Skylax in his *Periplus*,[4] dating from 338-335 B.C., still mentions the presence of Etruscans on the Adriatic coast between Umbria in the south, and the Spina mouth of the Po, while the Gauls were already settled in the river delta between the two mouths of Spina and Adria. In a few years the conquest would have been completed, and the Gauls would everywhere have won permanent possession of the country. The Anamari, the Boii, and the Lingones settled in Emilia between the pass of Stradella and Ravenna, while the Senones occupied the strip of Adriatic coast between Ravenna and Ancona.

In this general debacle, what became of the Etruscan

---

[1] P. Ducati, in **LXIII**, XX, 1911, 357-727; **CXL**, 453-55.
[2] **CXL**, 319-24; **CXLI**, 72.   [3] **CXL**, 99; **CXLI**, 72.
[4] Scyl., I, 17 (G.G.M., I, 24-26).

people and their civilization? The Etruscan element, composed of a conquering minority, had never been very numerous in North Italy, and the Celtic advance was largely facilitated by that circumstance. Of the Etruscan survivors, some migrated to Rhætia, where they maintained their independence and national identity for a long time. But the majority, doubtless, remained in the land which had been theirs for more than half a century; traces of their presence and influence can be detected much later at Verona, at Mantua,[1] and in Emilia.[2]

As for their civilization, far from disappearing, it was soon adopted by the conquerors, though in varying degrees in the different districts. In Emilia and in the Adriatic region, where Etruria had stamped her impression deeply, the Gauls readily allowed themselves to be seduced by the attractions of this higher culture; witness the necropolis of Montefortino, near Arcevia, in the land of the Senones. Beyond the Po, in regions more remote from the focus of Etruscan civilization, and thus less affected by it, the Gauls long remained much more faithful to their old habits and national traditions, as the cemetery of Ornavasso (Province of Novara) among the Lepontini proves.[3]

In the middle of the fourth century B.C. the two outposts of the Etruscan Empire—Campania in the south and the Po Valley in the north—had been captured by the Samnites and the Gauls respectively, and were irretrievably lost. Etruria proper was herself no longer intact, and her enemies —the Gauls on the north, the Greeks on the west, and the Romans on the south—were preparing a triple assault. By 474 Hiero, the victor of Cumæ, had laid hands on the Island of Ænaria, the modern Ischia. In 453 the Syracusan fleet captured Elba and pressed on to Corsica. With Dionysius the Elder and the revival of Syracusan imperialism associated with his name the offensive gained in intensity and speed. Dionysius landed on the Etruscan coast, sacked Pyrgi, the port of Cære, and a sanctuary of Leucothea, reconquered Elba, which had been lost in the second half of the fifth century, and proceeded to the seaboard of Corsica.

On the north the Gauls, now masters of the Po Valley,

---

[1] Virg., Æn., X, 201-3. [2] **XX**, III, 297.
[3] See p. 171 below.

were invading Etruria herself. In 391 B.C. they came and laid siege to Clusium, and were distracted only by Roman intervention. They reappeared again in the following years, while the Etruscans were never able to check their invasions.[1] Finally to the south, Rome had occupied the whole of Southern Etruria from the Tiber to the Ciminian Forest and the Sabatine Mountains by the first years of the fourth century. Veii, Capena, and Falerii were lost for ever.[2] Soon it would be the turn of the great cities of Central Etruria, Tarquinii, and Volsinii, which were now neighbours of the Romans.

If Etruria revealed herself to be completely bankrupt abroad, at home her incurable decay was no less patent. Rivalries between the cities had become chronic, and in the crisis preceding the fall of Veii and the loss of Southern Etruria, the federal tie was shown to be loose and ineffectual. Party strife everywhere was attaining frenzied fierceness. The traditional kingships were overthrown during the fifth century by the assaults of the aristocracies, which ended by concentrating in their hands the monopoly of political and social power.[3] But on the very morrow of their victories the aristocracies saw the lower classes rising against them, resolved to share in the government from which they had been jealously excluded. Democrats and demagogues initiated an agitation for the transformation of the constitutions of the several cities in accordance with their political ideals. There were even attempts at social revolution; at Volsinii and Arretium, perhaps also at Volaterræ,[4] the lower classes, grasping the power, established a system of pure communism.

The warlike spirit which had inspired and made possible the great expansion of Etruria was rapidly melting away; the whole population, the aristocracy more than the rest, thought only of pleasure; the very concept of patriotism was extinguished by this mad hunt for pleasure at any price. Art itself betrays this increasing decrepitude.[5] From the

---

[1] Livy, V, 33-36; Diod., XIV, 113, 4; Dion., XIII, 11-12; **XX**, I, 434-44.

[2] Livy, V, 19-27.   [3] **XX**, II, 432-33.

[4] Livy, X, 3, 2, 5, 13; Val. Max., IX, 1, 2; Flor., I, 21; Oros., IV, 5, 3; Zon., VIII, 7; **XX**, IV, 306-8.

[5] **CCVI**, 47 *ff*.

middle of the fourth century Etruria was in full decay, and ceased to count seriously in Italy. Her inheritance would soon fall vacant.

II

The Decline of Hellenism

Parallel to and contemporary with the decay of Etruria went the decline of Hellenism.[1] The period from the seventh to the fifth century had represented an epoch of unparalleled prosperity and expansion for Western Hellenism in Sicily and Italy. With the fourth century decadence was to set in. Little as we know of the detailed history of the Greek colonies in the West, we can at least discern the general causes that conduced to their ruin and paved the way for their subjugation. In the first place they were forced to struggle against the non-Hellenic peoples of the interior. This struggle was not peculiar to the Greeks of the West. On all the coasts where the Greeks had settled, whether in Europe, Asia, Africa, or the islands, a conflict between the newcomers and the former inhabitants of the land had been the rule. Systematically cut off from the sea and penned up in the interior, the latter tirelessly strove to take their revenge, whenever opportunity offered. In this exhausting and unequal warfare the Greek colonies, despite their technical and cultural superiority, must in the end succumb.

The pressure was felt everywhere, but with variable intensity. In Sicily it was comparatively slight; for the aboriginal Sicanian and Siculan tribes pent up in the interior, and hemmed in by the continuous chain of Greek colonies, could rely on no support from abroad. In Italy it was more severe in view of the growing impetus of the Sabellians, which, as we saw, was in evidence all over the peninsula since the fifth century. From the eighth century onwards political and commercial relations between the Greeks of the coasts and the natives of the interior had been at length established. The advance of the Sabellians upset this equilibrium and reopened an era of crisis which ultimately resulted in the repulse and then the ruin of Hellenism. The conquest of Greek Italy by Rome, the heir of Italic tradi-

[1] **XX**, IV, 253-65, 313-35, 365-72; **XXVI**, II, 177-91, 344-79.

tions, was, in the last analysis, only the culmination of this age-long evolution.

The Greek cities offered the most energetic resistance to the peril that threatened them, but the peoples of the interior poured on in a continuous stream, and catastrophes followed one another closely. In Campania even before the end of the fifth century—in 420 B.C. on Livy's chronology[1]— Cumæ fell into the hands of the Samnites: a portentous disaster for Hellenism. Her neighbour, Dicæarchia, soon shared her fate. Of the Greek cities in Campania only Naples, Capreæ, and Ænaria succeeded in preserving their nationality somehow or other. Even Naples had to receive within her gates a Samnite colony and accord it the full rights of citizenship.

Farther south Posidonia, Velia, Pyxus, Scidrus, and Laus waged fierce wars with the Lucanians. Eventually, all save Velia succumbed one after the other. Thurii was defeated by these same Lucanians in 390 B.C., and Metapontium was destroyed. Rhegium, Locri, and Croton were forced to take the defensive and held out with difficulty. Tarentum herself, despite her power and the exceptional advantages of her situation, was not exempt from the general tribulation. Her attempt to found a vast continental empire from the Ionian Sea to Mount Gargano came to shipwreck on the obstinate resistance of the inland nations, the Messapians and the Iapygians, and in 473 the last named inflicted a serious defeat upon her, which Herodotus described as " the most terrible that the Greeks have ever sustained."[2] Cured of such illusions she returned to the paths of a more modest and safer policy; the Sabellian danger which threatened the Tarentines and Iapyges alike served to bring the former adversaries together and secured Tarentum a few years' respite at least. But the danger was not finally past. It was to return yet more insistently than ever in the middle of the fourth century.

In the direction of the Adriatic Greek civilization held its more firmly established footholds: notably the urban centres of Arpi and Canusium. Nevertheless, the whole land of the Peuceti, once Hellenized by Tarentum, became the prey of the Sabellians. In this common crisis only the union

[1] Livy, IV, 44, 12.　　　　[2] Hdt., VII, 170.

of the Greek colonies could have kept the Italic advance at bay, and perhaps have saved Western Hellenism. It had often been talked of; experiments in a federation centred round the temple of Hera on the Lacinian promontory had been tried. As early as 473 B.C. Tarentum and Rhegium had united for action against the Iapyges.[1] At the beginning of the fourth century, to confront the double danger from Dionysius of Syracuse and the Italici of the interior, the Greek cities, other than Locri, organized a federation with a common council and entrusted Croton with the direction of the war against the tyrant. But defeats at Laos and on the Elleporus, and perhaps still more internal dissensions, soon wasted the forces of this league, which ceased to count seriously.[2]

The second cause of the decline of Hellenism is to be found in the conflicts between the Greek cities.[3] There was no lack of reasons for hostility. Racial contrasts engendered discord between the Chalcidian colonies (Cumæ, Naples, Dicæarchia, Rhegium), the Achæan (Sybaris, Croton, and Metapontium), the Dorian (Tarentum), and the Ionian (Velia, Thuria). This racial division was reinforced or cut across by divergences in political ideals; aristocracies confronted democracies, and both opposed tyrannies. Finally, economic rivalry, a factor of the utmost importance, split up the several States. Magna Grecia already had her disputes about channels represented by that over the Strait of Messina.

The Chalcidian cities on its shores, Rhegium on the Italian coast and Messina in Sicily, controlled the passage and placed a thousand obstacles in the way of the commerce of their rivals, the Achæan cities on the Ionian Sea, Croton and Sybaris. And so, to rid her commerce of Chalcidian interference, the last named town had established a continental route across Bruttium, terminating in her colony Posidonia on the Tyrrhenian Sea. The Locrians had endeavoured to secure the same result by founding the colonies of Medma and Hipponium. Croton *versus* Locri, Sybaris, and Rhegium, Tarentum *versus* Metapontium and

[1] Hdt., VII, 170; Diod., XI, 52, 1-5; **CCII**, II, 123-34.
[2] Diod., XIV, 91-105; Pol., II, 39, 7; **XXVI**, II, 189-90.
[3] **XXVI**, I, 337-38.

Thurii, and a hundred other local rivalries divided the cities of Magna Grecia into hostile camps; from the seventh to the fifth centuries B.C. incessant wars and endless conflicts were the order of the day. Triumphing over Sybaris in 510 Croton put an end to her old rival's national existence by an act of brutality, razed her to the ground, and buried her ruins beneath the alluvial sands of the Crathis to prevent her resurrection.

Such struggles between the cities and the resultant state of chronic impotence inevitably produced their usual result, the intervention of the foreigner. Syracuse and Athens, two nascent imperialisms in search of territory and outlets, cast greedy glances on Magna Grecia. In 480, under the brilliant dynasty of the Dinomenids, Syracuse sought to extend her ascendancy in South Italy and win a commercial supremacy there at the expense of Carthage and the Greek colonies alike.[1] In 474 Hiero occupied the Island of Ænaria (Ischia) as an outpost on the Tyrrhenian Sea and in the direction of the coast of Central Italy. The fall of the Dinomenids did not stop the movement; in 453 the Syracusan admirals advanced as far as Corsica and set foot on the Island of Elba. The increasing decadence of Syracuse from the middle of the fifth century momentarily left room for a second imperialism, that of Athens. As the champion of the Ionians against the Dorians, represented primarily by Syracuse, Athens inaugurated a forward policy in the Ionian Sea. About 444 B.C. she founded the colony of Thurii, and a few years later sent a contingent of settlers to reinforce Cumæ's colony of Naples.[2]

Athenian imperialism suffered a mortal blow in the Sicilian disaster of 413, and finally came to shipwreck in the waters of Ægospotami in 405 B.C. Syracuse, under the dynasty of the Dionysii, proceeded to win back the supremacy in the western seas, of which Athens had robbed her for half a century. As soon as the defeat of Carthage left his hands free, Dionysius the Elder turned his eyes towards Italy, and for thirty-eight years (406-5-367 B.C.) he was trying to carry

---

[1] **XX**, II, 366-68; **CLXXIX**, I, 215 *ff.*; **CXXXIII**, II, 201 *ff.*; **CLIV**, I, 192 *ff.*

[2] Diodorus, XII, 9-10; Ps.-Plut., *X Orators*, III, 3 (p. 385); **III**, III, 523 and note 3.

out in this direction the programme of hegemony bequeathed to him by the Dinomenids.[1] He considered any means legitimate for the attainment of his ends. He made alliances with Locri against Rhegium, and with the Lucanians, the hereditary enemies of Hellenism, against Rhegium at Locri, and did not disdain the friendship of the Gauls, from whom he recruited numerous mercenaries.

The results of this astute policy were soon manifest. In 390 B.C. the allied Greeks were defeated by the Lucanians at the great Battle of Laos, and next year Dionysius in his turn crushed them on the banks of the Elleporus, near Caulonia; then he took Rhegium, and by control of the Strait of Messina solved in his own favour the old question of the channel. In 384 he crossed the Tyrrhenian Sea with a squadron, effected a landing on the Etruscan coast, where he pillaged Leucothea's rich sanctuary at Pyrgi, reoccupied Elba, and held the coasts of Corsica to ransom. He was not content with the hegemony in the Tyrrhenian and Ionian Seas, he made his way up the Adriatic, established colonies at Ancona and Adria on the mouths of the Po, which he took from the Etruscans, and established commercial relations with the Veneti. After his death in 367 his son, Dionysius II, continued his father's Italian policy. Two new colonies were set up on the coast of Apulia, and the Etruscan squadrons, sweeping the waters of pirates, re-established freedom of the seas as far as the head of the Adriatic.

This policy of Syracusan hegemony directly injured the interests of the cities of Magna Grecia, especially those of Tarentum. The fall of Dionysius II and the decadence of his country that it brought in its train delivered Hellenic Italy from the Syracusan danger, but, like other lands, she had learnt nothing and forgotten nothing; dissensions between cities soon broke out again more bitterly than ever. However, Tarentum was to enjoy a last epoch of splendour between the waning Syracusan hegemony and the imminent Roman conquest. Under the wise government of Archytas the town, already a rich commercial centre, became also a formidable military power, able to put thirty thousand infantrymen and three thousand cavalrymen in the field. But dissolution was close at hand; from the middle of the

---

[1] **XX**, III, 288-308; IV, 256-58; **XXVI**, II, 186-91; **CLIV**, II, 122-41.

fourth century the pressure of the Sabellians was redoubled. A few years later Rome installed herself in Campania. Henceforth Tarentum's days were numbered.

The last and not the least potent cause of ruin was intestine feuds. Within each city the factions were at each others' throats. Aristocrats and democrats waged a pitiless civil war, government followed government like marionettes on the stage, revolutions continually broke out, and tyrants started up everywhere: Aristodemus at Cumæ, Anaxilaos at Rhegium, and plenty of others. In the face of the countless dangers confronting them the colonies in Magna Grecia appealed to the mother-land. In the fifth century the Chalcidian colonies invoked the aid of Athens against the double danger from the Sabellians and from Syracuse. Thurii entrusted Cleandridas, father of Gylippus, the future defender of Syracuse, with the mission of warring against the Lucanians. By the middle of the fourth century interventions of this nature became quite common; we may mention Archidamos, Alexander of Epirus, Cleonymus, and Pyrrhus. It is a swift decline; the death agony will soon supervene.

III

THE GAULISH INVASIONS

From the racial standpoint the Gaulish invasions constituted the last great event of early Italian history. By the seventh century B.C. the Celts were in occupation of Gaul, or at least of Southern Gaul.[1] In the fifth century Herodotus attests their presence in Western Europe in a passage which probably refers to Spain, and by the fourth Ephorus will be able to term the Celts the greatest people of the West.[2] As far as Italy is concerned, two questions arise: when and how did they come? On the date of their arrival two different traditions existed in antiquity: according to some[3] that event belonged to the period of Tarquin the Elder, and so to the end of the seventh century B.C.; according to others

[1] On the Gaulish invasions of Italy, **CXCII**, II, 247-61; **XI**, I, 289-96; **XX**, III, 271-323; **CXLI**, 64-76.

[2] Hdt., II, 33, 3; Eph., cited by Str., IV, 4, 6, p. 199 C (=F.H.G., I, p. 245, frag. 43).

[3] Livy, V, 34, 1.

it was not anterior to the last years of the fifth or the first years of the fourth century.[1] Livy records both traditions side by side without taking the trouble to choose between them.   In reality the whole history of primitive Italy, and especially that of the Etruscan Empire in the north, combined with the archæological discoveries which must to-day be regarded as decisive evidence, categorically exclude the first alternative.   The Celtic invasion of Italy only dates from the last years of the fifth century B.C.   All the rest is anticipation and legend.[2]

Our main source of information as to the context of the event is Livy.   The hegemony in the Celtic world, the Roman historian tells us, belonged then to the people of the Biturges. As the country was overpopulated, King Ambigatus sent out two expeditions, led by his two nephews, Sigovesus and Bellovèsus respectively.   The first gravitated eastwards towards the Hercynian Forest and the Danube Valley; the second took the road for Italy.   It crossed the Alps, beat the Etruscans near the Tessina, and founded Milan.   Thereafter other bands came to join their compatriots and settled in their turn in Cisalpine Gaul; the Cenomani, under Etitovius, took the regions round Brescia and Verona, the Libici and the Saluvii made their homes on the shores of the Tessina.   When at length the Boii and Lingones, coming through the Pennine Alps and over the Great St. Bernard, arrived, they found the whole country north of the Po already occupied.   They crossed the river on rafts, defeated the Umbrians and Etruscans, and took possession of Emilia. Finally, the Senones pushed on right to the Adriatic seaboard, where they henceforth formed the advance-guard of the invading army.   Such in broad outline was the official Roman version of events followed by Livy and also by Trogus Pompeius judging by the fragments in Justinian.[3]

This account is supported by indisputable facts.   Certain tribes of Transalpine Gaul bore names identical with those of the Celtic tribes of the Po Valley.   That is the case with the Aulercian Cenomani in the Valleys of the Sarthe and the Mayenne, the Senones and Lingones of the Seine Valley, and

---

[1] Livy, V, 34-35, 3.
[2] **CXLI**, 68-69; **XI**, I, 286 *ff.*; L. Joulin, in **LXX**, 1915[1], 65 *ff.*
[3] Just., XX, 5, 7-8.

the Boii round Bordeaux. Moreover, we hear mention of racial relationship between the Insubres and the Ædui, and between the Vertamacori round Novara and the Voconci in Haut Dauphiné, and between the Libici and the Salluvii of Provence. On the other hand, the two chief passes over the Graian and Cottian Alps, the Little St. Bernard and Mont Genevre, were later in the hands of the Gauls. There is therefore no reason to doubt that the Celts of Cisalpine Gaul had really come from Gaul proper across the passes of the Western Alps, but, of course, this does not imply the authenticity of the whole tradition.

The curious parallelism between the expedition of Sigovesus to the Danube Valley and that of Bellovesus into Italy, and even the historical reality of King Ambigatus himself, remain open to suspicion. On the other hand, though the bulk of the Celtic emigrants seems in truth to have set out from Gaul, that by no means excludes the possibility of a contemporary or subsequent intrusion of other invaders from the Danube Valley across the Central and Eastern Alps,[1] notably across the low passes of the Julian Alps and the Brenner. A number of the Gauls in Eastern Cisalpine Gaul may very well have followed this route, and perhaps an origin east of the Rhine should be sought for those Celts in Italy, for whom homonyms are not discoverable in Gaul proper.

Finally, the invasion was not a single nor a simultaneous influx; it took place in several stages and, as previously with the Sabellian invasion, in several waves. Judging by the graves of Golasecca[2] and Sesto Calende[3] at the southern end of Lake Maggiore, it looks as if the vanguard of the Celts had crossed the Alps and come to settle in the foothills overlooking the Po plain by the late Hallstatt period at the end of the first Iron Age (sixth-fifth centuries B.C.).[4] The body of the invaders took the road about the end of the fifth century, and, lured on by their successes, other groups of emigrants

[1] **XC**, 20 *ff.*; **LXXXIII**, 139 *ff.*; **CXX**, II, 577, 1092-93; **XX**, III, 279-80.

[2] **CXX**, II, 536, 539-40, 614; III, 1086; L. Joulin, in **LXX**, 1914[1], 94; **XVI**, I, 231-50 (B. pls., 33-35); **CXLI**, 67-68.

[3] **CXX**, II, 536, 540, 720-21; **XVI**, I, 315-18 (B. pl., 62); **CXLI**, 67-68.

[4] L. Joulin, in **LXX**, 1914[1], 94; 1915, 69.

gradually joined them. Conquering the Etruscans, a minority who yielded to superior numbers, the Gauls settled in Gallia Cisalpina in the manner described above. Only the country of the Veneti, east of the Adige and north of the Po delta, escaped conquest, as it had avoided Etruscan domination a century earlier, and it only purchased its independence at the price of stubborn resistance and stern battles; for instance, we find the Veneti at war with the Gauls in 390, and again in 302 Padua had to take up arms to vindicate her autonomy.

Having mastered Gallia Cisalpina, the Gauls might have stopped there. But their wandering fancy and their appetite for plunder drew them on further along the path of conquest. Felsina, the Etruscan Bologna, was still holding out when the Senones from the Adriatic, the advance-guard of the Celtic army, advanced upon Central Italy. In 391 B.C. these crossed the Tuscan Apennines several thousands strong—Diodorus' tradition says thirty thousand[1]—and appeared before the Etruscan town of Clusium clamouring for lands. Since the conquest of Southern Etruria, Clusium belonged to the Roman sphere of influence. It was thus that the Roman and Gaulish worlds, hitherto mutually unacquainted, were to confront one another for the first time. Rome sent an embassy to offer mediation, but the ambassadors violated the rules of neutrality, and, through treachery or simply through clumsiness, drew down upon their fatherland one of the most violent storms from which it ever suffered.

Irritated by this interference, and, moreover, unable by themselves to take a fortified town like Clusium, the Gauls marched upon Rome (in 390, according to the annalistic chronology; in 387-6, according to the Hellenic reckoning). The Roman army attempted to bar their passage on the Allia, a small tributary of the Tiber, but was crumpled up and scattered in panic in all directions. Since the days of Porsenna Rome no longer possessed a wall of defence. The populace lost their heads; the majority deserted the city and took refuge at Veii. So the city was occupied without resistance and partially burned. Only the Capitol held out for some months, as much through the invaders' inexperience

---

[1] Diod., XIV, 113, 4.

at siege operations as because of its defenders' force, but famine at length overcame the garrison and the Romans, at the end of their resources, offered to treat for peace.

The Gaulish horde that had taken Rome had come not for conquest, but for plunder. Wearied by the long siege and a prey to hunger and summer fevers and threatened at home by a Venetian invasion,[1] the Gauls granted terms. Rome redeemed her liberty and her land at a cost of a thousand pounds of gold.[2] That was not a heroic termination, but it was, on the whole, a lucky one. Yet the annalists endeavoured to cloak its character and disguise its necessity by all sorts of inventions which do more credit to their imagination than to their honesty. All things considered, Rome had got off cheaply. Her alarm had been greater than the actual damage sustained.

This capture of Rome by the Gauls has retained its celebrity in history, but it should be regarded as just one of many episodes in the prolonged incursions of the Gauls into peninsular Italy. The texts show that they travelled along the maritime corridors on the Tyrrhenian and Adriatic coasts as far as Campania and Apulia, and Justinian, citing a passage from Trogus Pompeius, could write:

" Almost the whole of Italy has been occupied by the Gauls."[3]

The Gaulish invasion of peninsular Italy cannot, then, be regarded as a momentary incident. It was, on the contrary, a comprehensive movement on a large scale prolonged over two centuries. Hannibal's invasion during the Second Punic War was to be its epilogue.

Though their guiding principles and first phases were identical, the Gaulish invasions culminated in diametrically opposite results in the Po basin and in peninsular Italy respectively. In the Po Valley, after a period of wavering and hesitation, the Celtic invaders eventually settled down. There, and there alone, they achieved a solid and durable result.[4] Warriors and pastoralists they met there peoples far more advanced than themselves; the Ligures had long

---

[1] Pol., II, 18, 3.
[2] Pol., I, 6, 3; II, 18, 1-3; Diod., XVI, 115-16; **CLXXXV**, II, 221-96.
[3] Just., XXVIII, 2, 6-7.
[4] **XX**, III, 284-97.

ago reached the agricultural stage, and the Etruscans represented an infinitely higher civilization. In their dealings with both races the Gauls, following the example of the Etruscans more than a century previously, did not adopt a policy of extermination to any extent, they brushed their predecessors aside or mingled with them.

Numerous Ligurian bands had sought refuge in the Alps and the Apennines, and still later they remained the dominant element there. At the beginning of the Empire Strabo[1] drew a sharp line of demarcation between the territories of Gauls and Ligures. The former occupied the plain, the latter were relegated to the mountains. But at least a partial fusion had taken place between the two peoples: that happened notably with the Salassi and Taurini. In the Maritime Alps we hear of Celtoligures just as we find Celtiberians in Spain and Celto-Greeks in Asia Minor. The invaders acted in the same way towards the Etruscans; a certain number of these were driven into the Rhætian foothills, where we still find them at a later date under the name of Rhæto-Euganæans, but the majority stayed at home and soon mingled with the invaders as in Campania. We have already noted the survival of the Etruscan element around Brescia and Verona; even at the end of the Republic Mantua still passed for an Etruscan city, and that fact materially affected the attitude of the Cenomani towards Rome at the time of the great wars of independence.

The Celts had brought with them across the Alps the La Tène culture of the Second Iron Age. In their new home they found themselves in contact with the Etruscan civilization, and combined its essential elements with their own native culture in varying degrees in different regions. Firstly, they adopted habits of agricultural life.[2] Thanks to the adaptability, which was one of the most conspicuous characteristics of their race, the Gauls in Italy, on becoming attached to the soil and sedentary, quickly blossomed out into most successful husbandmen. Polybius, who knew the country well through having visited it in the

---

[1] Str., V, 13 (p. 211 C); for place names of Celtic origin, see **XVIII**, I, 477-80; **CXCII**, III, 177 *ff*.

[2] **CXX**, II, 915; L. Joulin, in **LXX**, 1915², 51, 68; **CXLI**, 72-75.

first half of the second century, has left a glowing account of it in that respect.[1]

The Gauls rapidly assimilated the Etruscan arts and eagerly adopted their habits of luxury. The bronze weapons, implements of all sorts, necklaces, bracelets, brooches, metal and earthenware vases, brazen candelabra and basins, mirrors, articles of apparel, ivory combs, perfume-flasks, and products of Etruscan industry or Greek imports found in the cemeteries testify to the strength and complexity of this cultural evolution, to which the Gauls let themselves be enticed without much resistance. The influence of Etruscan civilization, however, did not act everywhere with equal intensity. It was very strong in Eastern Emilia and on the Adriatic seaboard, as the necropolis of Montefortino, in the land of the Senones,[2] shows, while it diminished to the north and west in proportion to the distance from the focus of culture; the tombs of Ornavasso, in the Province of Novara,[3] one of our most valuable records of the Celtic civilization in Cisalpine Gaul, illustrate this very clearly.

If the Gaulish invasions led to a positive and lasting result in North Italy, their outcome in the rest of the peninsula was quite different. There the Gauls always appeared merely as adventurers; they came either as marauders in bands acting on their own account and under their own national chiefs, like the horde of Brennus which sacked Rome in 390, or as mercenaries in the pay of one of the several peoples or cities of Italy. Rome's enemies in Central Italy gladly resorted to the employment of their services in the fourth and at the beginning of the third century.[4] Glaring examples are afforded by the Latins (Velitræ in 367 and 357, Tibur in 361, and Præneste in 358) and by the Etruscans between 299 and 295 during the last struggle for independence, the fate of which was sealed at Sentinum. Nowhere in peninsular Italy proper did the Gauls

---

[1] Pol., II, 15, 1-7; Cic., *Phil.*, "*Flos Italiæ, firmamentum imperii populi Romani, ornamentum dignitatis.*"

[2] **CXX**, II, 1088-92, 1161-63; **XVI**, II, 731-43 (B. pls., 151-56); **CXLI**, 74-75.

[3] E. Bianchetti, in **XXVI**, VI, 1895; **CXX**, II, 1093-97, 1356-58. 1446-49; **XVI**, I, add.

[4] Livy, VI, 42, 4-8; VII, 11, 12, 15; VIII, 14, 9-10; IX, 29 *ff*.

settle down, but their incursions had none the less deep and decisive effects. Through their barbarity and depredations and through the supreme impartiality with which they injured allies and foes alike, they became the terror of Italy, and ultimately stirred up general resentment. In the face of the danger from which all suffered, the peoples of Italy began for the first time to entertain feelings of solidarity. And on that day, although still vague and indefinite, the idea of Italian unity was born never to perish. Rome, the champion of the national cause, would see to it that the idea came to fruition.

IV

THE REVIVAL OF ROME

Complete and sudden catastrophes are the lot of all great military powers, and indeed the very price of their existence and success. Rome was no exception to the general rule. The Revolution of 509 had already broken her hegemony for the first time and imperilled her very national existence. The disaster of 390 evoked an analogous and no less grave crisis. Rome had no lack of open or secret enemies in Central Italy, and they promptly raised up their heads.[1] The reaction was general. In the north Etruria revolted, beginning with Falerii and Fidenæ, which were soon followed by Tarquinii and even Cære, Rome's hereditary ally. In the south a Volscian insurrection was led by Antium and Satricum, and supported by the Latin colony of Velitræ. In the east the Hernici rebelled. Even in Latium itself a separatist movement developed, and the Latin League was broken up. Tibur and Præneste took the lead of the secessionists, while Tusculum and all the Latin cities in the south (Ardea, Aricia, Lavinium, Lanuvium, Cora, Norba, Setia, and Signia) remained loyal to the Roman cause. Finally, for forty-five years the Gauls did not cease interference in the affairs of Central Italy either as independent invaders or as mercenaries hired by Rome's enemies,[2] and so increased Rome's embarrassment in an almost desperate situation.

As after the Revolution of 509, Rome took the exceptional

[1] Livy, VI, 2, 1-4; Varr., *de Ling. Lat.*, VI, 18; **XX**, III, 315-16.
[2] Pol., II, 18, 6-9; Livy, VI, 42-VII, 26; **XX**, III, 312-13.

measures demanded by the gravity of the situation. By strength of will and patriotic energy she succeeded in surmounting the crisis in which her position as a great power and her very life were at stake for the second time. The necessary work of reconstruction must be directed to three ends—defensive precautions to prevent a possible recurrence of the disaster of 390, military reorganization, and, finally, the re-establishment of Roman hegemony in Latium and Central Italy.

At the time of the Gaulish raid the absence of a fortification wall had delivered Rome over helpless to the mercy of the invaders. Her citizens resolved to rebuild and modernize the old wall of Servius Tullius, the ruins of which still cumbered the ground. Under year 378 Livy[1] mentions a contract for work of this nature being let by the censors, and the archæological study of the remains of the Republican wall confirms the historian's account.[2] Wherever possible the remains of the old regal wall were utilized; these are the portions built on the Oscan foot of twenty-seven centimetres, while in building the newly constructed sectors the Roman foot of twenty-nine centimetres, made the legal standard at Rome since the days of the Decemvirs, was employed. In its final form the circuit of Republican fortifications had a perimeter of seven miles, and was pierced by sixteen gates corresponding to the main Roman roads.[3] When the Gauls returned a few years later the work was finished. They might prowl round the city, they could never enter it again.

In the face of an impulsive and keen adversary, the very incarnation of the genius of attack, on the battlefield of the Allia the heavy and clumsy Roman army had revealed its inadequacy for its function. And so it was subject to a complete reorganization, in which the Romans, faithful to their traditional habits, were guided by experience. The reform affected both armament[4] and tactics. To enable them to parry the strokes of the terrible Gaulish sword, the

---

[1] Livy, VI, 32, 1.

[2] P. Graffunder, in **LVI**, 1911, 83 *ff.*; *id.*, in **XXII**, *s.v.* "Rom," 1024-26; **CCXIII**, 746-53.

[3] X, *s.v.* "Murus Servi," 107; **VIII**; **IX**, 8-9.

[4] Livy, VIII, 8, 3; **XIV**, XI, 20-22; **CXXIV**, I, 255-73; **XX**, 337-40.

defensive arms were systematically strengthened. The leather helmet gave place to one of iron; a casing of bronze plates gave the shield the necessary resisting power. In the same way the national offensive weapon, the pilum, was perfected by the addition of an iron tip.

In the domain of tactics the phalanx,[1] an inheritance from the Etruscans, was replaced by the less rigid and more supple manipular formation.[2] Another innovation connected with the foregoing was introduced by the dictator, C. Sulpicius, in 358;[3] the several ranks, instead of all hurling their javelins simultaneously according to the traditional practice, henceforth discharged their missiles in relays, a far more efficacious and deadly procedure. Thanks to this plan of co-ordinated reforms, which marks one of the main stages in the history of the Roman army, the instrument was ready. The men who had forged it—Camillus before all others and with him the generals forming his school, T. Manlius Torquatus, M. Valerius Corvus, C. Marcius Rutilus, and C. Sulpicius—knew how to use it. Let us watch them at work.

In the north Etruria was promptly reconquered, with a rapidity which shows once more the decadence of the Etruscan world. In 387 B.C. four new tribes—Stellatina, Tromentina, Sabatina, and Arnensis—were created for Southern Etruria. That meant an official and final act of annexation. In 383 the establishment of a Latin colony at Nepete reinforced the strategic value of the Ciminian range, Rome's natural frontier in this direction. Cære and Tarquinii had to sign treaties of peace; the former for a hundred years in 353, the latter for forty in 351. In the south the Volsci, despite the support of their Latin allies, Præneste and Velitræ, were repulsed and then crushed. In 358 Rome annexed the Pontine Marshes, excellent wheat land, where two new tribes, Pomptina and Poblilia, were forthwith constituted. In 345 a coalition of Romans and Samnites beat the Aurunci, and about the same date the Volsci were beaten to their knees. The permanent occupation of the corridor between the Alban Hills and the Monti Lepini cut

---

[1] *Ined. Vatic.*, ed. Arnim, in **XLVII**, 1892, III, p. 121.
[2] Livy, VIII, 8, 3-18; **CXXIV**, I², 274-85.
[3] App., *Celt.*, 1.

off Præneste from the sea, but the struggle was not over; it broke out again a few years later and dragged on till the end of the Latin War (338 B.C.).

All this time the Gauls, lured on by their success in 390, were repeating fresh offensives. Tradition mentions 367, 361, and 360 as years when the invaders appeared before the very gates of Rome; in 358 and 350 they encamped upon the Alban Hills. Under date 349 some celebrated episodes, such as the exploits of T. Manlius Torquatus and M. Valerius Corvus, are recorded. But in all these narratives the chronology is very dubious, and legend occupies more room than sober history. Let us hold to the certain facts: the Gaulish wars had been prolonged for half a century, and a treaty between Rome and the Senones, signed in 351, put an end to them at least provisionally.[1]

Finally, Rome came to grips with her old allies, the Latins and the Hernici. Here her whole future was at stake; for the independence of Latium and the greatness of Rome were incompatible. But here, too, fortune smiled on the Roman arms. Vainly did the two chief promoters of the separatist movement, the great Latin cities of Tibur and Præneste, hire numerous bands of Gauls and offer them the strategic bases they needed in the very heart of Latium. In 358 B.C. Latium was subdued and compelled to accept a renewal of the old Treaty of Spurius Cassius, but now with such modifications in Rome's favour as her victories enabled her to insert. In the course of the succeeding years (358-354 B.C.) the remaining rebel cities submitted one after the other. Tibur was feign to re-enter the League. Præneste, Nomentum, and Pedum had to follow suit. The Hernici, defeated from 362 to 358, capitulated.

The old pact of equality was transformed in Rome's favour to a charter of hegemony, already almost of dominion. Less than forty years after the sudden disaster that had so nearly proved fatal, the Roman State was standing erect again and stronger than ever. The Latins and the Hernici, after their fruitless attempts at independence, were henceforth bound to her chariot wheels and condemned to follow her policy meekly. From the Ciminian Forest to Terracina, from the Tyrrhenian Sea to beyond the Apennines, over an

[1] Pol., II, 18, 9; **XXVI**, II, 260-61.

area of two thousand three hundred square miles, Rome's will was law.   She was now possessed of rich wheat lands in Southern Etruria and the Pontine Marshes; the sturdy yeomen of Latium and the Apennines fought under her banner.   In area, in the size of her population, and in all kinds of resources, Rome had become the chief power in Central Italy by the middle of the fourth century.

No doubt she owed that position to her material strength, but her moral force must not be overlooked.   Though arms played the leading part in the progress of Roman power in the fourth century, though Italian unity was created by blood and iron, that had not been the only factor.   The Gaulish peril, first used as a weapon against Rome by her enemies in Latium, soon showed itself to be a menace to the whole of Italy, and community of sufferings and fears caused by the invasion gathered round Rome her enemies of yesterday in a devoted band; in view of the hopeless incompetence of Etruria she became the bulwark of the peninsula against the northern invader and the standard-bearer of national independence, and it was with this programme that she crystallized about her and for her own profit that body of sentiments and interests which were to be the cradle of the first unity of Italy.

The results of this new state of affairs were not slow to manifest themselves in the international arena, and in the middle of the fourth century B.C. Rome found her political horizon abruptly enlarged.   Two decisive diplomatic steps show this.   In 354 Rome signed her first treaty with the Samnites;[1] for she had become their neighbour through the occupation of the Volscian land.   In 348,[2] what is still more important, she concluded a treaty with Carthage, again the first; Polybius has preserved its main stipulations, although he erroneously attributes it to the beginning of the Republic.[3]

We may now conclude.   The past history of Italy had assumed the form of a long duel between Etruria and Western Hellenism.   The collapse of the former and the decline of the latter had left a vacant place in the peninsula.   Now the

---

[1] Livy, VII, 19, 4; **XX**, III, 124.
[2] Livy, VII, 27, 2 (*cf.* Orosius, III, 7, 1); Diod., XVI, 69, 1.   For the treaties between Rome and Carthage, see pp. 211 *ff* below.
[3] Pol., III, 22.

Gaulish invasion had imperiously called for the filling of this place. By her geographical position, her political organization, and her military strength Rome had shown herself the only State in a position to fill it, and fill it successfully. No people is master of its destiny. But at least, and that is their eternal glory, the Roman people was ready when their hour came. Rome knew how to hold and consolidate that hegemony that fortune gave her.

G

CHAPTER III

THE WARS OF ITALIAN INDEPENDENCE

I

The Roman Intervention in Campania and the Unification of Latium

Less than half a century after the catastrophe of the Gaulish invasion, which had so nearly proved fatal to her, Rome had regained her former position in Latium, and had indeed substantially improved it. But despite all her efforts this time, as after the Revolution of 509, she had secured only a compromise peace. Now, such a peace by its very definition satisfies neither party. The Latin problem remained in its essence unaltered. Held as in a vice between the Etruscans on the north and the Latins on the south, Rome continued to revolve in the same orbit. To acquire freedom of movement she must escape at all costs. Two possible ways of escape lay open to her : she might break out northwards by the defeat of Etruria, or southwards by the subjugation of Latium.

Now Etruria, despite her sad decadence, was still capable of a successful resistance, provided she could secure internal harmony. Moreover, to strike at her heart with Latium in the rear would have been madness in the Romans, and would have imperilled their national existence. And so in the light

Bibliography.—Texts: Livy, VII, 29-X (down to year 293), *Periochœ* of books XI-XII (*cf.* Florus, I, 9-12; Eutropius, II, 7-10; Orosius, III, 8-15, 21-23); Polybius, II, 19-20; Dionysius of Halicarnassus, XV-XVIII (fragments); Diodorus, XVII-XXI; Dio Cassius, VII-VIII (fragments, *cf.* Zonaras, VII, 26-VIII, 2); Appian, *Samnit.*, frags. 1-6; Valerius Maximus, I, 1, 17; V, 1, 5; VII, 2, 17; IX, 1, 2; Frontinus, *Strat.*, I, 8, 3; *Ined. Vat.*, III; *de Viris Illustribus*, 26-34.

Inscriptions.—Fasti consulares (C.I.L., I², pp. 128-34); *Fasti triumphales*, especially years 343, 340, 339, 338, 319, 314, 312, 311, 309, 305, 304, 298, 294, 293, 281 (*id.*, p. 172); C.I.L., I², 6-7 (*Elogium* on L. Cornelius Scipio Barbatus, consul in 298, censor in 290).

*Principal Works.—***XX**, III, 152-69, 324-74, 382-88, 412-16; IV, 3-309; **XXVI**, II, 291-379; **XXV**, 14-24; **V**, 61-108; **II**, 207-8; A. Rosenberg, in **XLVII**, 1919, 171-73.

of experience, two definite ideas dawned in the mind of Rome : she must, before all else and at all costs, wind up the Latin business, and she could not do that without resorting to new methods, attacking Latium in the rear and encircling her. The application of this clever strategy and the enlargement of Rome's horizon that it entailed mark a decisive moment in the progress of Roman conquest and in the history of the first unity of Italy.

This policy, which was to prove so fruitful, was not, however, a sudden inspiration. Its precursors are detectable by the middle of the fourth century; the annexation of the Volscian land and the creation of the tribes Pomptina and Poblilia in 358[1] and the first treaty with the Samnites in 354[2] were already two important steps toward the encirclement of Latium. A few years later events in Campania opened to Rome the way to a full attainment of her aims. In the seventh book of his History, Livy[3] gives a minute account of the preliminaries to the Campanian manœuvre and of its development. Let us take him as our guide at least provisionally.

In 343 B.C. the Sidicini, threatened by the Samnites (evidently a mere incident in the age-long onrush of the Sabellians), had appealed for aid to their neighbours in Campania. The latter were defeated, driven back to their capital, Capua, and soon reduced to the last extremities.[4] Unable to extricate themselves by their own resources, they turned their eyes towards Rome, who had been for several years the leading power in Central Italy. A Campanian embassy presented itself before the Senate, and formally solicited Roman intervention.[5] The alliance with Capua offered many advantages, and Livy does not omit to emphasize these in the speech which he puts in the mouth of the head of the deputation.[6] The region was very rich, and Rome had every reason to desire to control it freely; at the same time it would allow Rome to take the Æqui and the Volsci in the rear, and thus reduce them to impotence. Finally, the annexation of Capua and Campania to the

---

[1] Livy, VII, 15, 11-12.   [2] Livy, VII, 19, 4.
[3] VII, 29-31.
[4] Livy, VII, 29, 4-7; **XX**, III, 166-69, 412-16.
[5] Livy, VII, 29, 7.   [6] Livy, VII, 30.

Samnite State would involve the gravest dangers to Rome in the future. These were political, military, and economic considerations which could not leave the Senate indifferent. On the other hand, the Roman Government had a treaty with the Samnites; naturally it shrank from violating it deliberately and in cold blood.

> "On the withdrawal of the deputation," Livy[1] reports, "the Senate deliberated upon their proposition. In the eyes of many members, this city (Capua), the greatest and wealthiest in Italy with its fertile lands and its proximity to the sea, seemed a resource against the chance of bad harvests and the granary of the Roman people. Nevertheless, honour outweighed all such advantages, and in the name of the Senate the Consul replied: 'The Senate adjudges you, O Campanians, worthy of protection, but by extending to you the hand of friendship it may not impair an older friendship and alliance. The Samnites are bound to us by a treaty; to attack them would be an outrage against the gods rather than against men, and that is why we refuse. But, as right and justice demand, we will send delegates to our friends and allies to beg them to do no violence to you.'"

The majority of the Senate, in spite of the ultimate advantages of the enterprise, bluntly refused to have anything to do with such an adventure, and held to the principle of non-intervention.

> "Then," Livy continues,[2] "the head of the Campanian deputation replied: 'Since you will not undertake the just defence of our interests against violence and injustice, you will at least defend your own. Accordingly, the Campanian people, the town of Capua, its lands, the temples of its gods, and all things human and divine do we deliver over to you; we give them to you, Patres conscripti, and to the Roman people. If hereafter outrage is done us, it is your subjects who are outraged.' That said, all with hands outstretched towards the consuls prostrated themselves in tears in the vestibule of the Curia."

At this spectacle the Senate consented to reopen the discussion, and in contradiction with its former resolution voted for intervention, diplomatic at first, then military if necessary.[3] The Roman historian summarizes the reasons for this reversal, which was destined to unleash the terrible Samnite wars and lead Rome to the conquest of Italy, in these terms:

[1] Livy, VII, 31, 1.　　　　　　　[2] Livy, VII, 31, 3-5.
[3] Livy, VII, 31, 7-12.

WARS OF ITALIAN INDEPENDENCE

"The Senators were overcome with emotion at this example of the instability of human destiny, seeing a people so rich and powerful and a city so haughty and proud that her neighbours had never appealed for her aid, now so downcast as to place themselves, with their possessions, in the hands of another. Thereupon it was believed that honour forbad the betrayal of a folk who gave themselves up, and that the Samnites would be acting in contravention of equity if they continued to assail a land and people made by this *deditio* the property of the Roman people."[1]

This narrative of Livy's requires some commentary and some correction. Naturally the pathetic scene at the end[2] must be set down to the account of the annalists; it bears their stamp clearly enough and betrays all too patently their procedure. But the vital fact which, according to Livy, determined the Senate's decision, the *deditio*, is open to grave suspicion.

It is possible that in the tradition of the Roman school there has been a confusion with the later *deditio* of Capua in 211 during the Second Punic War,[3] and that we are here confronted with one of those cases of anticipation so common in early Roman history. In 343 the Campanians, a free and independent people, probably contented themselves with offering a *fœdus* on sufficiently seductive terms to win over the Senate.[4] The considerations of pity and humanity which it has pleased Livy to invoke[5] did not, we may guess, weigh seriously in the debate. The brutal truth is that from the political, military, and economic standpoint the intervention in Campania promised substantial advantages.

In the oration which he puts in the mouth of the leader of the embassy, Livy mentions the agricultural wealth of the region;[6] Rome was to find there the wheat lands needed by her rapidly growing population. He appeals to the strategic argument, the opportunity of taking in the rear the Æqui and the Volsci, and so also the Latins, which had been the essential aim of Roman policy in the fourth century.[7] Furthermore, Campania offered prospects as a great pastoral

---

[1] Livy, VII, 31, 7-8. [2] Livy, VII, 31, 5-6.
[3] **XX**, III, 152-65, 382-88.
[4] Diodorus, XIX, 76, 5, referring to the revolt of 314, speaks of "τὴν προϋπάρχουσαν συμμαχίαν"; **XX**, III, 326-27.
[5] Livy, VII, 31, 6-7.
[6] Livy, VII, 30, 6. [7] Livy, VII, 30, 7-10.

country; the Roman army, always weak in cavalry, would be able to fill the long-felt gap with her aid. Stripped of pious words and phrases, intervention in Campania meant to Rome politically the encirclement of the Latins, militarily cavalry, and economically wheat.

No doubt the enterprise involved serious risks, and, in particular, a duel to the death with the Sabellians of the Apennines, as the Senate was well aware. The Senate, the responsible organ of Roman policy, weighed advantages and disadvantages coldly as was its wont; it decided upon intervention because the first seemed to outweigh the second. Rome could not resist the temptation of the Campanian lands. In accepting the Campanians' offers the Senate deliberately embarked upon the road of conquest and expansion. The people for their part unhesitatingly ratified the Senatorial decision.[1] A cold will on the part of the Senate and acquiescence on the part of the people were the essential features characterizing Rome's attitude towards this vital question at this decisive date.

The war was short. Energetically supported by the Latin cities, who were threatened by the Samnite advance as much as Rome herself, the Romans took full advantage of the occasion, and pressed on vigorously with their operations. The Samnites were defeated by M. Valerius Corvus at Mount Gaurus[2] and at Suessola. Not feeling themselves prepared, and consequently desirous of avoiding a decisive engagement, they did not continue the struggle. A peace, signed in 341 B.C., left the Romans in possession of Campania and Capua.[3] This first encounter between Samnites and Romans had been little more than a skirmish. The real victims were the Latins. For them a Roman Campania meant complete encirclement on the south and, accordingly, disaster at short notice. They soon became conscious of this, and the only wonder is that they did not perceive it sooner.

In 343 B.C. their attitude was made manifest by an act of ill-temper; without consulting the Romans they embarked upon a war with the Pælignians, and a little later took up

[1] Livy, VII, 32, 2.
[2] Livy, VII, 32-VIII, 2; *Fast. tr.*, under year 343.
[3] Livy, VIII, 2, 4.

arms against the Samnites again on their own account. The Latins' policy at this juncture does not betray any very conspicuous adroitness. The danger from the Samnites, real but remote, blinded them to another danger, graver and more immediate, threatening their independence through Campania's inclusion in the Roman sphere of influence. When Rome's rapid strides forward had at length unsealed their eyes, they resolved to act before it were too late. They presented a strongly worded list of grievances[1] to the Roman Government. They demanded equality of political rights both in respect of the franchise (*jus suffragii*) and of eligibility for office (*jus honorum*), the nomination of one of the two consuls, and half the seats in the Senate. The authenticity of these demands has often been called in question, but they form too logical a whole not to correspond to reality. Of the two parties united by a pact of theoretical equality, Rome had hitherto reaped all the advantages, while the Latin cities had seen little but the bill. For equality of obligations equality of rights—that positive and categorical formula might sum up Latium's policy in 340 B.C.

Grave though the event might appear, it did not take Rome by surprise. She knew that the Latin question must some day be settled at the point of the sword; she had determined to carry through her ancestral policy and to impose an undisputed supremacy upon Latium once for all. The moment seemed favourable. The Sabellian danger was, at least for the moment, eliminated, and the Latins themselves, by excluding the possibility of co-operation with the Samnites by their stupid policy, had worked for their own subjugation. Roman diplomacy had skilfully prepared the soil this time. Resolved to make an end of them, Rome bluntly rejected the Latins' demands. That meant war.

As a whole the Latin cities, and especially, as might be expected, the two most powerful of them, Tibur and Præneste, declared against Rome. The Volsci, the colonies of Setia, Circei, Velitræ, and Capua swept away by the democratic faction, and Cumæ in Campania joined them. On the contrary, Lavinium, Ardea, and the aristocracy even in Campania and probably also the Hernici remained loyal to the Roman cause. The Samnites, bound by their treaty of

[1] Livy, VIII, 5, 1-6.

alliance and ill-disposed towards the Latins, even sent their contingent. The allies had the advantage of numbers, but from the strategic standpoint Rome was in an immeasurably superior position. Caught as in pincers between her own territory, on the one hand, and her Campanian allies, the cities of Fundi and Formiæ, on the other, Rome's enemies were doomed to an irreparable defeat. Three Roman victories—at Suessa Aurunca,[1] at Campi Fenectani in the vicinity of Pedum, and near the River Astura—finished the confederates. It only remained to reduce the several cities in detail. In 338 Antium, the centre of Volscian resistance, succumbed. The Roman columns marched triumphantly through Latium, and the Senate could settle the conditions of the conquered this time as a master.

The combat was doubtless longer than tradition makes out,[2] but, emerging triumphant, Rome cut the Latin knot. The essential point of the new settlement was the disappearance of the triple entente of Romans, Latins, and Hernici, on which Roman foreign policy had been based for a century and a half. The Latin League itself was dissolved; it survived only in the religious organization for the festival of the Alban Mount. Any Italic federation between the cities of Latium was forbidden, even community of civil rights—marriage and property, *connubium* and *commercium*—was systematically refused to them. Rome thus condemned the Latin cities in their inter-relations to perpetual isolation and so to impotence.

But Roman policy was not limited to destruction; it aimed at construction, too. The old Treaty of Spurius Cassius gave place to an organization based upon a strong hegemony. Rome officially became the capital of Latium and the sole legal bond between its constituent elements. Just as she had treated separately with each of the Latin cities, so she applied differential treatment to them. Some—Aricia, Lanuvium Nomentum, and Pedum—were annexed and given the inferior citizenship, *civitas sine suffragio*, preserving a large degree of local autonomy. Others—Tibur, Præneste, and Cora—became allies of Rome, bound to her by separate

---

[1] Livy, VIII, 8, 19-11, 5; Diod., XVI, 90, 2; **XX**, III, 179-84, and for the topography of the battle, **XX**, III, 179, note 1.

[2] **XX**, III, 328-35, 363-68; A. Rosenberg, in **XLVII**, 1919, 171-72.

treaties on particularly harsh terms involving the loss of part of the territory. Privernum had already been deprived of two-thirds of her land by Rome in 341. Signia, Norba, Ardea, Circei, and Setia retained their former positions. Colonies, newly planted or reinforced, at Antium (338) and at Terracina (Anxur, 329) were entrusted with the mission of mounting guard over the vanquished.[1]

The Latin War was not an accident in Roman history, but a necessary and predestined culmination. This time the Latin question, pendant since the beginning of the Republic, was settled once for all. Rome had just crushed Latium and reduced her to a state of passive obedience; by that act she was enabled in the succeeding years to create the unity of Italy. But it is essential to remember that on becoming the centre of Latium, the head and heart of the Latin nation, Rome procured substantial advantages for the vanquished, her brothers by race and her companions in past tribulations. If community of civil rights between the Latin cities was abolished, it was preserved and consolidated as between the Latins and Rome in the form of complete *commercium* and *connubium*. Nor did Rome confine her generosity to civil rights; she unhesitatingly added political rights too. A Latin who came and settled at Rome acquired citizenship automatically.

Later on when she led the subject Latins to the conquest of Italy, the heavy burdens which she imposed upon them were not left unrequited. Though she always took care to keep the lion's share for herself, the Latin colonies scattered all over pensinsular Italy represented the part of Latium, and that no small part, in this gigantic enterprise, the costs and the profits of which were pooled.

II

ROME AND THE SAMNITES

Rome became mistress of Campania in 341 and of Latium in 338 B.C. In the following years she worked unsparingly to join up the two sections of her territory. Two routes led

[1] Livy, VIII, 11, 13-16; 14, 1-12; on the settlement as a whole, see **XX**, III, 185-94, 328-33, 351-74; A. Rosenberg, in **XLVII**, 1919, 172-3.

to Campania : one along the coast through the land of the Aurunci and Sidicini, the other inland through the Valleys of the Trerus and the Liris. With that methodical spirit and keen appreciation of immediate needs which she displayed on all occasions, Rome occupied each in turn. The control of the coastal route was secured by the subjugation of the Sidicini and Aurunci, followed by the foundation of a colony at Cales (334) that was designed to ensure permanently freedom of passage. The inland route was opened by the occupation of Fabrateria, near the junction of the Trerus and the Liris, and the planting of a colony at Fregellæ (328) near the modern Ceprano. The annexation of Campania and the several conquests that followed had advanced Rome's southern frontier as far as the Silarus. The area of the State, including annexed territory and allied countries, had been doubled since 343, and now covered four thousand two hundred and fifty square miles with a million inhabitants. It possessed no racial nor linguistic unity; Latins, Sabellians, and Etruscans were to be met there; three languages, Latin, Oscan, and Etruscan, were officially current. But both politically and militarily Rome had concentrated all power in her hands and ensured the necessary unity of control.

She had definitely broken through the limits of Latium to emerge in the world of great Italic States. She established regular relations with the cities of Magna Grecia and with Carthage beyond the Tyrrhenian Sea. To meet the economic requirements of her new situation she inaugurated the coinage of silver in Campania and began to mint copper at Rome itself. But this brilliant picture had its darker side. No doubt Roman statesmen had not yet conceived the idea of Italian unity, which only saw the light later, but by setting foot in Southern Italy Rome condemned herself to a future of struggles and efforts. The Samnite federation had been expelled from Campania, the possession of which was a matter of life and death; now it was silently plotting revenge. The curtain was about to rise on the decisive contest between the Sabellian bull and the Roman wolf for the supremacy in the peninsula.

The impulse towards unity, which was already, though still uncertainly, stirring in the blood of Italy and the symptoms of which we have already observed both in Latium and Etruria in the guise of federations, had likewise reached the Sabellian tribes in the mountains. Four federations arose there successively, those of the Hernici, the Samnites, the Lucanians, and the Bruttians. In the Apennines, as on the Tuscan plateau and the Latian plain, the idea of unity was on the march, and the old particularisms had to yield before the new political tendencies, though not without a struggle. Among the several Sabellian federations, that of the Samnites was the most powerful. It extended from the Sagrus on the north to the frontiers of Lucania. It had won a frontage to the Tyrrhenian Sea south of Campania, from Cape Campanella to the mouth of the Silarus.

Territorially the Samnite State exceeded the Roman in size. The Samnites, rugged mountaineers with the sturdy virtues of warriors, constituted an army worthy to match with that of Rome. But in the mortal combat which was to begin, Rome enjoyed undeniable advantages. Centralization was her first source of strength. The Samnites, on the contrary, were condemned by the geographical division of their country in the heart of the Apennines into isolated valleys blocked by snow several months each year, and by their pastoral and half-nomadic mode of life to particularism and the life of cantons. Unity among them never transcended the federal stage, and even such federation remained, despite the exigencies of the moment, incomplete and fluid. Though more extensive than the Roman, the Samnite State was its inferior both in numbers and in economic value. A mountainous tableland, Samnium lacked plains. The Apulian plain on the east and, since the Roman intervention, the Campanian plain on the west had both been withdrawn from her influence, and emigration, the last resource of poor countries, was constantly at work draining the land of its best elements.

In this connection we should note that a Sabellian became denationalized with vexatious ease. The Sabines who had come to Rome at the beginning of the Republic were quickly absorbed in the old Latin and Ligurian substratum of the Roman populace. The past of Campania offered a still more striking instance of this phenomenon. The Samnites who had won Campania from the Etruscans and the Greeks in the fifth century had rapidly been absorbed in the higher civilization of the conquered. They had soon been seen taking up arms against their one-time brothers, the Samnites of the hills, and invoking Roman intervention against their Sabellian kinsmen by their appeal to the Senate.

To sum up, then, we may put down to the account of the Samnites strong arms, obstinate resistance, ardent patriotism but desultory operations, squandered forces, deplorable desertions and little experience in warfare; on the side of the Romans, together with equal personal qualities, the training under the Etruscans, a long military tradition, unity of action, a head and a will. The two States, both in vigorous adolescence, both on the path towards unity, suddenly confront one another at the cross-roads. Which will have to yield? Shall Italy be Latin or Sabellian? It is the decisive moment when her whole future is at stake, an agonizing question which Rome will undertake to answer.[1]

A clash between the Samnite federation and Rome, both in the full sweep of territorial and political expansion, was inevitable sooner or later. The treaty of 354 B.C. had aimed at postponing the crisis by the establishment of spheres of influence bounded apparently by the territory of the Aurunci on the coast and the Liris Valley inland. In this friendly partition the country of the Sidicini and the whole of Campania had been excluded from the Roman sphere. But, as always happens in such cases, circumstances were too strong for the will of the contracting parties, and the buffer States so shrewdly interposed between the greedy rivals were swallowed up one after the other. Let us just note the main dates: in 345 the Aurunci were defeated by the combined Roman and Samnite forces; in the same year the city of Sora, later made a colony, was founded upon the upper Liris; in 343 Campania was occupied by the Romans, a proceeding followed by the First Samnite War; in 338 the Romans interfered at Fundi and Formiæ; in 328 a colony was planted at Fregellæ.

In the direction of the Tyrrhenian Sea only two outlets were open to the Samnites—the Valley of the Vulturnus in the south and that of the Liris in the north. Rome set herself to close them both; the Vulturnus Valley was blocked

[1] **XX**, IV, 266-83.

by taking possession of Campania, the Liris by the three strongholds of Sora, Fregellæ, and Cales. Since the peace of 341 the Samnites had been paralysed by the war which they were waging in the south against Alexander the Molossian in conjunction with their Lucanian and Bruttian allies. And so they had been forced to submit without a word. Alexander's death at length set their hands free. Cut off from the sea, hemmed in among the Apennines, and faced with the prospect of being stifled there, they demanded the abandonment of the colony of Fregellæ. Rome refused and war broke out; there ensued a war of devastation and extermination, a pitiless duel between two races such as ancient Italy had never known. Pyrrhus, traversing Samnium a few years later and finding there only dreary wastes, asked in astonishment

> " whether the country had ever been inhabited."[1]

Even in the last century of the Republic the Samnite Pontius Telesinus would call Rome

> " the forest lair of wolves that devour the peoples of Italy,"[2]

and Sulla on his part would not hesitate to proclaim:

> " Not a Roman will accept peace so long as the Samnites continue to inhabit their country."[3]

Such pronouncements, two centuries after the Samnite Wars, speak volumes for the mutual sentiments of the two adversaries and the inexorable nature of the antagonism that had set them at each others' throats.

This thirty-seven years' long conflict (327-290 B.C.) falls into two main periods. In the first (327-312) the Samnites alone fought Rome, but despite their heroic resistance were defeated and constrained to sue for peace; in the second they won over to their side the powerful peoples of Central Italy, the Etruscans, the Umbrians, and the Gauls. Through the formation of successive coalitions the Samnite War ended in a war of Italian independence. The theatres of war were multiplied as the issue at stake expanded. Entering the struggle as the mistress of Latium and Campania, Rome

---

[1] Dio C., IX, 40, 27. [2] Vell., II, 27, 1.
[3] Str., V, 4, 11 (p. 249 C).

would emerge crowned with the supremacy over almost the whole of peninsular Italy.

The Second Samnite War was no longer just a war for Campania, and therefore a localized war in which the Samnites strove to repair their reverse of 343 and to lay hands on the object in dispute. In any case, the first five years, which witnessed a series of surprises and raids, led to no decisive result. But in 322 the aspect of a war to the death became dominant, and Rome resolved upon a double offensive. She attacked Samnium abruptly from Campania, while a second army proceeded to Apulia to take the Samnites in the rear, applying afresh the tactics of encirclement which had been so successful in dealing with Latium. The disaster of Caudium in 321 and the disgrace of the Caudine Forks[1] were avenged by the victories of L. Papirius Cursor and Q. Publilius Philo, the two ablest soldiers of the day. In the direction of Apulia the capture and permanent occupation of Lucerii isolated the Samnites from the Adriatic.

After a brief truce of two years (318-316 B.C.) employed by both sides in military and diplomatic preparations, hostilities recommenced. The Samnites launched two offensives on a grand scale, two slashing attacks designed to free Samnium. One was aimed at Latium, the other at Apulia. The first captured Sora and opened the road to Rome by the victory of Lautulæ, the Thermopylæ of Central Italy. The Samnites laid siege to Terracina; Capua and Campania revolted. But soon the Roman army regained the upper hand, relieved Terracina, and drove the Samnites back into the Apennines again by reconquering Campania. The second offensive was no more successful; Lucerii, lost for a moment, was recaptured. As a result of these alternating successes, two great facts were established: the Samnite offensive had definitely failed, and Rome had laid hands upon Apulia. A continuous line of Roman strongholds from Sora to Aternus on the Adriatic slopes completed the isolation of Samnium on the north.

[1] Livy, IX, 1-12, 4; Dion., XVI, 3 *ff.*; **XX**, IV, 127-41, and 469-78 for the topography of the defile.

III

THE GREAT COALITIONS

At this moment the arena of the combat was abruptly enlarged and fresh elements entered the stage. Rome's rapid conquests were beginning to alarm the other peoples of Italy. The Etruscans and Umbrians in the north and the Hernici in the east were thinking of intervening before it was too late. Even the Greeks in the south, despite the friendly relations they had maintained with Rome since the expulsion of the Etruscan kings, and notwithstanding the generous and far-sighted treatment accorded by the Senate to the city of Naples after its defeat in 326 B.C.,[1] were on the alert. Tarentum, the great Hellenic city on the Ionian Sea, was particularly anxious; for she saw a direct threat to her independence in the Roman settlement in Apulia. The diplomatic activities of the Samnites did the rest. A vast coalition was formed. Tarentum, who was its soul, furnished the money; Samnites, Etruscans, Umbrians, and Gauls, the latter engaged as mercenaries, were to supply the men.[2] The Samnite War was thus converted into a war of Italian independence which was to last for twenty-two years (312-290).[3]

No doubt not all Italy responded to the call, and secular hatreds, skilfully fomented by Roman diplomacy, were not disarmed even in the face of the common foe. The majority of the cities of Magna Grecia, the hereditary enemies of the Samnites, took refuge in a neutrality which was intended to be prudent, but was really just inopportune. In Etruria, though the old Etruscan cities of Perusia, Cortona, and Arretium in the north declared against Rome, not all their compatriots followed their lead. The Italiotes of the Central Apennines—the Marsi, Vestini, Pæligni, and Frentani—refused to stake all in this last struggle. Among their neighbours and kinsmen, the Lucanians, the Samnites did not find the support they were entitled to expect. Finally, Tarentum, whose maritime supremacy and commercial great-

---

[1] Livy, VIII, 26, 6; Cic., *pro Balbo*, VIII, 21; XXIV, 55; **XX**, IV, 116-19.

[2] Livy, IX, 29-X, 47, and *Per.*, XI; Diod., XX, 35-36; XXI, 6.

[3] Zon., VIII, 1; **XX**, IV, 150 *ff.*, 296-301.

ness and perhaps her national existence, too, were at stake, faithful to her traditional habits of nonchalance, merely trifled without ever agreeing to make the effort requisite to secure final success under the circumstances. But despite such defections and refusals, an Italian standard was now in the field, and from this fact the contest assumed a material and moral significance which it had never hitherto known.

Condemned to a war on two fronts with a glaring inferiority in effective forces, Rome found herself obliged to face new military and financial requirements. A revolutionary genius in the person of the censor Appius Claudius came forward to provide the indispensable sinews of action (about 312-310).[1] To hold out against the coalition men and money were needed. By a radical reform of the organization into centuries, Appius Claudius produced both. The division of the citizens among the classes and centuries had hitherto been based exclusively on real wealth; with the censorship of Appius Claudius personal property also began to be taken into account. Both in respect of men and taxes the output of the machine was increased henceforth, and in virtue of this Appius Claudius might justly claim the proud title of organizer of victory. The army itself was systematically overhauled. Armament, tactics, and regulations underwent the modifications which the Samnite Wars had shown to be urgent. The organization of the Roman cavalry was completed, and the plebiscite of M. Decius in 311[2] creating the *Duumviri navales* gave Rome at least the nucleus of a fighting marine.

The instrument of victory thus forged Rome knew how to find within her ranks soldiers capable of using it—Q. Fabius Rullianus, L. Papirius Cursor, P. Decius Mus, and M'. Curius Dentatus. The first Italian coalition included the Hernici, the Etruscans, and the Umbrians in addition to the Samnites. Two Roman armies took the field simultaneously. The one under Q. Fabius Rullianus won the two great victories of Perusia and Lake Vadmon through a bold offensive in Etruria; the result was the submission of Central Etruria

---

[1] Livy, IX, 29-30, 3; 33, 3-34; 46, 10-11; Diod., XX, 36; Val. Max., I, 1, 17; **XIV**, IV, 4, 2, p. 84; K. J. Neumann, in **XXIV**, 396; **XX**, IV, 177-94; **II**, 109-19.

[2] Livy, IX, 30, 4; *Ined. Vat.*, in **XLVII**, 1892, III, p. 121; **II**, 207-8.

at least for the time (310 B.C.). The other army under the dictator, L. Papirius Cursor, beat the Samnites at Allifæ, systematically ravaged Samnium for four years, and at length forced the Samnites to sue for peace. The latter were allowed to retain their own territory, but obliged to enter the Roman federation on harsher terms than before (304). The other members of the coalition quickly followed their example.

Peace only lasted four years. In 300 the Samnites formed a fresh coalition, larger than before, with the Etruscans and Umbrians, now supported by the Gauls, the Sabines, and the Lucanians. Almost the whole of Italy took the field to defend her independence. As in the previous campaigns Rome had to fight on two fronts. In the north the Roman army triumphed at Volaterræ and curbed Etruria (298). In the south Q. Fabius Rullianus and P. Decius Mus overran Samnium victoriously (297). In 295 the coalition was crushed at Sentinum, the battle of the nations of pre-Roman Italy. That was the end. With Q. Fabius Rullianus dogging their footsteps, the Umbrians and the Gaulish Senones laid down their arms. The rest of the Samnite armies, defeated by the consul L. Papirius Cursor, son of L. Papirius Cursor, at Aquilonia and pursued by Q. Fabius Rullianus and M'. Curius Dentatus, surrendered in 290. The vanquished Samnites renounced their independence, and unconditionally accepted the position of allies of Rome with all the burdens that name implied. This campaign, the fiercest of all, had ended decisively. Samnium was put out of action, and Rome had her hands free in Italy.

However, not all the Sabellian peoples of the Apennines had displayed the same tenacity and heroism in this struggle for Italian liberty as the Samnites. The Marsi, the Frentani, the Pæligni, the Vestini, the Marrucini, and the Sabini had submitted to Roman supremacy without much resistance. Their co-operation, loyal but obscure—history, in fact, says very little about them—had been one of the essential factors in Rome's ultimate success. After the final submission of the Æqui the Romans established permanent contact with the people of the Abruzzi. In 304 they concluded a *fœdus* with Marsi, the Marrucini, the Pæligni, and the Frentani. In 302 a similar treaty was signed with the Vestini. In 299 the Picentes in their turn joined the Roman alliance, and the foundation of the colonies of Alba Fuccens (303) and Carsioli (302) consolidated the advances made. The submission of all these peoples, a masterstroke of Roman diplomacy, dealt a terrible blow to the Samnite cause. Samnium's northern flank was turned, as had already happened to the western and eastern owing to the Roman occupation of Campania and Apulia. M'. Curius Dentatus defeated the Sabines in 290, reduced them to submission, and annexed the greater part of their territory to the Roman State.

From the standpoint of strategy the wars of Italian independence mark a turning-point in Rome's military history. Driven by the remoteness and multiplicity of the theatres of war to operations of comprehensive scope, the Roman army that had hitherto had experience only of petty warfare learnt the art of manœuvring. In particular it learnt the stratagem of envelopment and that based on the use of internal lines. The campaigns in Apulia from 320 to 317 B.C.[1] illustrate the first, that of Sentinum in 295[2] the second.

We have reached the year 326 B.C. Rome decides to take the offensive against Samnium, but she knows all the dangers and hazards of a frontal attack; the disaster of the Caudine Forks five years later will justify her apprehensions. Hence she proceeds to seek in a more subtle stratagem—that of envelopment—the desired decision. Apulia, long exposed to the ravages of the Samnites, offers herself as an ally in the rear. The alliance is concluded for the first time in 326, but in 320 Apulia revolts, and a series of campaigns conducted by the consuls L. Papirius Cursor (320 and 319), L. Plautius Venox (318), and C. Junius Bubulcus (317) is needed to reduce her. In 317 the envelopment is finally achieved, and the manœuvre will exercise that decisive influence on the course of the Samnite War that the Roman general staff had expected.

The manœuvre of envelopment was supplemented by the use of internal lines. Down to 312 B.C. Rome had only the Samnites to deal with, and had consequently been able to take the offensive against Samnium vigorously. The forma-

---

[1] Livy, VIII, 25, 3; IX, 12, 9-20, 8.
[2] Livy, X, 27-31, 9; Pol., II, 19, 5-7; Diod., XXI, 6; Front., *Strat.*, I, 8, 3; *Fast. tr.*, under year 295; **XXVI**, II, 352-58; **XX**, IV, 60-70.

tion of the first Italian coalition constrained the Roman army to fight on two fronts and inspired a complete transformation of military strategy. A simultaneous offensive on the Samnite and Etruscan fronts was out of the question. With her usual determination Rome made her choice, a defensive action on the south, an offensive on the north. The invaluable device of the use of internal lines allowed her to concentrate all the requisite force on the vulnerable front at the opportune moment. Thus in 310 B.C.[1] the consul C. Marcius Rutilus was operating on the Samnite front, while his colleague, Q. Fabius Rullianus, was fighting in Etruria. Then C. Marcius Rutilus came to reinforce his colleague, and both jointly won the victory of Sutrium.

The campaign of 295, which culminated in the great victory of Sentinum, was analogous from the point of view of strategy, but more typical because its consequences were far more important. In 297 the two consuls, Q. Fabius Rullianus and P. Decius Mus, had been conducting a campaign of devastation in Samnium for five months.[2] In the following year P. Decius Mus, continued in office, remained at the head of the army in Samnium. But then the Samnites, led by a clever and energetic captain, Gellius Egnatius, and taught by the example of the Romans, resolved to manœuvre themselves. By a skilful feint they slipped away and, crossing the line of Roman forts in Central Italy, marched to join their northern allies.[3]

Rome, as usual, was at first surprised by the enemies' tactical initiative, but then hastily prepared to take the necessary steps to counter it. The proconsul L. Volumnius was entrusted with the command of the war on the Samnite front, two reserve armies under the propraetors Cn. Fulvius and L. Postumus Megellus, were protecting Rome against any possible surprise, while the two consuls, Q. Fabius Rullianus and P. Decius Mus, with the bulk of the Roman forces—four legions, numerous cavalry, and some allied contingents to the number of at least five hundred thousand men in all—conducted a vigorous offensive in the direction of Etruria. The confederates—Samnites, Etruscans, Umbrians, and Gauls—had surrounded and cut to pieces one

---

[1] Livy, IX, 33-40.   [2] Livy, X, 14-15.
[3] Livy, X, 16-23.

legion of the vanguard at Camerinum and then retreated
northwards. The Roman army followed them, but in
view of their numerical superiority did not venture to
attack.

An adroit manœuvre by the Romans brought the decision.
At the command of the two consuls Cn. Fulvius and L.
Postumus Megellus, at the head of the two reserve armies,

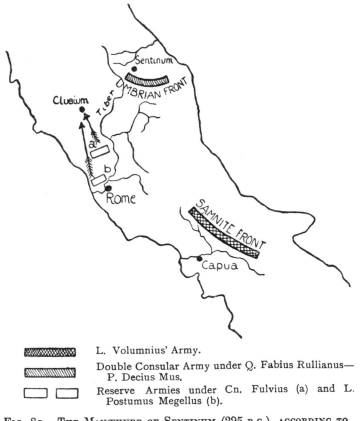

L. Volumnius' Army.

Double Consular Army under Q. Fabius Rullianus—
P. Decius Mus.

Reserve Armies under Cn. Fulvius (a) and L.
Postumus Megellus (b).

Fig. 8a.—The Manœuvre of Sentinum (295 b.c.), according to
Livy (X, 27-31) (First Phase).

hurled themselves upon Etruria and laid waste the territory
of Clusium. The Etruscans, followed by the Umbrians,
hastened to the defence of hearth and home. Weakened
by their departure the Samnites and Gauls succumbed upon
the battlefield of Sentinum.

WARS OF ITALIAN INDEPENDENCE

" The combat," writes Livy,[1] " was at first so equal that, had the Etruscans and Umbrians been present, the defeat of Rome would have been inevitable at whatever point they attacked, whether against the camp or against the army."

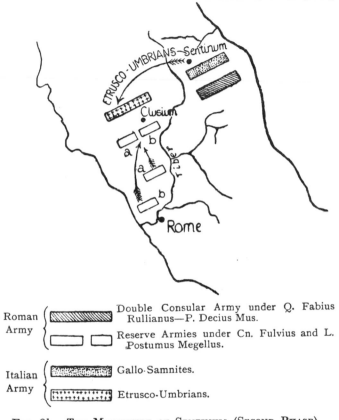

Roman Army	▨▨▨	Double Consular Army under Q. Fabius Rullianus—P. Decius Mus.
	▭ ▭	Reserve Armies under Cn. Fulvius and L. Postumus Megellus.
Italian Army	░░░	Gallo-Samnites.
	▥▥▥	Etrusco-Umbrians.

Fig. 8*b*.—The Manœuvre of Sentinum (Second Phase).

In other words, Roman strategy had had the last word to say, and Rome had won the victory because she knew how to manœuvre. And that is the point to remember.

[1] Livy, X, 27, 11.

IV

THE END OF THE RESISTANCE

Twenty years previously the war had ceased to be just a Samnite war and become an Italian one. And so it was prolonged even after the final submission of Samnium. A fresh coalition between the Etruscans, the Gauls, and the Lucanians was again formed. But the Romans, masters of the Samnite highlands and installed on three of its flanks in the Central Apennines, in Campania, and in Apulia, cut the coalition into two sections, and thus prevented concerted action. In 284 B.C. the Etruscans and Senones again succeeded in launching a vigorous offensive. They won a great victory at Arretium,[1] the revenge for the Sentinum, and their success provoked fresh movements of insurrection in Samniufn and Southern Etruria.

But Rome soon regained her advantage. Despite the intervention of the Boii, who hurried to the rescue, the confederates were crushed at the second Battle of Lake Vadmon by the consul P. Cornelius Dolabella (283). The Boii and Etruscans signed peace, while in the south C. Fabricius Luscinus reduced the Lucanians to complete submission in the next year. Rome annexed the territory of the Senones from the Æsis to the Rubicon and founded the colony of Sena Gallica (Sinigaglia) there.

Thus ended the first phase of the duel between the Romans and the Gauls, one of the vital facts in the history of primitive Italy. The Celts were pent up in Gallia Cisalpina or dispersed upon the Balkan peninsula, whence they invaded Macedonia (280), captured Thermopylæ, and pillaged Delphi (279), but for forty-five years they left peninsular Italy in peace. In addition to Samnium and the land of the Senones, Etruria, Umbria, the Sabine country, Picenum, Apulia, and Lucania were brought definitely within the sphere of Roman influence. Tarentum alone, reduced to impotence by the defeat of her allies, was preparing for the final struggle. Central Italy as a whole had become Roman for ever. Figures furnish the best and most eloquent commentary on the results attained. About 338 B.C. the Roman State, annexed terri-

[1] Pol., II, 19, 7-8.

tories and allied countries, comprised about 4,250 square miles; in 282 it covered some 31,600 square miles, nearly three-quarters of peninsular Italy.[1] Save for Magna Grecia and Bruttium, whose turn was soon to come, Italian unity was accomplished. Against this solid edifice Pyrrhus and Hannibal, those champions of worn-out particularisms, would break themselves in vain.

[1] **XXXIX**, 70-74; **XXVI**, II, 289, 365-66.

CHAPTER IV

THE ADVENTURE OF PYRRHUS AND THE CONQUEST OF MAGNA GRECIA

I

ROME AND SOUTH ITALY

IN the formation of Italian unity the Samnite Wars and the general submission of the Sabellian peoples open a new chapter, the conquest of Greek Italy. That was to take twenty years, and the fall of Tarentum in 272 B.C. marks its turning-point. By the incorporation of Samnium and Lucania in the Italic federation, the Roman State and the Greeks of the south were brought face to face.

Relations between the two worlds were of long standing, and had for long been particularly friendly. As we have seen, the Greeks of Cumæ had played a conspicuous part in the movement which had freed Latium from the Etruscans, and after the victory Hellenic civilization had replaced that of the vanquished in the Roman State. The occupation of Campania, by establishing for the first time a territorial contact between Rome and the outposts of the Greek world in Italy, notably Cumæ and Naples, had drawn tighter these traditional bonds. In 327 B.C. a dispute had arisen between Rome and the Hellenic colony of Naples,[1] and this had

Bibliography.—*Texts:* Livy, *Periochæ* of books XII-XV (*cf.* Florus, I, 13-16; Eutropius, II, 11-17; Orosius, IV, 1-5); Plutarch, *Pyrrhus;* Polybius, I, 6, 7, 10-13; Dionysius of Halicarnassus, XIX-XX (fragments); Diodorus, XX (fragments); Dio Cassius, IX-X (fragments, *cf.* Zonaras, VIII, 2-7); Justinian, XVIII, 1-2; XXIII, 3; XXV, 4-5; Pliny, *Hist. Nat.,* VIII, 16; Frontinus, *Strat.,* III, 3; Valerius Maximus, , II, 7, 15; IX, 1, 2; Festus, *s.v.* " Osculana pugna " (p. 214); *de Viris Illustribus,* 35-36.

Inscriptions.—*Fasti consulares* (C.I.L., I², pp. 134-36); *Fasti triumphales,* years 280, 278, 277, 276, 275, 272, 270, 267, 266, 264 (*id.,* p. 172).

Principal Works.—**XX**, IV, 309-444; **XXVI**, II, 380-429; **I**, III, 556 *ff.;* **CCII**, 163-77; **VII**, III, 67-75; **CXXIV**, I, 301-5.

---

[1] Livy, VIII, 22, 5-26, 6; Dion., XV, 5-8; **XX**, IV, 105-122, 454-68; *Fasti tr.,* under year 326.

been the pretext, if not the cause, of the rupture with the Samnites. Ill-supported by her allies, Naples fell after a long siege in 326, but the Senate did not abuse its victory. The city was gently treated and secured a peculiarly favourable *fœdus æquum*.

We may guess that political considerations had not been without their influence upon this generosity. For centuries Greeks and Sabellians had been confronting one another in South Italy, and their antagonism, at once racial, political, and economic, was the fundamental feature of its history. On the threshold of the Samnite wars, on the eve of a mortal combat with the Sabellians, Rome wished to ensure at least the neutrality of the Greeks in the conflict, and to prevent a coalition that might hinder the realization of her plans. In any case, she succeeded in doing so. In the middle of the fourth century a historian, Heraclitus of Pontus, bestowed upon Rome the title of Greek city, " πόλις Ἑλληνίς," the most flattering epithet that a Greek could imagine.[1]

Moreover, the decline of Western Hellenism, that had become irreparable since the fall of Dionysius II and the death of Dio, combined with the jealous and incurable parochialism of the Greek cities, gave substantial assistance to the Roman policy.[2] Disputes between the cities were multiplied, and intestine dissensions broke out in each of them. Tarentum, the powerful metropolis of South Italy, abandoned to demagogy after a last period of splendour, sunk in enjoyment, and pacifism was on the high-road to ruin. Since 346 B.C. the Sabellians had recommenced their tireless thrust southward.

In Sicily, Syracuse, the traditional bulwark of Hellenism on the western seas, had just enjoyed one of those periodical short spurts which compose her history, under the government of Timoleon.[3] By his victory on the Crimisus (about 340), Timoleon had once more repelled the menacing flood of Carthaginian invasion, but this revival did not endure long. Troubles broke out afresh after Timoleon's death, and Syracuse lived through another period of terrible anarchy lasting nineteen years till the accession of Agathocles to

---

[1] Heracl., quoted by Plut., *Cam.*, 22, 2.
[2] **XX**, IV, 313-322.
[3] **CLXXIX**, I, 319-38; **CLIV**, 190-218.

power.[1] The Samnite Wars and the enfeeblement of the
Greek world were two master cards in Rome's hand, and
she continued her regular and uninterrupted advance upon
Magna Grecia. Before reaching the place itself she deliberately occupied the approaches both on the west and on
the east; a Roman colony was planted in the Island of
Pontia (313) as a sentinel of the Latin world on the frontiers
of Italiote Hellenism, and on the east Apulia and the land
of the Iapyges were occupied (320-317).

This progress, slow but implacable as a phenomenon of
Nature, soon alarmed Tarentum. She made overtures to
her old foes, the Sabellians, and assisted to create the great
coalitions of the wars of Italian independence. At the same
time she came to an understanding with the tyrant Agathocles
of Syracuse. After the failure of his African enterprise the
latter came to seek compensation for his losses in the direction of Italy. He revived the great policy of his predecessors,
Hiero and the Dionysii, in Italy; Agathocles meant to ensure
the supremacy of Syracuse over the peninsula's coasts on
the Tyrrhenian, Ionian, and Adriatic Seas. We find him
successively in Bruttium, at Croton, and at Corcyra. But
two great and approximately contemporaneous events, the
Battle of Sentinum in 295 and the death of Agathocles in
289, wrecked Tarentum's hopes and marked a definite check
to her policy.

And all this time the Romans were steadily advancing
along both the Adriatic and the Tyrrhenian coasts. Having
conquered the Sabellians they constituted themselves the
heirs of the latter's policy and began to encroach upon
the Greek world. Between 286 and 282 B.C. they responded
to the appeal of Thurii when she was threatened by the
Lucanians, and made the town a member of the Italian
federation.[2] Locri, Croton, and Rhegium in turn received
Roman garrisons. By the occupation of the last named the
Strait of Messina passed permanently under Roman control,
and Western Hellenism was cut in half. Along the Adriatic,
too, the legions were pressing southward. By 319 the Roman
army, victorious over the Frentani and the Samnites, had

---

[1] **CLXXIX**, I, 352-53; **CLIV**, II, 218-25.
[2] Livy, *Per.*, XI; Dion., XIX, 13; Pliny, *Hist. Nat.*, XXXIV, 32;
XXVI, II, 375; **CXXXI**, 62; **XX**, IV, 334.

come out upon the slopes overlooking the eastern sea. In the course of the succeeding years the breach was enlarged, and victory after victory brought the Roman arms to the very frontiers of Magna Grecia.

But just at this juncture the Samnite Wars were in full swing, and Rome, anxious not to bring upon her head the arms of Greece, had the prudence to halt. In 303 she made a treaty with Tarentum.[1] An article in it formally forbade the Roman fleets to pass the Lacinian promontory (Capo di Nao), and consequently strictly excluded them from access to the Adriatic. Being embroiled with the Samnites the Senate was obliged to accept the unwelcome clause with the prospect of escaping its effects later. When Thurii, Rhegium, Locri, and Croton had fallen, Rome considered that the opportune moment had come. A Roman squadron of ten warships crossed the limit laid down by the treaty of 303 and deliberately sailed eastwards. One step more and the Adriatic problem would be solved in the interests of Rome.

For Tarentum it was a question of life or death. The Tarentine fleet sallied forth and attacked the Roman squadron unexpectedly. Four ships were sunk, one was captured, and the rest took to flight. The Tarentines had dealt an effective blow, but, the first moment of enthusiasm over, they soon recognized that they had embarked on a very perilous venture. By herself, or even with the help of such allies as she might recruit in the neighbourhood, Tarentum could not hope to cope with unified Italy led by Rome. One solution only, the traditional solution, was available—the appeal to the mother-country, represented in this case by her neighbour across the sea, Pyrrhus, the King of Epirus (280).

II

THE CAMPAIGNS OF PYRRHUS

An appeal to the metropoles of Balkanic Greece had always been the last resort of the Western Hellenes. In the course of her history, Tarentum had often had recourse to that procedure, and the employment of condottieri had formed one of the normal expedients of her policy in cases

---

[1] App., *Samn.*, VII, 1; **XXVI**, II, 347.

of danger from the Sabellians. Thus, about 346 B.C., she had turned to her metropolis, Sparta, who had sent her one of the kings, Archidamos. The latter at the head of a motley band of mercenaries had fought for several years against the Italici, and finally fell on the field of battle.[1] The Sabellian danger had been thereby intensified. In view of her utter decadence, nothing further was to be hoped from Sparta, and so, in default of her, Tarentum next appealed to an adventurer, Alexander the Molossian, King of Epirus, the uncle and brother-in-law of Alexander of Macedon.[2] He, too, wished to play the epic hero, and planned to carve himself out a vast empire in the heart of Western Hellenism. He at first fought successfully against the southern Italici, but his victories and his designs of personal aggrandizement soon aroused the suspicions of the jealous Republic, whose only wish was to see him depart with all speed now that the crisis was past. Fortune soon answered her prayers; Alexander was slain before Pandosia during a campaign against the Bruttians (about 331-330).

In 314 B.C. came the expedition of the Spartiate Acrotatos, son of King Cleomenes II, to Sicily,[3] and this was followed a few years later by the Italian expedition of his brother Cleonymos to South Italy. The latter landed with a strong army of mercenaries, made an alliance with the Messapians, and compelled the Lucanians to make peace with Tarentum. Then, like his predecessors, he launched out on adventures, aiming at his own private advancement. He tried to overthrow Agathocles, failed, and retreated to the Ionian Sea. There he occupied Corcyra, and lived as a pirate on the Adriatic. Eventually he regained his homeland without glory, but, at least, after appearing in many avatars (302).[4]

The history of these condottieri repeats itself monotonously again and again: Tarentum's appeal, repulse of the Italici, quarrels with the city on the morrow of the victory, disastrous end. Strabo[5] justly remarks that Tarentum had fallen out in turn with all the captains whom she had

---

[1] Diod., XVI, 62, 4-63, 1-3; 88, 3.
[2] Livy, VIII, 24, 1-18.
[3] Diod., XIX, 70, 4-71, 5; **XX**, IV, 327-28.
[4] Diod., XX, 104-5; Livy, X, 2, 1-15; **XX**, IV, 329-31.
[5] Str., VI, 3, 3 (p. 280 C).

summoned to her aid. The underlying cause of this lies in the chronic misunderstanding on which this co-operation was based. In appealing to them Tarentum thought only of herself; in acceding the military chiefs had only their personal designs in view.

The history of Pyrrhus is only another of these endless new beginnings. In an Italy on the high-road to unity only the sacrifice of local patriotism on the altar of common independence and the establishment of a solid military State with a monarchical organization could have checked Rome and saved Hellenism in Italy. The Etruscans and the Samnites had collapsed in turn through the failure to comprehend the new necessities and to realize the new political formula which they prescribed. Enlightened by their fall, could not Magna Grecia pull herself together and avoid their sad fate?

Pyrrhus was active and ambitious, but an intriguer and a mischief-maker. As nephew of Alexander the Molossian and son-in-law of Agathocles, he was the heir of the imperialisms of Epirus and Syracuse, and had conceived the idea of a vast empire—Epirus, South Italy, Sicily, and perhaps North Africa—of which the basins of the Ionian and Adriatic Seas would form the axis and link. The notion was attractive, and Pyrrhus was not without substantial means for its realization. He had at his disposal solid troops trained in the school of the Macedonian army, then the best in the world, and organized in imitation of it. Personally he had learned the art of war by continual practice, and possessed the energy, far-sightedness, and skill that make a good commander-in-chief. His realm of Epirus provided in itself an admirable base of operations. Pyrrhus had further extended it by the annexation of Illyria to the north, and Acarnania and the Island of Corcyra to the south. As master of two hundred and fifty miles of the Balkan coast from the mouth of the Drina to the Gulf of Corinth, he had a firm grip on one bank of the Straits of Otranto. The anguished appeal of Tarentum offered him a hold on the other. To these advantages may be added yet another, and by no means the least—the command of the sea and all the military and economic consequences involved in that privilege. Pyrrhus took care not to let slip the unexpected chance that fortune proffered. He came and landed at Tarentum amidst general enthusiasm.

As a good strategist Pyrrhus arrived with a plan of campaign already prepared. With his unaided forces—twenty thousand men, three thousand horses, and a few elephants—even supplemented by contingents of Southern Greeks he could not hope to crush the Italian federation in the form that Rome had given it. Like Hannibal later on he had really only one winning card in his hand—the disruption of the federation—and only one means of compassing that—by an offensive over a large area. The Romans, who this time were fully alive to the danger, left him no time and hastened to take the field in order to confine their adversary to the extremity of the peninsula. In this race of offensives the Romans succeeded in scoring the first point. By 280 B.C., even before Pyrrhus had been able to effect a junction with the whole of the Sabellian contingents, a Roman army under P. Valerius Lævinus reached South Italy; another was holding the Etruscans in check; a third was mounting guard over the Samnites in order to prevent them joining the forces of the King of Epirus; a fourth waited in reserve at Rome.

The superiority of its numbers and the immensity of its reserves thus assured the Roman State from the very start an incalculable advantage strategically and tactically. The southern army, on reaching the coasts of the Ionian Sea, met that of Pyrrhus, near Heraclea, between that city and Pandosia. Pyrrhus' strategic skill, the mettle of his troops, especially of his cavalry, and finally his elephants, disconcerted the Romans and gave him the victory. But it cost him dear. The legionaries had resisted stubbornly, his losses had been heavy—four thousand Epirotes as against seven thousand Romans; what was more alarming, the Roman army had retreated in good order into Apulia. Nevertheless, substantial results had been achieved. The Greeks of the south, the Bruttians, the Lucanians, the Southern Samnites, and the Apulians joined Pyrrhus *en masse*. The Romans had been outmanœuvred, and, thanks to this initial success, Pyrrhus was able to launch the offensive, from which he expected the decision. The whole issue of the campaign hinged upon one question: would Central Italy remain loyal to Rome, or would the Italian federation seize the opportunity offered and break up? Tarentum had kept in touch with Central Italy, and especially with the Etruscans, and might hope, without over-confidence, that a bold offensive would be the signal for a general defection.

To take full advantage of the surprise and make the fullest use of the liberty of action the victory of Heraclea had purchased, at least for the moment, Pyrrhus marched upon Central Italy by the shortest route. His goal was not the capture of Rome; for since the Gaulish invasion she had built a solid wall for her protection, and a siege would demand resources which he did not possess. He aimed merely at provoking by his presence a general defection of the allies, which alone could reduce the Roman people to capitulate. Crossing the close network of Roman and Latin colonies without pausing to reduce them, the King of Epirus reached Campania and marched upon Latium through the Valleys of the Liris and the Trerus. He stopped on the borders of Latium, at Anagni or Præneste—our authorities differ on this point. No one budged, and he did not dare to proceed further. The Etruscans, held in obedience, came to an understanding with Rome. The Roman armies were hovering on Pyrrhus' own rear to cut off his retreat, and he had not sufficient forces to ensure his long line of communications with Tarentum. The raid had failed. The Italian League remained unmistakably loyal to Rome. The bad weather was approaching. Pyrrhus hastily beat his retreat, and retired first to Campania, and then to Tarentum, his base.

He spent the winter in incorporating in his army the South Italian contingents of Greeks, Samnites, Lucanians, Bruttians, and Apulians, who had gone over to his cause. In the spring of 279 he was ready, and, faithful to his tactics of the offensive, one of the cardinal articles in the Macedonian military creed, he took the field again without delay. His first offensive along the coast of the Tyrrhenian Sea had failed, Latium had not stirred, and Pyrrhus himself had been unable to join hands with the Etruscans or the Umbrians. He intended to renew the attack, but this time along the Adriatic slopes; he would gain Central Italy under cover of the Apennine Ridge.

He advanced as far as Ausculum in Apulia, but the Romans had divined his plan and taken precautions in consequence. The Roman army lined the Aufidius (Ofanto), its flanks covered by the sea on the east and by the mountains and the fulcrum of Venusia on the west. Enlightened by experience, it was equipped with special engines of war, especially chariots to combat the elephants. Pyrrhus manœuvred to surround it. His generalship as much as the superior manœuvring qualities of his troops secured him the victory again. The way was opened, but the contest had been stern; Pyrrhus had lost three thousand five hundred men as against six thousand on the Roman side. The eventual issue depended on the power and the capacity of the victor to follow up his success. That point was soon settled. Despite the advantage gained, Pyrrhus dared not advance farther, and this time again retired upon Tarentum. The offensive along the Adriatic had failed, like that along the Tyrrhenian coast the preceding year. The Italian League as a whole remained intact.

As a result of this double check, which revealed to him the difficulties of his enterprise and the solidity of Rome's work, the King of Epirus sought to make peace on the basis of independence for Magna Grecia; such a formula would safeguard both Italiote Hellenism and his own projects for the future. A period of hesitation ensued at Rome, where a strong party inclined to peace. But a decisive factor turned the scale in the opposite direction. Carthage, anxious about her possessions in Sicily and desirous of getting rid of Pyrrhus, offered her alliance, and a Carthaginian fleet under Mago cruised off the mouth of the Tiber. By a memorable interposition in the debate Appius Claudius Cæcus, the leader of the die-hards, swept the majority of the Senate in his direction.[1]

Henceforth Roman policy had as its avowed programme the unity of Italy, and its practical application—no peace with Pyrrhus till he had quitted Italian soil. Pyrrhus and Rome represent two clashing wills, two contrasted programmes. One stands for the independence of Magna

---

[1] Ennius, quoted by Cic., *de Sen.*, 6, 16; Livy, *Per.*, XII; Plut., *Pyrr.*, 18, 5-19, 5; App. *Samn.*, 10, 2; Cic., *Brut.*, 14, 55 (=F.P.R., p. 80, frag. 44); **XX**, IV, 344-47.

THE CONQUEST OF MAGNA GRECIA

Grecia in the Macedonian form of a military monarchy, the other for the unity of Italy under the leadership of Rome. Between these two diametrically opposed plans no reconciliation nor compromise was possible. They meant a duel to the death, which could, and, in fact, did, only terminate with the utter ruin of one of the adversaries. Militarily and diplomatically fate had declared against the King of Epirus. He acknowledged it, and without persisting in an inevitably sterile policy of the defensive, he turned his regards elsewhere. Sicily offered; he hurried thither to a lighter task and one that was no less attractive from the standpoint of his personal interests.

III

ROME, PYRRHUS, AND CARTHAGE

The first phase of the conflict between Rome and Pyrrhus had provoked a new fact of far-reaching significance for the future history of Italy—the intervention of Carthage in the peninsula's affairs. To understand its scope and implications we must turn back for a moment.

Since the end of the sixth century the fate of the Tyrrhenian Sea had been the stake for which four great Mediterranean States—the Etruscans, Marseilles, Carthage, and Syracuse—had played. The Etruscans, a people of mariners and pirates who came to Italy in the eleventh or tenth century, had been the first to dominate this sea which was to bear their name. In the sixth century the Greeks of Marseilles entered the arena, and their compatriots, the Phocæans, came and planted the colony of Alalia in Corsica.[1] At the same time Carthage, who had taken up the Phœnician heritage in the West, appeared in Italian waters.[2] Finally, by the beginning of the fifth century it was the turn of the great Dorian metropolis of Syracuse, who soon claimed the leadership of Western Hellenism.[3]

So the four imperialisms of Marseilles, Etruria, Syracuse, and Carthage disputed fiercely for the supremacy in the

[1] **XX**, II, 364-65; **XI**, I, 213-20; **CXV**, 17 ff.

[2] **VII**, I, 424 ff.; **XX**, II, 362-63, 370.

[3] **XX**, II, 366-72; **CLXXIX**, I, 215 ff.; **CXXXIII**, II, 201 ff.; **CLIV**, I, 192 ff.

H

Tyrrhenian Sea. Of these the first, Massalian imperialism, soon disappeared. The recoil of the Battle of Alalia, the ensuing evacuation of Corsica by the Greeks, and the collapse of the Phocæan thalassocracy affected it. Marseilles was henceforth confined to the Gulf of Lyons, where she expanded magnificently, and no longer appeared in the Tyrrhenian Sea. The elimination of Marseilles left the field free for the Etruscans and the Carthaginians. For nearly sixty years the sea remained in their power. But by the end of the sixth century the decadence of Etruria had set in. First through the check at Cumæ, then through the loss of Latium, and in 474 through the naval battle of Cumæ the Greeks from the latter city and Syracuse finally wrested the empire of the sea from the Etruscans. In the fourth century Etruria collapsed. In the Tyrrhenian domain only Carthage and Syracuse were left as rivals. Their political and economic duel was pursued implacably for two centuries.

It was towards the end of the sixth century that Carthage, the heir of the Phœnicians, had first appeared in Sicily. By the beginning of the next century the conflict with Hellenism, represented by the great cities of Syracuse and Agrigentum, broke out. In 480 B.C. the victory of Himera delivered Sicily temporarily from the Carthaginian peril and laid the foundations of Syracuse's greatness. Carthage had failed through putting too much confidence in her own strength and underestimating that of her assailants. She took the lesson to heart. The sixty-two years following her defeat were a period of recuperation and active preparations for revenge. In 409 war recommenced. A furious struggle followed, in which the Semites of Africa were faced in turn by men of the stamp of Dionysius I, Timoleon, and Agathocles. But by the third century the hour of Syracusan decline had come. Agathocles' revolted mercenaries made themselves masters of Messina and threatened Syracuse. The Carthaginians came and besieged her by land and sea. What was worse, the Mamertines and the Carthaginians made an alliance against her. The great Dorian city was no longer a power to be reckoned with. The field seemed finally free for Carthage.

The traditional balance of power in the Tyrrhenian Sea had been converted into a political, naval, and economic monopoly by Carthage by the successive effacement of Marseilles, Etruria, and Syracuse. But at this precise moment a new element came into play; Italy, already partially unified by Rome, entered the scene. How did the contact between the Carthaginian Empire, on the one hand, and Rome and Italy, on the other, come about?

Relations between Rome and Carthage dated back to an early age. Polybius dates the first treaty concluded between the two cities to the consulship of L. Junius Brutus and M. Horatius, " the first consuls appointed after the expulsion of the kings "—that is, in 509 B.C. on the traditional chronology,[1] and gives the text of the treaty. But in view of the terms of the treaty themselves such a date is absolutely impossible,[2] and represents one of those cases of anticipation so common in early Roman history. This impossibility, however, by no means proves that some such treaty did not exist at this remote date or even earlier. At the end of the sixth century Etruscans and Carthaginians combined fought side by side against the Phocæans, and the alliance had been particularly close between Carthage and the Etruscans of Cære; the latter in turn were in regular relations with the Etruscan dynasty at Rome. It is accordingly possible that a treaty of alliance, or, at least, of friendship, between the Tarquins and Carthage had existed, but, in any case, by the time of Polybius its text was no longer extant. Moreover, Livy[3] mentions a treaty between Rome and Carthage in 348, and Diodorus[4] and Orosius[5] agree in asserting that it was the first. To this date really belongs the first of the treaties preserved by Polybius; this was the epoch when Rome had created the unity of Latium, and had thereby become the principal State in Central Italy.[6] In effect it dealt with the delimitation of spheres of influence assigning Africa and Carthaginian Sicily to Carthage and the whole of Latium to Rome.

[1] Pol., III, 22. In the same sense, E. Nissen, in **L**, 1867, 321-32; **XII**, II, 813-14; **CXCIV**, 52-56; **VII**, III, 67 *ff.*; M. Gelzer, in **XXII**, *s.v.* " Latium," 951.

[2] *Cf.* **CLXXXIII**, 320-28; **I**, III, 180, note 1; **XX**, III, 193, 399-401; IV, 373; **CCXXVI**, I, 254 *ff.*, and the summary table on p. 269; and, lastly, A. Piganiol, in **LXIV**, 1923, 178-88.

[3] Livy, VII, 27, 2.   [4] Diod., XVI, 69.

[5] Oros., III, 7, 1.   [6] **XX**, III, 193, 399-405; IV, 372-76.

A little later, probably in 343, when Livy notes the arrival of a Carthaginian embassy at Rome without mentioning a treaty,[1] Rome and Carthage signed a new pact designed to define the first more precisely; its text has likewise been preserved to us by Polybius.[2] Two vital points deserve notice in the second treaty: it no longer refers merely to the Carthaginians and their allies, the latter in a collective and anonymous way, but names specifically the inhabitants of Tyre and Utica; and, secondly, by forbidding the Romans from passing Points Mastia and Tarseion on the southern coast of Spain, the Carthaginians secure recognition for a new zone of influence in the south of that peninsula in addition to the others.

The two foregoing treaties were only treaties of friendship and for trade in which the two parties limited their respective spheres of influence. When and how did Rome and Carthage take the step which was to lead from commercial to political agreements? Under the year 306 Livy[3] mentions a treaty, and expressly says that it was the third. The historian Philinos of Agrigentum spoke of a convention which "closed the whole of Sicily to the Romans and all Italy to the Carthaginians." Polybius denies its existence,[4] but it seems none the less to have been a reality. In all probability both passages refer to one and the same diplomatic act, a distinctly political treaty belonging to the year 306 B.C.[5]

Finally, the invasion by Pyrrhus, through the very eventualities with which it threatened Carthage and Rome alike, inspired the conclusion of a genuine political alliance between the two States, supplemented, as was requisite, by a military convention. The provisions of the earlier treaties, Polybius tells us,[6] and therefore also those of the treaty of

---

[1] Livy, VII, 38, 2.

[2] Pol., III, 24; **XX**, III, 402-3; IV, 375. On the contrary, Mommsen, E. Taubler, and some other modern authors adopt 306 as the date of this treaty.

[3] Livy, IX, 43, 26.

[4] Pol., III, 26, 2-4; Serv., ad Æn., IV, 628.

[5] **VII**, III, 66-72; **CLXXIX**, II, 229; M. Cary, in **LIV**, 1919, 66-67; A. Piganiol, in **LXIV**, 1923, 187.

[6] Pol., III, 25; cf. Livy, Per., XIV; **XX**, IV, 375-76; **CCXXVI**, I, 254 ff.; **VII**, III, 72-73.

306, which he does not mention, remained in force, but they were supplemented by new clauses dictated directly by the exigencies of the moment. The text of these clauses, as given by Polybius,[1] is not always as clear as could be wished, and has given rise to many controversies: but at least we can discern their main lines, and that is the great thing. Rome and Carthage formally pledge themselves not to make a separate peace with Pyrrhus; they promise mutual assistance if either be attacked on its own territory on condition that a formal and express request be made. After these general principles the modes of their execution are specified.

> "Whichever of the contracting parties has need of help, Carthage shall provide the ships for the journey in both directions; provisions shall be supplied by each people to its own troops. On sea, too, the Carthaginians shall assist the Romans in case of need, but no one may compel the crews to land against their will."

Carthage desired, above all, by this treaty to prevent an eventual crossing to Sicily by Pyrrhus, and so to guarantee her possessions in the island. In fact, it depended on Rome alone whether the treaty came into force at once. At the time of the second offensive of Pyrrhus in 279 B.C. Carthage offered her co-operation. One of her admirals, Mago, came to cruise off the mouth of the Tiber with a hundred and twenty ships, and proposed to take action against the common enemy. The Romans declined the offer on the pretext that they were not accustomed to have recourse to foreign troops, but, in reality, because they had seen through the game of Carthage and intended to keep her from meddling in the affairs of the peninsula.[2] Conversely, when Pyrrhus crossed over into Sicily and began to conquer the Carthaginian portion of the island, Rome did not come to the help of Carthage, and the question was apparently not even broached.

At bottom Carthage was no more anxious to have a Roman army in Sicily than Rome was to have Etruscan

---

[1] Pol., III, 25. On the interpretation of the clauses, see **I**, III, 2, 401-4; **CCXXVI**, I, 264-68; **XX**, IV, 375-76; **VII**, III, 72-73.

[2] Val. Max., III, 7, 10; Just., XVIII, 2, 1-3; **XX**, IV, 376; **VII**, III, 73.

contingents in Italy. The two contracting parties only regarded the treaty as an emergency guarantee, and had only signed it in the firm intention never to let it become operative. Moreover, under a pretence of loyalty Carthage seems to have been playing a double game. The achievement of Italian unity under Rome's auspices caused her anxiety both for her maritime supremacy on the Tyrrhenian Sea and her possessions in Sicily. When his offer of co-operation had been declined by Rome, Mago turned to Pyrrhus and talked of mediation.[1] We shall meet a manœuvre of the same kind at the time of the siege of Tarentum a little later on.

While Pyrrhus was lingering over the Sicilian interlude, Rome was taking full advantage of his absence, and won a whole series of victories : the Lucanians, the Samnites, and the Bruttians were defeated; in 277 the consul L. Cornelius Rufinus recaptured Croton. Tarentum, left to herself, was on the brink of destruction. At this juncture she issued an agonized appeal to Pyrrhus, the last hope of Western Hellenism. He returned, but his army was no longer the same either quantitively—he had sustained heavy casualties during the previous campaigns—nor qualitatively—his best troops, the Epirotes, had been annihilated, and he had had to replace them by Italian recruits of far inferior mettle; the fleet, so essential for the security of his permanent communications with the home country, had been roughly handled and partly destroyed by the Carthaginians at the time of his return from Sicily. Enthusiasm and confidence in success had vanished; the Italic allies never forgave Pyrrhus for his temporary desertion.

In such circumstances only a great victory could restore his fortunes. He sought that through a new northward offensive, and tried to cleave a way to Campania through Apulia. But this time again the Roman army barred his path and awaited him near Malventum, the future Beneventum. The painful experiences of the past had taught it much, and the long respite that Pyrrhus had left it by his Sicilian expedition had given it time to master the lesson. The great superiority of Pyrrhus, which he owed to Hellenic military science, had always lain primarily in strategy. Now, his tactical devices had by this time become familiar,

---

[1] Just., XVIII, 2, 4-5.

and the effect of surprise had worn off; a whole system of strategy for use against elephants had been elaborated. Cured of its weaknesses and with its gaps filled the Roman army retained its traditional sources of success, numbers, courage, and ardent patriotism. Finally, it had at length found a captain capable of leading it to victory in the person of M'. Curius Dentatus. Thereafter the issue was a foregone conclusion. Pyrrhus tried to take the Roman army by surprise; he was defeated and barely succeeded in reaching Tarentum with a few stragglers. This time his mission in Italy was definitely ended. On the pretext of seeking reinforcements he departed, promising a speedy return. He at least took the precaution to make provision for the future. His lieutenant, Milo, occupied the citadel of Tarentum, and thus secured him the permanent possession of this powerful base. Despite his promises, Pyrrhus was destined never to return. Three years later the man who had threatened Rome and narrowly missed crushing Italian unity in the egg died ingloriously in a street fight at Argos (272).

IV

The Agony of Pre-Roman Italy

The fate of Magna Grecia had been sealed on the battlefield of Beneventum. The unity of peninsular Italy had been accomplished to the profit of Rome; it only remained to put the finishing touches to the work. Left to themselves the Southern Greeks submitted one after the other. Locri received a Roman garrison. Tarentum alone held out and fought to the last for her national independence. But there were dissensions within the city. In defiance of Milo, who held the citadel and the arsenal, the Tarentines demanded its evacuation; Milo refused. Then Tarentum played her last card; she appealed to Carthage, hoping by this diversion to preserve her liberty or, at least, to extort tolerable conditions from Rome under threat of the Carthaginian danger. A Carthaginian fleet came and anchored off the city while the Roman army under the consuls Sp. Carvilius and L. Papirius Cursor for its part was blockading the town by land.

The situation was a curious one. Tarentum, Milo,

Carthage, and Rome, with their four contrasting policies,
were all disputing for the possession of the great city that
then seemed the last fort of expiring Italian independence.
The attitudes of Tarentum and of Pyrrhus' lieutenant were
quite logical and excite no surprise, but the intervention of
Carthage, a veritable *deus ex machina*, might involve most
disastrous consequences for Roman policy. With Carthage
installed in South Italy Italian unity would have been postponed or even rendered impossible. Rome complained
bitterly, and declared that the attitude of Carthage was
contrary to the treaty and would be regarded by her as a
formal violation of former agreements. Looking at the
letter of the treaty alone Carthage had done no wrong whatever, but there are cases in politics, all too many alas, when
deeds alone count and the situation in question was one of
these. The solution of the problem lay in Milo's hands.
Surrounded at sea by the Carthaginian fleet and on land by
the Roman army, he could not hold out for long, but, though
his capitulation was inevitable, it remained to be seen to
whom and to whose advantage he would yield. And as this
event must involve also the surrender of Tarentum herself,
it is easy to see the exceptional importance of the decision
which he was called upon to take.

His choice fell upon Rome, and this decision is doubtless
to be explained by the very limited confidence Pyrrhus'
lieutenant reposed in the Carthaginians. The Senate, glad
to be quit of him so cheaply, granted him a safe conduct
with all the honours of war and all the treasure which
Pyrrhus had left in his care. The acropolis being occupied
by a Roman garrison, Tarentum capitulated in her turn.
She entered the Italic federation as an ally of Rome, but
under particularly burdensome conditions. In addition to
the loss of her national independence and sovereignty, she
had to dismantle her city wall, pay a war indemnity, and
receive a Roman garrison permanently into the citadel. She
had made Rome tremble, summoned Pyrrhus into Italy, and
imperilled the great Roman plan of Italian unity. Moreover,
Tarentum held the key to the door to the East, and this
door must be definitely closed against any subsequent
Hellenic interference. Rancour for the past and precautions
against the future were the principal causes of the excep-

tional rigour of the settlement imposed by Roman policy upon Tarentum in 272 B.C. Hellenism in Italy had not had the intelligence to sacrifice its parochial traditions to the higher necessities of national independence. The fall of Tarentum represented its definite collapse and constituted its death warrant.

With Tarentum the very soul of the anti-Roman resistance fell. The eight years (272-264 B.C.) intervening between the capture of the city and the opening of the Punic Wars were employed in a general pacification and winding-up. Rome took advantage of her victory, and completed the great work of the unification of peninsular Italy by a series of operations of detail. These closing scenes were enacted in three arenas—in the south, in Samnium, and in Northern Etruria. In South Italy Rome recovered Rhegium, whose Campanian garrison had mutinied during the war. To the Bruttians, Tarentum's allies, she granted tolerable terms. Between 269 and 266 B.C. she defeated the Messapians, conquered the peninsula of Otranto, and laid hands on Brundisium, where a Roman colony was planted in 244. By the possession of Rhegium and Brundisium, two complementary strategic points, one on the Strait of Messina, the other on the Straits of Otranto, she henceforth held the keys to the channels, and permanently ensured communications between her two great seas. The Lucanians made peace.

Samnium had been largely annexed to Rome and covered with Roman colonies, with the exception of the central region of the Pentri, who retained a certain independence and ceased to count. As a result of two successive expeditions, the Samnite Caracæni capitulated in 269 and Picenum in the following year. In Etruria Rome intervened successfully at Volsinii (265), then a prey to a social revolution. In Umbria she intervened against the Sarsinati, whom the consuls D. Junius Pera and N. Fabius Pictor reduced to submission. The establishment of a series of colonies at Beneventum and Ariminum (268), at Firmum (264), at Æsernia (263), and later at Brundisium (244), and the continuation of the Via Appia—first to Venusia; then to Brundisium and Tarentum—consolidated the results obtained and made them final. The conquest of Southern Italy, consequent upon the defeat of Pyrrhus and the fall of

Tarentum, had brought the area of the Italian federation's territory to more than 80,000 square miles.[1] The triumph of an idea and the work of a will, the unity of peninsular Italy up to the Macra on the west and the Æsis on the east was now realized. The history of primitive Italy closes, the history of Roman Italy begins.

[1] **XXVI**, II, 425.

THE ORGANIZATION OF ITALY BY ROME

I

ANNEXATION AND FEDERATION

THE organization of conquered Italy as we find it completed by the third century before our era was the result of a gradual process, which had not been carried out in a uniform manner. It had progressed at the same pace as, and step by step with, the conquest itself. For several centuries Rome had been learning, experimenting, and, as so constantly in her history, profiting by experience.

In default of the details which tradition, in its present state, too often withholds, we can at least discern the general ideas guiding it and record its results as exact and definite formulæ. Two great parallel systems, annexation and federation, came at length to be applied to the whole of peninsular Italy after having been tested first in the restricted domain of Latium, and then perfected and finished off on the wider field of Central Italy.

The system of annexation was the older; we find it in favour from the time of Rome's origins, but in the course of centuries it had evolved both in its form and in the manner of its application. At the start it included two fundamental varieties. The territory might be annexed and the inhabitants, when not annihilated by a general massacre or enslavement,[1] would be transplanted to Rome. This

---

Bibliography.—Texts: Texts are rare. Consult especially (*a*) for §§ I-III, Livy, VIII, 13, 10-14 (reorganization of Latium in 338); VIII, 17, 12; IX, 43, 24; X, 1, 2-3; Velleius Paterculus, I, 14-15 (general history of Roman colonization); Festus, *s.v.* " Municeps " (pp. 117 and 126), " Municipium " (p. 155); " Præfecturæ " (p. 262); Aulus Gellius, *Noctes Atticæ*, XVI, 13, 7; (*b*) for § IV, Polybius, II, 24, and VI (fragmentary), 19-42.

Principal Works.—**XIV**, VIII, 3-78; **XX**, III, 351-74; IV, 406-28; **XXVI**, II, 430-64; **LXXXIX**; **XXV**, 14-24.

---

[1] That had happened to Apiolæ (Dion, III, 49), Corniculum (*ib.*, III, 50), and later to Veii (see p. 150 above).

summary method presented the triple advantage of a territorial expansion, an increase to the city's population, and perfect security in the conquered territory. Primitive Rome treated certain places in her immediate vicinity, such as Politorum, Tellena, Ficana, Medullia, and, finally, Alba in this way.[1] The aristocracy, when it had made a timely submission, received the rights of citizenship, the rest of the population was sold into slavery or mingled with the plebs.

The alternative method was to annex the territory, but not to transfer its inhabitants, who were left at home. Such, according to tradition, was the fate of Antemnæ and Cænina in the days of Romulus[2] and of the cities annexed by the elder Tarquin—Ficulæ, Crustumerium, Collatia, and Nomentum.[3] In this case the Roman State confiscated a variable portion of the conquered territory, generally half or two-thirds, of which it disposed in various ways: when it was a question of specially important strategic points, such as Ostia at the mouth of the Tiber, the confiscated territory was allotted collectively to Roman colonies; alternatively it was granted to individual Roman citizens (*viritim*) to the extent of three, four, or sometimes seven *jugera* per head. Sometimes, again, the State kept the conquered territory as common land (*ager publicus*). The domain annexed to the Roman State was divided into tribes, the thirty-one rustic tribes, created successively in proportion to the annexations.

With the fourth century the *municipium* appears through a new transformation. This was a fruitful idea fraught with untold consequences, which meant the enlargement of the victorious city by the grant of civic rights to the conquered. But Rome knew how to use it with the necessary prudence and reserve. In 381 B.C., on the morrow of the revolt of the Latin cities following the capture of Rome by the Gauls, Tusculum was created the first *municipium*; Cicero[4] calls it *municipium antiquissimum*. It entered the Roman State and its inhabitants received the citizenship, but only in its

---

[1] Livy, I, 29-30, 2, 33, 1-2; Dion., 31, 43; Cic., *de Rep.*, II, 18, 33.

[2] Livy, I, 11, 1-3; Dion., II, 35. The inhabitants of these cities—who consented, adds Dionysius—were transplanted to Rome.

[3] Livy, I, 38, 1-4; Dion., III, 49-51.

[4] Cic., *Pro Planco*, VIII, 19; *pro Balbo*, XIII, 31; *de Orat.*, I, 11, 35; Fest., *s.v.* " Municipium," p. 155.

incomplete form; Rome granted them the private rights—the rights of marrying and trading, *connubium* and *commercium*—but not the public rights—the vote and eligibility for office, *jus suffragii* and *jus honorum*. The city further preserved a large degree of internal autonomy.

The system offered the double advantage of increasing Roman power through the incorporation of new citizens and of giving the vanquished a share in the greatness of the conqueror without placing them on a footing of absolute equality with the old citizens. And so it was soon extended. The Etruscan city of Cære, annexed in 353, was similarly treated. Then, after the dissolution of the Latin League, similar constitutions were granted to a number of cities in Latium (Aricia, Lanuvium Noventum, and Pedum), and outside (Cumæ, Capua, Fundi, Formiæ, and Suessula in 338, Atella and Catalia perhaps at the same time, Acerræ in 332, Anagnia in 306, Arpina and Trebula in 303, the Sabine cities in 290, and others, too).

The system of federation was no more a Roman invention than that of annexation; as we have seen, Latium had known it for ages. The model for this plan, which was to enjoy such an extraordinary career, was offered to Rome in the old Latin federations, particularly the Alban League, as it existed in the eighth and early seventh centuries, as well as that which the Etruscan kings had reconstituted in the sixth century round the federal sanctuary of Diana on the Aventine.[1] Shattered by the fall of the Tarquins, this federal idea reappeared in the shape of the triple entente of Romans, Latins, and Hernici, which remained the foundation of Roman foreign policy down to the middle of the fourth century B.C. Another parallel was also influential, though in a far smaller degree. In addition to the federal bond which united her to the Latins and the Hernici,[2] Rome had a very ancient treaty of alliance with the neighbouring city of Gabii, which tradition referred to Tarquin the Proud.[3]

After the sack of Rome by the Gauls the federation broke up; the Hernici and part of the Latins went their own ways, but Rome clung to this federal pact, which represented to

[1] Livy, I, 52, 4; Dion., III, 54; IV, 26, 5, 48; **CCXXVI**, I, 383-84.
[2] Pp. 145-48 above.
[3] Dion., IV, 58; **CCXXVI**, II, 380-83.

her at once a guarantee and an invaluable instrument. Through her victories she recreated the League in 358 B.C. In 338, after the great Latin War, Rome felt herself strong enough to put an end to it and reshape the federal system in her sole interests. Certain Latin cities which had not been annexed, such as Tibur, Præneste, and Cora, signed treaties of alliance with Rome, but separately. The principle of federation by means of special treaties between Rome and the several cities of Italy on the model of the old treaty with Gabii was thus invented. The wars of Italian independence would result in its extension to the whole of peninsular Italy.

Neither of the two systems on which the organization of Roman Italy was based in the last analysis was an original invention by Rome; they had long been known to Italy and the Mediterranean world in general. Sparta in particular had employed both in turn. But Rome made them doubly her own both through the form which she gave them and the equilibrium she managed to maintain between them. Under the system of annexation the new subjects were admitted to citizenship, but under the restrictions which experience and prudence indicated. On the federal plan the conquered were united by no legal bonds to one another, but were allied separately to Rome on varying terms. Equally wise was the balance which Rome struck between the two systems; both were skilfully meted out, and the formula governing their apportionment might be summed up in these terms: neither too many new citizens, lest the Roman State be swamped by their influx; nor too few, since Roman policy required ever larger contingents of citizens. Annexation must be pushed far enough to meet the ever-growing needs of the State and to counterbalance the influence of the allied States, but not too far to undermine the foundations of the traditional system of the ancient City-State, the base of Rome's whole political structure. Let us consider two specific examples. At the time of the great Italian coalitions Rome annexed the Sabine people in a body, and thus secured an effective supplement of a hundred thousand citizens, allowing her to bring to a successful conclusion the heavy task of creating Italian unity. At the end of the First Punic War, which inflicted severe losses on the citizen body, two new tribes—the Velina and Quirina (241 B.C.)—were created, designed to fill the gaps.

During the progress which led to the creation of Italian unity, Rome steadily set herself to maintain this balance which she had been clever enough to discover, and she succeeded. The figures, as far as they can be estimated in a very approximate way,[1] furnish the most eloquent and conclusive testimony in this respect. About 350 B.C. annexed territory comprised some 1,200 square miles, allied countries about 1,160; about 338, after the Latin war, the figures are: annexed territory 2,300 square miles and allied countries 1,930; about 300, 3,130 and 7,590 square miles respectively; about 280, 7,720 and 23,950 respectively; finally, after the war with Pyrrhus, annexed territory covered 7,900 square miles and allied countries 40,500. Annexation and federation were, therefore, the two fundamental systems which governed the organization of conquered Italy. In consequence of this double principle, unified Italy consisted of two distinct elements: the annexed territory and the allied countries. Let us glance at each in turn.

II

THE ANNEXED TERRITORY

The annexed territory was composed of areas taken from the vanquished States at the moment of their conquest. Its nucleus lay in Rome and Central Italy, but it was also extended to a varying degree to the rest of the peninsula. It was distinguished by one primary feature: it was by definition the domain of the Roman citizens.

We have said it was the domain of Roman citizens, but the citizens fell into two classes. Roman citizenship in its full form implied two kinds of rights: political (*jura publica*) and civil (*jura privata*). *Jura publica* involved two vital privileges: the vote—only a citizen could participate in assemblies, elect magistrates and legislate, all which rights in conformity with the ancient conception of citizenship could only be exercised at Rome herself in the *comitia cen-*

---

[1] **LXXXIX**, 75, 77; **XXVI**, II, 289, 342, 365-66, 425; note the reservations made by **CXXXI**, 80 and 84, note 27.

turiata or *tributa*—and eligibility for office; only the citizen was eligible for honours, magistracies, and that under the further condition that he had his real or fictitious domicile at Rome. *Jura privata* again involved two vital privileges: the right of Roman marriage (*jus connubii*), in the full sense of the word and with all its many implications, and the right to property (*jus commercii*); a citizen alone could hold property in right of quiritary ownership, acquire it by inheritance, or purchase and dispose of it by sale, bequest, or any other sort of alienation. Such are the essential rights implied in Roman citizenship. In Italy their possessor was a full citizen (*optimo jure*) of the first or superior class of citizens.

But below such there was a second class, an inferior category of citizens who possessed only the civil rights without the political rights; these were citizens with limited rights (*minuto jure*) or without the vote (*sine suffragio*). However, no impassable barrier sundered the two classes. A man might be degraded from the superior to the inferior class, though that was an exceptional event, or might rise from the second to the first, and we find in practice that such promotion was quite common down to the first years of the second century before our era.

All full citizens, and they alone, were grouped within a common structure, the thirty-five tribes which formed from this period territorial units comparable to our counties or parishes. The oldest of these tribes, the four urban tribes, dated back, according to tradition, to the end of the regal period; the Republic had created thirty-one others, the thirty-one rural tribes, and the process ended in 241 B.C. with the creation of the two last Roman tribes, Velina and Quirina. The figure was thenceforth fixed at thirty-five.

The first four or urban tribes corresponded to quarters of the city of Rome proper, and bore geographical names: Palatina, Esquilina, Suburana, and Collina.[1] Later on, in 495 B.C., according to tradition, the immediate vicinity was divided among sixteen rural tribes (Æmilia, Camilia, Claudia, Cornelia, Fabia, Galeria, Horatia, Lemonia, Menenia, Papyria, Pollia, Pupinia, Romulia, Sergia, Voltinia, and

---

[1] Dion., IV, 14.

Voturia).[1] All these bear the names of patrician *gentes*, but these names had, however, a geographical sense, at least, indirectly; they denoted the districts where these several *gentes* had the bulk of their property. In 494 a seventeenth rural tribe appeared named Clustumina, a purely topographical appellation this time.[2] Then a century's pause ensued. After 387 the steady extension of Roman territory inspired the creation of fourteen new rural tribes, nearly all christened with local names; in 387 four were created, Stellatina, Tromentina, Sabatina, and Arnensis; in 358 two, Pomptina and Poblilia; in 332 two, Mæcia and Scaptia; in 318 two, Ufentina and Falerna; in 299 two, Aniensis and Teretina; and, finally, in 241 two, Velina and Quirina.

The inhabitants of the annexed territory were divided among two classes of settlements; some lived in urban centres, colonies or *municipia*, the rest in rural centres of varying kinds and magnitudes. Among the urban centres Roman colonies occupied the first rank. Cicero[3] gives us a complete and exact definition of a Roman colony:

> "For the establishment of their colonies our ancestors chose sites so convenient and so well adapted to guaranteeing them against all dangers that they seemed to be not so much cities of Italy as bulwarks of the Empire (*ut esse non oppida Italiæ, sed propugnacula imperii viderentur*)."

The colonies were, in fact, bodies of citizens settled at a strategic point in hostile or doubtful country and designed before all else to serve as garrisons. Tradition attributed the oldest of these colonies—that of Ostia—to the reign of Ancus Marcius; we have seen above what this assertion is worth. Then came Labici, in 318, we are told; then Antium, formerly a Latin colony, in 338; Terracina (Anxur) in 329; Minturnæ and Sinuessa in 296; Sena Gallica and Castrum novum in 283. Down to the middle of the third millennium B.C. the number of Roman colonies remained very limited; it was substantially augmented during the following century. We may mention Æsium and Alsium in 247; Fregenæ in 245; Pyrgi before 191; Puteoli, Volturnum, Liternum, Salernum, Buxentum, Sipontum, Tempsa, and Croton in 194; Potentia

---

[1] Livy, II, 21, 7; Dion., VII, 64; **XXVI**, II, 19-21.
[2] **XIV**, VI, 192-94.
[3] Cic., *de Lege Agr.*, II, 27, 73.

and Pisaurum in 184; Parma, Mutina, and Saturnia in 183; Graviscæ in 181; Luna in 177; and Auximum in 157.

Scattered all over Italy these Roman colonies had in essence nothing Italian about them. The colony was constituted as a whole by the despatch of colonists from Rome. Under the command of the commissioners, who had led them, the newcomers built a town and encircled it with a rampart to overawe the native population. It was a miniature copy of Rome, *quasi effigies parvæ simulacraque populi Romani*, as Aulus Gellius suggestively defines it.[1] The Roman colony was composed exclusively of Roman citizens of the superior class (*optimo jure*) generally three hundred strong. It possessed local institutions modelled on those of Rome— a popular assembly (*comitia*), magistrates (*duoviri* or *prætores*), a senate (*ordo decurionum*), and priests (*flamines*) —and· was granted complete administrative autonomy. Moreover, these colonists sent out by Rome remained closely attached to their birthplace; in addition to their rights as colonists they retained all their political rights at Rome, to the vote and to office, on the same terms as their compatriots in the metropolis. The native population, on the other hand, received either immediately or after a period of probation the inferior citizenship without the vote.

The colony, the nucleus of which was a body of citizens sent from Rome, was contrasted to the annexed Italian city, or *municipium*. The latter was normally a centre of population, the inhabitants of which, in contrast to the Roman colony, were not natives of Rome, but enjoyed the rights of citizenship. Such Italians who had become Roman citizens were still only half-citizens without the vote, *sine suffragio*. They possessed the civil rights, but not the political ones. A considerable number of them sooner or later rose to the full citizenship. That might come about individually or collectively. Every inhabitant of a *municipium* who had held any office in his town as duumvir, ædile, or quæstor automatically obtained the full citizenship both for himself and his descendants. Or the citizenship might be conferred directly on a whole *municipium*; thus the Sabine cities which had received the citizenship *sine suffragio*

---

[1] A. Gell., *Noct. Att.*, XVI, 13, 9.

in 290 B.C. attained the full citizenship in 268.[1] Formiæ, Fundi, and Arpinum were similarly treated in 188.[2] From the beginning of the third century the process of promotion was rapidly and continuously applied to the whole of the *municipia*.

From the point of view of internal administration *municipia* might be divided into two classes; the more favoured towns possessed administrative autonomy with an assembly of the people, a senate, and magistrates. The second class *municipia*, on the other hand, were deprived of such autonomous administrative organs and governed by the same magistrates as Rome as dependencies of the city; these were the *præfecturæ*, cities which Rome thought it necessary to restrain or punish for some fault, such as Anagnia and the other cities of the Hernici in 306[3] or Capua after its rebellion in 216.[4] They were administered by circuit-judges (*præfecti juredicundo*) nominated by the *comitia tributa* (in the case of Cumæ, Casilinum, Volturnum, Liternum, Puteoli, Suessula, Atella, Calatia, Capua, and Acerræ) or merely appointed by the *prætor urbanus*.[5] The rustics of the annexed territory inhabited either villages or hamlets (*vici, conciliabula*) or isolated farms.

III

THE ALLIED COUNTRIES

The territory not annexed, the allied country subject to the political and military domination of Rome, was distinguished from the foregoing by two main characteristics: its inhabitants were not Roman citizens, but in the eyes of Roman law, foreigners or *peregrini;* secondly, like half-citizens, they remained outside the thirty-five tribes. These allied countries comprised two distinct categories: Latin colonies and allied peoples or cities.

Originally the term Latin colonies, as contrasted with Roman colonies, was used to designate the colonies founded by the old Latin League before its dissolution in 338; how-

[1] Vell., I, 14, 6. [2] Livy, XXXVIII, 36, 7-8.
[3] Livy, IX, 43, 23; Fest., *s.v.* " Præfecturæ," p. 262.
[4] Livy, IX, 43. [5] Festus, *s.v.* " Præfecturæ," p. 262.

ever, Romans as allies might participate in such, beside Hernici and Latins. Tradition, which should only be accepted with caution, referred the four oldest—Signia, Circei, Suessa Pometia, and Cora—to the regal period. They were followed by Velitræ (494), Norba (492), Antium (467), Ardea (442), Satricum (385), Nepete and Sutrium (383), and Setia (382), in all twelve colonies founded by the first Latin League before its disappearance in 338. After its destruction and the establishment of Roman predominance in Latium, Rome, in virtue of her new position as the capital of Latium, continued to plant so-called Latin colonies, which differed from the earlier ones in two respects: firstly, they were founded by Rome alone; and, secondly, in contrast to the Roman colonies, no Romans dwelt in them.

Such was the second Latin League, which, by a series of successive foundations, proceeded to spread gradually all over peninsular Italy. The movement began only four years after the disappearance of the old Latin League with the foundation of the colony of Cales (334); then came Fregellæ (328), Luceria (314), Suessa, the colony on the island of Pontia, and Saticula (313), Interamna Lirinas (312), Sora and Alba Fucens (303), Carsioli (302), Narnia (299), Venusia (291), Hatria (289), Cosa and Pæstum (273), Ariminum and Beneventum (268), Firmum (264), Æsernia (263), Brundisium (244), Spoletium (241), Placentia and Cremona (218), Copia (193), Vibo Valentia (192), Bononia (189), Aquileia (181), and Luca (180).

In contradistinction to the Roman colonies, which were essentially coastal, the Latin colonies were almost all situated inland. As independent States allied to Rome, their mother-city, by a perpetual treaty, the Latin colonies further enjoyed the rights of intermarriage and trade (*jus connubii* and *jus commercii*) on the same terms as the allied Latin cities. They possessed complete autonomy and their own proper institutions.

The allied cities and peoples embraced the bulk of the population of Italy. Their positions were regulated by formal treaties (*fœdera*) concluded at the moment when they had been forced to acknowledge the supremacy of Rome. We shall return to them again in a moment.

IV

What Rome Demanded of Italy

Of the Italians Rome asked three things : their liberties, men, and money.

As far as national liberties were concerned, two parallel cases corresponding to the two systems of annexation and federation arose. In the case of annexed territory the solution was simple and radical. Such countries just ceased to exist from the national standpoint, and were incorporated in the Roman State. The case of the allied cities was far more complex. The systematic suppression of leagues, such as the Hernician League after the revolt of 306 B.C., or their retention in a purely religious form, like the Latin League after 338 or the Etruscan League, was a first blow to the sovereignty of Italian cities. In other respects distinctions must be drawn. The *fœdus* which bound each city to Rome theoretically regulated their legal and political status. And so in this respect several categories of allied cities existed. The most favoured of all, allied cities in the fullest sense, had treated with Rome on a footing of equality, and had concluded a *fœdus æquum* with her. As examples, we may mention Naples,[1] Præneste, and, no doubt, also the majority of the Etruscans, Umbrians, and peoples of the Central Apennines (we have even the expression *æquissimum*), such as Camerinum in Umbria[2] and Heraclea in Magna Grecia, whose exceptional *fœdus* is qualified by Cicero as " *æquissimum* " and " *prope singulare*."[3] Such cities preserved their sovereign rights, notably that of coining copper, their local institutions, their magistrates, their tribunals, and their language. These cities and the Latin colonies, the best treated of all, enjoyed full community of civil rights with Rome (*connubium* and *commercium*); their inhabitants might even obtain the full citizenship provided they came to reside at Rome, as we have seen.[4]

[1] Livy, VIII, 26, 6; Cic., *pro Balbo*, VIII, 21; XXIV, 55.
[2] Cic., *pro Balbo*, XX, 46; Livy, XXVIII, 45, 20.
[3] Cic., *pro Arch.*, IV, 6; *pro Balbo*, XXII, 50.
[4] The non-Latin allied cities did not possess *connubium* with Rome, but it is probable that a certain number of them, the best treated, did enjoy *commercium*.

This first class was contrasted with a second composed of cities and peoples, whose treaty with Rome was not a *fœdus æquum;* the city or people in question had contracted an alliance with the Roman people, but as an inferior. The provisions of such a *fœdus* would vary from case to case, but as a general rule a double principle was observed. The sovereignty of the contracting city was relatively restricted in virtue of the article " *ut is populus* (the people concerned) *alterius populi* (the Roman people) *majestatem comiter conservaret* "[1]—a vague and elastic clause which could be interpreted by Rome just as she liked. In fact, treaties of this type constituted veritable pacts of clientship or protectorateship. Allied cities of this category, and they formed the great majority, surrendered all autonomous foreign policy, all private military power, and, in a word, all national independence. In this respect the Latin colonies were usually assimilated to allied cities, but Rome did not treat them alike otherwise. The oldest of them enjoyed the right of minting copper money. This right was restricted or withdrawn in the case of the last twelve Latin colonies planted between 268 and 181 B.C. The second principle observed in dealing with the allies was to leave all classes of allied cities an autonomous administration and their own institutions.

Such, as far as the allies were concerned, was their legal position as strictly regulated by the *fœdus.* But the actual situation must also be considered, for it is no less important. In practice the federal system was perverted from the outset owing to the inequality of the two parties in power and the continually increasing greatness of Rome. The very foundation of the system was that the isolated cities were bound to Rome alone, and had no political or legal link with each other. Thus Roman Italy appears from the first as a medley of cities enjoying different rights, whose situation was regulated with regard to Rome alone. This disproportion only became more accentuated when conquests beyond Italy began and the provinces were created as the exclusive domain of Rome, from which the Italian federation had nothing to hope. And so Rome exerted a crushing predominance within the League. Its political, military, and financial management was legally in her hands, but at least

[1] Cic., *pro Balbo*, XVI, 35; **CCXXVI**, I, 63.

theoretically the internal affairs of the cities were outside her competence.

In practice, however, she did not hesitate to interfere, particularly by introducing an aristocratic régime everywhere. In the Italian cities the effective power was exercised by a senate recruited, like that of Rome, from the old families, and, again like the Roman, regularly hostile to new men. The democratic party, suspect for its loyalty to national traditions, was jealously watched and kept from all control of policy. The local aristocracies only maintained their positions by favour of Rome, and were well aware of the fact; and so vital personal interests kept them loyal to her. On two occasions—during the wars with Pyrrhus and with Hannibal—they prevented defections from spreading, and their loyalist attitude saved Roman dominion. In spite of all appearances, national liberties were still alive in Italy.

Secondly, whether as the result of annexation or in virtue of the several federal pacts, Rome demanded men from Italy. All males in Italy owed her military service, but on different terms, according to the two great categories of Italians: citizens and non-citizens.

A Roman citizen served in the legion and had no option. There was only one exception : down to the third century B.C. Roman citizens from colonies, being regarded as permanently on service, were exempt from conscription (*vacatio militiæ*). In 207, as a result of exceptional circumstances (Hasdrubal's arrival in Italy), all colonists were compelled to serve, with the exception of those of Ostia and Antium,[1] and the old legal exemption was probably withdrawn after the end of the Punic Wars. In 191 certain colonies—Ostia, Fregenæ, Castrum novum, Pyrgi, Antium, Terracina, Minturnæ, and Sinuessa—refused to serve at sea. The Senate overruled their objection, declaring that they had no right to exemption from naval service.[2] All Roman citizens, therefore, served in the legion, but this class might be subdivided according to the manner in which service was rendered. Full citizens (*optimo jure*) and those of the citizens *sine suffragio*, whose towns had preserved their autonomy and local institutions, were enrolled in the legions proper. On

---

[1] Livy, XXVII, 38, 4-5. [2] Livy, XXXVI, 3, 4-7.

the other hand, the inferior class of citizens belonging to *municipia* without an autonomous administration formed special legions, such as the Campanian Legion, which behaved so disgracefully at Rhegium during the war with Pyrrhus. As the latter class disappeared through the promotion of its members to the full citizenship, the special legions were abolished, and all Roman citizens without exception served thereafter in ordinary legions.

Let us turn next to the inhabitants of allied cities, the non-citizens. By virtue of the *fœdus*, which bound them to the Roman State, the towns or peoples of territory that had not been annexed had to supply Rome with a contingent of soldiers or, in the case of maritime cities, of marines. A specific article in the *fœdus* fixed the number of effectives. The whole of these confederate troops represented the allies (*socii*) in opposition to the citizen troops, the Roman legions. Polybius[1] describes the mechanism of the levy and the army organizations in the second century B.C. Every year at the same time as he proceeded to raise the Roman troops, the consul laid down the number of effectives to be supplied by each allied city, the place of muster, and the date of mobilization. Rome considered only the total. It was left to the local magistrates to arrange for the delivery of the requisite number of men and horses under the prescribed conditions.

The proportion between the allied contingents and the Roman troops may be calculated, especially from several passages in Polybius.[2] In general the effective strength of the allied infantry was approximately equal to that of the Roman infantry, but in the case of the cavalry the ratio was normally three to one. At the Battle of Trebia in 218 B.C., when two consular armies of four legions fought on the Roman side, the total strength of the Roman infantry amounted to thirty-six thousand legionaries, of whom sixteen thousand (Livy says eighteen thousand) were Romans and twenty thousand allies.[3] For estimating the total effectives mobilizable in Italy we possess one invaluable document, the list of Italians capable of bearing arms in 225 B.C., which is known at once from Polybius,[4] Diodorus,[5] Livy,[6] the Elder

---

[1] Pol., VI, 19-26. [2] Pol., III, 107, 10-13; VI, 26, 6-10; 30, 1-2.
[3] Pol., III, 72, 11-12; Livy, XXI, 55, 4.
[4] Pol., II, 24. [5] Diod., XXV, 13. [6] Livy, *Per.*, XX.

Pliny,[1] Eutropius,[2] and Orosius.[3] The two last named historians, who are here using the lost text of Livy, add a valuable item of information—namely, that this statistical list was taken from the annalist Fabius Pictor, a contemporary who had just copied an official paper, the muster-roll of Italy on the eve of the Second Punic War. In view of its exceptional importance, it will be well to reproduce it in the fullest form, which has come down to us—*i.e.*, as given by Polybius.[4]

> " The consuls had brought with them four legions, each composed of five thousand two hundred foot and three hundred horse; they were both accompanied by allied troops totalling thirty thousand foot and two thousand horse. In addition there were four thousand horsemen and more than fifty thousand foot soldiers provided by the Sabines and the Etruscans, whom the danger had brought to the help of Rome. . . . The mountaineers of the Apennines, Umbrians, and Sarsinati had put into the field nearly twenty thousand men, and the Veneti and the Cenomani twenty thousand likewise.
>
> " At Rome a reserve corps was held in readiness against a surprise; it numbered twenty thousand infantrymen and fifteen hundred Roman knights, and auxiliaries of thirty thousand foot and two thousand horse. The rolls which had been drawn up showed eighty thousand foot and five thousand horse among the Latins, seventy thousand foot and seven thousand horse among the Samnites, fifty thousand foot and sixteen thousand horse among the Iapyges and Messapians combined, and twenty thousand foot and four thousand horse among the Marsi, Marrucini, Frentani, and Vestini. There were besides two legions each composed of four thousand two hundred foot and two hundred horse designed to guard Tarentum and Sicily. The enrolments of the Roman and Campanian populations gave nearly two hundred and fifty thousand infantrymen and twenty-three thousand cavalrymen. . . . Hence the total of men capable of bearing arms exceeded seven hundred thousand foot soldiers and about seventy thousand horsemen."

According to this document the forces mobilized, or capable of mobilization at the disposal of the Italian federation at the end of the third century B.C., may be tabulated as follows :[5]

---

[1] Pliny, *Hist. Nat.*, III, 138. [2] Eutr., III, 5.
[3] Oros., IV, 13, 6-7. [4] Pol., II, 24.
[5] The figure for the maritime contingents furnished by the *socii navales* is lacking. To these forces belonging to the Italic federation proper must be added the 20,000 allies from the Veneti and Cenomani.

ROMAN CITIZENS: Infantry		...	...	299,200	
,, ,, Cavalry ...	...	.·.	26,100		
	Total	...	...	...	325,300
ALLIED TROOPS: Infantry ...	...	...	360,000		
,, ,, Cavalry ...	...	...	43,000		
,, ,, Umbrians-Sarsinati	...	20,000			
	Total of Allies ...	...	423,000		
	Grand Total	...	...	748,300	

Thus the total force was made up of 43 per cent. of Roman troops and 57 per cent. of allied troops. The Romans were thus in a minority in the Italic army, a fact naturally explained by the numerical superiority of the non-citizen population, but which was nevertheless of considerable importance from the military and political standpoint.

Recruited by the local authorities, the allied contingents were led to the place of muster under a native captain, accompanied by an officer in charge of their pay. Once concentrated these troops were entirely withdrawn from the control of the city that had raised them, except in respect of the provision of their pay and the maintenance of their equipment, which remained charges upon the Italian cities. Food for men and horses was provided by Rome. Rome reserved an autonomous organization for her allies' contingents; they were not amalgamated with the Roman troops in the legions. Rome even left natives in charge of them as non-commissioned officers, but she kept the higher ranks in her own hands. The allied infantry was divided into two "wings," the right wing and the left wing (*ala dextra*, *ala sinistra*), so called because they operated on the flanks of the Roman army; the strength of each was ten cohorts of about four hundred men each. The cavalry was divided into six "wings," subdivided into squadrons or *turmæ*.

The cohort was commanded by a cohort-prefect, the *turma* by a decurion, both native officers. The higher officers in command of *alæ* of infantry and cavalry, the prefects of the allies, belonged to Roman cadres. Under such circumstances no hope of promotion was held out to the native subalterns. The Italian cities had no control over their troops, and, since they paid them, they bore all the burdens of military service without any of its compensations. Their situation was aggravated later. The allies were, for the most part, sturdy mountaineers, and from the military point of view were worth as much as the Roman troops themselves. They fought in Roman style, and fought well, but that did not prevent Rome from treating them as inferiors. The division of the booty is a good instance. The allies, as a rule, received less than the Roman citizens.

At the time of the triumph of C. Claudius Pulcher over the Ligures in 177 B.C.,[1] every soldier who had taken part in the campaign received a gratuity; each Roman soldier was given fifteen denarii, and each of the allies only half as much. And so, Livy tells us, the latter followed the triumphal car in silence to display their discontent. In 173 allotments were made from the Gaulish and Ligurian lands; ten *jugera* per head were given to the Romans, only three to the Latin allies.[2] In the face of such facts one conclusion is inevitable: military service was harder for the allies than for the Romans; for on the campaign the commander did not spare them. And as an aggravation they had no substantial compensation either immediately or in the future; for they received only a limited share in distributions of booty and allotments of land, and the political and economic profits to be derived from the war were practically monopolized by Romans alone.

Finally, Rome demanded from the Italians money. Italy paid both direct and indirect taxes.

In the case of direct taxation, as of military service, the difference between citizens and non-citizens, between the inhabitants of annexed territory and allied cities or peoples of all kinds, was fundamental. The Roman citizen of whatever class, be he *optimo jure* or *sine suffragio*, paid a direct tax in the form of the *tributum*, a comprehensive impost upon capital, to which the whole fortune of each head of a household was liable. For many centuries only real wealth, represented by landed estates in the town and country, rural domains (with or without buildings), buildings in the city (houses and premises used for habitation or trade), and the appurtenances of such property (slaves, horses, cattle, asses, or mules), was recognized at Rome. And so originally it alone was taken into account in assessing the capital tax.

[1] Livy, XLI, 13, 7-8. [2] Livy, XLII, 4, 4.

Later on the great events which marked the first centuries of the Republic, the conquest of Central Italy, followed by the creation of Italian unity, the development of trade and industry, and the growing importance of money, resulted in the birth of a new factor in wealth—personal property. It was natural that the treasury should come to pay attention to this form of wealth, and to take advantage thereof in balancing its budget. In 312 B.C. the censor Appius Claudius used it for the first time for the statistics of the census as well as for the assessment of the *tributum*.[1] Thereafter direct taxation was levied not only on real property as in the past, but also on the whole personal estate of the taxpayer—cash, bullion, chattels, and jewellery.

To be a member of the classes, to serve in the army and to pay the capital tax were synonymous terms. Hence arose two exemptions from taxation, founded on age and on wealth respectively. Minors, fatherless orphans (*orbi*), widows (*viduæ*), and wards (*pupillæ*), who, by definition, did not figure in the census lists, were exempt from paying the *tributum*, but all four paid an equivalent in the shape of a special tax, the *æs hordearium*, earmarked for the maintenance of the cavalry horses. This impost, according to our authorities, had been established by Tarquin the Elder and retained in the system of Servius Tullius. Temporarily remitted by Valerius Publicola after the expulsion of the kings, the duty was reimposed by Camillus during his censorship, and continued to be exacted thereafter. The second exemption applied to poor persons whose rateable estate did not reach the minimum legal figure for the census, that of the fifth class—eleven thousand or twelve thousand five hundred *as*. The State, being anxious to swell the roll both of taxpayers and soldiers, was soon obliged to lower the limit. It was reduced to four thousand *as* by the middle of the second century B.C., and perhaps to fifteen hundred *as* only later on.

The capital tax at Rome was neither permanent nor regular. Its purpose was essentially military; it was only imposed in special circumstances and for a specifically defined object. When it chanced that there was neither a war in progress nor an army to maintain, or when the State com-

---

[1] K. J. Neumann, in **XXIV**, 396; **II**, 109 *ff*.

manded adequate funds derived from other sources, the tax was not levied. It even happened in exceptionally lucky years that the treasury reimbursed taxpayers for the total of their contributions; that happened, for instance, in 503[1] and in 187 B.C.[2] Nevertheless, this contingent reimbursement always remained an act of grace on the part of the State, and never became a right of the taxpayer. It would be wrong to infer, as some have done, that the capital levy at Rome was just a sort of forced loan. As an extraordinary impost the raising of the capital levy required the direct interposition of the public authorities, represented in this case not by the assembly of the people as at Athens, but by the consuls and the Senate. It was for the consuls to take the initiative, the Senate merely decided as to the necessity for the levy and the total to be raised.

The official census lists revealed as exactly as possible the total wealth of the taxpayers. At the same time the Senate knew the amount which was indispensable. It thus fixed the rate of the tax to be payed by each person liable; the normal rate was one-tenth per cent. (*tributum simplex*), but it might rise to two or three-tenths (*tributum duplex* or *triplex*) if the financial needs of the year were particularly heavy. The impost was assessed on a strictly proportional principle. Each payed in proportion to his wealth, save that in practice a progressive rate intruded exceptionally and indirectly.

The assessment was based upon a declaration by the taxpayer. The declaration was made by the head of the household every five years in the presence of the censors under conditions of quite exceptional solemnity. The obligation to make the declaration extended to all Roman citizens possessed of real or personal property, and had to be fulfilled in person by the head of the family unless he could offer an excuse accepted as legitimate. Absentees who had not been excused and could offer no valid excuse (*incensi*) incurred the rigours of the law. The supreme control of all matters relating to the declaration was vested in the censors. They were not limited to merely receiving passively the declarations of the taxpayers, but might intervene actively, and did not fail to exercise their rights. In cases of doubt they cross-

---

[1] Dion., V, 47.
[2] Livy, XXXIV, 7, 4; **XIV**, X, p. 210, note 2.

examined the declarers, encouraged informers by the offer of rewards, and ordered any enquiries they judged needful. Other factors, such as celibacy, considerations of morality, or the like, might induce the censors to impose a supplementary tax. Finally, they had the option of increasing the rate of taxation upon certain articles, a procedure which resulted in a relatively substantial progression in the rate of taxation. The *tributum* was collected by tribes; it was the business not of State officials, but of notables taken from the ranks of citizens of the second census class, the tribunes of the treasury (*tribuni ærarii*) perhaps elected by each tribe and responsible for all receipts upon security of their personal estates. They paid all sums received to the magistrates charged with the administration of the treasury, the quæstors.

Italians who were not citizens were not liable to the capital tax, but they paid an equivalent in specie and in kind. Of course, only the impost due to Rome is here considered, apart from the local contributions which they paid to the treasury of their city, and with which Rome could not interfere. Specie payments took the form of the dues paid by cities which held a portion of the Roman public domain (*ager publicus*). By right of conquest Rome habitually confiscated part of the lands of a vanquished city; it became domain land, belonging to Rome in full right of ownership. Now Rome might lease out these lands, and often did so either to communities of citizens, Roman colonies or *municipia*, or to allied cities, and peoples in return for the payment of a regular rent (*vectigal*). Dues in kind assumed the form of imposts; for instance, Italians were obliged to entertain and defray all the expenses of Roman magistrates on circuit in Italy. This was a heavy burden, which was often aggravated by its beneficiaries' requirements and misuse of power.

On the other hand, all Italians, citizens, and non-citizens alike, were subject to the same indirect tax, the customs-duties (*portoria*). There had been a tariffs at Rome in the regal period, and Livy reports that the Senate freed the Roman people from all customs and all tribute at the time of Porsenna's invasion.[1] We also know that there were

---

[1] Livy, II, 9, 6.

customs-houses in Campania, at Puteoli and Capua[1] in 199
B.C. The system of tariffs was later completed; the censors
of 179[2] and the Gracchi created new ones. The tariff barriers
were naturally extended step by step with the advance of
conquest. When Italy was at length unified, the cordon of
customs-houses placed at the frontiers of the Roman State,
which had been steadily advanced at the same time as the
State itself grew, had been carried to the very borders of
the peninsula.

V

What Rome gave Italy

If Rome created Italian unity by blood and iron, if she
permanently imposed upon the peninsula heavy burdens, loss
of national liberties, military obligations, and financial contributions, these sacrifices were nevertheless not left unrequited. At the beginning of the third century B.C., the
unification of peninsular Italy was barely finished, and
naturally the benefits of Roman rule were only just beginning to become apparent. But they were soon made
manifest, and largely explain the loyalty of the Italian
federation at the two great crises of Roman history in the
third century, the war with Pyrrhus and later that against
Hannibal.

Rome's gift to Italy was in the first place the *pax
Romana*. As long as she could remember, Italy had known
nothing but war. The normal state of the peninsula before
the advent of Roman supremacy had been one of wars with
foreigners, wars between neighbours and civil wars in the
heart of the cities and peoples. The part played by war
with foreigners is sufficiently illustrated by the long series
of invasions by Italici, Veneti, Iapyges, Etruscans, Greeks,
and Gauls, which had followed one another from the dawn
of Italy's history, not to mention the long ages of the prehistoric period. This era was now over. The unification of
Italy had put an end to it. No doubt there were to be other
invaders—the Gauls and Hannibal—but the former did not
pass Etruria, and the second effected no permanent modifica-
tion in the political organization or the ethnographic map

[1] Livy, XXXII, 7, 3.   [2] Livy, XL, 51, 8.

of peninsular Italy. The closing of the gates to the barbarians abroad and the protection of her coasts from pirates by a line of Roman colonies were the first benefits conferred by the peace of Rome.

Internecine war had formerly raged. The limits of the city were narrow. Two neighbouring cities might belong to the same race, worship the same deities, and speak the same language; they none the less formed two States, mutually foreign and often hostile. In primitive Italy stranger and enemy, *hostis* and *peregrinus*, were synonymous terms in the testimony of Cicero[1] and Varro.[2] The chronic division of Italy, favoured by the general geography and the mountainous configuration of the soil, only disappeared very late. Rome put an end to it by the creation of Italian unity.

Finally, civil wars had everywhere been common. Factional conflicts raged among the ranks of the peoples and within the walls of the cities; aristocrats and democrats were at each others' throats. Rome did away with this perpetual state of crisis by making order reign and establishing everywhere a moderate aristocratic government. Her activity as peacemaker had been made manifest early; when Volsinii[3] and Arretium[4] had been given over to social revolution and communism, Rome had intervened to re-establish peace. All over Italy the Roman soldier acted as policeman—a rough one, doubtless, but beneficent; the peoples themselves desired and demanded his presence. Italian unity under the leadership of Rome therefore represented a guarantee of order and stability, an insurance against invasion from without or revolution within. It is not, therefore, surprising that once she had experienced its benefits, the peninsula resolutely refused to abandon that unity to go back to a revival of her immemorial local jealousies.

Secondly, by her enlightened policy, Rome had contrived to give the whole of Italy an interest in maintaining Italian unity. The Italic federation, as we have seen, was in no sense a league of the Italians among themselves. The Roman

---

[1] Cic., *de Off.*, I, 12, 37.   [2] Var., *de Ling. Lat.*, V, 3.

[3] Livy, *Per.*, XVI; Val. Max., IX, 1, 2; Flor., I, 21; Oros., IV, 5, 3; Zon., VIII, 7; *Fast. tr.*, under year 264.

[4] Livy, X, 5, 13.

State, which had treated individually with each people and city, took the supreme and exclusive control of it; outside it there was only a medley of isolated and impotent cities. An Italian of Tarentum, for instance, voted, married, and held property in virtue of the Tarentine laws just as legally as a Roman citizen under Roman laws, but his political and civil rights remained purely local. He was neither an elector nor eligible for office in any other city than his own; his marriage was only legally valid if he contracted it in the city of which he was a citizen, where he was domiciled and in acordance with the laws proper to his tiny fatherland. In the eyes of the law he could only hold property, sell, or buy within his own city's territory, otherwise possession, purchase, or sale would be void. This traditional legal division, which interposed impassable barriers between the cities, had been carefully maintained by Rome, and at times even exaggerated in the interests of her own rule.

But such a policy involved one great danger. There was a risk lest, if it had taken an absolute form, equality in impotence might inspire a unanimity of anger and hatred against Rome. After the conquests the number of Italians in the federation exceeded that of their conquerors. To leave a minority of citizens face to face with an overwhelming majority of non-citizens, deprived in the eyes of the conquerors of all political and civil rights, would have been a blunder that might have proved fatal. The Roman Government had the wisdom to see this, and to take the necessary steps to eliminate the danger. At the top of the ladder were Roman citizens in enjoyment of all the rights implied in that status, at the bottom the mass of Italian non-citizens. Without obliterating this fundamental distinction, the very basis of the system of the ancient city, Rome's own interests, clearly perceived, required that the distinction should be softened down through the creation of a series of intermediate grades so as to undermine the unanimity of Italian claims. Among the Italians who were and remained outside the citizen body, some were better treated than the rest in virtue of their *fœdus*, and the Latins, the *socii Latini nominis*, obtained a privileged place within the federation. A considerable number of other Italians received the citizenship without the political rights, the *civitas sine suffragio*.

Finally, full citizenship rewarded the privileged ones at the top of the ladder.

Such differences of treatment by fostering mutual jealousies among the Italians consolidated the dominant position of Rome. They offered a further advantage; such hopes dangled before the eyes of non-citizens reconciled them to their new status and bound them to the cause of unity. The status of Roman citizen conferred a host of advantages on its possessor. An Italian, apart from Latins and probably also, as far as *commercium* is concerned, natives of a certain number of legally privileged cities, was in the eyes of the law confined to his own town; a Roman citizen enjoyed his political and civil rights throughout the Roman State. If he desired to marry, to buy, to sell, or to trade, the Roman law protected him everywhere. The rights of citizenship, therefore, represented to an Italian both the amelioration of his lot through the guarantee of Roman law and the sole available way of escape from that chronic isolation which was so disastrous for him.

That was not all. In addition to the collective advantages which might appeal to the mass of the Italians, the contingent advantages peculiar to the several classes in the population must be taken into account. In Italy, as in Rome, there were rich and poor; each of these classes in society saw different benefits to be attained through the acquisition of Roman citizenship: the rich, who were ambitious and galled by their inferior legal status, were tempted primarily by the political rights, eligibility to magistracies, and promotion to higher ranks in the army; the poor were enticed by the alleviation of the burdens of military service, admission to an equal share in the booty, and participation in the foundation of colonies and in public largesses. Rome knew all this, and so she had determined to open the way to this salutary advancement. But, according to her wont, she opened it cautiously, and carefully arranged a series of intermediate stages. The whole of the population of the annexed territories had received the right of half-citizenship with the possibility of rising to the higher rank of full citizenship when they had proved their claims. All the peoples of Italy might thus hope, in the long run, to attain the citizenship. This bait, which Rome dangled before the eyes of the vanquished, represented one of the constituent moments—and not the least weighty—in the first unity of Italy.

Finally, Rome gave unified Italy the economic machinery she had hitherto lacked, save in a few rare cases, such as in Etruria or among the Southern Greeks. We see the Roman roads[1] then appearing, those railways of the ancient world: the Via Appia was constructed from Rome to Capua by Appius Claudius during his censorship (312), and prolonged from Capua to Brundisium; the Via Latina duplicated the foregoing in its northern section; the Viæ Salaria and Flaminia and Clodia and Aurelia at the end of the fourth and the beginning of the third century were the first of those arteries of a network which, continued till the end of the Republic, did not reach its final form till the days of the Empire.

In addition to the Roman roads we must mention works of public utility—the construction of drains, aqueducts and bridges, the regularization of rivers, the deepening of harbours, to say nothing of the perfecting of agriculture and the development of trade. In all these benefits conferred by Rome the new Italy found increasing satisfaction for her material needs.

In creating Italian unity, Rome had struck out quite a new line. This composite league, a motley aggregate, wherein half-a-dozen races jostled one another and as many languages were current, was unprecedented and not destined to be paralleled in the ancient world. Doubtless this edifice still manifested imperfections and gaps at the beginning of the third century—only the contrary would be surprising; the usual work of time was still needed. But already Italian unity stood forth, solid and cemented by a master's hand both politically and militarily. Community in the Carthaginian danger and the economic advantages which Rome took care to reserve for the Italians in the exploitation of the world ultimately made its constituents forget their parochial past and, by tightening up the bonds which united them to the Roman State, rendered the work indestructible. After undergoing unification Italy resigned herself to accept it and then, convinced by the advantages she found in it, ended by willing it. But one fact already stood out. With

---

[1] V. Chapot, in **IV**, *s.v.* " Viæ," 793-98.

her 47,200 square miles and 750,000 men capable of bearing arms, the Italic federation, forged in the rough school of the wars of independence, represented the most formidable military power in the whole Mediterranean basin. She only lacked consciousness of her power and the will to use it. The Punic Wars already brewing would give her both.

BOOK III
THE BIRTH OF ROMAN IMPERIALISM

CHAPTER I
FROM ITALIAN UNITY TO THE MEDITERRANEAN PROGRAMME

I

THE CONSEQUENCES OF UNITY

By virtue of her natural configuration and her geographical position, a unified Italy was inevitably confronted with three vital problems—those of the Tyrrhenian Sea, of the Adriatic Sea, and of the Continent. Contemporary Italy has been experiencing them for half a century. The case of Rome on the morrow of the first unification of Italy recorded in history was identical.

Owing to its relatively modest size and the succession of islands—the Tuscan Archipelago on the north, Corsica and Sardinia on the west, and Sicily on the south—which frame

Bibliography.—Texts: Texts are rare (compare the bibliographies to Chapters II and III). It may be well to note in particular: for the whole question, Livy, Books XXI-XLV, and Polybius, Books, I-V (intact) and VI-XL (fragmentary); for the East, in addition to these two main authorities, Appian, *Syriaca*, 1-47, 66-67; for Spain, Appian, *Iberica*, 3-62; for Africa, Appian, *Lybica*, 1-135, and all the international treaties by which Rome attained her supremacy in the Mediterranean—treaty with Carthage in 241, Pol., I, 62; III, 27; App., *Sic.*, 2; treaty with Carthage in 201, Pol., XV, 18; Livy, XXX, 37; App., *Lib.*, 54; treaty with Macedonia in 196, Pol., XVIII, 44; Livy, XXXIII, 30; treaty with Ætolia in 189, Pol., XXI, 30, 1-5, 32; Livy, XXXVIII, 9-10; treaty with Antiochus III in 188, Pol., XXI, 17, 43; Livy, XXXVIII, 38; App., *Syr.*, 38-39; treaty with the Jews in 161, I, *Macc.*, 8, 23-30.

Inscriptions.—Treaty with Cibyra shortly after 188 (Ditt., I.O., II, 792).

Principal Works.—**CCI**; **CXXXI**, 128-242; **XXVI**, III-IV. Instruments of Imperialism: (*a*) Diplomacy and Treaties, **XXVI**, IV. 519-23; **CCXXVI**, I; **CCXXXV**, II, 465-515; (*b*) Army, **XIV**, XI, 22-137; **CXXIV**, I, 409-32; (*c*) Finance, **XIV**, X, 190-258, 311-34, 340 *ff.*; **CLVI**, 161 *ff.*

it, the Tyrrhenian Sea forms one of the best defined secondary seas in the world. In the whole western basin of the Mediterranean it has its separate life and its peculiar function. That was even more true in antiquity than to-day; the natural protection against the great storms of the deep ensured by the broad ridge of the two great western islands, the habits of coasting dear to ancient navigation, and the great trade routes which intersected in it conferred upon it a first-class importance both politically and economically. For centuries Etruscans, Greeks, Phœnicians, and Carthaginians had been fighting over the straits and passes which command the approaches to it. Now unified Italy, a new factor in the Tyrrhenian cock-pit, also claimed her say. Blocked by Carthage, who mounted guard like a vigilant sentinel over the shores of Corsica, Sardinia, and Sicily, Italy wanted breathing space, wanted to break the island circle which was choking her, and to win freedom of communications with the open sea by dismissing her gaolers.

The second problem confronting unified Italy, that of the Adriatic, was conditioned by three essential elements all specifically geographical in nature. In the first place, the narrowness of the Adriatic is such that its two coasts share in common their vicissitudes, and intercourse between them, whether peaceful or hostile, is peculiarly easy. The second feature, which is still more important, is that the characters of the Italian and Balkan coasts are extraordinarily different. The Italian coast, lacking the semicircle of islands which forms a protecting girdle off the Tyrrhenian seaboard and without good natural harbours, is exposed defenceless to every threat from the east. On the contrary, the Balkan shore, rocky and deeply indented with its medley of islands and its labyrinth of channels, possesses an exceptional importance both politically and economically. Strabo, the great geographer of the Augustan Age, had already noted the fact with his accustomed acumen and exactitude:[1]

> "The whole coast of Illyria, mainland and adjacent islands alike, abounds in excellent harbours, and in this respect is in striking contrast to the Italian shore opposite which is totally lacking in such."

---

[1] Str., VII, 5, 10 (p. 317 C).

Lastly, the Adriatic is characterized by being virtually a closed sea. The channel connecting it with the rest of the Mediterranean, the Straits of Otranto, is only twenty-six miles wide. Hence freedom of passage lies absolutely within the discretion of the coastal powers, and unified Italy was predestined by an inevitable necessity to place the question in the forefront of her agenda of vital subjects as soon as she resolved to make herself at home on the Adriatic.

The continental problem may be summed up in a word. The domain of the Italian federation did not extend beyond the line of the Apennines on the north. Only the acquisition of the Alpine frontier could allow Italy to achieve her unity finally and completely.

The solution of these three problems was, we repeat, forced upon ancient Italy, but she could not hope to tackle all simultaneously. Which would she take in hand first once her unity had been cemented by the defeat of Pyrrhus? To our modern eyes it looks as if the continental problem was so urgent that it ought to have been accorded priority. But let us not be misled by the theory of natural frontiers so dear to us. It was quite a long time before the Romans came to regard the Alps as the necessary geographical boundary of Italy, and they never assigned a more than relative value to that conception. It must not be forgotten that the Alpine regions were conquered only under Augustus, and that even in the days of the Empire the whole Italian slope of the Alps was not included in Italy for administrative purposes. Moreover, the great danger of Celtic invasions had ceased since the middle of the fourth century. The Gauls had settled down in Gallia Cisalpina, and these incorrigible nomads, checked by Rome and allured by the incomparable wealth of the country which they owed to conquest, were no longer dreaming of fresh adventures—at least, for the moment. Rome's wisdom in dealing with them and the respect she showed their chiefs had caused ancestral hostility to give place to neighbourly relations equally beneficial to both parties. Provisionally, at least, the Senate asked for nothing better. Besides, the conquest of Gallia Cisalpina looked a very serious affair, on which one would only wish to embark after careful preparation and at a favourable moment. There was no hurry in this direction; the continental question could wait. We shall see the seemingly paradoxical spectacle of the legions landing on Illyrian isles and fighting on the soil of Africa before crossing the Po and entering Milan.

The question of the Adriatic, too, did not arise in a pressing form on the eve of the Punic Wars. The two Balkan powers most concerned in an ultimate settlement, Epirus and Macedonia, were for the moment out of court. Rome's good fortune had decreed that on this side she should have no serious complications to fear—at least, temporarily. On the death of Pyrrhus the Greater Epirus, of which he had dreamed and which he had partially realized at the point of the sword, passed out of the sphere of practical politics. His son and successor, Alexander II, was glad enough to save his ancestral patrimony without reviving his father's pretensions in the basin of the Ionian Sea. In the direction of Macedonia the situation was rather different. Antigonus Gonatas, the founder of a new dynasty, planned to raise Macedonia out of the mire of decadence and aspired to reconstitute her former power in the Adriatic as elsewhere. But this work of national resurrection, which must take many years, was only just beginning. For Roman policy, the results of the final eclipse of Epirus and the temporary effacement of Macedonia were the same; no danger threatened in the direction of the Adriatic, and here, too, Rome could wait.

The Tyrrhenian problem was left. Now, Rome had grown up in an essentially Tyrrhenian atmosphere, and consequently this question touched her much more closely than the others. Moreover, the steady advance of Carthage constituted a peril which was no longer problematical nor even remote, but permanent and immediate, for unified Italy. By the time of the expedition of Pyrrhus, Carthage's offensive in the Tyrrhenian Sea was in full swing. At the beginning of the third century B.C. that is the essential fact to bear in mind. About 280 she occupied Lipara in the Æolian Islands, an invaluable observation post at the entry to the Strait of Messina on the very approaches to the peninsula, and at the same period there was a momentary danger of her establishment at Rhegium. "What a fine battle-field we are leaving to the Romans and the Carthaginians," Pyrrhus is alleged to have said on leaving Sicily. This historic phrase has doubtless no more value than the majority of such epigrams. None the less, it gives expression to an indisputable truth of tremendous import.

Syracuse no longer counted. Carthage not only recovered her lost ground, but she was ceaselessly advancing while Rome, for her part, was completing the conquest of South Italy. In the years following Pyrrhus' death causes of friction were multiplied and relations between the two States became strained. We have already referred to the suspicious part played by Carthage at the time of the siege and capture of Tarentum in 272 B.C. Two years later Rome recovered Rhegium from the mutinous Campanian mercenaries and thus permanently secured a frontage opposite Sicily and the control of the Strait of Messina, one of the great ways of communication between the eastern and western basins of the Mediterranean. Carthage, who had been unable at the last moment to prevent the unification of peninsular Italy to the advantage of the Roman State, intended at least to bar Rome's access to Sicily, the key to the Carthaginian colonial empire. The destined hour of conflict approached; the affair of the Mamertines was to give the signal for it.

During the period of anarchy which followed upon the death of Agathocles, his Campanian mercenaries, the Mamertines, had seized Messana, which they made their arsenal and lair. Syracuse had taken the field against these inconvenient neighbours, and her general, Hiero, had won a victory over them near the River Longanos (not far from Milazzo). He had taken advantage of this success to make himself tyrant. Rome, always a realist in her policy, did not hesitate to recognize the new sovereign as a friend and ally. The first intervention by Rome in the affairs of Sicily was, as may well be imagined, very disagreeable to Carthage, and she was not to forget it. Meanwhile, Hiero had resolved to make an end of the Mamertines, and had commenced the siege of Messana, while the Carthaginian general, Hannibal, on his side, had managed to introduce his soldiers into the town's citadel. Rome and Carthage thenceforth stood armed and face to face on the opposite shores of the strait. At this moment, when only a spark was needed to kindle the conflict, the Mamertines appealed to Rome as the guardian of Italian interests and solicited her intervention. From this step the Punic Wars arose.

The Tyrrhenian question which provoked the terrible duel between Rome and Carthage, and for the first time drew Italy outside the frame of the peninsula, was in essence a struggle for Sicily. But soon the problem came to assume much vaster proportions through the extension and multiplication of theatres of war; Corsica, Sardinia, and Africa during the First Punic War, and Gallia Cisalpina, Southern Gaul, and Spain during the Second, were included one after the other within the zone of operations. The war for the Tyrrhenian Sea gave place to a war for the Mediterranean. At least, when Carthage was vanquished and made peace in 201, the question was definitely settled; Rome had won the supremacy in the whole western basin of the Mediterranean. But the Punic War had had other consequences too. Romans and Carthaginians had been fighting in Gallia Cisalpina and in Spain; in Africa, Massinissa, as an ally of Rome, had co-operated in the decisive operations against Carthage. Roman policy, which had been strictly Italian before the Punic Wars, has now overstepped its original limits. The issues before it are no longer just Sicily, Sardinia, or Corsica; the questions which engage Roman statesmen throughout the first half of the second century B.C. are labelled Africa, Spain, and Gaul. The Italian horizon, immeasurably enlarged by victory, merges in the Mediterranean horizon on the west.

The same process, with the same results, transformed the Adriatic problem. At the beginning of the third century B.C. Rome approached the question without any predetermined plan, but with that keen appreciation of realities—at least, immediate realities—which she always displayed in dealing with matters of State. One hard fact immediately caught her attention; she found herself as an Adriatic power caught up in the mechanism of her own conquest. The Straits of Otranto, that indispensable way of communication between the two Italian seas that unification had made Roman, was in the hands of Hellenism; on the east, Pyrrhus, King of Epirus, who was also master of Southern Illyria and the Island of Corcyra; and on the west, Tarentum, the Greek metropolis in South Italy, held the keys to the passage. The problem of the Adriatic, therefore, presented itself to Rome first in a purely defensive form; freedom of passage and the necessary guarantees to ensure that were the first aims of Roman policy. Only later, when this original end had been attained and this necessity met, did Rome aim higher and farther. Her claims rose in proportion to her success, and the defensive programme of the first years gave place to a more ambitious plan of domination and supremacy. By the conquest of South Italy and the systematic occupation of the seaboard during the first third of the third century, Rome accomplished her designs on the Adriatic and effectively ensured freedom of the passage. But by this time, as happens so often in politics, yesterday's programme no longer corresponds to the realities of to-day and still less to the needs of the morrow. Half a century had passed since the Roman legionaries had first set foot on the coast of the eastern sea. Young Italy, unified by Rome's will and banded together under her sway, awoke to consciousness of her destinies and saw hitherto unsuspected vistas opening up before her on the Adriatic as elsewhere.

In the second half of the third century B.C. Italy, with Rome as her mouthpiece, for the first time faced the problem of the Adriatic squarely. In what spirit did she approach it? What solution did she propose? The solution is written on the map itself. The leaders of Roman policy in quest of a plan of action had only to decipher it, and they found the surest and quickest road to a solution just because geography herself had dictated its terms as sovereign. Italian supremacy in the Adriatic, the new object in view, obviously required two bases for stability: these were mastery of the Straits of Otranto and dominion over the Dalmatian coast. The surest, indeed the sole, way to the realization of this programme was to gain a permanent foothold on the Balkan shore and to establish there solid outposts to be Italy's rampart against Hellenism and the best guarantee for the maintenance of her recent unity. Local resistance in this region of Illyrian tribes was hardly to be expected, the main difficulty was—or, rather, might have been—international complications. But the only two Balkan powers directly affected by the question, Epirus and Macedonia, were, as we saw, out of court for ever or temporarily. And so locally no insurmountable obstacles were to be feared, while internationally Rome might expect freedom of action, at least temporarily. These considerations weighted the scales in favour of the enterprise. The aim Rome set herself was attained in the two Illyrian campaigns of 229 and 219.

The international consequences of this new situation were soon manifest. Down to the Second Punic War the two basins of the Mediterranean had led separate lives, though this view must not be exaggerated.

> "Hitherto," writes Polybius,[1] "the several events happening in the world had not been interrelated; no enterprise was planned, no project executed save for reasons peculiar to it. An action only affected the country where it was done. But after this epoch all affairs become, as it were, members one of another, those of Italy and Africa are confused with those of Asia or Greece and all converge upon the same end."

Rome had as yet only occasional relations with the East, it was the Adriatic problem which established direct and increasingly permanent contact between the eastern and the western basins of the Mediterranean. From the day when Rome first set foot on the Illyrian coast she was confronted by an Eastern question. Exactly what form did it assume in the eyes of Roman statesmen?

It meant, firstly, the establishment of increasingly constant relations with the several States of the Hellenistic world. Let us listen to the words of Polybius:[2]

> "At this conference (the conference of Naupactus in 217) the affairs of Greece were for the first time envisaged as linked to those of Italy and Africa. Henceforth Philip and the chiefs of Greece, who made war and peace amongst themselves, no longer were guided in their conduct by what happened in Greece, but all turned their eyes and their thoughts towards Italy. This change in policy rapidly spread to the islands and Asia. Philip's enemies and some of the opponents of Attalus no longer turned to Antiochus or Ptolemy in the south or east; they looked to the west and sent their ambassadors to Rome or to Carthage. The Romans in their turn sent embassies to the Greeks; for Philip's audacity alarmed them, and they feared to see him taking advantage of the embarrassments which encompassed them."

The political system of the East since the death of Alexander had been dominated by the friendly or hostile

[1] Pol., I, 3, 3-5.   [2] Pol., V, 105, 4-8.

relations of the three great Hellenistic monarchies sprung from the dismemberment of his empire—Macedonia, the realm of the Seleucids, and the kingdom of Lagids. From the Second Punic War Rome was to find herself gradually entangled in the affairs of the Eastern Mediterranean, until nothing could happen in the Orient without her claiming first to have her say and in the end to have the controlling voice.

Secondly, in its more concrete form the eastern question meant a conflict with the great Balkan monarchy of Macedonia. The Treaty of Naupactus in 217 B.C., by putting an end to the Social War had restored to Macedonia full freedom of action. Philip took advantage of it to raise anew the banner of national rights and to reclaim in the name of his country that frontage on the Adriatic that had been lost for a century. In 215 B.C. he allied himself with Hannibal to win a triumph for his pretensions. Roman diplomacy replied by rekindling war in Greece, and in 205 the Peace of Phœnice guaranteed to Rome the maintenance of her privileged position on the Adriatic.

Three years later Philip of Macedon and the Seleucid, Antiochus III, concluded a treaty of alliance against Ptolemy V (Ephiphanes) of Egypt, which was a regular pact for the partition of the Lagid monarchy. This caused fresh complications which led Rome little by little to the supremacy in the East. It was only a step from the question of the Adriatic to the complex problems of the Oriental world. Roman imperialism, whether willing or reluctant, did not hesitate to take the step when the moment came.

II

Defensive Policy and Preventive War

The expansion of Roman power beyond Italy from the third century B.C. and the gradual conquest of the Mediterranean basin are facts of history. But was there such a thing as Roman imperialism, and, if so, what were its underlying principles, and how ought its birth and successive stages of growth to be conceived? A throng of theorists, eager to justify the past or even to foretell it, press upon us and deafen us with their discordant clamour. Some propound a theory of deliberate conquest; Rome cold-bloodedly plans the subjugation of the world and methodically realizes her ambitious projects in the teeth of storms and tempests. Others are more sentimental and invoke philhellenism, which would reach its zenith in the proclamation of the Isthmian Games and find its natural corollaries in the war with Antiochus and the Roman intervention in Asia Minor. Others advocate a theory of defensive imperialism; Rome only attacked in self-defence, and it was in spite of herself that she ended by extending her sway over the whole Mediterranean world. Such is the theory, let us examine the main arguments adduced in support of it.

Rome, threatened by neighbouring peoples like the Etruscans, Volscii, and Sabellians, had to subdue them in order to secure peace in Latium. Menaced by invasions of Celts she was forced to assume the leadership of the Italians to ward off the invader, and the conquest of Gaul by Julius Cæsar was itself only the last episode in this long war. The war with Pyrrhus would be defensive and necessary to the achievement of Italian unity. The war with the Semites of Africa would again be defensive; for they represented a first way of Mohammedanism before Mohammed, and their religious fanaticism and mercantile cupidity threatened to overwhelm Italy, and all Europe after her. So, too, with the war against the pirates of Illyria, which was indispensable to secure freedom of trade and the safety of the Adriatic coasts. The war with Hannibal was defensive as a war for territorial integrity and national independence. Similarly with the wars in Spain and Greece, the natural corollaries of the Punic Wars, and attributable, like the latter, to Carthaginian imperialism. Finally, the wars in the East would be defensive, for they resulted from the aggressive policy of Philip and Antiochus, and were acts of self-preservation forced upon unified Italy. No doubt there was a Roman imperialism—it would be thankless to deny it—but at least in its intentions this imperialism had always remained strictly defensive.

Then we are offered a theory of Machiavellianism; for the attainment of her programme Rome displayed a diplomatic astuteness and a political foresight such as mankind has never known before or since. Again, there is the theory of contingence; Roman policy was passive and always followed events; Roman conquest was the result of pure chance explicable by the mere interplay of circumstances; and, in a word, everything in the world conspired to further Roman greatness save the Romans themselves. The list might be continued by the theory of militarist imperialism, the theory of economic imperialism, and a host of others.[1]

To orientate ourselves in this maze of theories, as many as varied, it may be helpful to lay down a few primary truths as stepping-stones. Consider first the geographical factor. Through her situation in the centre of the Mediterranean basin, with her double coastal frontage on the Tyrrhenian and Adriatic Seas facing west and east, Italy seemed destined by Nature herself to play a dominant part in the history of the Mediterranean. Though this is an indisputable fact, it must not be exaggerated. It was merely a promising possibility which the human factor might or might not transform into a reality. The human factor was in this case, firstly, general circumstances, and, secondly, the temperament of the people fated to exploit these. Rome appeared at her predestined hour between the Oriental world already on the steep slope to decadence and the Western world still sunk in barbarism. The first of all the great Mediterranean countries to transcend the limits of the City-State, Rome had been able to create in a stable form a national unity of a larger type. The Balkan unity, momentarily established by Macedonia, had preceded that of Italy by more than a century in the form of the League of Corinth (338-37), but it had remained incomplete, and, worse still, it had not lasted despite all subsequent attempts at its resurrection. Through this accident, the field was left open to Rome and Italy. As for the Roman people themselves they will remain what we have found them in the hour of the conquest of Italy. Let us not picture the Roman as a stupid boor nor as a superman. His character was dominated by two traits—practical common-sense and lack of imagination. The Roman had no subtle and far-reaching programme of foreign policy. When he was thinking of the future, he did not look beyond the

[1] On these several theories, see especially **CXIV**, 97-172; **CXXXI**, 139-89; **CCI**, 63-75; **CLIII**, 306-34; **XXVI**, IV, 25-27.

morrow. He did not care to burden his mind with a mass of possibilities the majority of which would never become realities. As a practical man he did not bother about sentiment. His policy was governed by his interests and was realistic, aiming at specific ends near at hand. In these circumstances it is natural that foreign policy appeared primarily as a series of defensive problems.

In 264 B.C. Rome intervened in Sicily and thus gave the signal for the Punic Wars; she did so under the impression of a danger from Carthage:

> "The Romans," says Polybius,[1] "beheld the Carthaginians already masters of Africa, of a great part of Spain, and of all the islands washed by the Tyrrhenian and Sardinian Seas. If the same people seized Sicily it was to be feared that they would be extremely inconvenient and formidable neighbours who were encircling Rome and threatening all the coasts of Italy. Now, it was obvious that they would quickly subdue Sicily unless help were given to the Mamertines; for with Messana in their hands they would not take long to capture Syracuse, their sway being already established in almost the whole of Sicily. That is what was foreseen at Rome when it was found necessary not to abandon Messana nor to allow the Carthaginians to use it as a bridge for reaching Italy."

The memory of the great Syracusan tyrants and their policy of active interference in the affairs of the peninsula was too vivid at Rome for men to remain blind to a similar menace. It was just the same in 201 B.C., when the Senate embarked upon the second war with Macedonia, which drew Rome on step by step to the conquest of the whole East. After the first defeat of Carthage and the satisfactory settlement of the Tyrrhenian question, it was generally believed at Rome that Italy was henceforth inviolable, and this feeling soon became a dogma. Hannibal's invasion came as a rude shock and had brusquely opened men's eyes. Hence, peculiarly quick as the Romans were to profit by the lessons of experience, the possibility of a similar danger, coming this time from the east and originating in Macedonia, had soon alarmed public opinion. The Senate, with its coolness and wider information, did not perhaps share these fears, but there was a real danger nearer home, and therefore more serious, which it had resolved to eliminate one day. The

---

[1] Pol., I, 10, 5-10.

Balkan peninsula was at least as populous as Italy. If united it could put as many soldiers into the field. For the sake of Italy's greatness—nay, for her very safety—it was essential to prevent at all costs the revival of that Balkan unity once created momentarily by Philip and Alexander, with new guarantees for stability and permanence. It might seem premature, but it was really prudent to intervene before Macedonia had been able to realize her designs.

The same anxiety for defence was the dominant note at the time of the war with Antiochus. Rome, who had ruined Macedonia's plans upon Greece, did not intend that a new military power should get a footing in the Balkans. To deliver Italy from such a possibility, she did not hesitate to cross over to Asia and cut the wings of the Seleucids' European ambitions by the treaty of 188. Finally, seeing herself threatened sooner or later with revenge by Macedon, she uprooted the evil by suppressing Macedon herself through the war with Perses.

In the history of all great military powers, it is certain that the interconnection of events has always played a prominent part. Every victorious campaign paves the way for another through its consequences and repercussions, and the conquering State finds herself led on to further conquests, be it only for defensive considerations. Rome was no exception to the general rule. But, at least in her case, though the theory of defensive imperialism explains much, it does not explain everything. In that long concatenation of interventions and conquests there were decisive moments when Rome had to decide and the offensive depended on her and on her alone. Three such cases deserve attention—the beginning of the Punic Wars in 264 B.C., the declaration of war upon Macedon in 200, and the final conflict with Carthage in the middle of the second century. Apart from any theories, however attractive, what was the attitude of the Roman Government in these concrete cases? If we wish to follow through all its phases the genesis of the idea of conquest at Rome some details are here necessary.

In 264 B.C., with Pyrrhus out of the way, Carthage threatened to submerge all Sicily. Syracuse was decadent and could not stop her. Carthaginian forces had been smuggled into the citadel of Messana by a trick. No doubt this advance was a threat to the young unity of Italy, and Polybius,[1] as we have seen, says so explicitly. But defensive measures might have sufficed. As for the danger of a Carthaginian invasion of Italy, if it is remembered that, after two centuries of fierce fighting, she had not succeeded in conquering the whole of Sicily, we are justified in remaining sceptical about such a possibility. In deciding to assist the Mamertines, Rome deliberately adopted an offensive policy, whatever her reasons or her pretexts. On the day when the legions crossed the Strait of Messina, Roman imperialism, whether wittingly or not, inaugurated the long series of colonial wars and launched out upon the conquest of the Mediterranean world.

In 200 B.C., a year after the treaty of peace ending the Second Punic War, the Roman Senate placed upon the agenda for the comitia the question of the declaration of war upon Macedonia.[2] It knew from experience that one day the Adriatic question would provoke a conflict between the two powers, and the alliance between the King of Macedonia, Philip V, and the Seleucid Antiochus III concluded two years previously had only aggravated her fears. From the standpoint of defence, however, there was no urgency, and Rome, behind her network of outposts in Illyria, had time for thought. Nevertheless, the Senate took the first step. Politically and militarily the moment was particularly propitious. Antiochus was detained in Asia by his conflict with Egypt, and his hands were therefore tied. On the other hand, schooled by the stern trials of the Second Punic War, the Roman army was in exceptionally good condition, such as might never recur. Throughout the eighteen years of the war with Hannibal the whole of Italy had been kept in a continual state of mobilization, and her citizen army had thus acquired the value of a professional machine. Moreover, there had always been one particularly weak point in the Roman organization—the high command suffered both from incompetence and instability. Now, thanks to the long Punic Wars, both these chronic vices had been, if not permanently eliminated, at least temporarily alleviated. The superior officers had had leisure to train themselves in the field; Scipio Africanus and Flamininus, the future victors of

[1] Pol., I, 10, 5-10.　　　　　[2] Livy, XXXI, 6, 1.

Zama and Cynoscephalæ, who were military tribunes at twenty, had served their apprenticeship to large-scale warfare on the battle-fields of Italy, and in this trial had prepared the triumphs of the future.[1] And so the Senate, fully conscious of the advantages of the moment, chose to settle the Macedonian affair on the spot and acted accordingly.

Finally, it was the same on the eve of the Third Punic War. Rome cold-bloodedly passed the sentence of death on Carthage; her decision was largely influenced by the possibility of the capture of the town by Massinissa, a grave danger for the future which Rome meant to eliminate once for all. On that day she took the initiative and the offensive was due to her, whatever motives she might invoke.

But we, too, are acquainted with this theory whereby war with your neighbour is in the long run inevitable, and which recommends forestalling him as soon as you have—or think you have—all the trumps in your hand. It is just the theory of preventive war, the pet child of all imperialisms, and we know from experience that all lovers of conquest at all times and in all places have always had a weakness for it. According to it you label preventive the war with Carthage in 264, that with Macedonia in 200, that with Perses in 171, and that with Carthage in 149. That Rome had aimed at the conquest of the world from the end of the third century is, of course, a theory due to over-simplification and merely childish, *pace* Bossuet. No doubt even on the morrow of the defeat of Carthage in 201, the Roman Government had not resolved upon a policy of conquest nor annexation. Admit that considerations of defence always occupied the first place in her deliberations : after all, it remains none the less true that a logical concatenation of events led Rome from the unification of Italy to the conception of an ever-expanding Mediterranean programme and that, with the assistance of the system of preventive war, the ultimate outcome of this programme must mean in the long run the subjugation of the whole Mediterranean world.

The Senate, the organ of Roman foreign policy invested with the powers of a veritable dictatorship since the Second Punic War, bears the main responsibility. No doubt is pos-

[1] On the function of the Second Punic War in training the officers, see Plut., *Flam.*, I, 4.

sible upon this point. The declaration of war upon Macedonia in 201 B.C. had been almost unanimously rejected by the centuries.[1]

> "The citizens," says Livy,[2] "were tired after such a long and disastrous war (the Second Punic War), and weariness of dangers and fatigue had naturally impelled them to this refusal. Moreover, the tribune of the plebs, Q. Bæbius, reviving the old practice of recriminations against the senators, accused them of stirring up war after war to prevent the people ever tasting the fruits of peace."

The Senate insisted, had the question restored to the agenda for the comitia,[3] and finally secured a favourable vote.[4] Again in 171 and 149 the Senate, and it alone, took the initiative in the rupture with Perses and then with Carthage. But the people also had its share, a very considerable share, in the responsibility for the direction of Roman foreign policy. As a rule, from the third century onwards it allied itself fully to the Senatorial policy, although less through a true appreciation of the international position as through a care for its own economic interests. A reduction of the capital tax or even its practical remission (from 167), a low cost of living through the reduction of the price of grain, distributions and largesses and fêtes, and spectacles of all kinds were the principal advantages which the populace saw in conquest. And so, apart from its quite passing fit of ill-temper in 200, the people ratified the Senate's proposals without a murmur—for instance, in 191[5] and 171[6] at the time of the declaration of war with Antiochus and with Perses. Sometimes even it exhibited greater intransigeance than the Senate itself. The First Punic War offers two good illustrations of this attitude. In 264 B.C. the Senate hesitated to accede to the appeal of the Mamertines, it deliberated long without coming to any decision.

> " But the people, ruined by the previous wars and ready to jump at any sort of opportunity for repairing its losses and at the same time swayed by the considerations of public interest and the substantial advantages which the consuls held forth to each individual, declared for the expedition. By the decision of the people

---

[1] Livy, XXXI, 6, 3.
[2] Livy, XXXI, 6, 4-5.
[3] Livy, XXXI, 6, 5-6; 7, 1 *ff*.
[4] Livy, XXXI, 8, 1-2.
[5] Livy, XXXVI, 1, 6.
[6] Livy, XLII, 30, 11.

one of the two consuls, Appius Claudius, was placed in command of a relieving army and was ordered to cross the straits to help Messana.''[1]

At the end of the war in 241 B.C., it was the people and not the Senate who rejected as unsatisfactory the provisional terms negotiated by Lutatius Catulus. A commission of ten senators dispatched at their instigation modified and aggravated the terms.[2] Imperialism crowned with victory was beginning to get a hold on the public mind.

III

MILITARIST IMPERIALISM AND ECONOMIC IMPERIALISM

The Second Punic War, the sternest trial that Rome had yet endured, marks the critical moment in the formation of Roman imperialism. After fighting for eighteen years for their very lives, Rome and Italy have ended by winning a complete victory. The power of Carthage is broken and nothing in the West can resist them. In the East, on the other hand, the great Hellenistic Oriental monarchies are still intact. The phalanx, the enigma of the moment, still retains its enormous prestige unimpaired, and in the Greek world many still believe in the dogma of its invincibility. The day of Cynoscephalæ dispelled that last illusion, not only in the eyes of the Greeks, but also of the Romans, which was more important.[3]

After her victory over Carthage and Macedon, the two first military powers in the Mediterranean, Rome knew—for a double test had taught her—that henceforth she was all-powerful through her army. From the ability to the will is a short step, and it was soon taken, since imperialism had not received her due. National intoxication and the dizziness of greatness, but also more prosaic and material considerations, as the study of the economic factor will shortly show, swept Rome along the path. Statesmen—I will not say parties, for at this period there were none left—might squabble over domestic policy; in the domain of foreign policy they were

---

[1] Pol., I, 11, 2-4. [2] Pol., I, 63. 1.
[3] See the parallel between the phalanx and the legion in Polybius, XVIII, 28-32; **CXXIV**, I, 409-32.

agreed. The Scipios, who for the first fifteen years of the second century exercised a predominant influence, and their implacable enemy Cato, worked hand in hand when Rome's greatness was at stake. The idea of imperialism gripped the whole city; in this unanimity the secret of its power and the irresistible force of its expansion are to be found.

And here a serious question arises: How far did the economic factor contribute side by side with the political causes to the formation and growth of Roman imperialism? We shall shortly see its rôle in the middle of the second century B.C., but to what extent did it influence Roman policy during the first half of that century? On this point two conflicting theses are advanced. To some, Roman imperialism was governed primarily by mercantile aims throughout this period. First the great campaigns in the East, and then the simultaneous destruction of Carthage and Corinth, played into the hands of the Roman merchant and speculator. According to others, imperialism at Rome was strictly military in form and was affected by economic considerations either not at all or to a negligible degree.[1] Which party is right? We answer, neither; both theses are too rigid and fail to take into account the natural complexity of the problem and the historical evolution by which it had been conditioned.

No doubt, both through the environment in which it was born and the conditions which had governed its early growth, Roman imperialism was essentially militarist in nature. The contrast between Roman imperialism—that of a nation of soldiers—and the Carthaginian—the imperialism of a nation of shopkeepers—is patent. At Carthage the economic aspect was a motive; at Rome it seemed an incidental result. Such a result was twofold. The first consequence appears by the end of the Second Punic War. Through the numerous large military contracts of all kinds which it involved, the latter had resulted in the rise of a class of capitalists, whose importance increased during the next fifty years and who appear as a group apart by the age of the Gracchi.

Secondly, in proportion to her expansion in the Orient as well as in the West (Spain and Africa), Rome was becoming

[1] T. Frank, in **XXX**, 1912-1913, 233 *ff.; id.*, **CXXXII** ,108-18; **CXLIV**, 369-75; **XXVI**, IV¹, 26 and note 58.

a great centre of capital. In the form of booty, war indemnities, and the products of the legal or illegal exploitation of the conquered countries, trade and banking, wealth poured to Rome abundantly. Part of this wealth was scattered among private individuals, part came into the treasury, but did not stay there, as we shall shortly see. In less than two generations Italy became the richest country in the Mediterranean world. For the most part, this capital was not left in Italy. The Italian and the Roman loaned it out abroad, and made it bear fruit by investing it in countries where capital was scarcer. Hence, as the practice spread, the exportation of Italian capital became a factor to be reckoned with by Roman statesmen, whether they liked it or not. Thirdly, parallel with the influx of wealth, the mercantile spirit and the taste for trade were growing up in the peninsula. Many Romans or Italians who had left the plough to go to the war were enticed by the bait of quick profits and transformed themselves into merchants. They bought a ship and set up business with their share in the booty or with the cash realized by the sale of the paternal holding. They are found at Delos by the first third of the second century.

The exploitation of the world which conquest had thus brought in its train therefore assumed the guise of a huge and profitable business from which all classes of the population might draw dividends. To the aristocracy imperialism represented primarily honours, triumphs, provincial governorships, the exploitation of the conquered territory, and speculations in public lands, or, in other terms, power, glory, and riches. To the equestrian class it meant the farming of taxes, public contracts (for military supplies and public works), and banking operations. The profits from such investments were not restricted to the class of capitalists proper, and especially lavish censorships like that of 174 represented a veritable rain of gold for the whole population of Italy. In an extraordinarily important passage Polybius discloses this as affecting the middle of the second century B.C.:

> " In Italy there are many works, contracts for which are let by the censors, such as the construction and upkeep of public buildings too numerous to count, and the working of water-courses,

ports, mines, gardens, and lands, and, in a word, everything under the control of Rome. The Roman people is in charge of all these enterprises, and almost everyone participates in them through the contracts to which they give rise and the benefits they produce. Some contract for them with the censors, others go into partnership with the former, others go surety for these, and others again pledge their property with the treasury as guarantors."[1]

Let us not forget the peasant who supplied victuals or raw materials, and the rest of the people to whom the policy of expansions meant the remission or reduction of the *tributum*, some share in the booty, regular employment, and all sorts of material advantages. It is, then, fair to say that all classes in the community shared not only in the glory but also in the business of the fatherland. Hence it is not surprising that the economic factor acquired an ever-growing influence on the direction of Roman foreign policy during the first half of the second century, and that, while not yet the sole nor even the dominant consideration, it, at least, lent imperialism the considerable weight it could already command.

IV

The Methods of Roman Imperialism

There is no doubt that Roman imperialism represented a brutal and often pitiless system. But in default of panegyrics, which scarcely become it, it can at least put forward some excuses. We may, of course, at once dismiss the justifications in which Roman tradition revelled contrasting the generosity, loyalty, and clemency of Roman statesmen and soldiers with the egoism, cruelty, and habitual treachery of their adversaries. When Tacitus[2] makes Claudius say " that the Romans had learnt from their ancestors to display as much clemency to suppliants as firmness towards their enemies," or puts into the mouth of Tiberius the words, " The Roman people does not take vengeance upon its foes by guile nor through conspiracies, but openly with arms in its hand," we must eschew taking them literally. When Virgil enshrines in his treasure-house " *parcere subjectis et debellare superbos* "[3] as the guiding principles of Roman

---

[1] Pol., VI, 17, 2-4. [2] Tac., *Ann.*, XII, 20,; II, 88.
[3] Virg., *Æn.*, 853.

policy, let us recall that in the eyes of the Romans the *superbi* were just the peoples who dared to fight to the last gasp in defence of their national liberties. At least one point must be remembered in extenuation of Roman imperialism. Its extreme methods, such as devastation of lands, confiscation of territory, and deportation of inhabitants were current coin in the ancient world, and the Roman, not being naturally inventive, was no more an innovator in this respect than in others. That is an attenuating circumstance, if you will, but nothing more. To judge Roman imperialism at work we may appeal to words or deeds.

For the words let us quote Polybius. Referring to Roman policy in regard to Achæa, he writes:[1]

> "The Senate recognized that the advice of Callicrates would be profitable. It grasped that the partisans of the Roman cause must be supported and its opponents abased. This was the first time that it adopted the plan of humiliating the ardent patriots in every city and exalting the spokesmen of its own cause." "Such is, in fact, the common policy of Rome; she takes advantage of the inadvertence of others to extend and consolidate her own sway while always having the air of befriending them and doing them a service."[2]

The same note is struck in describing the relations of Rome with Carthage:

> "The Romans showed no regard for equity, and the Carthaginians had to yield to necessity."[3] "As for the second war, which led to the treaty about Sardinia, no reason nor pretext could be found to justify it. It must be acknowledged that the Romans were guilty of an abuse of power in forcing the Carthaginians to cede Sardinia and pay the considerable sum of which we have spoken in the teeth of all principles of justice."[4]

Or, again, he writes:

> "The Romans always decided against Carthage, not because such a decision was just, but because it seemed to suit their interests."[5] "It (war with Carthage) had been for long a foregone conclusion; they were just awaiting a favourable opportunity and a pretext that should seem plausible in the eyes of the world."[6]

Such testimony assumes an additional value in the mouth of Polybius, who was anything but an enemy of Rome in

[1] Pol., XXIV., 10, 3-5.   [2] Pol., XXXI, 10, 7-8.
[3] Pol., III, 10, 3.   [4] Pol., III, 28, 1-2.
[5] Pol., XXXI, 6-7.   [6] Pol., XXXVI, 2, 1.

general, and of the governing aristocracy in particular. But we have yet stronger evidence, that of the facts. Rome would later do great things for humanity, but it would be a mistake to transpose dates or distort her intentions. It would be a flagrant anachronism to picture the Roman legionary who conquered the world as a champion of right or a knight of chivalry. Roman imperialism, like all imperialism, had gone on growing more domineering in proportion to its triumphs and step by step with the advance of general enslavement. It had, indeed, at no time shrunk from acts of severity that were necessary or judged so, but after Zama, Cynoscephalæ, and Magnesia it found the whole world at its feet and henceforth knew no bounds. Everything must yield before it, and for the attainment of the result at which it aimed all means—brutal force, perfidy, and on occasions even frightfulness—were lawful. Acts of violence, often useless and sometimes even frankly ill-timed, were heaped up; in 151 B.C. the two prætors of Spain, L. Licinius Lucullus and S. Sulpicius Galba, set out for their provinces charged with a mission of pitiless repression; its fulfilment in the guise of wholesale massacres soon bore fruit. And against the heartless methods of the new aristocracy, against the deliberate atrocities of the Spanish War, not one voice was raised in protest at Rome, save that of old Cato, a man of a bygone age and almost a ghost. One reservation must be made: S. Sulpicius Galba's crime, by its very enormity, provoked a storm of disapprobation, but even in this case public condemnation did not find vent in the application of any sanction, and the culprit was left unpunished. Three instances seem typical in this connection—the sack of Epirus by Æmilius Paulus in 167, the felony of Sulpicius Galba in Spain in 150, and the destruction of Carthage in 146.[1]

At the end of the Third Macedonian War the Senate handed over the cities of Epirus to the victorious army for pillage to reward it. Let us note that these cities had returned to Roman allegiance before the collapse of Macedonia, and that this extenuating circumstance might have secured them some indulgence. Æmilius Paulus was en-

---

[1] Pol., XXX, 15; Livy, XLV, 34, 1-7; Plut., *Æm. Paul.*, 29; Str., VII, 7, 3 (p. 322 C); App. *Ill.*, 9; Plin., *Hist. Nat.*, IV, 39.

trusted with the unenviable mission of executing the Senate's decree. He arrived in Epirus and summoned ten of the chief citizens from each town. After ordering them to bring all the gold and silver they possessed on an appointed day, he sent them home, each accompanied by a centurion and a detachment of troops. Those who had to travel to the remotest places set out before the rest so that all might reach their destinations on the same day. The tribunes and centurions had received precise instructions. On the appointed day at the fourth hour the signal for pillage was given everywhere. The troops spread simultaneously among the several cities, looting and carrying off everything they could lay hands on. In one hour seventy towns were plundered and a hundred and fifty thousand men enslaved and sold. Out of the proceeds of the booty each horseman received four hundred denarii as his share, and each infantryman two hundred. Livy[1] reports the episode without a word of reprobation. Plutarch[2] insists upon the atrocity of the action by which

> " a whole nation had been ruined just to procure a modest gain for each soldier."

He tries to exculpate at least his hero Æmilius Paulus, by adding :

> " this expedition was repugnant to the gentleness and humanity of his character."[3]

We should stigmatize it as an act of brigandage committed in time of perfect peace, the barbarity of which was aggravated by the perfect orderliness and the methodical manner of its execution.

Seventeen years have passed. We reach Spain,[4] where S. Sulpicius Galba has just arrived as prætor to take up the governorship of the further province. After a campaign, in which he displays no conspicuous military talent, he signs a peace with the Lusitanians and offers them good lands to

---

[1] Livy, XLV, 34, 1-6.   [2] Plut., Æm. Paul., 29, 4.
[3] Ibid., 30, 1.
[4] Livy, Per., XLIX (Epit. Oxyr., 1, 83, p. 131 R); App., Iber., 59-60; Cato, quoted by A. Gell., N. Att., I, 12, 17; XIII, 25, 15 (=M. Cat. frag., ed. H. Jordan, pp. 27-30); Cic., de Orat., I, 53, 227-28; Brut., 23, 89; pro Mur., X, 59; **XXVI**, IV¹, 480-83; **CCXXI**, 352.

colonize. Relying on the word and the signature of the Roman general applicants flock in. Galba divides them up into three groups, which he carefully isolates, and after this precaution lets loose his soldiers upon them. The men are massacred, the women and children sold as slaves. The booty goes to swell his patrimony. Such a violation of a solemn treaty and the savagery displayed by Galba for once aroused a wave of emotion at Rome. In 149 B.C. the tribune of the plebs, L. Scribonius Libo proposed to bring Galba before an extraordinary tribunal, and the old Cato lent the project his weighty support. However, nothing was done. Galba invoked the pity of the people. We may also suspect that the senatorial aristocracy, having been converted to these new methods, was secretly working to spare him the disgrace of a condemnation. The proposal was lost. The Lusitanians who had been sold into slavery, and to whom at least reparation might have been made, were not even set at liberty.

Finally, the destruction of Carthage in 146 B.C. is the most typical instance of all.[1] For half a century after the Second Punic War, despite the incessant provocations of Massinissa and the at least equivocal attitude of Rome, she had duly fulfilled the term of the treaty of 201. In 150, driven to extremities by her insatiable neighbour after a vain appeal for protection to her suzerain, she resolved to oppose force to force. No doubt on a strictly literal interpretation of the text she thereby violated the peace treaty, but under the circumstances she was not without excuses. Rome chose this moment for interposition. Cato, sent as ambassador to Carthage, found the city populous and prosperous. He also—perhaps chiefly—realized the danger Rome would run in the event of the occupation of the great metropolis by Massinissa. At all events, shortly afterwards the Senate in a secret session cold-bloodedly decreed the annihilation of Carthage. The treachery and hypocrisy accompanying its execution only made this cynical decision more odious.

Bluntly to announce the death-sentence would be to

[1] Pol., XXXVI, 2-7; Livy, *Per.*, XLIX (*epit. Oxyr.*, ll. 88-142 (K), pp. 131-37 R); App., *Lib.*, 74-92; Diod., XXXII, 1, 3-6; Zon., IX, 26-27, 29-30; **VII**, III, 340-51.

provoke a dogged resistance, which the Senate, as a thrifty steward of Rome's interests, intended to avoid. The Carthaginians must be induced to disarm themselves. Thereafter the irrevocable resolutions of Rome might be announced safely, if not gloriously, and the executioner might fulfil his task with ease. Carthage, knowing naught of this, but yet conscious of the impending peril, sent an embassy to Rome to inquire what was required of her. "To give satisfaction to the Roman people," came back the reply. A second embassy was sent to obtain an explanation : What satisfaction ? "Carthage knows well enough," and once more the Senate dismissed the envoys without any show of a hearing. War was voted, and the two consuls crossed over into Sicily with the army. A third embassy set out for Rome with plenipotentiary powers; Carthage put herself absolutely at the discretion of the Senate. Then the president of the Senate, the prætor urbanus on this occasion, enumerated Rome's conditions. "The Carthaginians shall keep their freedom, their territory, their laws, and their possessions, public and private; within thirty days they shall dispatch to Lilybæum three hundred hostages, sons of members of the Senate and the Council, and for the rest they shall obey the orders which the consuls will give them." Two points in this schedule were pregnant with danger—the Carthaginians were mentioned in it, but not a word was said of the city of Carthage; secondly, what could those mysterious orders of the consuls be to which the Roman Senate referred the envoys ? Nevertheless, Carthage obeyed. The hostages set out for Lilybæum. The consuls, for their part, refused any explanation, averring that they would only reveal their will when in Africa.

The expedition crossed the sea without encountering the least opposition from the Carthaginian fleet and disembarked at Utica. A fresh deputation came to repeat the submission of the city and to implore the disclosure of the famous terms so obstinately hidden. The consuls revealed their instructions on one point only. Carthage must surrender all her arms and engines of war. Two hundred thousand weapons of all kinds and two thousand machines were transported to the Roman generals' quarters. A further Carthaginian embassy followed, composed this time of thirty of the leading men of the Republic. This time the consuls who had crossed to Africa without hindrance and had reduced the city to helplessness by disarmament thought they had really nothing more to fear. At last they condescended to speak : the Carthaginians must evacuate their city and retire at least eighty stades (nine miles) from the sea. To pronounce such a sentence upon a nation of traders and mariners was to signify bluntly a desire for its death. Horrified, the Carthaginian ambassadors begged for a postponement; in default of justice they appealed to pity. "I have formal instructions," replied the consul brutally, "and I have fulfilled them." Apart from the last desperate resistance of three years, which had not been included in the Roman programme, the sentence was executed literally. This destruction of Carthage, compassed with a truly diabolical treachery, is one of the most odious incidents in the progress of Roman imperialism towards the conquest of the Mediterranean world. And it was to be followed by other illustrations of the method and samples of the system—Corinth and Numantia.

CHAPTER II

ROME AND CARTHAGE

I

THE WAR FOR SICILY

DURING the summer of 264 B.C. the consul Appius Claudius received orders to cross the straits and march to the help of the Mamertines.

Carthage had only one reply to make to this step—a declaration of war. She could not allow the Romans to gain a footing in Sicily. With her fleet in the straits and her troops in Messana, she did not lack means of hindering it. Yet she hesitated to embark upon a conflict which promised to be terrible; and the Carthaginian generals at the front, left without instructions, or perhaps warned not to risk a serious engagement, avoided compromising themselves by a too energetic action, as always happens in such cases. Without loss of time Rome set herself to make full use of such a favourable situation. The Roman troops crossed the straits and relieved Messana, the Carthaginian

Bibliography.—Texts: Livy, *Periochæ* of books XVI-XX (from 264 to the beginning of the Second Punic War); XXI-XXX (Second Punic War) (*cf.* Florus, I, 18-22; Eutropius, II, 18-III, 23; Orosius, IV, 6-19); Polybius, I-III (down to 216), VII-XV (fragments); Diodorus, XXI-XXVII (fragments); Dio Cassius, XI-XVII (fragments, *cf.* Zonaras, VIII, 8-IX, 14); Plutarch, *Fabius Maximus, Marcellus;* Appian, *Illyr.* (VII-VIII), *Iberic.* (III-XXXVIII), *Hannibal, Libyc.* (1-67), *Macedon.* (frag. 1), *Sicil.* (frags. 1-5); Cornelius Nepos, *Hamilcar, Hannibal;* Justinian, XXIX, 1-4; Festus, *s.v.* " Sardi venales," pp. 428 and 430; Frontinus, *Strat.,* II, 3, 16; *de Viris Illustribus,* 37-50.

Inscriptions.—Fasti consulares (C.I.L., I², pp. 136-42); *Fasti triumphales,* under years 264-146 (*id.,* pp. 172-76), C.I.L., I², 25 (rostral column of C. Duilius); *id.,* 8-9 (*elogium* of L. Cornelius Scipio, consul in 259, censor in 258).

*Principal Works.—***VII**, III, 67-296; **CLXXIX**, II-III; **XXVI**, III¹·², 91-432, 1-688; **CXLIX**; **CLXXI**; **XI**, I, 444-503; **XXV**, 33-42; **V**, 121-76; **CLXVII**, III, 1 and 2, maps 1-14; **CXXIV**, I, 304-406; for the campaigns in Illyria and relations with the Greek world in particular, **XVII**, II, 281-86, 436-38, 465-561; **CLIII**, 97-305.

garrison having evacuated the citadel.[1] In the following year Hiero, whose capital was threatened, deserted the Carthaginian cause and allied himself with Rome (263).[2] With the defection of Syracuse the curtain falls upon the prologue, the main drama begins.

The plans of the two adversaries were in contrast from the start. The Romans' programme was the conquest of Sicily; they aimed at expelling the Carthaginians from the island and taking their place. To attain this result it was thought that the operations of the land army alone would be sufficient, and that the support of a fleet would not be indispensable. The Carthaginian programme was quite different: war on land by itself could not bring about a decision; the Carthaginian army must keep on the defensive; the vital point was to preserve freedom of communications with the metropolis, and consequently to retain the undisputed mastery of the sea.

At first everything played into the hands of the Romans perfectly. Agrigentum herself fell in 262 B.C., but soon the long series of disillusionments began. The great Carthaginian strongholds on the coast—Eryx, Panormus, Solus, and Lilybæum—remained impregnable. This resistance suggested salutary reflections at Rome, and men came to ask whether the plan of operating only on land was capable of producing the desired result. Two centuries of Sicilian wars furnished the answer; neither Gelo nor Dionysius nor, more recently, Pyrrhus, despite the repeated victories of their armies, had been able to tear Carthage from Sicilian soil just through the want of a fleet capable of wresting from her the mastery of the sea. To an observant people like the Romans, the lessons of experience had the force of laws. The Senate was convinced that they had been hitherto pursuing the wrong track, and that no lasting result was to be obtained without supremacy at sea.

Willing the end, it willed the means; the construction of a great fleet was decided upon, and preparations were made for carrying the war on to the sea as soon as the ships should be ready. This abrupt change of front towards the whole plan of campaign created a profound impression throughout

[1] Pol., I, 11, 9-12; Livy, *Per.*, XVI; **XIX**, IV, 337-74.
[2] Pol., I, 16; Livy, *Per.*, XVI.

Italy, and the ancient writers have not failed to give voice thereto. They relate many varied and picturesque anecdotes in this connection : the Romans possessed no workmen sufficiently expert to build ships with five tiers of oars, and they were consequently seriously embarrassed. Fortunately, the enemy himself came to their aid; a Carthaginian quinquereme fell into their hands and furnished the necessary pattern. It remained to train the crews. Someone was inspired with the idea of drilling them on land, and it was, we are told, on terra firma that they learnt to handle oars.[1]

In point of fact such details belong more to the realm of legend than that of history. The solution of the problem, intricate though it was, offered far fewer difficulties than tradition pretends. If the rugged landsmen of Latium and mountaineers of the Apennines had only the most distant acquaintance with the sea, Rome could count on a number of maritime allies—the *socii navales*, such as the Etruscans of the coast, the Volsci of Antium, and the Greeks of the south, and by this time also Hiero of Syracuse—whose naval traditions were not to be despised. In men and material, thanks to the brilliant maritime past of some of her cities, Italy controlled the necessary forces for the creation of a great fleet. The problem was, therefore, primarily one of organization, and in that direction the Romans had no rivals, nor would have for many centuries. Moreover, the idea of making her début as a maritime power by attacking Carthage, " who had enjoyed an undisputed supremacy at sea since the days of their ancestors,"[2] denoted an undeniable audacity, and such a decision by itself would do honour to the assembly that did not shrink from taking the heavy responsibility therefor. Success was swift and complete. In 260 B.C. the consul C. Duilius crushed the Carthaginian fleet at the Battle of Mylæ. The victory at Sulci in 258 and the action, at least indecisive, off Tyndaris in 257 preserved to the Romans the maritime supremacy they had just gained for the first time.

The exaltation of victory soon gave place once more to grave despondency. Despite the success of the naval policy,

[1] On these preparations, consult especially **XXVI**, III¹, 123-25; **VII**, III, 77; **XIX**, IV, 377-80.

[2] Pol., I, 20, 12-13.

no headway was being made in Sicily. The Senate, return-
ing to the traditions of Agathocles, decided to settle the
matter by a frontal blow delivered at the heart of the
Carthaginian Empire in Africa. The expedition was ready
by the spring of 256, under the command of the consuls
M. Atilius Regulus and L. Manlius Vulso. A great naval
victory off Cape Ecnome, on the southern shore of Sicily,
opened the way to Carthage, and the Roman troops were
able to disembark on the shores of Africa without hindrance. But disillusionment soon began. They had counted
on a general insurrection among the subjects of Carthage,
but the commander-in-chief, Regulus, was a sorry diplomat
and a poor politician, and by no means the man for the
occasion. The expected revolt did not eventuate. To gain
time Carthage entered into negotiations for peace. Dio
Cassius[1] enumerates the conditions then offered to her : the
surrender of Sicily and Sardinia and the payment of the
expenses of the war, an annual tribute, the release of all
prisoners without ransom, prohibition against declaring war
without Rome's sanction, and the duty of assisting her in
time of need, and a strict limitation of the Carthaginian fleet.
Doubt has very properly been cast upon the authenticity of
such conditions, for they simply meant the end of Carthage's
independence and her disappearance as a great power. At
least, we know from Polybius[2] that the terms of Regulus
were rigorous, and that the Carthaginian plenipotentiaries,
far from wanting to subscribe to them, could not even listen
to them calmly. Negotiations were broken off. A little later
the Carthaginian army was reorganized by Xanthippus, and
crushingly defeated the Roman army, and the Senate, under
the pressure of public opinion, ordered the recall of the
remnants of the expedition. The African experiment had
failed, and the Romans returned to Sicily and naval warfare.
But disasters at sea followed one another in quick succession ;
there were reverses at Camarina in 253 and 249 b.c., at
Cape Palinurus in 253, and at Drepanum in 249. Sickened of
naval warfare, which brought only losses, Rome went back
to her original plan.

The earlier experience was repeated. Rome held the
land, Carthage dominated the sea; it was a duel between the

---

[1] Dio Cas., XI, 43, 22-23. [2] Pol., I, 31, 5-7.

whale and the elephant, in which a decision seemed impossible. Without a fleet the Roman generals could attempt no serious operations against the Carthaginian strongholds of Lilybæum and Drepanum. Deprived of an army the Carthaginian commanders, despite their undeniable ability, found themselves excluded from any sweeping operations. In 247 Carthage sent her greatest soldier, Hamilcar Barca, to Sicily, and he initiated a subtle but exhausting war for position, first at Mount Heircte and then on Mount Eryx.[1] The war dragged on, and operations made no headway. Polybius, our main authority, admirably sums up the position in 246 B.C. :

> "This campaign is comparable to an encounter between two boxers of exceptional strength and courage contesting for the prize. They smite one another continually, and it is no longer possible for them or the spectators to count or follow the blows interchanged."[2]

Again he writes :

> "The belligerents remind one of two of those valiant birds which fight desperately, so exhausted that they can no longer use their wings, but, sustained by their courage alone, they grapple again after a moment's respite and overwhelm one another with blows until one be vanquished. Thus the Romans and Carthaginians, broken by a ceaseless conflict, exhausted and ruined by prolonged expenditure and continual taxes, seemed to have become unconscious of the blows that they interchanged."[3]

What was the cause of this deadlock? On the Roman side the enthusiasm evoked by the first naval victories had soon given place to a profound despondency. A series of sad experiences had shown that the Roman generals dressed up as admirals, if capable of forcing victory on the battlefield, were none the less sorry sailors, and their self-complaisance in dealing with trained mariners only aggravated their responsibility. At the time of the first disaster at Camarina the pilots had not spared their warnings, but the high command had simply refused to listen to them. The catastrophe at Cape Palinurus in 253, the second defeat at Camarina, and the disaster at Drepanum in 249 were solely

[1] Pol., I, 56 *ff.*
[2] Pol., I, 57, 1-2; **CLXVII**, III, 4-39 and map 2.
[3] Pol., I, 58, 7-9.

due to this incapacity in manœuvring. This was well known at Rome both among the populace and in high places, and this conviction had set up a current of opinion against the naval war which, for the moment, was hard to stem.

On the Carthaginian side the great defect was the absence of that quality which Rome had always possessed in such a high degree, the offensive spirit. Carthage had only embarked upon the war in defence of her person. She had not had the sense to cover the Strait of Messina, her first line of defence, and, when hostilities had broken out, she had kept to an almost passive defensive attitude. In the course of the first years of the war no serious effort had been made to carry the war into Italy, to involve the Cisalpine Gauls, a diversion which might have been decisive, or to attack Rome on her own ground. A still graver and irreparable mistake was that for fourteen years (255-241) Carthage remained mistress of the sea, and let slip this unique opportunity of regaining the initiative by an offensive on a large scale. In fact, save when she was obliged to fight on her own African territory, Carthage had conducted the First Punic War just as if it had been merely a colonial war. Two main causes explain this attitude. From the material point of view, her military and naval resources were always limited, and far inferior to those of Italy. From the standpoint of morale, this Republic of merchants, in which money played the leading part and had always the last word, only desired military policy within the bounds of her commercial interests. But at Rome militarism was not, as at Carthage, just a means. Carthage possessed only the army of her policy, Rome had the policy of her army. Faltering, only transient at Rome, was a chronic condition at Carthage. Rome, a young and lusty organism, could recover, Carthage, old and worn, ultimately died thereof.

For these various reasons the war had come to a stalemate. Some escape had to be found. Only Rome could compass a decision, and that only by a revival of the naval war. Rome at last took this in, and in 242 resolved upon a desperate effort.[1] A fleet of two hundred ships took the sea under the command of the consul C. Lutatius Catulus. In the spring of the following year it won a decisive victory

[1] Pol., I, 59.

over the Carthaginian squadron at the Ægatæ Islands. This time Carthaginian Sicily was lost. No doubt, as Polybius remarks,[1] Carthage would still have ardour and courage to pursue the conflict, but she was running short of the material means, especially money, and, moreover, a continuation of hostilities was thereafter pointless. The strongholds in Sicily, Drepanum and Lilybæum, had been blockaded for a year and were in dire straits. A counter-offensive, even if successful, would come too late to save them, and their recapture was out of the question. The mastery of the sea might have enabled Carthage to preserve them, but with the military superiority won on land by the Roman army, their eventual loss seemed inevitable. In such circumstances at a loss for any better plan, Carthage left the decision to Hamilcar, and gave him a free hand. Hamilcar declared for peace, and immediately made overtures to the Romans. C. Lutatius Catulus welcomed these gleefully. With the expulsion of the Carthaginians from Sicily, Rome would have achieved her essential object in the war. Thereafter to drive Carthage to extremes would have been an ill-timed and foolhardy policy on her part.

Animated by an equal desire for a settlement, the negotiators agreed upon the following preliminary terms of peace :

> " With the reservation that the present draft shall be submitted for ratification to the Roman people, friendship is re-established between Rome and Carthage on the following terms: The Carthaginians shall evacuate the whole of Sicily and pledge themselves not to make war upon Hiero nor to take up arms against the Syracusans or their allies; they shall restore without ransom all Roman prisoners, and, further, shall pay an indemnity of one thousand two hundred Eubœan talents payable in twenty years."[2]

In brief the loss of Sicily and the payment of a substantial war indemnity constituted the price to be paid by Carthage for her defeat. No doubt this fell far short of the demands of Regulus. No doubt, too, Rome would have been glad to wrest Sardinia also from her adversary, and so secure a final and satisfactory settlement of the Tyrrhenian question at

---

[1] Pol., I, 62, 1-2.

[2] Pol., I, 62, 7-9; **VII**, III, 98; **XXVI**, III[1], 188-89; **CCXXVI**, I, 188-90.

one blow. Nevertheless, the terms imposed appeared to be the maximum possible to Lutatius Catulus, and Carthage would doubtless have preferred a continuation of hostilities to any substantial additional sacrifices. However, Lutatius was well aware of the discontent that the preliminary draft would provoke at Rome, and took care to initial it only on an express stipulation for a reference to the comitia.[1]

He was not mistaken. The people, not finding the material gains on which they had long counted in the draft treaty and with their warlike ardour rekindled by the victory of the Ægatæ, withheld ratification, and sent a commission of ten deputies to Sicily to wring additional concessions out of the Carthaginians. The ten commissioners were soon convinced, like Lutatius Catulus himself, that they would have to abide by the agreed terms on the whole, but they managed to make them more drastic in two respects : the indemnity was increased by a thousand talents, and the period of grace was curtailed by a half. It was, moreover, expressly laid down that, in addition to Sicily, Carthage should abandon all the islands lying between Sicily and Italy—that is the Æolian Islands (Lipari Islands). The article obliging the Carthaginians not to make war upon Hiero nor to take up arms against the Syracusans or their allies was tightened up and reinforced by a new clause forbidding either of the contracting parties to raise mercenaries on the other's territory—a prohibition which, in practice, was solely aimed at Carthage.[2] On being laid before the comitia for the second time, no doubt after the Senate had taken the necessary steps to insure its ratification, the remodelled treaty was voted by the people, but without enthusiasm, and apparently even regretfully.[3]

And yet the peace of 241 B.C. offered Rome advantages which the wildest optimist would not have dreamed of twenty years earlier. Carthaginian imperialism, which had defied all the efforts of Syracuse in a conflict lasting over two centuries, had crumbled away under the blows of unified Italy. Rome, the successor of the Dionysii and Agathocles

---

[1] Pol., I, 6, 2, 8.

[2] Pol., III, 27, 1-6; App., *Sicil.*, 2; **VII**, III, 98; **XXVI**, III,[1] 190-91; **CCXXVI**, 188-90.

[3] Pol., I, 63.

and the heir of their policy, drove the Semites back to Africa, and thus secured the hegemony in the western basin of the Mediterranean for seven centuries. A decisive page in the history of Italy and of the world had been turned.

II

Towards Greater Italy : Sardinia, Cisalpine Gaul, and Illyria

Sicily had become Roman by the treaty of 241, but the two other great islands of the Tyrrhenian Sea, Sardinia and Corsica, still belonged to the Carthaginian sphere of influence. Doubtless the Senate of those days would have asked for nothing better than to wrest them from the Semites of Africa, but that would have involved a continuation of a war of which everyone was tired at Rome. However, fortune soon intervened to give the Romans for nothing the two great islands, the conquest of which, by force of arms, they had, for the moment, renounced.

When the "inexpiable war" broke out in Africa, the mercenaries garrisoning Sardinia soon joined the movement, and revolted against the Carthaginians established in the island.[1] In spite of reinforcements tardily despatched by the metropolis, the mutineers were soon masters of the whole island. The greatest danger to Carthage lay in the possible attitude of Rome. What was the Senate going to do? From the outset the events in Sardinia caused certain difficulties between the two States, especially over the question of contraband; for the Italian merchants had not observed an unimpeachable neutrality.[2] However, the friction led to no farther results, and Rome even answered the appeal for help sent by the mercenaries in Sardinia by a formal refusal. When the revolt in Africa had been crushed, thanks to Hamilcar's energy, Carthage planned to restore her sway in Sardinia at the earliest possible moment. But the Roman Government had decided not to tolerate this, and knew that Carthage was too exhausted to ignore its veto. It bluntly announced that the Carthaginian preparations for the reconquest of Sardinia appeared an unfriendly

---

[1] Pol., I, 79, 1-6. [2] Pol., I, 83, 6-8.

act and constituted a *casus belli*. In the conditions in which Carthage was then placed, a war would have been suicidal. She had to yield and abandon the island, and, to add insult to injury, was even forced to pay a supplementary indemnity of twelve hundred talents (238).[1]

Through the capitulation of Carthage Rome secured a free hand in Sardinia. It only remained for her to conquer the island, and, being anxious to make full use of the favourable moment, she set to work forthwith.[2] The Phœnician cities on the coast which constituted the bases of the Carthaginian dominion—Caralis, Sulci, Nora, Tharrus, and Olbia—were first occupied by the consul Ti. Sempronius Gracchus, probably in 237 B.C. Then the Roman army embarked upon the conquest of the interior, a peculiarly thankless task which Carthage had never completed. The consul T. Manlius Torquatus in 235, the prætor P. Cornelius with the consul Sp. Corvilius Maximus in 234, and the consul M'. Pomponius Mato in 233 won a series of victories. In 232, as the situation had grown worse, the two consuls M. Æmilius Lepidus and M. Publicius Maleolus took the field, but obtained no decisive results. In 231 the consul M'. Pomponius Mato earned an unenviable notoriety by inaugurating the employment of man-hunting dogs against the Sardinians. At all events, he succeeded in pacifying the whole of the island for some years. But about 226, in consequence of its organization as a Roman province, and perhaps also at the instigation of the Carthaginians, Sardinia was again seething with revolt. In 225, at the time of the last Gaulish offensive, the consul C. Atilius Regulus occupied the island with two legions in order to forestall any possible Carthaginian intervention, but he found no occasion for action in default of enemies to fight. On the eve of the Second Punic War Sardinia had been conquered from end to end, with the exception of a few mountain tribes in the interior, which preserved an actual independence; it would take half a century of supplementary campaigns to reduce these.

In Corsica,[3] where the Carthaginian occupation had never

---

[1] Pol., I, 88, 9-12.   [2] **XXVI**, III[1], 280-83.

[3] On the Roman campaigns in Corsica as a whole, see **XXVI**, III[1], 280-83.

been firmly established, the Romans carried out an analogous and parallel task. They had appeared on the eastern coast of the island during the First Punic War, but then, distracted by other anxieties, had abandoned it in the following years. At the moment when they interfered in Sardinia, they returned to Corsica and consolidated their footing, particularly at Alalia. Then they tackled the conquest of the interior. The consul for 236, C. Licinius Varus, reduced some native tribes at the cost of flagrant treachery. The consul Sp. Carvilius Maximus in 234 and the consul C. Papirius Maso in 231 pushed ahead vigorously. A durable peace was concluded, which divided the island into two spheres of influence. Rome took the coasts, the highlands were left to the natives, although perhaps the Roman protectorate nominally rather than actually embraced the latter region also.

Rome had embarked upon the war for the settlement of the Tyrrhenian question in the belief that the other two vital questions—those of Gallia Cisalpina and the Adriatic—could wait, and her belief was justified. No unpleasant surprise had been in store for her on either of these sectors throughout the period of the First Punic War. Wars in Gallia Cisalpina only broke out anew in 283 B.C., and in the Adriatic the situation would not become delicate before the day chosen by Rome herself for beginning operations.

In dealing with the Gauls, Rome had pursued a policy of prudence and forbearance throughout the course of the hostilities with Carthage; for a diversion from this quarter in the thick of the Punic War might have had disastrous consequences. On the conclusion of peace the position soon changed. By forbidding the Carthaginians raising mercenaries in Italy, the peace of 241 closed a brilliant and lucrative career to the Gaulish youth.[1] The new generation, which had not tasted the terrible lessons of Sentinum and Vadmon, thought only of revenge, and prayed only for war.[2] Otherwise the moment was as ill-chosen as possible. Not having had the sense to act in co-operation with Carthage, or at least simultaneously with her, the Gauls were about

[1] App., *Sicil.*, 2. [2] Pol., II, 21, 1-3.

to hurl themselves upon the united Roman forces and to give their hereditary foes an opportunity of settling the question of Gallia Cisalpina once for all.[1] A campaign conducted by the Romans against the Apuans and the neighbouring Ligurian or Celto-Ligurian tribes furnished the desired pretext for a rupture.

In 238 B.C. the Boii defeated the consular army of P. Valerius Falto. In 236, reinforced by contingents from beyond the Alps, they came to besiege the bulwark of Central Italy—Ariminum—but in the course of the siege quarrels broke out in their own ranks, they fell to fighting one another, and after suffering heavy losses, retreated to their own territories in disorder.[2] The attack had failed. The moment seemed ripe for Rome to launch a counter-offensive, and to complete the unity of Italy by the conquest of the Po Valley. But Rome had not the courage. The memory of the Gaulish inroads was ingrained in everyone's mind. Carthage, installed in Spain, was making feverish preparations for revenge, and nobody wanted to face difficulties, the gravity of which was generally exaggerated, unless it were absolutely inevitable. And so things were left at that. The Senate merely took advantage of the favourable moment to embark upon the conquest of Liguria; that meant mountain fighting, a hard and unprofitable task, but, owing to the numerical weakness of the various tribes and their lack of cohesion, exposed Rome to no serious risks. After a series of hard campaigns the Ligurians of the south at least partially submitted, and Roman posts were established at the most important strategic points on the coasts— Luna (near the Gulf of Spezia) and Genua (Genoa). Before attacking Gallia Cisalpina, Rome had begun by encircling it on the south.

The Gauls there, seeing the danger, anticipated it. The Boii, Insubres, Lingones, Taurini, and Gesati from across the Alps formed a coalition and took the offensive. Rome replied by preparations on a formidable scale; all the contingents of the Italian federation—approximately seven hundred and seventy thousand men—were mobilized or ordered to hold themselves in readiness. The invaders advanced into Southern Etruria as far as Clusium, but,

[1] **XXVI**, III[1], 186-91, 304-20.   [2] Pol., II, 21, 4-6.

caught between the consular armies of L. Æmilius Papus on the south and of C. Atilius Regulus on the north, they

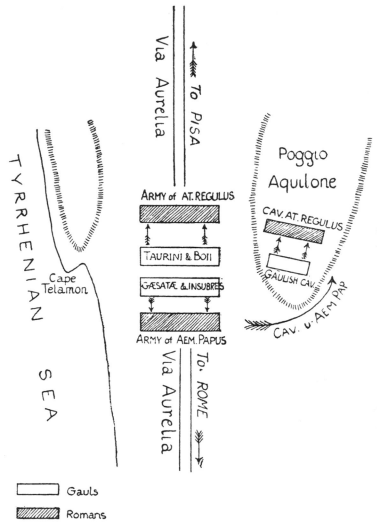

F<small>IG.</small> 10.—T<small>HE</small> M<small>ANŒUVRE OF</small> T<small>ELAMON</small> (225 B.C.) <small>ACCORDING TO</small> P<small>OLYBIUS</small> (II, 27-31).

suffered a terrible disaster on the Tuscan seaboard, not far from Cape Telamon.[1] Only a few stragglers managed to regain North Italy. The Battle of Telamon, wherein nearly

[1] Pol., II, 27-31; **XXVI**, III[1], 308-11.

a hundred thousand men had been engaged, had far-reaching consequences. It meant the end of Gaulish invasions, the spell of Gaul was for ever broken. Flinging off her former timidity, Rome proceeded to take the offensive. Just as Sentinum had given her the hegemony in Central Italy, so Telamon enabled her to conquer Gallia Cisalpina and complete the unification of Italy.

In 225 B.C., the very year of the victory, the consul L. Æmilius Papus crossed the Apennines and carried the war into the land of the Boii.[1] In 224 the consuls T. Manlius Torquatus and Q. Fulvius Flaccus renewed the onslaught. The Boii and Lingones made peace, and had to cede part of their territory. The Insubres remained beyond the Po, covered, as they thought, by the defensive barrier of the river. In 223 the consul C. Flaminius Nepos crossed that stream near the confluence of the Adda, and by a bold flank march effected a junction with his allies the Cenomani. The combined forces won a great victory on the banks of the Clesis (the modern Chiese, a tributary of the Oglio), which opened their path to the Insubres' capital—Milan. At the beginning of the next year (222) the Insubres sued for peace. The Senate, however, having resolved to make an end of the danger in this quarter, rejected their petition, and the two new consuls, Cn. Cornelius Scipio and M. Claudius Marcellus, both valiant generals, pushed on vigorously with the operations. After crossing the Po they proceeded to lay siege to Acerræ (Gela, near Pizzighettone), an important strategic point commanding the ford of the Adda. The Insubres replied by creating a diversion in the direction of Clastidium (Casteggio, nor far from Piacenza), one of the Roman army's bases. Far from abandoning the siege of Acerræ as the enemy had expected, the consuls prepared to fight on both fronts: Marcellus marched to relieve Clastidium, on the way beat the Insubres and Gesati, who were trying to bar his passage, and raised the siege of the beleaguered city. Meanwhile his colleague, Scipio, had captured Acerræ and, anxious to make the most of the occasion, attempted a raid on Milan. However, he failed there and had to retreat upon Acerræ, where the Gauls

---

[1] On the first conquest of Gallia Cisalpina, see Pol., II, 31, 8; 35, 2; **XXVI**, III¹, 312-18; *Fasti trium., ann.,* 225, 223, 222.

promptly surrounded him. The cavalry of Marcellus raised the siege, the Gaulish army was routed, and the Romans entered Milan on the heels of the fugitives. The capture of Milan sealed the fate of Gallia Cisalpina. The Insubres opened negotiations, ceded part of their territory, gave hostages, and were constrained to join the ranks of Rome's clients under the name of allies. Shortly afterwards the Anamari capitulated in their turn.

A series of supplementary operations directed against North-East Italy rounded off the results achieved.[1] The Cenomani and the Veneti had long ago joined the Roman alliance. Istria and the land of the Liburni south of the Arsia were left. In 221 the two consuls P. Cornelius Scipio Asina and M. Minucius Rufus subdued Istria and the adjacent regions. In 220 their successors, L. Veturius Philo and C. Lutatius Catulus, made their way up to the line of the Julian and the Carnic Alps. Save for the Ligurian countries—Piedmont and Liguria proper, the conquest of which was only a matter of time—the whole of North Italy had acknowledged Rome's hegemony. Colonization began on the very morrow of victory. Two military colonies—Placentia and Cremona—rose armed to the teeth as sentinels guarding the Po (218). It was high time. At this very moment Hannibal was crossing the Alps and debouching upon Italy.

The unification of Italy had made Rome an Adriatic power for the first time. The logical consequences of this new position were soon made manifest. As a first symptom, about 266 B.C., the city of Apollonia, on the Balkan coast, entered into diplomatic relations with Rome,[2] and these overtures were perhaps followed by the conclusion of a treaty of alliance or, at least, of friendship, though proof of this is lacking. Some thirty years later, probably about 239, Justinian[3] describes at length an interposition by Rome on behalf of the Acarnanians when they were threatened by the

---

[1] **XXVI**, III, 319-20.

[2] Val. Max., VI, 6, 5; Dio Cas., X, 42; Zon., VIII, 7, 3; Livy, *Per.*, XV; **CXIV**, 35-36; **CLIII**, 1-5.

[3] Just., XXVIII, 1-2; **CLIII**, 5-22.

Ætolians. The historicity of this event has been questioned, but the arguments adduced in support of the negative thesis are far from conclusive.

In this development of the Adriatic question, Roman intervention in Illyria marks a turning-point. Among the nests of pirates swarming in the Eastern Mediterranean, one of the most lively and vicious was that of the Dalmatian Archipelago. The Illyrians of Dalmatia were bold mariners, and lurking in the maze of islands subjected Greek and Italian commerces to regular exactions.[1] They went further. They attacked the town of Epidamnus and laid hands upon the Island of Corcyra, which commanded the very entry to the Straits of Otranto. Merely from the defensive standpoint, Rome could not tolerate this definite attack on the *status quo* in the Adriatic without compromising her future and sacrificing her more immediate interests. Military measures were resolved on. Queen Teuta had to capitulate, to cede part of her territory to Demetrius of Pharos, and to pay a heavy war indemnity to Rome. The Illyrian State of Demetrius being thus created, the Greek cities of the coasts (Epidamnus, Apollonia, and Oricos), the Islands of Corcyra and Issa, and some barbarian tribes in the vicinity (the Parthinians and Atintanes) became Roman protectorates.[2] The Illyrian Wars had both reopened the question of the Straits of Otranto and raised the question of Dalmatia. The treaty which ended them settled both, naturally in the best interests of Rome and unified Italy (228).

From the international standpoint, the settlement of 228 B.C. gave rise to no serious difficulty. Epirus had been out of court since the death of Pyrrhus, and the Greeks were too thankful to be rid of the Illyrian pirates to raise the least objection. There was only Macedonia to consider. She was engaged by affairs in Greece, where she was confronted by the hostility of the Ætolians, and, for the moment, her hands were tied, but her kings, with their gaze always fixed on the Adriatic, were only waiting for a favourable moment to strike. That was soon demonstrated. Active diplomatic negotiations were soon opened up between Antigonus Doson, King of Macedonia, and Demetrius of

[1] Pol., II, 8, 1-2.
[2] Pol., II, 11-12; **XXVI**, III¹, 229-304; **CLIII**, 97-112.

Pharos,[1] who had enlarged his dominions in Illyria since the settlement of 228, and found the Roman protectorate irksome. It is probable that a plan of joint action was worked out, and that the conspirators counted on the Punic War breaking out anew, and preventing Rome from intervening effectively in the Adriatic domain. The two allies were, therefore, equally interested in postponing the rupture. But the infatuation of Demetrius spoilt everything. In 220 he violated the treaty of 228, seized the stronghold of Dimale in the land of the Parthinians, and set out on a career of piracy on the Ionian Sea at the head of a substantial fleet.[2]

The moment was as ill-chosen as possible for such a stroke. Rome was still unfettered in the direction of Carthage, and had all her forces at her disposal. And, as Polybius justly remarks,[3] a prompt settlement of Adriatic affairs was all in her interests. In Macedonia Antigonus Doson had just died, and the accession of Philip V, a youth of seventeen, to the throne of Alexander could only facilitate the needful operations. Demetrius, left to himself, was doomed. The Senate sent an army under the consul L. Æmilius Paulus across into Illyria. Operations did not hang fire. Dimale was recaptured, Pharos capitulated, and Demetrius was deposed and fled to the court of Macedonia. Pharos passed under the Roman protectorate. Though momentarily shaken, the Roman supremacy on the eastern coast of the Adriatic was re-established firmer and more secure than ever (219 B.C.).[4]

In some forty years Rome had solved, as far as was necessary, the three vital questions raised by the unification of Italy on the eve of the Punic Wars. The Tyrrhenian question had been settled by the conquest of the islands of the Western Mediterranean—Sicily, Sardinia, and Corsica. The continental question had been eliminated by the annexation of Gallia Cisalpina. Finally, the Adriatic question had been resolved by the establishment of a protectorate over Illyria and the conquest of Istria. Greater Italy ceased to be a project, and became a reality.

[1] Already before 223, probably by 225, Pol., III, 16, 2-3; **CLIII**, 130-35.

[2] Pol., III, 16, 3; 18, 1.   [3] Pol., III, 16, 4.

[4] Pol., III, 16, 7-19, 13; **XXVI**, III¹, 322-27; **CLIII**, 135-39.

III

HANNIBAL'S CRUSADE

The First Punic War had been the conflict of two nations. The Second appears primarily as a duel between Rome and one man—Hannibal.

> " There is no need," writes Polybius,[1] " to dwell on the contest between Rome and Hannibal and the defeats he inflicted on her, for it was not to any superiority in armament or tactics that the Carthaginians owed their success, but to the talent and genius of their general. . . . As soon as the Romans secured a leader equal to Hannibal victory quickly inclined in their direction."

Appian, having to give a name to the Second Punic War, christened it simply " Hannibal's War." Yet this point of view needs to be corrected by a word of explanation. It is often alleged that in the course of the war Hannibal did not find adequate support in the Carthaginian Government, and that the Hanno faction, the relentless opponent of that of the Barcids, conspired to thwart his victorious activity in every possible way. Specific instances are adduced: At the time of the affair of Sagontum, Hannibal involved Carthage against her will; before Cannæ she left her general without support, and after the victory she gave him reinforcements with a niggard hand. All that is pure legend. In point of fact, Hannibal conducted the war in concert with the legitimate Government of his country; from the outset Carthage stood shoulder to shoulder with him, and during the campaign she followed his lead docilely. She gave him as lieutenants the officers whom he himself selected; for example, his two brothers Hasdrubal and Mago. She did all she could for him everywhere in Italy, Spain, Sicily, Sardinia, and later in Africa. Hannibal's commandership was a veritable dictatorship.[2] But Carthage had only very limited resources at her disposal. Apart from the Numidian cavalry, the recruits raised in Africa were worthless, what was worse, and was indeed to prove fatal, was that the

---

[1] XVIII, 28, 6-9. Sketches of Hannibal's character, Livy, XXI, 4; Pol., IX, 22, 24-26; XI, 19; Diod., XXIX, 19; Dio Cas., XIII, frag. 54; Just., XXXII, 4, 10-12.

[2] **VII**, III, 143-44.

means for recovering the mastery of the sea, lost half a century previously, no longer existed. Rome commanded infinitely superior resources, human and material, and the real question for her was not to find them, but how to employ them.[1] To attack the Roman colossus under such circumstances might seem madness, and here we touch the heart of the problem—Hannibal's plan :

> " So," writes Polybius,[2] " Hannibal's tactics in this respect must excite surprise, and it may unhesitatingly be asserted that, had he begun by attacking the rest of the world so as to finish with the Romans, he would have fully attained his end, but he started where he ought to have finished up, so that his first enterprise was also his last."

Although rather strained, as expressed by the historian, the notion is, nevertheless, right. A less hazardous and surer plan can be imagined, and there is nothing to prove that Hamilcar, Hannibal's father, had not formed such a plan. Not only prosperity, but also life itself was impossible for Carthage without supremacy at sea ; that must be won back at all costs. But this vital aim was unattainable unless Carthage became a great continental State, a military power of the first rank capable of fighting with Rome herself when the day came. The conquest of Spain first and then of North Africa must have appeared as the two main stages on this road to recovery. An abrupt attack, such as Hannibal loved, would be all very well provided reserves of forces were available to enable it to be driven home. Hannibal's army once in Italy, Carthage ought to have been able to put irresistible subsidiary forces into the field, and by recovering the mastery of the sea to maintain that permanent co-operation between the general and the mother-country, without which no success was in the last analysis possible.

Now such reserves were non-existent, and Hannibal knew that better than anyone else. He was aware of the formidable strength of Rome and of unified Italy who followed in her train ; he knew that the city of Rome was fortified and virtually impregnable with the technical means of the day. He recognized that with the effectives under him he

---

[1] On the whole strategic problem, see **CXXIV**, I, 345-73.
[2] Pol., XI, 19, 6-7.

could not secure a line of communications on land six hundred miles long, that the Romans would easily keep the mastery of the sea, and that, once in Italy and cut off from his bases in Spain and Africa, he must find himself in the air and impotent. And yet, in spite of all, he took the risk. That was because this gambler had, or, what came to the same thing in the elaboration of his plans, thought he had, two master cards in his hand. Carrying on the policy of Tarentum and Pyrrhus, he counted on the dissolution of Italian unity through the revival of parochialism, which would have put Rome at his mercy, or, at least, on the formation of a vast Mediterranean coalition, beneath the weight of which Rome must ultimately have succumbed. Were these eventualities certainties? No, indeed, they might at best rank as two possibilities, two hypotheses, both equally rash, neither of which was to be realized. Hannibal's crusade quickly degenerated into an adventure; in fact, it had never been anything else.

At first the effect of surprise was complete. Hannibal crossed the Alps and debouched upon Italy, while the Roman troops in utter confusion were hastening to block the mountain passes. Thereafter his path was a triumphal progress—Tessina, Trebia, and Trasimene.[1] The supreme moment was at hand. Hannibal was only eighty miles from Rome; he had but to descend the Tiber Valley, and he enjoyed equal freedom on either bank. There was no serious force ahead of him. The Carthaginian general had his goal within his grasp, and yet he suddenly turned aside. He marched into Umbria, then into Picenum, and through the land of the Marrucini reached Apulia. Why? Through the need of resting his troops, say some; through the desire to seize a port in Southern Italy, so as to establish communications with Carthage, say others. Neither explanation is convincing. Hannibal might just as well have halted in Etruria, or even in Campania, while, given the chronic incompetence of Carthage to recover mastery of the sea, a port in Italy would lose much of its value to Hannibal. In reality, Hannibal turned aside from the path to Rome just as Pyrrhus had once done, and for the same reasons. He

---

[1] Livy, XXI, 39-XXII, 8; Pol., III, 60-86, 6; **CLXVII**, III, 45-312 and maps 3-6.

knew that a surprise attack upon the city would have been
fruitless, that the city was prepared to withstand a long
siege, and that he lacked the men and machines necessary to
bring such a siege to a successful termination. The "lion's
whelp" of Hamilcar feared to break his teeth against the
granite of the Italian federation.

And so came 216 and Cannæ, Hannibal's strategic masterpiece, which has remained the classic model of envelopment
by wings.[1] That battle, one of the most frightful disasters
that the Roman army had ever suffered, did not have the
decisive results that might have been expected, and on the
whole its effects remained very limited. The victory was
subject to the grave disadvantage of having been won too
far from Rome, and the Senate held strong forces in reserve.
This time again Hannibal dared not advance upon the city,
and, as on the morrow of Trasimene, the compact mass of
Central Italy continued to face his onslaughts.

In risking his offensive, Hannibal had counted on two
last chances—the dissolution of the Italic League and the
formation of a Mediterranean coalition against Rome. But
from the moment of his arrival in Italy disillusionment had
begun, and his hopes had been evaporating. Hannibal expected an insurrection among the Gauls; the latter had no
love for Rome, and had proved it, but they knew her power,
and hesitated to march against her. They ended by declaring
for Hannibal, and a number of them joined his army. Nevertheless, despite his efforts, the revolt never assumed the form
of a great national movement. Scarcely had Hannibal
plunged into Central Italy and communications with him
been interrupted when the Gauls returned to their initial
passivity and left him to his fate. After his victory at
Trasimene, in the very heart of peninsular Italy, Hannibal
counted on a general rising among the Italians of the central
region (Etruscans, Umbrians, and Samnites) and of the
south (Lucanians, Apulians, and Greeks). Through the impotence of some, the distrust of others, and the general
appreciation of the benefits of unity, no one responded, and
Rome could organize the resistance at her leisure.[2]

[1] On Cannæ, see Livy, XXII, 46-52; Pol., III, 110-118; App., *Hann.*,
18-26; **XXVI**, III², 131-66; **CLXVII**, III, 278-338, and map 8.
[2] **XXVI**, III², 43 *ff.*

Finally, Cannæ, by the sheer immensity of the triumph, shook the loyalty of the Italians; the great part of South

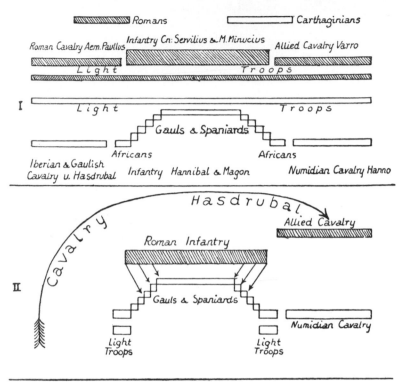

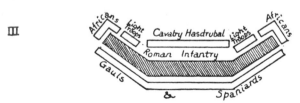

FIG. 11.—THE MANŒUVRE OF CANNÆ (216 B.C.) ACCORDING TO POLYBIUS (III, 113-16) AND LIVY (XXII, 45-49).

I, First phase; II, second phase; III, third phase.

Italy—Samnium (save for the Pentri), Lucania, Bruttium, and part of Apulia and Magna Grecia, the very regions which had previously supported Pyrrhus—and Campania, with its rich capital Capua, deserted the federation and went over to Hannibal.[1] That was no doubt a heavy blow to Rome, but far from fatal. Hannibal led his army to Capua, established winter quarters there in a fertile country close to Rome, and awaited developments.[2] But the essential fact was that the loyalty of Central Italy was unshaken, and this attitude was, in the last analysis, the decisive factor in the final check of Hannibal. What are the reasons for it? No doubt in the very heart of the Italian federation not all were Rome's friends. There were people who inveighed against her militarism, and, in particular, the democratic parties, rigidly excluded from political influence in favour of the rival aristocracies, had never forgiven Rome for their eclipse. But Hannibal, carried away by his success, mistakenly believed these cracks in the edifice of unity much graver than they really were, and hence inferred the possibility of a collapse of the League.

Apart from the fact that she possessed the material means of enforcing obedience, Rome, confronted with Hannibal, the standard-bearer of democracy and parochialism, could rely upon the support of the local aristocracies. Livy has a characteristic phrase on this subject: "It looked as if the disease would spread to all the cities of Italy. Everywhere the people and the leading citizens were divided in opinion: the Senate was for Rome, the people declared for Carthage."[3] Finally, if the Italians as a whole remained faithful to the federal pact, that was also, and perhaps primarily, because they found it to their interests. Though it involved heavy burdens, the Italian federation still offered solid compensations, political, social, and economic; the former isolation had not been without grave disadvantages, and nearly a century of life in union had developed in the peninsula, in default of the sense of community of race, which could not exist in Italy, at least a feeling of a new community in needs and interests. In contrast to Hannibal, Rome stood for the modern notion of Italy and unity. It was not only force which won the victory, but also the ideal.

In any case, even after Cannæ, the movement of defection

[1] Livy, XXII, 61, 1-13; XXIII, 2-10; Pol., VII, 1.
[2] Livy, XXIII, 18, 10-16; 45, 4; Str., V, 4, 13 (pp. 250-51 C).
[3] Livy, XXIV, 2, 8-9.

soon stopped and remained strictly localized. In 211, at the moment when Capua, besieged by the Roman army, was about to fall, Hannibal marched upon Rome, not so much to try and take the city—a feat about which he cherished no illusions—as to try once more to raise Central Italy. His enterprise failed, and Capua fell beneath his very eyes. Two years later Tarentum's turn came (209), and Fabius Maximus reconquered the town. Rome made terrible examples of these two cities, and this put an end to any inclinations to revolt on the part of waverers, if any were left. As a whole, the Italian federation had stood fast. On this first and principal point, Hannibal had been mistaken.

His second idea, the Mediterranean coalition, was doomed to a like fate. Hannibal had counted on Syracuse and, above all, on Macedonia. He at first succeeded in both directions. On the death of Hiero, Rome's faithful ally, his successor, Hieronymus, denounced the treaty and went over to the Carthaginian side (215). Since the peace of Naupactus (217) Philip V of Macedonia had been struggling to take advantage of Rome's embarrassments to settle the question of the Adriatic in his own favour. In the spring of 216 he attempted a surprise attack on Roman Albania, but failed lamentably. Warned by this disastrous experience and hoping to find the needed support in Carthaginian co-operation, he concluded a formal treaty of alliance with Hannibal in 215. Macedonia's share in the victory, upon which both parties counted, was to be the exclusion of Rome from the Balkan seaboard. The treaty, as preserved by Polybius,[1] provided :

> " If the gods grant us victory in the war we are waging against the Romans and their allies and if the Romans decide to sue for peace and friendship, we shall grant it only upon these conditions : that you shall be included in the scope of the treaty, that the Romans shall not be permitted to declare war upon you ever, and that they shall be masters neither of the Corcyreans, nor of the Apolloniates, nor of the Epidamnians, nor of Pharos, nor of Dimale, nor of the Parthini, nor of Atintania."

The article was then perfectly explicit : Rome was to lose everything she possessed on the Balkan coast, her protectorate over Dalmatia, as well as her Albanian territories.

[1] Pol., VII, 9; **XXVI**, III², 407-9; **CLIII**, 181-84.

In a word, the whole Adriatic question was to be settled
without her and against her. Rome replied to Hannibal's
successful intrigues for a coalition by redoubling her efforts.
While persisting in her system of a war of attrition in Italy,
she intervened vigorously in Sicily, and rekindled war in
Greece in order to paralyse Philip (212).[1] In the same year
Marcellus took Syracuse, and two years later the Carthaginians evacuated Sicily for good. In 205 Philip was
exhausted and signed the Peace of Phœnice, whereby the
Roman protectorate over the Albanian coast, including the
towns of Apollonia and Epidamnus and the Island of Corcyra,
was recognized, and only Atintinia was left to the King of
Macedonia.[2] The Peace of Phœnice was a death-blow to
Hannibal. He had played his only two cards—the disruption of the Italian federation and the formation of a Mediterranean coalition against Rome—and he had lost. Two years
earlier (207) his brother Hasdrubal had fallen on the battlefield of Metaurus,[3] and Scipio, the future Africanus, had
just completed the systematic conquest of Spain in 206. By
force of energy Hannibal could still hold his own in Italy,
but since the war had become hopeless, desertions had been
growing common, and he only kept his last allies in hand by
terrorism. After thirteen years of agony the Romans had
nothing more to fear from him. The hour for a counter-
offensive had come.

Thereafter developments were rapid. In 205 B.C., repeating the experiment of Regulus, Rome decided to carry the
war into Africa. Scipio won a victory over Carthage and her
ally Syphax, and Hannibal hastened precipitately to Africa
in response to the despairing appeal of his country, only to
be crushed himself by Scipio at Zama, or apparently, to be
precise, at Naragarra, a small town near by.[4] This time
Carthage had to capitulate, and the treaty of 201 B.C.
registered her complete surrender. As far as territory was
concerned, she renounced all claims to Spain, where she left
the Romans a free hand, and recovered her African domains

---

[1] Livy, XXVI, 24; **XXVI**, III², 413; **CLIII**, 208-15.

[2] Livy, XXIX, 12; Pol., XVIII, 1, 14; **XXVI**, III², 435-39; **CLIII**,
276 ff.

[3] Livy, XXVII, 47-50; Pol., XI, 1-3; **CLXVII**, III, 424-94, and map 8.

[4] **VII**, III, 255-80; **XXVI**, III², 588-616; **CLXVII**, III, 599-702, and
maps 11, 13, 14.

of 218, subject to rigorous restrictions. In particular she pledged herself not to recruit mercenaries abroad, surrendered all her elephants, being prohibited from keeping any in the future, and paid a war indemnity of ten thousand talents, payable in fifty years. She was forbidden to make war outside Libya, and even in Libya without the consent of the Roman people. Finally, as a last precaution, Rome forced an alliance upon her.[1]

In 241 Carthage had lost Sicily; in 237 Sardinia and Corsica were wrested from her, and therewith the whole Tyrrhenian Sea; but she kept her national sovereignty and her prerogatives as an independent State, and all the means for an eventual revenge. The treaty of 201 marks the end of Carthage as a great power. She no longer had any foreign possessions, for she had to abandon Spain, and even in Africa her hands were tied. Militarily and financially ruined, closely watched by the Numidian prince, Massinissa who was careful to keep her impotent in his own interests, fettered by a permanent treaty of alliance with Rome, in a word, subject to a Roman protectorate, Carthage was henceforth only a rich commercial town. With the mastery of the sea, her old rival, Rome, had definitely acquired predominance in the western basin of the Mediterranean.

[1] **VII**, III, 288-90; **CCXXVI**, I, 190-202; **XXVI**, III², 556-60, 616-23.

CHAPTER III

TO THE CONQUEST OF THE WORLD—
EAST AND WEST

I

THE EAST—MACEDONIA, THE SELEUCIDS, EGYPT, AND GREECE

SINCE the Second Punic War the relative insolation in which the two basins of the Mediterranean had lived for centuries was broken down. Spain, Africa, and Southern Gaul in the west, and Macedonia, the Greek States, and the Seleucid and Lagid kingdoms in the east, were henceforth caught in one current of political life, which became increasingly

Bibliography.—Texts: Livy, XXXI-LXV (down to 167); *Periochæ* of books XLVI-LII (*cf.* Florus, I, 23-33; Eutropius, IV, 1-14; Orosius, IV, 20-V, 4, and the new data furnished by the Oxyrrhynchus Epitome for the period 150-146, in **LVI**, Beih. II, 1904, pp. 21-27, 112-15, and ed. Rossbach, 131-39); Polybius, XV-XL (fragments); Diodorus, XXVIII-XXXII (fragments, *cf.* Zonaras, IX, 15-31); Plutarch, *Flamininus, Philopœmen, Æmilius Paulus, Cato;* Appian, *Iberic.,* 39-62; *Libyc.,* 68-135; *Illyric.,* 9-11; *Syriac.,* 66-67; *Macedonic.,* frags. 2-19; Cornelius Nepos, *Cato;* Justinian, XXX-XXXIV, XLIV; Pausanias, VII, 7-16; *de Viris Illustribus,* 51-61.

Inscriptions.—(a) Latin: *Fasti consulares,* C.I.L., I², pp. 142-48; *Fasti triumphales, ibid.,* pp. 174-76; *Elogia* on the Scipios, *ibid.,* 10-15, decree of Æmilius Paulus, prætor in Further Spain, 191-189, C.I.L., II, 5041; dedication of the statue of Æmilius Paulus at Delphi, C.I.L., III, Suppl., p. 2316, no. 14203, and Ditt., *Syll.³,* II, 652.

(b) Greek (see Ditt., *Syll.³,* II, pp. 71-260): Letter from Flamininus to the inhabitants of Cyretiæ in Thessaly (196 or 194), I.G., IX, 388, Ditt., *l.c.,* 593; letter from the prætor M. Valerius Messala to the inhabitants of Teos in 193, C.I.G., 3045, Ditt., *l.c.,* 601; the inscriptions concerning M. Acilius Glabro and Roman policy towards Delphi (191-180), Ditt., *l.c.,* 607-15; letter from L. Manlius Volso to the inhabitants of Heraclæa in Latmos in 188, C.I.G., 3800, Ditt., *l.c.,* 618; the *senatus consultum* relating to the Thisbeans in 170, I.G., VII, 2225, Ditt., *l.c.,* 646; the *senatus consultum* about Delos in about 164, Ditt., *l.c.,* 664; the *senatus consultum* of Narthakion (150-147), I.G., IX, 2, 89, and the additions Ditt., *l.c.,* 674; list of Epidaurians slain at the battle of the Isthmus in 146, I.G., IV, 894.

Principal Works.—(i) Rome and the East: **XXVI**, IV¹, 1-406 (down to 167); **XVII**, II, 562-770; III, 1-359; **CXIV**; **XCV**, I, 341-401; II, 1-54;

focussed about unified Italy. As a result of this new situation Roman conquest during the first half of the second century B.C. advanced simultaneously on the eastern and western fronts, but the two phases of its progress were not strictly parallel nor equally important. Down to 150 B.C. the eastern front occupied the foremost place and formed the centre of gravity of Roman policy. Only with the beginning of the Third Punic War and for some fifteen years thereafter did the western front take its place. And, secondly, the eastern front, being the most important, determined the general scheme of the development, events on the western front merely keeping step with its rhythm. The following table of synchronisms will illustrate this essential point :

EAST	WEST
200–197. Second Macedonian War.	
	197–191. Roman offensive in Gallia Cisalpina.
	195–192. War in Spain.
191–188. Wars against Antiochus, the Ætolians, and the Galatians.	
	185–173. Campaigns against the Ligures.
	187–179. War in Spain.
	178–177. War in Istria.
	177–176. War in Sardinia.
	174–173. War in Corsica.
171–167. Third Macedonian War.	
	166–154. End of the Ligurian War.
	156–155. War in Dalmatia.
	154 and following years. End of the war in Spain.
149–148. Andriscos' revolt in Macedonia.	150–146. Third Punic War. Destruction of Carthage.
147–146. Achæan War. Sack of Corinth.	

XCVI, 123-346; L. Homo, in **LXXIII**, 1916[1], 241-79; 1916[2], 1-32; **XXV**, 44-47; **V**, 177-224; **CLIII**, 306-34.

(ii) Rome and the West: (a) Gallia Cisalpina, Corsica, and Sardinia, **XXVI**, IV[1], 410-41; (b) Spain, **XXVI**, IV[1], 441-85; **CCXX**ter and **CCXXI**; (c) Massalia and Southern Gaul, **XI**, I, 518-24; **CXV**, 40-41; (d) Africa, **VII**, III, 297-407. For the general criticism of the sources for this period, see **CXCVI**; **CLXII**; A. Klotz, in **XLVII**, 1915, 481-536, and for the military history, **CLXVII**, II and III[2].

TO THE CONQUEST OF THE WORLD

In 200 B.C. Rome declared war upon Macedonia. This was a turning-point in the growth of Roman imperialism, and an act fraught with incalculable consequences for the future of Rome and the world. The plan of campaign adopted by the Roman general staff was founded primarily on the utilization of the Illyrian coast as a base of operations. The army, mustered at Apollonia, had to push eastward and invade Macedonian territory through the region of the Lakes of Okhrida (Lake Lychnitis) and Presba. With a well-organized base of operations, little likelihood of local resistance, and a certainty of native support it looked as if all precautions had been taken to ensure a swift campaign which it was hoped would be short and decisive. In 199 the Roman troops under P. Sulpicius Galba advanced as far as Lyncestis, but could not penetrate to the heart of Macedonia nor strike a mortal blow at Philip. The consul led back his forces to Apollonia to winter. His successor, P. Villius Tappulus, found the army seething with discontent. By kind words he succeeded in recalling it to obedience. At the same moment the new commander-in-chief, T. Quinctius Flamininus, reached headquarters.

In deciding to take action against Macedonia, the Senate had no intention of conquering Greece; it had been guided by an essentially defensive idea. The creation of a solid Balkan unity might, in the long run, have proved a grave and even deadly peril to Italy, for Hannibal's invasion was still fresh in men's minds. The realization of such unity, whether under the auspices of Macedonia or any other power, must at all costs be prevented. That was the fundamental conception which dictated Roman interference and governed her attitude towards the settlement of Hellenic affairs. Her aim was attained in two stages. The defeat of Macedonia sealed the doom of the Macedonian plan of union. The organization of the Greek world under a Roman protectorate prevented the recurrence of such a possibility in the future, and, by converting Greece into a solid defensive barrier, freed Italy from all worries about the East. As for the philhellenism, which is so freely attributed to the Senate in general and to its mouthpiece, Flamininus, in particular, lets us make no mistake. In Greece, as elsewhere, Rome's policy was dictated simply and solely by her interests, and the skilful way in which she contrived the impotence of the country proves it. Now, Roman policy and the national aspirations of Hellas coincided in one point—both aimed at the maintenance of traditional separatism. Hence, in pursuing a philhellenic policy, Rome was primarily serving her own ends. To her philhellenism, the safest way of conciliating the Greeks, was only a convenient instrument and nothing more.

In the spring of 198 B.C., Flamininus, the new general, repeated the attempt of P. Sulpicius Galba, this time following the Valley of the Aöus (Viosa). He made his way right into Thessaly, but Philip again succeeded in closing the approaches to Macedonia.[1] A double trial had proved that Macedonia was invulnerable on the west; the weak point in her armour lay in the direction of Greece. Flamininus comprehended this, and by a masterly change of front transferred his base of operations on to Greek soil. Thereafter diplomatic and military successes followed in quick succession. The Achæan League, adroitly handled, deserted Philip's side and joined the Romans. Nabis, tyrant of Sparta, and the Bœotian League quickly followed their example. Finally, in the spring of 197 the Macedonian army was routed in the Battle of Cynoscephalæ.[2] Philip signed a treaty of peace which excluded him from Greece and imposed upon him a heavy indemnity.[3]

Macedonia having been eliminated, it remained to organize the Greek world. The first article of the peace treaty had laid down the essential principle of the new order, at least as far as the Greek peoples not subject to Philip were concerned: all those in Europe and Asia alike were "to be free and governed by their own laws." The remainder—i.e., the Greeks who had previously been dependent upon Philip and the cities occupied by his troops— were in their turn solemnly declared free in the famous proclamation of the Isthmian Games (196).[4] If the general rule of liberty was applied simultaneously to both classes, it was not applied under the same conditions. The first had

---

[1] **CLXVII**, II, 33-57, and map 2.
[2] **CLXVII**, II, 57-94, and map 4.
[3] **XXVI**, IV¹, 94-97; **CCXXVI**, I, 228-39.
[4] **XVII**, II, 650-51; **CCXXVI**, I, 231-32; **XXVI**, IV¹, 98-100.

secured their liberty by an international act, the treaty with Macedonia; the latter enjoyed it owing to a purely Roman decision, an act of grace which might be revoked. In practice the result was the same. Under cover of philhellenism, Rome had revived the good old Macedonian plan and had imposed her protectorate upon the Greek world. Roman policy had the end within its grasp. One element of unrest was left in Greece, Nabis, the tyrant of Sparta. With that affectation of disinterestedness, which was an integral part of her Greek policy, Rome was cunning enough to contrive that the Greeks themselves should declare war upon him.

> "It was not for the Romans," solemnly declared Flamininus to the Congress of Corinth (spring of 195), "to decide whether war should be declared against Nabis. It was for the Greeks to signify whether they would leave Argos in his hands. Rome was content to execute their decisions."[1]

War was voted unanimously, the Ætolians alone dissenting. The confederate army marched upon Sparta, while the fleet, under Lucius Flamininus, blockaded the coast and compelled Gythium to surrender. Nabis yielded, and, despite the opposition of the majority of the allies, Flamininus granted him terms. The tyrant quitted Argos and paid a substantial indemnity. He at least kept his throne, and that was his main concern. The treaty of 195, in which Rome, while pretending to demand nothing except for her allies, secured recognition for her protectorate over Greece, was a purely Roman work. The Greeks clamoured for the dethronement of Nabis. Rome took care not to yield. Nabis, maintained at Sparta, formed a counterpoise to the Achæan League and an insurmountable obstacle to the formation of Peloponnesian unity. Despite words and appearances Roman policy pursued its implacable way.

No one was duped in Greece, and the Ætolians in particular gave free vent to their discontent. Roman garrisons had been in occupation of the strategic points of Chalcis, Corinth, and Demetrias for two years, and, despite reiterated endeavours, Flamininus had not been able to obtain the Senate's authorization for their evacuation. At last the Senate made up its mind in March, 194, when allotting

---

[1] Livy, XXXIV, 22-24.

the provinces; Flamininus received orders to evacuate Greece altogether and to conduct the army back to Italy. He convoked the allies at Corinth to announce the news to them formally :

> " Rome had been accused of desiring to perpetuate her dominion in Greece. That was a pure calumny. He was about to set out for Italy and to take the whole army with him. Within ten days the Greeks should learn of the evacuation of Chalcis and Demetrias. As for the Acrocorinthos, he would restore it to the Achæans himself on the spot and under their very eyes."[1]

Even before the assembly dispersed the Roman garrison evacuated the Acrocorinthos, restored the citadel to the townspeople, and quitted the city. A few days later not a Roman soldier was left in Greece. But at least the specific objects at which Roman policy had aimed in entering upon the campaign were fully attained. With Macedonia excluded from the Greek world, Nabis kept in power at Sparta, and the Greeks left to their immemorial jealousies in the name of philhellenism, Balkan unity was impossible, and through the establishment of a Roman protectorate Hellas formed a buffer to the east of Italy similar to that which had been secured a little earlier on the west by the conquest of Spain. Freed from the Carthaginian peril and the Macedonian danger, and protected on both flanks by solid outposts, Italy thought she might at length breathe freely. She had reckoned without Antiochus.

Ascending the throne of the Seleucids in 223 B.C., Antiochus III had set himself a very definite line of policy to pursue. He meant to restore Seleucid power over the whole area ruled by the founder of the dynasty, Seleucus. From his accession he had been systematically carrying out this programme. As a preliminary measure, he suppressed a revolt of the satraps in Upper Asia, and, after a disastrous war with Egypt, undertook a campaign which brought him to the Indus. The alliance, concluded in 202 with Philip of Macedon, allowed him to advance his frontiers farther. As a result of the victory of Panion he won Cœle Syria back from Egypt and thus secured the Seleucid kingdom that

---

[1] Livy, XXXIV, 49, 4-7.

Syrian frontier which was necessary both militarily and economically. Then he returned to the north; in 197 he advanced in Asia Minor as far as Ephesus, which he captured. In 196 he crossed the straits and occupied the towns of Sestos and Lysimachia, which latter city had been almost entirely destroyed by the Thracians shortly before. He thus embarked upon the conquest of Thrace, to which he laid claim as the successor of Seleucus Nicator.

It was this Thracian question which brought him into conflict with Rome. The latter laid down her conditions by the mouth of Flamininus and the ten commissioners at Corinth in 196, and then at the conferences at Lysimachia:[1] Antiochus must abandon the cities of Asia which had formerly belonged to the Lagids or to Philip, must leave the Greek cities in Asia Minor free, and, above all, must not meddle in the affairs of Europe. Thus, on the specific issue of Thrace, the plans of Rome and Antiochus came into open conflict. The latter, nevertheless, firmly continued the prosecution of his programme. He secured the cession to himself of Cœle Syria, and sealed his reconciliation with Egypt by the marriage of his daughter Cleopatra to Ptolemy Epiphanes. That was a crucial moment; henceforth Antiochus would have a free hand in the north. He hastened to profit by the opportunity.

Seleucid policy, strictly Oriental in aims and traditions, aimed neither at a conflict with Rome nor even the hegemony in European Greece. But finding Rome in his way in settling the Thracian question, which alone interested him on the continent, Antiochus was firmly resolved not to retreat, even though the price of constancy might in the long run be war. Hannibal, who had taken refuge at his court,[2] naturally urged him to the conflict, but for different reasons. At the Syrian court he preached a crusade against Rome and the formation of a vast Mediterranean coalition in which Macedonia, Carthage, and the Spanish rebels would eventually be ranged side by side with Syria. This plan was inspired by a rational idea which Hannibal himself had worked to realize during the Second Punic War. Only a huge Mediterranean coalition could still nip Roman expansion in the bud,

---

[1] M. Holleaux, in **LXXII**, 1913, 5-11.
[2] M. Holleaux, in **XLVII**, 1908, 296 *ff.*; **XXVI**, IV[1], 143 *ff.*

if it were not already too late. The Ætolians on their side, dissatisfied with the share allotted to them in the spoils of Philip, invited Antiochus to Greece and predicted a general movement in his favour. As a realist Antiochus doubtless attached only a relative value to these promises and fancies. Hannibal's anti-Roman policy and the Ætolians' Hellenic programme only interested him in so far as they might serve his immediate ends.[1] He let them talk and held his hand. The impatience of the Ætolians, who were determined to involve the King of Syria even in spite of himself, precipitated events. In 192 B.C. they opened hostilities by a triple offensive against Demetrias, Chalcis, and Sparta. Antiochus yielded to the accomplished fact. He landed in Thessaly with the troops he had ready, some ten thousand men all told.

Faced with such an occurrence, Rome did not disguise her policy. She intended, at all costs, not to let Antiochus get a footing in Greece and imperil the protectorate she had established over the country as a result of the previous campaign. She succeeded in gathering about her a regular Hellenic coalition, comprising the Achæan League, Eumenes of Pergamon, Rhodes, and even Philip of Macedon. Through its lack of unison, the Greek world, thus split once more into two camps, threw away the opportunity—perhaps the last—of saving its liberty. The war comprises three acts and an epilogue—campaigns against Antiochus in Greece, against him in Asia, against the Ætolians, and against the Galatians.

Beaten on land at Thermopylæ and on sea in the encounters of Corycos, Side, and Cape Myonnesos, and crushed at Magnesia[2] (end of 190 or beginning of 189), Antiochus signed peace to prevent the total collapse of his empire. He abandoned Asia Minor west of the Taurus and paid a heavy indemnity. Antiochus being eliminated, the turn of his allies, the Ætolians and the Galatians, came next. As after the second war with Macedonia, Rome pretended to be keeping nothing for herself as direct possessions, but through the limits she imposed on the activities of the

[1] On these divergences, see **CLXVII**, II, 127 *ff.*; **XXVI**, IV¹, 141-47.
[2] On the Battle of Magnesia, see **XXVI**, IV¹, 197-203, 390-95; **CLXVII**, II, 179-205, and map 6.

Seleucid monarchy, she obtained confirmation of her protectorate over European Greece, and, as an additional safeguard, proceeded to the establishment of a new balance of power thoroughly favourable to her interests. Cynoscephalæ had given her European Greece, Magnesia yielded her the East. In Greece the Ætolian League was finally crippled, its historic rôle was over. As for Philip and the Achæans, who had loyally fulfilled their duties as allies during the war, Rome contrived that they got as little as possible. In Asia Eumenes and Rhodes were entrusted with the task of mounting guard over Antiochus and seeing that he did not come to life again, and both received substantial additions to their territories. After the successive defeats of Macedonia and Syria, and in view of the incurable decadence of Egypt, Rome no longer found any power capable of standing up against her in the Hellenistic world. The West was ahead of the East, and " divide to rule," the favourite motto of Roman imperialism, inscribed a fresh victory in its list of triumphs.

Victorious over Antiochus, Rome had had to reward her two chief allies in Greece—Philip of Macedon and the Achæan League—with substantial extensions of territory. Philip received several fresh slices, less than he hoped for, but still a goodly estate. The Achæan League at last attained its long-cherished ambition—the unity of the Peloponnese.[1] This double enlargement, to which Rome had only resigned herself of necessity, contained the germ of fresh complications in the future. It was through conflicts with both her old allies, the war with Macedonia in 171 and that with Achæa in 146, that Rome was destined to achieve the mastery of the Oriental world in less than forty years.

Though beaten at Cynoscephalæ and excluded from Greek affairs, Macedonia had not resigned herself to defeat, and Philip had promptly begun to plot revenge. The war with Antiochus, in which his own interests and the impossibility of any other attitude had thrown him into the arms of Rome, had allowed him to press on with his military preparations and give his army the needed training under colour

L   [1] **XXVI**, IV[1], 229-31.

of an alliance. His second son, Demetrius, inclined to the Roman side. Philip did not hesitate to sacrifice him to the exigencies of the national cause and the public weal. When he died himself in the winter of 179-178, leaving his throne to his son Perses, Macedonia was ready. The vital question was: would she be left alone on the day of the supreme combat for independence and Hellenism? If he had ever cherished any illusions on this head, Perses was quickly undeceived, and he could soon see from the failures of his diplomacy that the Greek world would remain as incurably disunited as ever. When the time came he would find sympathizers in Greece and at Rhodes, especially among the poorer classes, but no national enthusiasm nor even any substantial support. The Achæan League and Eumenes of Pergamon were attached to Rome. Egypt and the Seleucid monarchy were absorbed in their own concerns, and were shortly to fall into Rome's hands. Perses was left alone. Rome, who had had a hand in compassing this result, was well aware of it, and soon drew the practical conclusions that this favourable situation implied.

As we have seen, Roman imperialism was already familiar with the theory of preventive war. Perses' isolation offered a magnificent opportunity for applying it once more. In 172 B.C. Eumenes came to Rome with warnings of the dangerous designs of Macedonia, and the next year war was declared. For three successive campaigns the Roman army, badly drilled and led by inexperienced generals, was unable to force a decision. Perses even won some distinct military and diplomatic victories. The King of Illyria, Gentius, joined his cause, and Rhodes was soon emboldened to offer her mediation, a gesture which the Roman Government contemptuously ignored. The tide of anti-Romanism was rising in the East; it was time to put an end to the war. Æmilius Paulus, an able organizer and an energetic general, was appointed commander-in-chief with a thoroughgoing offensive programme. Thereafter events moved rapidly. Perses was crushed at Pydna (168), the Macedonian State collapsed and its king capitulated.[1] To nip any subsequent attempt at revenge in the bud, the Romans

---

[1] On the Battle of Pydna, see **CLXVII**, II, 310-34 (map 9); **XXVI**, IV[1], 326-30.

dethroned the dynasty and broke up the Macedonian national unity. The country was parcelled out among four separate Republics, artificial States foredoomed to impotence with no roots in the past and no hopes for the future.[1]

After Pydna, as after Cynoscephalæ and Magnesia, Rome proceeded to a general settlement of scores in Greece and the East. The Ætolian, Acarnanian, and Bœotian Leagues, which had supported Macedonia or had at least adopted an ambiguous attitude, were weakened, but it was a sign of the times that on this occasion Rome also castigated her allies—the Achæan League, Rhodes, and Eumenes—and even neutrals, such as the Seleucid King Antiochus IV (Epiphanes). In Achæa, where voices had been raised on behalf of Perses during the war, at Rome's instigation Callicrates, the head of the Roman party, drew up a list of a thousand Achæans, who were banished to Italy and interned without trial in different cities in the peninsula. Rhodes painfully expiated her abortive attempt at mediation. The heads of the nationalist party, responsible for this ill-fated overture, were condemned to death by their fellow-citizens, and at Rome there were even some intransigents who demanded a declaration of war.[2] Even as it was, Rhodes lost her continental possessions in Caria and Lycia, and the creation of the free port of Delos dealt a mortal blow to her commercial supremacy in the Ægean.

If Rome was unsparing toward her allies, that was not in order to humour the neutrals. The King of Syria, Antiochus IV (Epiphanes), from his accession, had maintained cordial relations with Rome, and throughout the whole war had preserved a benevolent attitude towards her. While Macedonia was succumbing, he had conquered Egypt, save for Alexandria, which he was besieging. Immediately after Pydna, the Roman ambassador in Rome's name, brought him the formal summons to evacuate the country (168). His message's content was harsh, its form was still harsher, and the celebrated circle of Popilius remains the most brutal

[1] For this work of reorganization, see **XXVI**, IV[1], 331-65, and pp. 344-46 below.

[2] Pol., XXX, 4-9; 21-23, 31, 10-11; Cato, quoted by Aul. Gel., *Noct. Att.*, VI (VIII) (=*M. Cato frag.*, ed. H. Jordan, pp. 21-25); Livy, XLV, 10, 20, 4-25; Dio Cass., XX, frag. 68, 2-3.

of ultimatums within the memory of diplomacy. The days were come when everything must bow to Rome's will. In complying with such an injunction, Antiochos, the head of the last great power surviving in the Mediterranean basin, officially acknowledged Rome's political supremacy. In his person the whole Hellenistic world publicly announced its abdication.

The series of executions closed with Eumenes of Pergamon. Despite the services which he had constantly rendered to the Roman cause, he was treated still more harshly than the Rhodians. In 167 the Senate formally forbad him access to Rome, and in Asia Minor stirred up against him his neighbours—the Kings of Bithynia, Pontus and Cappadocia —and his hereditary foes, the Galatians. With Macedonia destroyed and the Seleucid monarchy prostrate, the King of Pergamon had ceased to be necessary, and might become dangerous. So his position was disclosed to him peremptorily.

The last scene is at hand. During the twenty-two years intervening between the defeat of Pydna and the annexation of Greece, the Greek peoples and the Hellenistic monarchies were beating the air, mere puppets which Rome, the despotic mistress of the Mediterranean basin, was content to manipulate. In the East the Senate pursued its policy of dismemberment with its usual tenacity, and Pergamon, Syria, and Egypt wittingly or unwittingly played its game through their mutual rivalries. At Pergamon the public humiliation inflicted upon Eumenes bore fruit; after his death his son, Attalus II (159-138), bowed his head submissively and was content to obey. In Syria internal policy came to occupy the foremost place, and the menacing shadow of dissolution darkened the landscape. A double Eastern reaction, represented by the Parthians on the east and the Jews on the west, imperilled the very unity of the Seleucid monarchy. There ensued an additional calamity, a competition for the throne. Antiochus IV (Epiphanes), dying in 164, left the power to his son, Antiochus V (Eupator), a child of nine. His cousin, Demetrius I, dethroned the boy king after a reign of two years, but himself perished twelve years later

(150) through the machinations of a usurper, Alexander I (Bala), supported by the Kings of Pergamon and Egypt—Attalus II and Ptolemy VI (Philometor). The Seleucid monarchy was on the slippery slope to anarchy,[1] and in 161 Rome concluded her first treaty of alliance with the Jews.[2] Finally, in Egypt, with Ptolemy VI (Philometor) (181-145), the process of decay, already incurable, was accelerated. Rome did her best to aggravate the disease. In 163-162 the Senate awarded Cyrenaica and Cyprus to Ptolemy VII Euergetes II, brother of the King of Egypt, a dismemberment, which struck a mortal blow at the old monarchy of the Lagids.[3]

From the East, in Africa and Asia, Rome had nothing more to fear; impotence and servility reigned everywhere. But in the Greek world, two foci of resistance were still left; Macedonia could not resign herself to lose her independence and forget her glorious past, and the Achæan League had not yet felt the weight of Roman arms, so that national feeling quickly rebelled there against the growing tyranny of Rome. Side by side with Lycortas, a man of the past who followed the policy of Philopœmen, and in his dealings with Rome at least managed to combine a proper dignity with the necessary submission, stood Callicrates, the head of the Roman party, who stood for unconditional and passive obedience. Lycortas' disappearance, the excesses of Callicrates and the return of the banished Achæans after seventeen years of exile in 150 B.C., at last caused a complete revolution in the direction of Achæan policy. Damocritos, Critolaos, and Diæos, fanatics determined to combat Roman demands even by arms if it came to that pass, came into power. At this very moment the Third Punic War broke out in the west, a last opportunity of saving or, at least, trying to save, Hellenic independence, which the patriots could not let slip. But even this last rising was again only partial; according to their wont the Greeks went into battle with disunited ranks. Macedonia and the Achæan League, with some peoples from Central Greece, alone entered the

[1] **XXVII**, III, 219-65; **XCVI**, 307-46.
[2] I *Macc.*, 8, 17; **XCVI**, 320-21; **CCXXVI**, I, 47, 239-54.
[3] Pol., XXXI, 10; Livy, *Per.*, XLVII; **XVII**, III, 205-12, **XCV**, II, 32-36.

lists, and even these two countries, the leaders of the national movement, could not co-ordinate their efforts.

Macedonia gave the signal in 149 B.C. A certain Andriscos, who had taken the name of Philip and gave himself out to be a son of Perses, raised the populace, beat the local forces several times, and inspired a general insurrection with a frenzy of patriotism. In the absence of Roman troops the Achæan contingents had to be called upon for the defence of Greece, but none the less Andriscos defeated the prætor P. Juventius and invaded Thessaly. But that was the limit of his successes. A Roman army under the prætor Q. Cæcilius Metellus arrived in 148. The King of Pergamon, Attalus II, lent it effective support, and Andriscos, vanquished at the second Battle of Pydna, was taken prisoner (148).[1]

The fate of Macedonia was already sealed when the Achæan League in its turn took the field. In 148 B.C. a new separatist movement broke out at Sparta. Without waiting to consult Rome, the Achæans took arms against it. The strategos Damocritos beat the Spartiates without, however, being able to take the city. Nevertheless, the Senate replied to this act of independence by a brutal decision; it detached Sparta, Corinth, Argos, Orchomenos, and Heraclea in Œta from the League, and a Roman embassy came to communicate the Senate's will to the assembly at Corinth (147). It meant plainly the destruction of Peloponnesian unity, the whole edifice of Achæan policy. This announcement provoked an outburst of patriotism. The Roman envoys were maltreated, and the Achæan League resolved upon war.

In all Greece only Bœotia, Phocis, Locris, and Eubœa promised help. Under such conditions the issue of the contest could not be doubtful, despite the heroism displayed by the last defenders of Greek liberty. Victorious over Critolaos at Scarphæa, and after the latter's death in a second encounter at Chæronæa, Metellus reconquered the whole of Central Greece. His successor, the consul Mummius, crushed the League's last army at the isthmus of Corinth, and the strategos Diæos committed suicide rather than behold the ruin of his country. The Achæans did not defend Corinth,

---

[1] On Andriscos, see G. Cardinalli, in **LXXV**, 1911, 1-20.

but, nevertheless, the town was given over to pillage, its population enslaved, and the whole city systematically destroyed.[1] By this terrible example the Senate meant to discourage any inclination to resistance in the future. Its aim was fully attained. At least, in default of a success which was impossible, the leaders of the Achæan movement had saved their honour and fallen facing the foe.[2] Not all the Greek States in Europe or elsewhere had earned such a eulogy.

II

The West: Gallia Cisalpina, Spain, Southern Gaul, and Africa

Gallia Cisalpina, first conquered between 225 and 219 B.C., had been lost at the beginning of the Second Punic War. When this war ended with the defeat of Carthage in 201, Rome found that the whole task must be begun afresh. We have little information as to the details of the wars in this direction. Save for some fragments Polybius fails us here, and the annalistic writers, Livy's main authorities for these events,[3] as usual abound in falsifications and errors. But though the details remain often suspect, we can at least discern clearly the general character of the conflict and the essential phases of the campaigns, and these are, after all, the main points.

The ancient historians, enamoured of decisive battles and bright descriptions, had nothing but contempt for these wretched campaigns in Cisalpine Gaul and Liguria, and for those in Sardinia or Corsica. No doubt these wars were not very exciting, but they were none the less very severe and bloody.[4] The Gauls, Ligurians, and Istrians fought with the courage of despair, and only Rome's technical and numerical superiority eventually overcame their fierce resistance.

---

[1] **XVII**, III, 350; **CXIV**, 328-629.

[2] The instigators of the last Achæan War are very harshly judged by Polybius, XXXVIII, 17-18; Pausanias, VII, 14, 6; and Diodorus, XXXII, 26. Fustel de Coulanges, in **CXXXIV**, 99-100, strikes a more moderate and juster note.

[3] Books XXXI-XL. On the value of annalistic tradition about such events, see **CXCVI**; **CLXII**; A. Klotz, in **XLVII**, 1915, 481-536.

[4] On the wars in Gallia Cisalpina as a whole, see **XXVI**, IV^1, 410-38.

During the ten years from 201 to 191 their heroic perseverance inflicted very substantial losses on the Roman army. When all was lost, the Boii could not make up their minds to submit, but emigrated in a body to escape the conqueror's yoke. During the war in Istria (178-177) at the siege of Nesactium the besieged, rather than surrender, slew their wives and children upon the ramparts, and then killed themselves, with their King Æpulon at their head, upon the corpses of their dear ones. The Romans punished their tenacity with pitiless repression. In Liguria the legions conducted a regular campaign of devastation. The vines were cut down, the crops burnt, the villages razed to the ground, the populace transplanted bodily to the plains or even into other depopulated regions of Italy, such as Samnium. In Sardinia the prisoners were sold in droves, and their number was such that the expression " Sardinians for sale "—*Sardi venales*—eventually became a proverb.[1] In conformity with the geography of North Italy, these wars, which lasted nearly half a century, were waged in three distinct arenas : Gallia Cisalpina proper in the centre, Liguria in the west, and Venetia in the east. The campaigns in Corsica and Sardinia were contemporary and similar in character, but of secondary importance.

In Gallia Cisalpina the Romans at first temporized. The Second Macedonian War had just broken out and absorbed their attention, and the people, who had only reluctantly voted for it, were in no mood to duplicate it by a second war in Italy without urgent need. But the Gauls, who had let the auspicious moment slip by, failing to support Hannibal wholeheartedly, perceived that their turn would come after Macedonia had been eliminated. The hour for the last struggle for independence had struck.[2] The Boii, Insubres, and Cenomani armed and threw themselves upon the colonies of Placentia and Cremona, the outposts of Romanization in the north. Placentia fell, but Cremona held out, and the whole Celtic flood broke itself beneath the ramparts. The war dragged on for ten years with fluctuating fortunes. The loyal support of the Veneti allowed the Romans to attack the enemy in the rear. In 197 B.C. the consuls C.

[1] Fest., art., " Sardi venales," pp. 428-29.
[2] Livy, XXXI, 10-38, 7 ; 39, 3.

Cornelius Cethegus and Q. Minucius Rufus, aided in the task by the defection of the Cenomani, crushed the Boii and Insubres on the banks of the Mincio. In the following year the consul M. Claudius Marcellus overwhelmed the Insubres near Lake Como and imposed peace upon them. The Boii suffered the same fate, only five years later. Yet when it came to executing the terms of the treaty their hearts failed them, and in 191 B.C. the remnants of the nation crossed the Alps to seek a new home on the banks of the Danube.[1]

In Liguria, Corsica, and Sardinia, as in Gallia Cisalpina, the Second Punic War had meant the loss to the Romans of all the conquered territory. To recover it a series of strenuous campaigns was needed, and these dragged on for over half a century.[2] The work was finished by 150 B.C. Finally, to the North-East of Italy, after the reconquest of Cisalpina, the Romans returned to Venetia without encountering any opposition. The Veneti accepted the accomplished fact, and the old treaty binding them to Rome was easily transformed into a pact of vassalage. The Roman army met more stubborn resistance in Istria, whose inhabitants had taken advantage of Rome's momentary eclipse in order to regain their liberty and create a national unity. As the result of a two years' war, the hero of which was King Æpulon, the land was conquered up to the line of the Arsia. Beyond that river lived the marauding tribes of the Dalmati. The consul C. Marcius Figulus beat them in 156, and in the next year P. Cornelius Scipio Nasica completed their subjugation by the capture of their chief town, Delminium.[3] Italy had now everywhere reached her natural frontiers in the region of the Upper Adriatic.

With the conquest of Gallia Cisalpina, Liguria, and Venetia, Rome's programme in North Italy, was fully realized. The country was conquered; it only remained to improve it and Romanize it. As the heirs of the Etruscans, the Romans continued the great works of public utility, the foundation-stones of which had been laid by their pre-

[1] Str., V, 6 (pp. 212-13 C).

[2] Livy, XXXI, 2, 11-XLI, 22, 5-8; *Per.*, XLVI and XLVII; *Fast. tr.*, for years 177, 175, 166, 158, 155; **XXVI**, IV[1], 418-23, 438-41.

[3] Livy, XLI, 1-5; 9, 1-3; 10-11, 13, 6; *Per.*, XLII; App., *Illyr.*, 11; *Fast. tr.*, for years 177 and 155.

decessors; they dug channels for the water-courses, drained the swamps, and cleared the forests. Agricultural life blossomed out marvellously. A network of Roman roads, serving both military and economic ends, linked up peninsular Italy with the Po Valley. In 187 the Via Flaminia from Arretium to Bononia and the Via Æmilia from Ariminum to Placentia were built, in 148 the Via Postumia from Genua to Aquileia through Placentia, Cremona, and Verona was opened, and other branch roads were subsequently joined on to these.[1]

The two old colonies of Placentia and Cremona, which had been reinforced by fresh colonists in 190, were supplemented by the Roman or Latin colonies of Bononia (189), Mutina and Parma (183), and Aquileia (181), and, in Liguria, by the Latin colony of Luca (180) and the Roman colony of Luna (177). Numerous centres and markets—*conciliabula et fora*—enjoying a large measure of autonomy and serving as the embryos of future communes — Pollentia (Pollenza), Hasta (Asti), Valentia (Valenza), Iria (Voghera), Industria (Monteu da Po), Faventia (Fænza), Forum Livi (Forli), Cæsena (Cesena), Forum Popili (Forlim), and many others— implanted in North Italy the germs of that flourishing urban life which more than twenty centuries later still remains one of its most essential characteristics.[2] Immediately after the conquest the process of fusion between victors and vanquished began. Though the last to be embraced in the union, Cisalpine Gaul none the less very rapidly became an intense focus of Romanization. The land which a century later gave birth to Catullus, Livy, and Virgil deserves a place of honour in the golden book of Latinity.

Finally, the definite annexation of Gallia Cisalpina meant the completion of the first unity of Italy. From the Alps on the north to the Straits of Messina on the south, the political frontiers of the peninsula had come to coincide with its geographical boundaries. Unity was achieved, and when, in 179, the Senate answered the Carnic Gauls' requests for land by a summons to retire across the Alps instantly,[3] it

---

[1] Livy, XXXIX, 2, 6; 10; V. Chapot, in **IV**, *s.v.* "Viæ," 793-98; **XXVI**, IV[1], 427-28

[2] **XXVI**, IV[1], 422-26.

[3] Livy, XL, 53, 5-6; **XXVI**, IV[1], 429.

was not merely acting as the mouthpiece of Roman policy, but also as the organ and interpreter of a national consciousness already awake.

The first conquest of Spain by the Romans[1] had been a mere incident in the Punic Wars. But though Carthage was beaten and eliminated by the treaty of 201, the Romans had no intention of evacuating the country; they installed themselves there permanently as Carthage's heirs. The peninsula's economic value, particularly its silver-mines, obviously influenced this decision.[2] However, the essential reasons for it were not economic, but political and military. To abandon Spain would not have been to leave it to itself, but to reopen it to Carthage. Here the Romans judged rightly. Through failure to recognize the possible function of Spain in Carthaginian schemes of revenge, Rome had come to the brink of destruction. Now, if she was often short-sighted, her memory was always long. Against the hypothetical danger there was only one guarantee—the permanent occupation of the country. The Senate did not hesitate to adopt this solution. However, in their view, it was not yet a question of conquering the whole peninsula. To exclude Carthage from access to Spain it seemed at once necessary and sufficient to occupy the Mediterranean coastline. A permanent but limited occupation was the Senate's guiding idea after the defeat of Carthage. In 197 B.C. Hither Spain in the north and Further Spain in the south were constituted as provincial governorships on the model of the earlier provinces of Sicily and Sardinia. The Saltus Castulensis, the present Sierra Morena, formed the boundary between them. Besides the strip of coast from the Pyrenees to the Straits of Gibraltar, with its towns of Saguntum, Tarraco, and Carthagena, the Roman territory did not comprise much more than the lower valley of the Ebro below Osca (Huesca) in the north, and Andalusia between the Anas (Guadiana) and the sea on the south.

[1] For the criticism of our sources for the conquest of Spain, see CXCVI; CLXII; and A. Klotz, in XLVII, 1915, 481-536; for the Celtiberian Wars, CCXXter, and especially CCXXI, 112-353.
[2] CCXXI, 318.

THE BIRTH OF ROMAN IMPERIALISM

The plan of restricted occupation, despite its attractive appearance, soon showed itself deceptive and hazardous. Rome's hold on the Mediterranean coast of Spain, the danger point, was not definitely secured, and for some ten years Spanish history is a record of successive revolts, followed by punitive expeditions. In 197 an insurrection, in which we may suspect the hand of Carthage, broke out simultaneously in Hither and Further Spain. It took seven years of campaigns, among which that of Cato, in 195, was particularly famous, to pacify the coastal region. About 190 the subjugation of the seaboard was almost complete. But the plan of limited occupation, as applied by the Romans hitherto, involved a further defect still graver than the first; the peoples of the interior persistently and importunately meddled in the affairs of the coast. As allies the Celtiberians and the Lusitanians from the high plateau descended to help the rebels of the coast, or else just to pillage on their own account. Despite the repugnance felt at Rome to any extension of the sphere of operations in Spain, it was ultimately perceived that only the occupation of the tableland would permit of the attainment of lasting results.

About 180 B.C. Rome had set foot on the central tableland after a series of victories over the Celtiberians and Lusitanians, but she could not occupy it permanently for lack of the necessary numbers. The methods of warfare followed for the last twenty years were evidently insufficient by themselves to secure the regular occupation of the country. Rome proceeded to seek by diplomatic means the results which arms could not bring. Tiberius Sempronius Gracchus, appointed prætor in 180, arrived as the representative of the new policy. Conquering the Celtiberians, while his colleague in Further Spain, Sp. Postumius Albinus, crushed the Lusitanians, Gracchus concluded peace with the vanquished on moderate terms. He won their affection by his tolerance and humanity. Thanks to this sage policy pacification spread to the interior, and the foundation of the town of Gracchuris on the Upper Ebro indicates the scope of his achievement in this direction. When Gracchus laid down the governorship of Spain, the whole eastern half of the peninsula east of a line roughly marked by the Pampelo (Pampeluna), the Upper Douro, the Sierra de Guadarrama, and the lower course of the Guadiana had been brought within the sphere of Roman influence.[1]

The period of twenty-four years following the departure of Sempronius Gracchus represented for Spain an era of general peace, disturbed only by a few local risings of no account. But if it brought solid benefits in its train, Roman dominion irked the conquered people through its habits of sternness and oppression. The governors' pride and rapacity ultimately aroused general discontent. The Spaniards complained to Rome. No serious attention was paid to their protests. Their only alternative was to take up arms. The national revolt, allayed for a quarter of a century, broke out afresh, more savage and obstinate than ever. In 154 B.C. the Lusitanians gave the signal. The Celtiberians[2] quickly followed, and soon the insurrection became general. Thus opened the last struggle for national independence, which lasted for twenty-one years. The Spaniards displayed their traditional qualities of courage, stubbornness, and fiery patriotism. The Roman army, very often reduced to insufficient numbers, discouraged by guerilla warfare—the " fire-war " of Polybius[3]—monotonous, savage, and constantly reigniting, and led by incompetent officers, remained inadequate for its task, and could only triumph at the cost of exceptional efforts. Fighting took place in two distinct theatres of war ; there was a Celtiberian war and a Lusitanian war.

The campaign against the Celtiberians opened with a succession of reverses.[4] At Rome the populace responded with the utmost reluctance to the call for recruits, and the aristocracy itself felt little enthusiasm for a war in which there were more blows to be received than spoils to be collected or glory to be won. However, the Senate recognized that a decisive effort was necessary. M. Claudius Marcellus, a good general who had already fought in Spain, was raised to the consulship for the third time, and entrusted with the direction of the Celtiberian War. With great skill

---

[1] **XXVI**, IV[1], 462-64.   [2] App., *Iberi.*, 44 *ff.*; **CCXXI**, 332 *ff.*

[3] Pol., XXXV, 1, 6; **CCXXI**, 200 *ff.*

[4] That was notably the case with the offensive campaign of Q. Fulvius Nobilior (**CCXXI**, 343-45); the winter camp discovered between 1909 and 1912 on the slopes of la Gran Atalaya, near Renieblas, about four miles from Numantia, is a monument of this campaign (*ibid.*, 316).

Marcellus revived the policy of Gracchus, and the majority
of the Celtiberian tribes, allured by the moderate conditions
offered to them, laid down their arms. Unfortunately,
Marcellus' policy encountered the Senate's opposition. It
was disowned, and the war party having regained the
ascendant a new general, L. Licinius Lucullus, the consul
for 151, was sent out to Spain with directions to stamp out
every spark of resistance. He enjoyed little success, and
after his governorship the Celtiberian War dragged on for
another eighteen years. The capture and destruction of
Numantia by Scipio Æmilianus in 133, one of the most
bloody deeds and most ruthless gestures of Roman imperialism, constituted its last episode.[1]

In Lusitania the same strategy was pursued, and the like
result attained. The prætor Servius Sulpicius Galba, despatched from Rome with the same instructions as Lucullus,
sustained a terrible defeat, but avenged it in the following
year and forced the Lusitanians to sue for peace. The
honour of Roman arms thus vindicated, the time seemed to
have come for a revival of the prudent policy of moderation
so successfully applied by Gracchus, and more recently by
Marcellus. Galba preferred to act with a high hand. By
an act of unheard-of treachery in contravention of his sworn
word, he massacred the men in a body and sold the women
and children as slaves (150).[2] The consequences were not
long delayed. The war broke out again fiercer than ever
under the leadership of one of the Lusitanians who had
escaped the massacre—Viriathus. The peasant had in him
the makings of a soldier. In 147 his compatriots acknowledged him as their chief,[3] and thanks to his perfect knowledge of the country he initiated a bloody guerilla war, in
which the Roman troops lost their bravest soldiers. For
five years Viriathus beat all the Roman generals sent against
him. The Romans only overcame him in 139, and still they
only managed to get rid of him by assassination.

The death of Viriathus and the fall of Numantia marked
the end of the war of independence, the last act in the great

[1] **CCXX***ter* and **CCXXI**, 332-75.
[2] See pp. 267 *f.* above.
[3] *Epit. Oxyr.*, in **LVI**, Beih, II, 1904, 96-97; App. *Iber.*, 62; A.
Schulten, in **L**, 1917, 209-37, and **CCXXI**, 353.

Spanish drama. But the conquest was not finished. In 138 B.C. the consul D. Junius Brutus Callaicus advanced to the mouth of the Tagus, and for the first time the Roman legions encamped on the shores of the ocean. Fifteen years later the consul Q. Cæcilius Metellus took possession of the Balearic Islands after having virtually exterminated the population. On the north the Astures, Cantabri, and Vascones still retained their independence; they were only reduced in the time of Augustus.

So soon as Rome secured a definite footing in Spain, the unfettered control of the Gallic coast of the Mediterranean, the sole safe and permanent line of communications with her new conquest, became an absolute necessity to her. And, in fact, the establishment of such control was soon effected through a gradual process. The traditionally cordial relations maintained between Rome and Marseilles (Massalia), the key to the route, facilitated Rome's progress in this direction to an exceptional degree. After the collapse of Syracusan and then of Carthaginian imperialism, Marseilles was left alone to face Rome after the Second Punic War. The pact of alliance which had united the two cities since the fourth century was doubtless a treaty of equality, a *fœdus æquum*,[1] but in practice Marseilles was henceforth condemned to follow in the wake of the new mistress of the seas.[2] She had the wisdom to resign herself to this fate, and when she had to face the combined attacks of the Ligurians and Gauls a couple of years later she appealed to Rome. In 181 B.C. Æmilius Paulus beat the Ligurian Ingauni in the vicinity of Genoa. In 154 the same fate overtook the Ligurian tribes of the region of Var, the Oxybii and Deciati, and Massalia inherited part of their territory, thanks to Rome's generosity. The formation of the province of Gallia Narbonensis was delayed for another thirty years, but from the middle of the second century Rome's word was law on the southern coast of Gaul. In the benign but practical form of a protectorate, the land road from Italy to the Spanish provinces, which was the fundamental aim of Roman policy in those parts, was henceforth fully assured.

[1] Just., XLIII, 5, 3, 10; **CXV**, 35.   [2] **XI**, I, 518-24; **CXV**, 37.

THE BIRTH OF ROMAN IMPERIALISM

Carthage survived the Second Punic War for more than half a century, but she was only the shadow of her former self. Though she remained a rich commercial town, she had ceased to count as a military power, and the treaty of 201 had subjected her to a Roman protectorate. Rome, having attained her war aims in the Western Mediterranean, did not desire the annihilation of her former rival, at least provisionally. Carthage, for her part, conscious of her impotence, did not dream of revenge, the bare idea of which looked like sheer madness. Correct relations were established between the old rivals, of whom the one was satisfied, the other resigned whether she liked it or not. Carthage regularly fulfilled her obligations under the treaty; she paid the annuities of her tribute as they fell due. In 201 she repudiated Hamilcar, a Carthaginian officer left in Gallia Cisalpina, condemned him to exile and confiscated his property. At the time of the wars in Macedonia and Syria, she provided Rome with substantial supplies of wheat and barley. She sent a contingent of six galleys for use against Antiochus. Rome, on her side, made a point of displaying an equally correct attitude. In 188 a Carthaginian embassy passing through Rome had been insulted by a pair of young madcaps. The Government ordered the surrender of the culprits, a courtesy which the delegates magnanimously declined.

Nevertheless, such interchange of courtesies could produce no illusion. Rome had her eye on Carthage, and in the latter there were patriots who forgot nothing. Their chief was Hannibal. Placed at the head of affairs he embarked upon a programme of radical reforms designed to restore his country. He modified the constitution in a democratic direction, reorganized the army, and took pains to place finance upon a sound basis. That is not to say that he was preparing for a Third Punic War; for no genius was needed to see that such was impossible, common sense alone was enough. He knew that in the state of permanent disarmament, in which she had been placed by the treaty of 201, Carthage by herself could not resume the struggle against Rome, in which she had twice been worsted, but she might perhaps have her part to play in some future coalition. Hannibal intended that Carthage should be ready when the day came. And that was all. Despite the correct attitude that Hannibal was at pains to observe, Rome soon became alarmed at his activity. In 195 she made representations to Carthage on this head, and demanded Hannibal's surrender. The Carthaginians bowed to the threat; at least, they spared themselves the crowning disgrace of surrendering their national hero, and let him retire freely into exile.

Carthage might have lived provided she always yielded and made no attempt to escape from her condition of servitude. But if Rome was far away, at her very doors in Africa itself she had an enemy who was resolved to rob her of this last chance of preserving her national existence for the very good reason that he coveted her heritage. This was Massinissa, King of the Numidians, an intelligent, ambitious, unscrupulous, semi-barbarian who dreamed of founding a great empire in North Africa. The treaty of 201 had solemnly guaranteed Carthage her African frontiers as in 218,[1] but an explicit clause accorded the Numidians' king the right of reclaiming all that his ancestors or he had ever possessed, even within these boundaries. Now, Massinissa's theory was delightfully simple: as an intruder, Carthage had stolen from the natives all that went to make up her territory; rightfully they could recover it all from her. Really Massinissa aimed primarily at the city of Carthage itself, for he looked forward to its being the capital of his future African empire. Naturally Rome could not share such a view; for she had not crushed Carthage in order to let the African peril arise anew in a fresh and yet more menacing shape. The Roman Government reserved to itself the right of interposing its veto upon the king's plans.

But for all their disagreement on the ultimate end in view, Roman and Numidian policy coincided on at least one point: it was equally in the interest of both parties to keep Carthage under surveillance and in a state of chronic weakness. Rome might safely leave Massinissa to see that his part of the bargain was carried out. An article of the treaty of 201 forbade Carthage to make war even in Libya without the authority of the Roman people. And so the Numidian king cynically and with impunity took advantage of such a favourable situation. From the beginning of the

[1] Pol., XV, 18, 1; Livy, XXX, 37, 2; **VII**, III, 286 *ff.*

second century, on the very morrow of the peace, frontier disputes began, and lasted for fifty years. In 195, 193, 182, 174, 172, 157, 153, and 152 Massinissa stripped the Carthaginian artichoke leaf by leaf.[1] The process was always the same: Carthage, tied by the treaty, complained to Rome. The Senate answered with smooth words; sometimes, as in 172, when it feared lest she might take the field on the side of Perses, it declared solemnly that it would not tolerate her spoliation, or, alternatively, it made no answer, a more elegant solution. Massinissa kept what he had taken, meaning to recommence his depredations on the next opportunity.

However, a day at last came when Carthage, sick of this policy of hypocrisy and pin-pricks, lost patience. In 150 B.C. Massinissa had again invaded Carthaginian territory, and had laid siege to the stronghold of Orosco. A Carthaginian army marched out against him. It was defeated, and Carthage had to yield as usual.[2] But the really serious thing on this occasion was that Carthage had violated the letter of the treaty of 201 by taking up arms in self-defence. No doubt she could plead valid excuses, and it might have been supposed that she would have been allowed to bear her heavy cross a few years longer, but at this very moment a sudden revival of interest in Africa had taken place at Rome. Carthage was condemned to death, and Rome prepared to execute the sentence without delay. What prompted this new attitude? Fear of revenge perhaps, but also the dread lest Carthage should ultimately fall into Massinissa's hands, and, in this case, the best way of eliminating the danger once for all was to destroy her. Economic considerations, too, doubtless affected the decision. At all events, Cato and the party of *delenda Carthago* won the day.

As we have already seen,[3] in executing the sentence, Rome acted with a perfidy and Machiavellianism which remain grievous blots on her record. None the less, in spite of all the precautions she had taken, and, contrary to all expectations, she had to overcome a desperate resistance. The Carthaginian people would not die. The capital held out for three years (149-146). Unfortunately, in this hour

[1] **VII**, III, 312-22. [2] **VII**, III, 323-28.
[3] Pp. 268-70 above; **VII**, III, 340-3405; **CLXVII**, III, 705-84, and map 15.

of crisis Carthage did not find the leader that her brilliant military traditions seemed to promise. She needed a Hamilcar or a Hannibal. The best she could discover was a Hasdrubal, a mediocrity and a coward, who, after fighting badly, did not even know how to die. Rome for her part possessed a man, Scipio Æmilianus, "the only sage among the flitting shades," as old Cato said with his customary frankness. In 148 he was elected to the consulship for 147. Then, before the driving force of his energy, the whole situation changed. The army was reorganized and properly drilled. Carthage, strictly blockaded, soon felt the pinch of famine, and her surrender seemed only a question of days. She had only one hope left—the reserve army in the camp of Nepheris. Scipio made it his business to rob her of this. He marched upon the camp of Nepheris and took it. Carthage had lost her last army, and the Libyans, who had remained faithful, submitted. The death agony began. In the spring of 146 Scipio at last delivered his assault. The city was taken, and at the express behest of the Senate was razed to the ground. Carthage disappeared, and so the plans of the Numidian princes were frustrated. Rome had killed two birds with one stone and by the annihilation of her old rival realized two items of her African programme simultaneously.

CHAPTER IV

THE POLICY OF ANNEXATION AND THE POLICY OF PROTECTORATES

I

THE FIRST PROVINCES

THE successive cessions of Sicily (241), Sardinia and Corsica (237) by Carthage, on the one hand, and the victorious campaign in Illyria (229-228), on the other, had raised a serious new problem for Rome—that of the organization of her domain outside Italy. The unification of Italy had been followed by the conquest of the Mediterranean basin. How would the Roman State—and it alone, for the Italic federation, whatever its part in the conquest of these lands, had no voice in their organization—proceed to solve this problem? Once more the Roman genius, practical and realistic as it was, did not turn to any pretty abstract theories, but to its practical experience of men and affairs for solutions. These solutions were discovered almost simultaneously during the fourteen years intervening between the end of the First Punic War (241) and the definite organization of Sicily and Sardinia (about 227). During this brief period Rome laid the foundations and fixed the principles of an administrative system which was to govern the Mediterranean world for more than six centuries. She devised the system of provinces and the system of protectorates, two parallel schemes, two complementary ideas.

By the treaty of 241 Carthage abandoned her Sicilian possessions to Rome. It then became necessary to give the conquered territory some permanent organization. Rome

Bibliography.—Texts: Texts are rare (see the bibliographies to Chapters II and III). In the first place, Livy, books XXXI-XLV (down to 167), notably XLV, 29-30; 26, 12-15 (organization of protectorates in Macedonia and Illyria), and Polybius, books I-V (intact) and VI-XL (fragmentary down to 146).

Principal Works.—**XIV**, IX, 48-56, 57-63, 64-68, 203-7, 211-29, 450-51, 462-68; **CCXXVI**, I, 427-58; **CXIV**; **CVII**; **CCXX**bis; K. J. Neumann, in **XLVIII**, 1917, 1-10.

intended to keep the country under her direct control in view of its strategic situation in the centre of the Mediterranean basin and of its exceptional economic importance. Hence of the only two plans which she knew, and which she had applied in the organization of Italy, those of federation and annexation, the first must obviously be dismissed. Annexation alone was practicable. The Roman State proceeded to apply the principle to her new conquest, but with the adjustments and additions that the special case required. As in Italy, she annexed the land and its inhabitants, save that she left the cities a large measure of municipal autonomy. But annexation as practised in Italy involved as a corollary the extension of the right of citizenship. That was out of the question in the case of a distant country whose inhabitants were alien to the Roman people in race, language, traditions, interests, and everything else. Rome had not annexed Magna Grecia to the citizen body, *a fortiori* she could not think of incorporating the Sicilians. At the same time at this very moment after the creation of the last tribes—Velina and Quirina—in 241, she had begun to restrict grants of citizenship. A second characteristic feature of annexation in Italy was that the annexed countries were under the immediate control of the central governmental machinery of the city of Rome, the comitia, magistrates, and Senate, without the intervention of any regional or local representatives. But such a scheme was inapplicable to distant countries like Sicily, Sardinia, and, later, Spain. The Roman State must be represented there by permanent agents. Just as the precedent of Italy had suggested the principle of annexation, so it inspired the idea from which the institution of governorships was to arise by a natural evolution.

In truth the problem had already arisen, although in a more modest form, when the inordinate expansion of the Roman State had begun to burst the old traditional city framework. In two directions it had been necessary to strain the venerable principle according to which the magistrates, the only officers capable of administering the State in the name of the Roman people, must exercise their authority at the seat of citizen Government—that is, at Rome itself; on the one hand, the prefects *jure dicundo*, whom we find in many localities in the Sabine territory, in Etruria, in Campania, and elsewhere; on the other, the Italic quæstors (*quæstores classici*) of Ostia, Cales, and Ariminum were pro-

FIG. 12.—ROMAN ITALY IN 146 B.C.

ducts of the new situation, the first having been created by the fourth century, the second since 267. Accordingly, even before the Punic Wars, there were in Italy delegates, direct or indirect, of the Roman people who did not exercise their functions in the capital; they were local representatives of

THE POLICY OF ANNEXATION

Rome, a seemingly modest but really portentous innovation, which we shall find reacting upon the elaboration of the provincial system. The administrative precedent upon which the idea of provincial governors was to be modelled accordingly existed, but it was a far cry from these still modest personages, the prefects *jure dicundo*, or even the Italic quæstors, to the mighty provincial governors, and it may well be imagined that the Romans did not pass from one to the other without feeling their way cautiously.

Appian[1] alleges that Sicily was administered by a prætor from 241, the very year of its formation as a province. Livy, on the contrary, states that that system was only instituted fifteen years later (about 227 B.C.), when the number of prætors was raised from two to four, the two new officers receiving the governorships of the two provinces of Sicily and Sardinia-Corsica.[2] Of these two statements the second is indisputably the sounder. Consequently, from 241 to 227 approximately, some temporary system must have been devised for Sicily; in all probability, one of the Italic quæstors, with his seat of jurisdiction at Lilybæum, directed the administration of the island. But the imperfections of this scheme were soon recognized at Rome. From the end of the First Punic War Sicily had formed Rome's chief military base for offence and defence in the Mediterranean. To be able to fulfill his functions the governor must enjoy the full *imperium*, but such *imperium* did not attach to the quæstorship. It was, therefore, planned to entrust the government of Sicily and also of Sardinia, which had been lately ceded by Carthage, to a magistrate invested with *imperium*. Only the consulship or prætorship could meet this requirement. Now the number of consuls was strictly limited by the constitution to two. Hence there was only the prætorship to fall back upon, and that is why the number of prætors was doubled about 227, as Livy states.[3] By the creation of provincial prætors the problem of provincial administration was solved, if not ideally, at least, in a generally satisfactory way. The annexation of Syracusan Sicily in 210 involved no change in the general

[1] App., *Sicil.*, II, 1.
[2] Livy, *Per.*, XX; **XIV**, III, 227; **XXVI**, III², 197-200.
[3] Livy, *Per.*, XX.

arrangements previously adopted, save that the governor's authority henceforth embraced the whole island.

So from about 227 B.C. the people had every year to elect four prætors : two for the urban and peregrine prætorships respectively, and two for the provinces of Sicily and Sardinia-Corsica. In accordance with the hallowed rule of annual tenure, all four were elected for one year, and drew lots amongst themselves for the several provinces. The provincial governor, the supreme representative of the Roman people, was thus in the last analysis chosen by election. As the junior colleague of the consuls and the equal of the other prætors, the provincial governor of prætorian rank enjoyed the plenitude of the *imperium*, involving, according to the principles of the constitution, administrative, military, and judicial functions. From the administrative standpoint, the governor, representing the majesty of the Roman people, directed the general administration of the province. He supervised the local authorities and had supreme control of public works. In his military functions, in the absence of any separation of powers, the governor commanded all the land and sea forces in his province, called out recruits, and ordered requisitions as necessary. Finally, he was supreme judge both in civil and criminal cases. A large staff assisted him in his duties ; there was a quæstor (in Sicily, as an exception, there were two after the completion of the conquest in 210), in charge of the financial business, a legate, and various subordinate officers.

The governor clearly enjoyed very substantial powers. He was restrained neither by the opposition of his colleagues, the magistrates at Rome, nor collegiality, nor the tribunician veto, nor, save where Roman citizens were concerned, by the right of appeal, but at least in law he was subject to one permanent check, the local liberties represented primarily by the cities' privileges. Their general status had been defined at the time of the conquest by the *lex provinciæ*, the official charter of the province, and the governor was bound to respect its general principles. In Sicily, for example, Rome had divided the sixty-five cities into three categories, differing widely in numerical content, according to their respective attitudes or her own interests : there were three allied cities (*civitates fœderatæ*)—Messana, Tauromenium, and Netum—then five free cities (*immunes*)—Centuripæ, Halæsa, Segesta, Panormus, and Halicyæ—and, finally, fifty-seven subject cities (*decumanæ*). The allied cities, the most favoured of all, were simply bound to Rome by a *fœdus*, and were regarded as outside the province. They thus were exempt from the governor's authority. The free but not allied cities had retained their liberty, not in virtue of a synallagmatic treaty like the foregoing, but by a mere law granted as an act of grace by the Roman people, and as such revocable at any time. Finally, the subject cities, having passed under Roman sway by way of conquest or through a *deditio*, were subject to the governor's authority without any limitations.

For the provinces, conquest had involved loss of their national independence, and this condition of inferiority was expressed in the very presence of the representative of the Roman State—the governor. What did Rome demand of these first two provinces of Sicily and Sardinia-Corsica? As an almost universal rule she made no military demands upon them; in contradistinction to the system applied in Italy, she did not impose the obligation of military service upon the provincials. She demanded merely a few auxiliaries, and these only in restricted numbers and in cases of necessity. Rome had very little confidence in the military value of such provincial contingents, and judged it safer to entrust the defence of her empire to Italian troops recruited from citizens or allies. The burdens with which she saddled the provinces were primarily financial in character. Italy provided the men, it was for the provinces to find the money.

The conquered territory had become the property (*dominium*) of the Roman people. The provincial soil was, therefore, liable to direct taxation, a liability inherent in its very nature and not to be eradicated. As the methods of financial administration were different in Sicily and in Sardinia, it is desirable to consider the two provinces separately.

Sicily[1] paid three kinds of taxes—the revenue from the public domain, the direct tax, and indirect taxes. At the

[1] On the financial organization of Sicily, consult especially **CV** and **CVII**.

conquest the State reserved to itself a private domain (*ager publicus*),[1] which it leased either to communities or to individuals, and the yield of which was taken by the treasury. To this category belong the rents from cultivated lands (*vectigal*), pastures (*scriptura*), and mines or quarries (*metalla*). The direct tax was the tithe established by Hiero's legislation which the Romans had retained, though they supplemented or aggravated the charges.[2] To the tithe proper were added supplements in kind (*accessiones*)—the three fiftieths, *tres quinquagesimæ*—or in money and forced sales, a Roman innovation—the " bought wheat," *frumentum emptum* designed for the consumption of the plebs and the *frumentum in cellam* supplied in return for payment for the support of the governor's household.[3] In regard to the indirect taxes in their several forms, the various Sicilian cities were differently situated.[4] Allied cities were only subject, and that only partially, to the system of forced sales. The five " immune " cities had to pay in addition the tithe and its supplements. Finally, the fifty-seven cities termed *decumanæ*, besides the foregoing burdens, paid yet another special tax. Rome had accordingly taken over the whole system of Hiero, but had aggravated its terms and burdened it with new obligations to be paid for by the prosperity of Sicilian agriculture. The indirect tax meant essentially the customs dues (*portoria*). Sicily formed a customs district, and all commodities crossing its borders were subject to an *ad valorem* duty of five per cent.[5]

The second province—Sardinia-Corsica—enjoyed a far less favourable political and financial status than Sicily. A large part of the country had been confiscated at the time of the conquest, and was reduced to the level of public domain land; the rest paid the tithe in kind and a heavy tribute besides. No town enjoyed the privileged status of an allied city nor even that of a free city, and Cicero,[6] referring to the last century of the Republic, tells us that Sardinia was the only province to be placed in this position of unenviable legal inferiority. Two new provinces—Further and Hither Spain—were created in 197, and thereafter the Roman State

---

[1] **CVII**, 239-49.
[3] **CVII**, 172-204.
[5] **CV**, 80.
[2] **CVII**, 77-120.
[4] **CVII**, 205-54.
[6] Cic., *pro Balbo*, XVIII, 41.

possessed four, a number which did not vary till the middle of the second century.

With the organization of the provinces the systematic exploitation of the Mediterranean world by Rome began. Keeping strictly to the letter of the law indeed, the burdens which she imposed on her provinces remained very moderate, especially when it is remembered that she did not require of them the heaviest tax of all—the tax of blood. But theory is one thing, practice another, and viewed from this angle the aspect of affairs changes considerably. By their offices, governors and tax-collectors were in a position to exploit the provinces on their own account, and they did not let such a rich harvest slip. As far as the governors are concerned, their attitude was conditioned by the Roman political system and intimately connected with the conception of magistracy. A provincial governorship represented, at least, to some magistrates, the provincial prætors, one stage in their official career, the *cursus honorum*. Every prætorian governor had already held the offices of quæstor, of ædile, and, sometimes, if he were a plebeian, of tribune; he aspired to the consulship. Now all these magistracies were honorary, and, moreover, they entailed considerable expenditure both in election costs and in all sorts of largesses during the term of office. Nor yet was any regular salary attached to a provincial governorship. And so the office seemed, and came to seem more and more, an invitation to refill one's purse and restore one's fortune at the expense of the provincials. Governors changed every year, and, worst of all, despite the legal restrictions imposed by the provincial charter or the Senate's instructions, they acted in their provinces almost as despotic sovereigns, and disposed at pleasure of the properties and even of the persons of those under their care.[1] In fact, the central Government left the observation of the laws to them, and allowed them a discretionary power in dealing with provincials. On the spot there were none of those constitutional checks upon their activity to which a magistrate in Rome or Italy was exposed; the governors' power was limited neither by being shared with a colleague, nor by the right of appeal, nor by the tribunicial veto. Nor were they accountable to any

---

[1] **CVII**, 121-71.

effective judicial authority, to which the provincials might appeal. Theoretically any complaints must be addressed to the Senate, but the senators, being themselves all either ex-governors or potential governors, were careful to shut their eyes to abuses from which they had profited in the past or hoped to profit in the future. The provincial governor might, therefore, safely repair his fortunes at the risk of having to share the spoils at a pinch with some of his influential colleagues in the Senate. Under such circumstances it may easily be understood that the complaints of the provincials were, as a general rule, fruitless.

At the end of the third century and at the beginning of the second the evil was not yet great. As there were still only four provinces—Sicily, Sardinia-Corsica, and the two Spains—supervision by the central Government was easy. And, on the other hand, as long as independent States existed in the Mediterranean basin, Rome spared the provincials for reasons of prudence. But with the advance of the Roman monopoly of power these guarantees gradually disappeared and the defects of the provincial system latent in it from the first creation of the provinces, and implicit in the very conception of these, became glaring. Robbed by the administration in the form of senatorial governors, the provincials were equally plundered, though in a different way by the tax-collectors, whom the governors were powerless to restrain even when they were not their accomplices.[1] The brutal exploitation of the conquered lands, one of the darkest blots in Republican administration, did not reach its height till the second century. But the evil was deeply rooted in the preceding period, and in this respect again the era of the Punic Wars marks a decisive moment in the organization of Rome's domain outside Italy.

II

THE PROTECTORATE SYSTEM

Of the two plans that had guided the organization of the Italian federation the one, annexation, had suggested the basic principles of the provincial administration, as we

[1] **CVII**, 77-107.

have just seen. The system of federation gave birth to the protectorate system. In Illyria, after the war against Teuta, Rome did not directly annex the country, but established a wide sphere of influence, the main constituents of which were the State of Demetrius of Pharos, the Greek cities on the coast (Epidamnos, Apollonia, and Oricos), the Islands of Corcyra and Issa, and the barbarian tribes of the neighbourhood (Parthini and Atintanes).

Without any annexation or permanent occupation of the country, Roman omnipotence was really established under cover of local powers. Such in Illyria by 228 B.C. was the classical system of protectorate, which was to flourish so luxuriantly at the beginning of the succeeding century. Why was this plan adopted? Its merits are self-evident. The interference of the suzerain power was thereby reduced to a minimum, no administrative staff was required, its operation was elastic, and, in a word, it offered the maximum of advantages with the minimum of burdens and risks. These qualities inherent in the system, which distinguish it at all times and everywhere, obviously would not escape the notice of observant and experienced men like the rulers of Rome. But there were further advantages. Rome was still a city, and scarcely capable of imagining any larger political organism. She, therefore, did not possess the military or administrative machinery which the formation of too many provinces would entail, and she knew that the creation of such machinery would undermine her traditional institutions. She had only a limited number of citizens at her disposal; she could not increase the army without giving a larger share to the Italian element, and so upsetting that cunning balance between citizens and non-citizens within the federation that she had at all times been at such pains to maintain. On the other hand, the Roman nobility, from whose ranks the superior administrative staff must be recruited, formed a very small close corporation, and it could not be abruptly augmented without seriously endangering its whole constitution. Under these circumstances the protectorate system was not only convenient, but absolutely necessary for Rome. The high favour Rome accorded it, and the intense and obstinate reluctance with which she ultimately abandoned it, are at once explained by this vital observation. While after Sicily, Sardinia, and the Spains were constituted provinces, the protectorate system, under the convenient label of federation, was generally applied in both basins of the Mediterranean. Carthage, the Numidian realm of Massinissa, and Marseilles in the west, and Greece, Macedonia, the kingdoms of Asia Minor (Pergamon, Bithynia, and Cappadocia), the Seleucid monarchy, and Egypt in the east, at various dates, but sooner or later, relapsed into the condition of protected countries. From being allies they became vassals.

In the second century B.C., therefore, the protectorate system was in vogue from one end of the Mediterranean to the other, but in respect both of the foundations on which they rested and the principles governing their application, the several protectorates differed profoundly from one another. In the West, where Syracuse and Marseilles had been brought within the Roman sphere of influence even before the Second Punic War, only Carthage preserved intact her rank as a sovereign power over against Rome. The treaty of 201, which sealed her political abdication, had at the same time laid the foundation of the definite supremacy of Rome in the west. In this respect it constituted the charter of the Roman protectorate in the Western Mediterranean. The clause forbidding Carthage " to make war upon anyone outside Libya, and even in Libya to make war without the consent of the Romans," was, from a legal standpoint, equivalent to the establishment of a permanent protectorate.[1]

In the east, where the protectorate régime was systematized and lasted longest, three diplomatic deeds of first-class importance give official expression to the progress of Roman domination, and reveal its successive stages. These are the treaty with Philip of Macedon in 196, the treaty with the Ætolians in 189, and the treaty with Antiochus in 188. The treaty with Macedonia, as given by Polybius and Livy,[2] includes three sets of clauses : territorial, military, and financial respectively, but, in contrast to the treaty of 201 between Rome and Carthage, no provision for a protectorate. Two articles given by Livy—the prohibition against maintaining more

[1] Livy, XXX, 37, 4; Pol., XV, 18, 4; **CCXXVI**, I, 198.
[2] Pol., XVIII, 44; Livy, XXXIII, 30; **CCXXVI**, I, 228-39.

than five thousand men and against keeping elephants, and the interdiction of wars outside Macedonia unless authorized by the Senate—are annalistic forgeries, and so deserve no credence. From the legal standpoint Philip's sovereignty was left intact; although conquered, humiliated, and diminished Macedonia was not yet ripe for that first instalment of servitude represented by a protectorate.

The same remark applies to the treaty between Rome and Antiochus[1] (pourparlers in 189, signature in 188), and the same conclusions may be drawn from it, notwithstanding the insertion of permanent restrictive provisions, such as the fixation of a tcrritorial limit to the military activities of the Seleucids, and the prohibition against possessing war elephants and more than ten decked ships. Finally, we reach the treaty with Ætolia of 189, the character and scope of which are very different from the foregoing. Three articles in it have an exceptional significance. Firstly, in the preamble, the Ætolian nation acknowledges " the empire and the sovereignty of the Roman people ";[2] then " it will regard as friends and foes those of the Roman people";[3] and, finally, " if the Romans be at war with any other people, the Ætolians will be bound to take up arms against the latter."[4] It is no longer a question of a treaty of equality, a *fœdus æquum*, as in the two previous cases, nor even of a *de facto* protectorate, but of an official and legal protectorate, the first that a great State of the Eastern Greek world had accepted.

The protectorate system could, therefore, rest upon formal documents, as in the case of Carthage in the west, or of the Ætolians in the east. On the other hand, it might develop out of a simple state of fact. That is what happened to the countries to which Rome was bound by a *fœdus æquum*—a treaty of friendship (*fœdus amicitiæ*) or of alliance (*societatis*)—those whom Rome had not reduced by force of arms, and who, therefore, did not figure, at least

[1] Pol., XXI, 17, 1-8; 43; Livy, XXXVIII, 38; **CCXXVI**, I, 46-48, 101-3.

[2] Pol., XXI, 32, 2; Livy, XXXVIII, 11, 2; **CCXXVI**, 62-64.

[3] Livy, XXXVIII, 11, 3; there is here a lacuna in the text of Polybius which may be filled in with the aid of Livy; see ed. Th. Büttner-Wobst, IV, p. 66.

[4] Pol., XXI, 32, 4; Livy, XXXVIII, 11, 4.

theoretically, as vanquished, such as the Achæan League in Greece or the Kings of Bithynia, Pergamon, and Egypt in the east. For such a protectorate, based on alliance, there was an official term, the expression always on the lips of the Senate or its representatives : " the friendship of the Roman people." As the disturbance of the balance between the Roman power and the rest of the world became accentuated, these treaties of equal alliance degenerated into contracts of clientship and ever narrower pacts of protectorate in Rome's favour.

The great Eastern Wars against Philip of Macedon, Antiochus, the Ætolians, and Perses in the second century mark a series of successive stages on this road. In contact with hard realities the disguises of diplomacy fell away, and, despite all theoretical equality, the dependence of her fellow-signatories upon Rome became more patent every day. Not only did kings, like Ptolemy VI (Philometor)[1] or Ariarathes V of Cappadocia,[2] invite the Senate to renew treaties of alliance or friendship, but often they actually besought it. So the King of Syria, Antiochus IV (Epiphanes), sent an embassy in 173 with these instructions :

> " Apollonius, the leader," writes Livy,[3] " adduced many good reasons to excuse the king for the delay in the payment of the tribute. . . . The king in his own name implored the renewal of the alliance and friendship which had subsisted between Rome and his father. He prayed the Roman people to command of him all that could be commanded of a king who would show himself a good and faithful ally. He would never be weary of serving the Republic."

In such circumstances, in whatever diplomatic phraseology the treaties might be couched, the Roman Government had no longer to deal with equals, but with clients and vassals. The history of Rome's relations with the Achæan League during the last fifty years of Greek independence offers a peculiarly striking example of the general transformation. Take first the political programme of the nationalist party, the head and the great man of which, till his death in 182, was Philopœmen ; Polybius[4] puts these words into his mouth :

[1] Pol., XXVIII, I, 7-8.　　[2] Pol., XXXI, 3.
[3] Livy, XLII, 6, 8.　　[4] Pol., XXIV, 13, 6.

> " A day will come when the Greeks will be obliged to yield and
> obey. I know that full well, but should we desire to see it arrive
> as soon as possible or as late as possible? The later the better in
> my opinion."

And so he fought with all his might at least to postpone
this inevitable doom.

> " Whenever a demand of the Romans was in conformity with
> the laws and the terms of the treaty of alliance, he endorsed it and
> unreservedly complied with it, but if it trespassed beyond those
> limits he was not the man to yield voluntarily. The magistrates,
> he said, should first plead their case, and next try prayers, and,
> if they had no success, and only then, should they yield and obey
> calling the gods to witness."[1]

Since the Roman intervention against Philip, which so
profoundly altered the conditions of political equilibrium in
the Balkan peninsula, Philopœmen began to appear like a
man of the past. In opposition to the party he represented,
a new one was formed adapted to the times, with Aristenes
as leader. The inevitable end, which Philopœmen was
struggling might and main to postpone, Aristenes did not
hesitate to accelerate.

> " He went out of his way," says Polybius,[2] " to do everything
> that could be helpful to the Romans, sometimes even forestalling
> their demands. He tried, indeed, to seem to obey the laws and
> assumed an air of respecting them, but he yielded when one of
> their provisions was in flat contradiction with the demands of
> Rome."

And Polybius mournfully concludes :

> " that the policy of Philopœmen was noble, but that of Aristenes
> prudent."[3]

Times had changed.

But, as might have been expected, Aristenes himself was
soon outstripped on the road to servitude. The spokesman
of the new party was Callicrates, whose programme at least
possessed the merit of frankness. He advocated " yielding
and letting neither laws nor decrees nor anything else weigh
against Rome's will."[4] Polybius puts into his mouth the

[1] Pol., XXIV, 11, 6-8.
[2] Pol., XXIV, 11, 4-6.
[3] Pol., XXIV, 13, 8.
[4] Pol., XXIV, 8, 6-7 : 9, 2.

M

following typical statements, accentuating his attitude by depicting him as speaking before the Roman Senate itself:

> "It was the Romans' own fault if the Greeks did not obey them and laughed at their written or verbal commands. In all the republics there were at the moment two parties: the one urged submission to the wishes of Rome, without allowing any law or decree or anything whatsoever to stand in their way; the other was continually invoking the laws, the oaths, and the decrees, conjuring the people not to transgress them. The latter policy was much more to the taste of the Achæans and better adapted to tickle the fancy of the mob. And so the partisans of Rome were little esteemed and disparaged by the crowd, while their adversaries enjoyed the opposite fortune. If the Senate manifested some vexation, the rulers would soon be found ranging themselves on the side of Rome, and the masses would follow their example through fear, but if it omitted to take this precaution, everybody would endorse the opposite policy which the multitude found the nobler and the more honourable."[1]

The Senate was not inclined to reject such sage advice, and went so far as to declare explicitly that "it was to be hoped that men like him should be found in the Governments of all the States."[2] A little later Callicrates was appointed strategos. His political influence grew in proportion to the progress of Roman power. When, after the defeat of Perses, Rome wished to strike down her open or covert enemies in Achæa, it was her jackal Callicrates who undertook the filthy business on her behalf. In 154-153 he was found opposing a plan for sending help to the Rhodians on the plea that "without the consent of the Roman people war should not be declared upon anyone nor help sent to any with whomsoever they might be embroiled."[3] And he remained the master of the Government in his country until the democratic reaction which precipitated the final crisis. Some kings gave proof of an equal servility. In 190 B.C. the King of Egypt, Ptolemy V (Epiphanes), invited the Senate to send the Roman army to Asia, and added that he was ready to do whatever they desired.[4] A little later Prusias II, at the time of his visit to Rome in 167, earned a place of honour in this gallery of lackeys, and by his servility became immortalized as the type of the class.[5]

[1] Pol., XXIV, 9, 1-8. [2] Pol., XXIV, 10, 7-8.
[3] Pol., XXXIII, 16, 7. [4] Livy, XXXVII, 3, 9-11.
[5] Pol., XXX, 18; Livy, XLV, 44, 4-21.

Every system of government needs special organs, and the protectorate system as applied by Rome in the first half of the second century had its organs. At the top stood the Senate, which concentrated in its hands the whole foreign policy of Rome, and so exercised supervision over the protected countries. The effective execution of this mission presupposed the existence of intermediate agents. Like the other nations of antiquity, Rome was not acquainted with the system of permanent diplomatic representation. There were neither foreign ambassadors resident at Rome nor Roman ambassadors accredited to the Governments of foreign States. To fill this gap expedients were resorted to, and of these the special embassy was the favourite. Embassies from abroad were constantly coming to Rome to lay before the Senate their offers of service or to prefer their complaints or excuses. In 183, Polybius says,[1] " more embassies from Greece than ever before were concentrated at Rome, and deputations from Macedonia and Pergamon besides." A little later envoys from the Lacedæmonians, from the Lacedæmonian exiles, from the Achæans, from Eumenes, from Arairathes, and from Pharnaces[2] were gathered together. Under the date 167 Livy speaks " of the great number of embassies from kings, nations, and peoples " who thronged Rome and received audience of the Senate in turn.[3] Conversely, Roman envoys were constantly on the spot, either carrying the wishes of the Senate or merely conducting investigations or on tours of inspection. For such confidential missions the most qualified specialists were naturally chosen; in 192, on the eve of the war with Antiochus, Flamininus made a diplomatic tour through Greece to spy out the lie of the land and to rally wavering friends.[4] Finally, in default of strictly official representatives, Rome had agents and confederates in the various States. The Attalids of Pergamon were little better than spies in her pay, and for fear of social revolution local aristocracies did not scruple to play the traitor at a pinch.

One remark in conclusion. The protectorate system, very flexible in theory and in operation, might, when combined with territorial readjustments or partitions, be invested with

[1] Pol., XXIII, 1, 1.
[2] Pol., XXIV, 1, 1-7.
[3] Livy, XLV, 19, 1.
[4] Livy, XXIV, 23, 5.

a peculiar efficacy and become the equivalent of annexation pure and simple in the hands of Roman policy. The case of the Ionian Islands—Corcyra in 229, Zacynthus in 191, Cephallenia in 189, and Leucas in 167—is typical of this procedure.[1]

III

FROM PROTECTORATE TO ANNEXATION

And yet, notwithstanding these undeniable advantages, the protectorate system began gradually to disappear. The decay of the system dates from the victory of Pydna. Rome believed she had found in the protectorate an instrument of hegemony at once economical and efficacious. She saw in it a means of retaining her political predominance permanently, and assuring most cheaply a balance of power in the Mediterranean entirely favourable to her interests. She was mistaken, and proofs of her error soon became glaringly apparent. The balance she thought she had established in the east by the concurrent action of arms and diplomacy soon revealed itself to be unstable. On all sides the current of national life, damned or diverted for an instant by Roman intervention, resumed its imprescriptible rights. Macedonia *versus* Pergamon, the Achæans *versus* Sparta and Messenia, Pergamon *versus* Bithynia, Cappadocia *versus* Cappadocia Pontica, Seleucids *versus* Lagids, State against State, city against city, and faction against faction, there were difficulties and frictions everywhere, even where there were not open conflicts, and the result of this gigantic bankruptcy was universal chaos.

Rome, the slave of her creation and obliged to ensure its safety, at once loathed and despised as a foreigner by those Greeks whose liberties she had in theory assured, while in practice she reduced them to a humiliating vassalage, was forced to interfere constantly. She did so usually in accordance with her habitual methods under diplomatic forms and by dint of many envoys, but less and less attention was paid to her commissioners, and some were even done to death. Only Rome's legions were feared, and her repugnance to

[1] On Corcyra, see above, pp. 286 *f.*; for the other three islands, see Livy, XXXVI, 31, 10-12; 32; XXXVIII, 28, 5-11; 29; XLV, 31, 12-13; Plut., *Flam.*, 17, 4; L. Homo, in **LXXIII**, 1916[2], 22-23.

risking them on the stormy sea of Hellenism was no longer a secret. And yet her repeated and often brutal interventions, by always injuring some interest, only aggravated the trouble, exacerbated the general hostility, and gave rise to fresh incidents. In Macedonia, in Achæa, at Carthage, at Rhodes, and even at Pergamon, hitherto her loyal ally, Rome encountered ever-growing national resistance, a potent weapon in the hands of the factions which her diplomacy only exasperated, and which the force of arms alone was capable of stamping out, as she began to see. In practice, therefore, the protectorate system did not produce the results anticipated by the Senate. Instead of order it engendered only anarchy. The war with Perses, in which anti-Roman sentiment had had free play in many quarters, had revealed the danger to Rome of this general disturbance of balance. A day came when action was essential. Once embarked upon an active policy, Rome found herself drawn on and on, and compelled to eliminate once for all every possibility of subsequent conflict by means of annexation.

But though political considerations were uppermost down to the middle of the second century, they were not the sole ones. They were now reinforced by economic causes. The development of Roman power since the Punic Wars had resulted in a very large increase in the activities of the equestrian class and an extraordinary enlargement of their field of action. Tax-farming, contracting for public supplies, and banking, the three constituent elements in its wealth, thus found a new domain. Let us consider some specific cases. In 199 B.C. the censors P. Cornelius Scipio and P. Ælius Pætus leased to the publicans the great Italian customs of Capua and Puozzuoli.[1] In 179 the censors M. Æmilius Lepidus and M. Fulvius Nobilior created fresh ones.[2] The successive formation of provinces—Sicily in 241, Sardinia and Corsica in 238, and the two Spains in 197—involved the creation of fresh customs barriers, to the advantage of the knights who farmed them. Secondly, the extension of the Roman domination resulted in the multiplication of public works and supplies for the State, for which the knights again contracted. In 169, during the Second Macedonian War, we find the prætor C. Sulpicius

---

[1] Livy, XXXII, 7, 2-3.   [2] Livy, XL, 51, 8.

letting contracts for the supply of six thousand togas, thirty thousand tunics, and some indispensable horses.[1] Finally, for the same reason, the publicans' banking operations assumed an ever-growing importance. At the beginning of the second century the comedies of Plautus introduce us to a whole world of bankers at work and already rolling in wealth. However, the movement was not confined to the equestrian class. The passage in Polybius,[2] showing us " almost all " the Romans sharing directly or indirectly in the public contracts, belongs to the second century.

It was not only in Italy that the growing influence of the economic factor made itself felt, but also abroad. From the day when union had, for the first time in her history, made her a nation, Italy began to spread abroad, above all, towards that east the wealth and refined culture of which were so alluring.[3] Lucanians, Apulians, and Campanians, heirs of the traditions of Magna Grecia, took the road of the Ægean Sea, as the inscriptions of Delos show with peculiarly illuminating testimony.[4] The first Italians, whose presence in the island, about the middle of the third century, is disclosed by epigraphical data, were still humble personages : like Novius,[5] an agricultural labourer, who, about 250, was engaged to brand with red-hot iron the flocks grazing on the sacred properties ; or Serdon, a juggler ; or Agathodorus, a juggler or an actor. Then, as time goes on, the number of such grows. We read, among others, of Marcus, Publius, Vibius, Quintus, Titus Mentius, and Sotion, some expressly described as " Romans " (to be read as Italians), Marcus Sestius of Fregellæ, and Agathon of Petelia. And now business men, such as Heracleides of Tarentum or Nymphodorus of Syracuse,[6] begin to figure among these Italians. From 167-166, the date when Delos, having been restored to Athens and created a free port, became a considerable commercial centre in the Ægean, the Italian colony assumed an ever-growing importance.[7] Now the leading place was taken by the *negotiatores*, merchants, industrialists, and, above all,

[1] Livy, XLIV, 18, 16, 4.   [2] Pol., VI, 17, 3.
[3] **CXLIV**, 18 *ff*.
[4] J. Hatzfeld, in **XXXVIII**, 1912, 5-218.   [5] *Id.*, 102.
[6] *Id.*, 102-3 ; **CCXX**, 12, 75-76.
[7] J. Hatzfeld, in **XXXVIII**, 1912, 103 ; **CCXX**, 75-76.

financiers. About 150 they felt the need of coming into closer contact and uniting. At this date the clubs of Italians were formed, and established themselves in the agora of the Competialistæ, close to the port and the commercial quarter of the town. At first these *negotiatores* had been primarily isolated individuals, but soon a more potent and active element joined them, the agents of the great companies of Roman publicani, the representatives of high finance, whose influence went on growing down to the last years of the Republic.

Together with the social importance of the capitalists, embodied primarily in the equestrian order, grew their influence upon foreign policy. These moneyed men, eager to swell continually the figures of their balances, worked tirelessly to open new outlets, and urged on the policy of expansion. But it was a long time before they came to have the last word. The dispute over the mines in Macedonia in 167 proves this. After the defeat of Perses the question of legislating for the use of the mines came up. The equestrian order desired them to be leased, expecting great profits therefrom. But the Senate met them with a blunt refusal.

> " It was resolved," says Livy,[1] " to abolish the leasing of the mines in Macedonia, which constituted a very substantial source of revenue, and also that of the public lands, because that system could not be applied without the assistance of the *publicani*, and to have recourse to the *publicani* meant either compromising the rights of the State or sacrificing the liberties of the allies."

The liberty of the allies—that was the key-word. Under the protectorate system, whatever means of pressure she had at her command, Rome's hands were not absolutely free, and had they been, in the state of suppressed hostility subsisting between the senatorial and equestrian orders, the Senate would not have failed to take refuge behind such a convenient pretext. And so, to break down any obstacle in whatever quarter, the knights urged on the policy of annexation. If they did not, as is probable, play the leading part in the simultaneous destruction of Carthage and Corinth in 146, we may at least be sure that their weight had been thrown into the support of the double enterprise, and that they exerted all their strength to secure its success.

[1] Livy, XLV, 18, 3-4; *cf.* 29, 10; **CXLIV**, 223-24.

THE BIRTH OF ROMAN IMPERIALISM

Nevertheless, the Senate hung back a long time before entering resolutely upon the course of annexation, which the attitude of the Hellenic world itself made indispensable. It at first thought it possible to escape the necessity that it dreaded by introducing the necessary refinements into the traditional protectorate system and hedging it in with more substantial guarantees than heretofore in the light of acquired experience. After the fall of Perses there were politicians who advocated the annexation of Macedonia and Illyria. Cato, Æmilius Paulus, and the whole traditionalist party opposed this plan, and the Senate endorsed their attitude. The protectorate system was applied to both countries, but it was stiffened by new arrangements designed to guarantee peace and prevent any subsequent attempt at revenge. The reorganization involved two features in particular—the deposition of the dynasties and the disruption of national unity. Perses in Macedonia and Gentius in Illyria lost their thrones, and their exclusion was extended to embrace their whole families.

The two countries were deliberately split up: Macedonia into four districts, with their respective capitals at Amphipolis, Thessalonica, Pella, and Pelagonia (probably Heraclea in Lyncestis)[1]; and Illyria into three, the first including Lissus and the lands of the Taulantii and Pirusti, the second the territory of the Labeati, with Scodra, and the third the coastal region north of Olcinium as far as the Naro (Narenta) and the adjoining districts.

These new republics continued to enjoy independence, at least in theory, and to coin money, a symbol of their sovereign status. Each of the Macedonian republics was governed by a magistrate, presumably annual, assisted by an elected council, the Σύνεδροι. Both sat at the capital of the district. But this nominal sovereignty was curbed by political, military, and financial limitations. Politically, in order to break finally every link between the several regions, Rome prohibited any rights of intermarriage (*connubium*) between them and any common system of ownership (*commercium*) in so far as land was concerned. Militarily, the traditional army, the author of Macedonian nationality and

---

[1] **XXVI**, IV, 338, and n. 260. On the territorial reshuffle, see Livy, XLV, 29, 5-10 (Macedonia), and 26, 12-15 (Illyria).

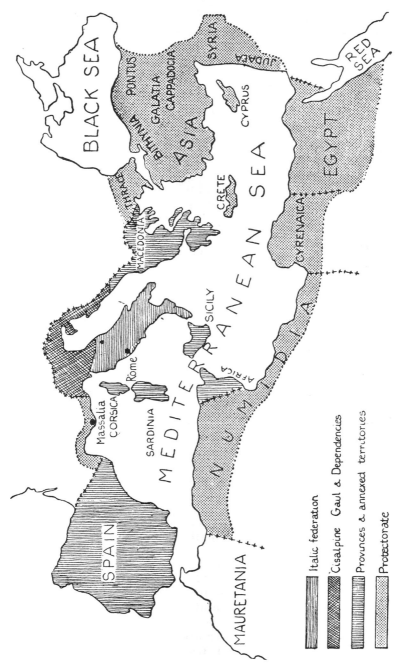

BLACK SEA

PONTUS

BITHYNIA
GALATIA
CAPPADOCIA

SYRIA

JUDAEA

RED SEA

ASIA

CYPRUS

EGYPT

THRACE

MACEDONIA

CRETE

MEDITERRANEAN SEA

CYRENAICA

SICILY

Rome

AFRICA

NUMIDIA

CORSICA

Massalia

SARDINIA

SPAIN

MAURETANIA

Italic federation

Cisalpine Gaul & Dependencies

Provinces & annexed territories

Protectorate

Fig. 13.—The Roman State in 146 b.c., Provinces and Protectorates.

the foundation of its greatness, was abolished. Only frontiers guards were permitted, few in numbers and, as was soon proved, inadequate in practice. Financially, the exploitation of the gold and silver mines was forbidden, and, furthermore, the several Macedonian republics had to pay an annual tribute of one hundred talents to Rome, which incidentally represented only half what they had paid to the former kings.[1] Illyria was similarly treated.[2]

This reinforced protectorate system, however, enjoyed little success. Even on the day when, from the height of his tribune, Æmilius Paulus solemnly announced the new system to the Macedonians, his audience was not filled with unmixed joy :

> "This declaration, made on the first day of the assembly," writes Livy,[3] "was received with mixed feelings. The freedom unexpectedly granted and the reduction of the annual tribute caused lively satisfaction. But seeing their country split up into districts and their commercial relations interrupted the hearers likened themselves to a body torn up into many members which could only exist together."

There are national unions that can be reduced, but that it is vain to try and break up. Macedonia belonged to this category, and the Senate itself came to realize it after twenty years' experience. It learnt the same lesson in Achæa, at Carthage, and elsewhere. And so the day dawned when Rome awoke to the fact that, from the military and political standpoint alike, certain protectorates involved more inconveniences than advantages to the suzerain State. At the same time Roman imperialism, essentially military, came to be duplicated by an economic imperialism, which, beginning with the voice of a suppliant, eventually adopted the tone of a dictator.

The events of 149-146—the insurrection in Macedonia, the shock from Achæa, and the Third Punic War—raised the old problem anew, but this time in its full amplitude. At least, in the Balkan peninsula and in Africa the protectorate system was bankrupt. Experience had declared irrevocably against it, and Rome, always attentive to its lessons, bowed her head and modified her traditional policy accordingly.

[1] Livy, XLV, 29, 4-14.   [2] Livy, XLV, 26, 12-15.
[3] Livy, XLV, 30, 1-2.

THE POLICY OF ANNEXATION

In 148-147, on the very morrow of the fall of Andriscos, Macedonia was reduced to a province on the Roman plan; only a few towns—Amphipolis and Thessalonica in Macedonia proper, Abdera and Ænos in Thrace, and Apollonia and Epidamnos on the Illyrian coast—retained their independence as a special favour by the conqueror. Macedonia was now subject to an annual governor, but she at least received some compensations: the dismemberment imposed upon her after Pydna vanished, and she recovered under Roman rule her traditional unity, and was even augmented by the inclusion of regions which wholly or partly had once moved within her orbit—the Thracian coast on the east and Southern Illyria and Epiros in the west.[1] In Africa, after the destruction of Carthage, the same programme was applied with the same results.[2] The territory of Carthage became a province under the name of Africa—the sixth in the Roman world (146). Only seven cities were declared free as a reward for the attitude in the past and received some of the conquered lands; an inscription of 111 B.C., the Agrarian Law, enumerates them as Utica, Hadrumetum, Thapsus, Leptis, Acholla, Theudalis, and, doubtless, Usilla.[3]

The reduction of Macedonia and Africa to the status of provinces in less than two years was an event of first-class importance in the evolution of Roman imperialism. It meant the introduction of the provincial scheme into two domains which had hitherto been immune from it—Africa and the Balkan peninsula. But still a warning too often disregarded is needed; it would be a mistake to overestimate its importance. In the development of Roman imperialism and the march towards the system of annexation, the year 146 marks an important stage, but nothing more. In the future the Senate still cherished its prejudices in favour of the protectorate system whenever it could be applied without compromising the State's interests. The settlement of the Jugurthine War furnishes a striking proof of this; for Rome annexed the smallest possible bit of Africa—Tripolitana—in 105 B.C. The great annexationist policy was not due to the senatorial aristocracy, but to the military chiefs of the

---

[1] **XVII**, III, 335-37; **CXIV**, 639-40.   [2] **VII**, III, 403-4.
[3] C.I.L., I, 200, l. 79; **VII**, III, 353, n. 1.

last century of the Republic : Pompey in the east and Cæsar in Gaul and Africa. Even then plenty of protectorates still survived, and the last of them—Thrace in Europe; Galatia, Cappadocia, Pontus Polemoniacus, Lycia, Pamphylia, and the Syrian principalities in Asia; and Numidia and Mauretania in Africa—did not disappear till the full imperial age.

On the other hand, Rome introduced into Greece a hybrid régime, a compromise between the two opposing systems. Eubœa, Bœotia, and part of Corinth's territory, all the countries vanquished in the war, were treated as provinces and paid tribute. The federations were dissolved everywhere, the cities methodically isolated, and in all the States Rome gave the power to local aristocracies. At the price of these limitations Greece, as a whole, nominally escaped the status of a province, and at least in appearance preserved her former autonomy.[1] But this autonomy was, in truth, a pure fiction, and the concessions granted her were essentially precarious in nature. From his official residence at Thessalonica, whence he supervised the whole Greek world of the East, the Roman governor of Macedonia kept his eye upon the country always ready to intervene in the interests of the Romans in case of need. Rome made sure of the realities and took the necessary precautions while safeguarding the principle of Greek freedom, the traditional basis of her Hellenic policy. No more practical nor more elegant solution could have been found for this intricate problem.

[1] On this reorganization as a whole and the host of questions it raises, see Paus., VII, 16, 9, 10; **XVII**, III, 352-59; **CXIV**, 640-66; **CXCV**, 423-44; **CIX**, 31-53.

CONCLUSION

OUR conclusion will be brief. The facts as we have tried to set them forth in the foregoing pages speak clearly enough by themselves. Republican Rome bequeathed to the world two political formulæ it had not previously known—Italian unity and Mediterranean empire. By the year 146 B.C. these two formulæ already corresponded to facts, but the realization of both was still incomplete. How and why? "The Romans," wrote Bossuet in a still famous phrase, "did not proceed to the conquest of the world by chance, but by conduct." The antithesis is meant to be striking, but, taken strictly literally, neither of its terms correspond to historical truth. If chance alone do not account for the marvellous destiny which the Roman people had enjoyed, it is at least proper to vindicate for it a very considerable share, and to acknowledge that without an extraordinary conjunction of circumstances Rome would never have attained to that pinnacle of greatness in history that fortune had assigned her. And, on the other hand, by speaking of "conduct," there is the danger of suggesting the idea of methodical continuity and farseeing plan, a late notion, an anachronistic conception, a retrospective philosophy nurtured in the fertile imagination of moderns. But in default of a general "conduct," the Romans at least pursued special "lines of conduct," in the shape of political problems, ever wider, ever more comprehensive, sprung from the necessities of the hour or the morrow which they successively faced with their practical common sense and realistic genius, and endeavoured to solve one after the other. It might seem paradoxical that they should have intervened in both basins of the Mediterranean before completing the unification of Italy. This paradox, which is wholly apparent, is explained just by the absence of any idea of the whole in the directors of Roman policy, and by the strictly realist method adopted in practice.

By the middle of the second century B.C. Italy had achieved her political unity, but she possessed neither administrative unity nor linguistic unity; the creation of

349

these took some centuries more, and was only finished under the Empire. It was just the same with the Mediterranean State; if the legions' victorious sword had carved out its frame, it still lacked the definite frontiers and the uniform organization that the military chiefs of the late Republic and the dynasties of the mature Empire would succeed in giving it.

The explanation at the bottom of this double lacuna must be sought in the causes which inspired the conquest and the methods which had guided its realization. For the sake of security in Italy and to safeguard the unity she had given to the peninsula, Rome had become embroiled in ever more far-reaching adventures in the Mediterranean, but, being a prudent realist, no more susceptible to the entice-ments of chimeras than to the mirage of ideals, she had gone to work gradually step by step. She did not intend to proceed to the conquest of North Italy in order to com-plete the unification of the peninsula until she had secured her flanks by an at least temporary settlement of the Tyrrhenian and Adriatic questions. Nothing here is so decisive as the solid and eloquent testimony of the dates: 241, annexation of Sicily; 238, annexation of Sardinia and Corsica; 229-228, establishment of a Roman protectorate over Illyria; 224, beginning of the great offensive in Gallia Cisalpina. Hannibal's crusade shook and partly demolished the whole edifice. As soon as Carthage had been crushed Rome rebuilt it more solidly, but according to the same general plan: 197, formation of two provinces in Spain; 197, overthrow of Macedonia at Cynoscephalæ; 197-191, conquest—this time final—of the Po Valley and extension of Roman domination to the natural barrier of the Alps.

This method, so admirably adapted to the Roman temperament, had one immense advantage: it allowed Rome to rear a solid and durable structure in Italy. But, like every medal, it had its reverse. Through the reper-cussions abroad of her Italian programme, Rome found her-self involved in a policy of intervention in the Mediterra-nean, both complicated and premature. If you grasp too much and grasp it too quickly there is the danger that your grip will be but weak. The Roman people, like many others after them, learnt this eternal truth by painful experience. When that universal empire which Rome had neither dreamed of theoretically nor pursued systematically became a reality, she had to preserve it and organize it. For this gigantic task she was not equipped, and only four centuries of a personal régime allowed of its being brought to a successful conclusion.

But in the life of nations, as of individuals, lost time cannot be regained. Rome's work, however brilliant it may seem, was destined always to remain incomplete. It would always bear one indelible blot for which the Oriental mirage that dominated the orientation of Roman imperialism in the second century must shoulder the burden of responsibility. In 200 B.C., after the collapse of Carthage, Rome's true future lay in the West. With Carthage out of the way, the gates of Gaul, Spain, and Western Africa, new countries with boundless economic possibilities, were wide open to her influence. To enter them would doubtless have meant a heavy and thankless task, but one in which Rome's immense military and cultural superiority guaranteed certain success. In those vast regions, generally thinly populated, the peasant of Italy, who had been ruined by the growth of the capitalist class and the competition of the large estate, might have found the outlet he needed, and have implanted with the Latin tongue Roman nationality and patriotism beyond the seas. The Roman Government, standing like Hercules at the parting of the ways, did not perceive these possibilities open before it, or rather these necessities imposed upon it.

The East, that El Dorado of brilliant civilization and infinite riches, that land of easy triumphs and prodigious booty, dazzled and blinded it. For fifty years Rome devoted to the East the best of her resources, and concentrated upon it the main exertions of her policy. The West, on the other hand, till the middle of the second century a Cinderella, experienced interminable and aimless wars, genuine colonial expeditions conducted without method, with inadequate forces, and under leaders who were all too often either mediocrities or ciphers. We must wait till the last years of the Republic for the Western question to be seen in its true light. Cæsar, the conqueror of Gaul, and Augustus, the pacifier of Spain, the great colonizers of Narbonensis

CONCLUSION

and Bætica, secured it the place which logically ought to have belonged to it at the beginning of the evolution of Roman imperialism.

It was too late. The civil wars, mowing down men and dissipating energy, had accomplished their deadly work. Depopulated and impoverished Italy could no longer devote the essential contingents of men to the assimilation of the West. Between the Romanization of Italy and that of the Mediterranean world there should have been an intermediate stage, the Romanization of the West, which could not be omitted without endangering the whole result. Rome at length perceived this, but a century and a half too late, when the time lost had made the disease incurable. An indispensable link was always missing in Rome's work. By sacrificing at the crucial moment the possibilities of the West to the mirage of an alien, and, in fact, inassimilable East, Roman imperialism had let slip the substance to grasp at the shadow. That fatal error Rome could never repair, and of it she died in the end.

BIBLIOGRAPHY

I. SOURCES

(A) LITERARY SOURCES

Abbreviations.	Authors.	Works.
A. Gell.	Aulus Gellius	*Noctes Atticæ.*
Ant.	Anticlides	in Arrian, ed. C. Muller, Paris, 1846, pp. 147 *ff.*
App.	Appian	*Historia Romana (Basilica, Celtica, Hannibalic War, Iberica, Illyrica, Libyca, Macedonica, Samnitica, Sicilica, Syriaca.*
Arist.	Aristotle	*Politics,* ed. O. Immisch, Leipzig, 1909.
Aristox.	Aristoxenes	
Cat.	Cato	*Origines, Orationes.* (Catonis *Præter librum de Re rustica quæ extant,* **ed.** H. Jordan, Leipzig, 1860.)
Cæs.	Cæsar	*de Bello Gallico.*
Cic.	Cicero	*Brutus; de Lege Agraria; de Legibus; de Officiis; de Oratore; de Republica; de Senectute; Philippics; Pro Archia; Pro Balbo; Pro Murena; Pro Plancio.*
Corn. Nep.	Cornelius Nepos	*de Illustribus Viris.*
Dion.	Dionysius of Halicarnassus	*Antiquitates Romanæ.*
Diod.	Diodorus Siculus	*Bibliotheca Historica.*
Dio Cas.	Dio Cassius	*Historia Romana.*
Enn.	Ennius	*Annales (Ennianæ poesis reliquiæ,* ed. J. Vahlen, 2nd ed., 1903).
Eph.	Ephorus	*Historia.*
Epit. Oxyr.		*Epitome Oxyrhychos,* ed. E. Kornemann, in **LVI**, Beiheft II, Leipzig, 1904; ed. Rossbach, Leipzig, 1910.
Eus.	Eusebius	*Chronica,* ed. A. Schöne, Berlin, 1866-1875.
Eutr.	Eutropius	*Breviarium.*
Fest.	Festus	*de Verborum Significatione,* ed. M. Lindsay, Leipzig, 1913.
F.H.G.		*Fragmenta Historicorum Græcorum,* ed. C. Muller, Paris, 1849-1853.
Flor.	Florus	*Epitome.*
F.P.R.		*Fragmenta Poetarum Romanorum,* ed. A. Behrens, Leipzig, 1868.
Front.	Frontinus	*Strategemata.*
G.G.M.		*Geographici Græci Minores,* ed. C. Müller, Paris, 1857-1880.
Gr. Lat.		*Grammatici Latini,* ed. H. Keil, Leipzig, 1857-1880.

BIBLIOGRAPHY

Abbreviations.	Authors.	Works.
Heracl.	Heracleides Ponticus	de Anima.
Hdt.	Herodotus	History.
Hier.	Hieronymus	Chronicle, ed. A. Schöne, Berlin, 1866-1875.
H.R.F.		Historicorum Romanorum Fragmenta, ed. H. Peter, 1883.
H.R.R.		Historicorum Romanorum Reliquiæ, ed. H. Peter, 2nd ed., 1914.
Ined. Vat.		Ineditum Vaticanum, ed. d'Arnim, in **XLVII**, 1892, pp. 119-22.
Just.	Justinian	Summary of Trogus Pompeius.
Livy		History.
Lucil.	Lucilius	Satires.
Macr.	Macrobius	Saturnales.
Oros.	Orosius	Historiæ adversus paganos.
Paus.	Pausanias	Græciæ descriptio.
Pind.	Pindar	Pythians.
Plut.	Plutarch	Parallel Lives; Roman Questions.
Pol.	Polybius	History.
Polyæn.	Polyænus	Strategicon.
Pompon.	Pomponius	Liber enchiridii (to Digest, I, 2, 2, 2).
Quint.	Quintilian	Institutio oratoris.
Scyl.	Scylax	Periplus.
Scym.	Scymnos	Descriptio mundi.
Serv.	Servius	ad Æneidem
Sil. Ital.	Silius Italicus	Punica.
Str.	Strabo	Geography.
Suet.	Suetonius	Cæsars.
Tac.	Tacitus	Annales
Theop.	Theopompus	Hellenica.
Thuc.	Thucydides	History.
Tim.	Timæus	Historia.
Val. Max.	Valerius Maximus	Factorum ac dictorum memorabilium libri IX.
Vell.	Velleius Paterculus	Historia Romana.
Virg.	Virgil	Æneid.
de Vir. Ill.		de Viris Illustribus.
Zonaras		Chronicle.

(B) EPIGRAPHIC SOURCES

Abbreviations.	Works.
C.I.E.	Corpus Inscriptionum Etruscarum, by C. Pauli, O. A. Danielsson, G. Herbig, and A. Torp, Leipzig, 1893 ff.
C.I.G.	Corpus Inscriptionum Græcarum, by A. Böckh, continued by J. Franz, E. Curtius, A. Kirchoff, and H. Röhl, 1828-1877.
C.I.L.	Corpus Inscriptionum Latinarum, consilio et auctoritate Academiæ regiæ Borussicæ, Berlin, 1863 ff.

BIBLIOGRAPHY

Abbreviations.   *Works.*

Ditt. *Syll.*   Dittenberger (W.), *Sylloge Inscriptionum Græcarum*, **3rd** ed., Leipzig, 1915-1923.

Fast. cons.   *Fasti consulares*, in C.I.L., I, 1, 2nd ed., pp. 79-167.

Fast.   *Fasti triumphales, id.*, pp. 168-81.
trium.

I.G.   *Inscriptiones Græcæ editæ consilio et auctoritate Academiæ regiæ Borussicæ*, Berlin, 1873 *ff.*

I.G.A.   *Inscriptiones Græcæ antiquissimæ præter Atticas in Attica repertas*, ed. H. Röhl, Berlin, 1873.

I.O.   W. Dittenberger, *Orientis Græci inscriptiones selectæ*, Leipzig, 1903-1905.

II. GENERAL WORKS

K. J. BELLOCH, *Griechische Geschichte*, 2nd. ed., Strasburg, 1912-1916   **I**

G. BLOCH, *La République romaine. Conflits politiques et sociaux*, Paris, 1913   **II**

G. BUSOLT, *Griechische Geschichte*, 2nd ed., Gotha, 1893-1904   **III**

DAREMBERG and SAGLIO, *Dictionnaire des Antiquités grecques et romaines*, Paris, 1877-1918   **IV**

G. FERRERO and C. BARBAGALLO, *Roma Antica*, Florence, 1921   **V**

A. GERCKE and E. NORDEN, *Einleitung in die Altertumswissenschaft*, III, 2nd ed., Berlin, 1914   **VI**

ST. GSELL, *Histoire ancienne de l'Afrique du Nord*, Paris, 1913-1920   **VII**

L. HOMO, *Lexique de topographie romaine*, Paris, 1900   **VIII**

————, *Rome antique*, Paris, 1921   **IX**

CHR. HUELSEN and H. KIEPERT, *Formæ Urbis Romæ antiquæ*, 2nd ed., Berlin, 1912   **X**

C. JULLIAN, *Historie de la Gaule*, Paris, 1908-1920   **XI**

E. MEYER, *Geschichte des Altertums*, 1st to 3rd eds., Stuttgart, 1893-1913   **XII**

B. MODESTOV, *Introduction à l'histoire romaine*, translated by M. Delines, Paris, 1907   **XIII**

T. MOMMSEN, J. MARQUARDT, P. KRÜGER, *Manuel des Antiquités romaines*, French translation, 19 vols., Paris, 1887-1907   **XIV**

T. MOMMSEN, *Histoire romaine*, translation by C. A. Alexandre, 8 vols., Paris, 1863-1872   **XV**

O. MONTELIUS, *La civilisation primitive en Italie depuis l'introduction des metaux.* Texte: I, *Italie septentrionale*, 1895; II, *Italie centrale* (Part I), 1910, and 3 vols. of plates, Stockholm   **XVI**

BIBLIOGRAPHY

B. Niese, *Geschichte der Griechischen und Makedonischen Staaten seit der Schlacht bei Chœronea*, Gotha, 1893-1903 . . . . **XVII**

H. Nisson, *Italische Landeskunde*, Berlin, 1883-1902 . . **XVIII**

E. Pais, *Ricerche sulla storia e sul diretto pubblico di Roma*, Rome, 1913-1916 . . . . **XIX**

————, *Storia critica di Roma durante i primi cinque secoli*, Rome, 1913-1920 . . . . **XX**

————, *Storia d'Italia dai tempi più antichi sino alle guerre puniche: I, Storia della Sicilia e della Magna Grecia*, Turin, 1914 . . . . **XXI**

Pauly-Wissowa, *Real-Encyclopädie der klassischen Alter-tumswissenschaft*, Stuttgart, 1894 (notably the articles "Etrusker," by G. Körte and F. Skutsch, 1907; "Italia," by H. Philipp, 1918; "Latium," by M. Gelzer, 1924; and "Rom," by P. Graffunder, 1914) . **XXII**

T. E. Peet, *The Stone and Bronze Ages in Italy and Sicily*, Oxford, 1909 . . . . **XXIII**

J. v. Pflugk-Hartung, *Weltgeschichte* (in the *Weltgeschichte des Ullsteinschen Verlags*), I, *Altertum* (K. J. Neumann, *Die hellenistischen Staaten und die römische Republik*, pp. 329 *ff.*), Berlin, 1909 . . . . . **XXIV**

A. Rosenberg, *Geschichte der römischen Republik*, Leipzig, 1921 . . . . **XXV**

G. de Sanctis, *Storia dei Romani*, Turin, 1907-1923 . . **XXVI**

III. PERIODICALS

Abhandlungen der königlichen Gesellschaft der Wissen-schaften zu Göttingen, Phil.-hist. Klasse, Berlin . . **XXVII**

Abhandlungen der bayerischen Akademie der Wissenschaften, Munich . . . . **XXVIII**

Allgemeine Zeitung, Munich . . . . . **XXIX**

American Economic Review, Cambridge, Mass. . . **XXX**

American Journal of Archæology, Baltimore . . **XXXI**

Annali dell'Instituto di Corrispondenza archeologica, Rome . **XXXII**

L'Anthropologie, Paris . . . . . . **XXXIII**

Archäologische-epigraphische Mitteilungen aus Œsterreich-Ungarn, Vienna . . . . . . **XXXIV**

Athenæum, London . . . . . . **XXXV**

Atti della Società di Archeologia e belle arte per la provincia di Torino, Turin . . . . **XXXVI**

Berliner Philologische Wochenschrift, Berlin . . . **XXXVII**

Bulletin de correspondance hellenique, Athens . . **XXXVIII**

BIBLIOGRAPHY

Bulletin de la Société linguistique de Paris, Paris . . **XXXIX**

Bullettino della Commissione archeologica communale di Roma,
Rome . . . . **XL**

Bullettino dell'Instituto de corrispondenza archeologica, Rome **XLI**

Bullettino di Paletnologia italiana, Parma . . . **XLII**

Classical Philology, Chicago . . . . . **XLIII**

Comptes-Rendus des séances de l'Académie des Inscriptions et
Belles-Lettres, Paris . . . . . . **XLIV**

Denkschriften der k. Akademie der Wissenschaften zu Wien,
Phil-hist. Klasse, Vienna . . . . . **XLV**

Göttingische gelehrte Anzeigen, Berlin . . . . **XLVI**

Hermes, Berlin . . . . **XLVII**

Historische Zeitschrift, Munich and Berlin . . . **XLVIII**

Jahrbuch der k. d. archäologischen Instituts, Berlin . . **XLIX**

Jahrbücher für Philologie und Pädigogik, Neue Jahrbücher
für das klassische Altertum, Leipzig . . . **L**

Jahresbericht über die Fortschritte der klassischen Altertumswissenschaft (C. Bursian), Leipzig . . . . **LI**

Journal of the Royal Anthropological Institute of Great Britain
and Ireland, London . . . . . . **LII**

Journal of Hellenic Studies, London . . . . **LIII**

Journal of Roman Studies, London . . . . **LIV**

Journal des savants, Paris . . . . . **LV**

Klio, Berlin . . . . **LVI**

Mélanges d'archéologie et d'histoire publiés par l'École fran-
çaise de Rome, Rome . . . . . . **LVII**

Memorie della classe di scienze morali, storiche e filologiche
della R. Accademia dei Lincei, Ser. III (1877-1884), Rome **LVIII**

Memorie della R. Accademia di archeologia, lettere e belle arte
di Napoli, Naples . . . . . . **LIX**

Mémoires de la Société linguistique de Paris, Paris . . **LX**

Mitteilungen des k. d. archäologischen Instituts, Athenische
Abteilung, Athens . . . . . . **LXI**

Id., Römische Abteilung, Rome . . . . . **LXII**

Monumenti antichi pubblicati per cura della R. Accademia dei
Lincei, Milan . . . . **LXIII**

Musée belge, Liège and Paris . . . . . **LXIV**

Notizie degli scavi di antichità, Rome . . . . **LXV**

Nuova antologia, Rome . . . . . . **LXVI**

Philologus, Stolberg . . . . . . **LXVII**

Prähistorische Zeitschrift, Berlin . . . . . **LXVIII**

BIBLIOGRAPHY

Rendi conti della R. Accademia dei Lincei, classe di scienze morali, storiche e filologiche, Rome . . . **LXIX**

Revue archéologique, Paris . . . . . **LXX**

Revue critique, Paris . . . . . . **LXXI**

Revue des études anciennes, Bordeaux . . . **LXXII**

Revue historique, Paris . . . . . **LXXIII**

Rheinisches Museum für Philologie, Frankfort-on-Main . **LXXIV**

Rivista di filologia e d'istruzione classica, Turin . . **LXXV**

Rivista di storia antica, Padua . . . . **LXXVI**

Scientia, Paris and Bologna . . . . . **LXXVII**

Sitzungsberichte der k. preuss. Akademie der Wissenschaften, Berlin . . . . . **LXXVIII**

Sitzungsberichte der k. Akademie der Wissenschaften zu Wien, phil-hist. Klasse, Vienna . . . . **LXXIX**

Wiener Studien, Vienna . . . . . **LXXX**

Wochenschrift für klassischen Philologie, Berlin . . **LXXXI**

Zeitschrift für vergleichende Sprachforschung, Berlin . **LXXXII**

IV. INDIVIDUAL WORKS

H. D'ARBOIS DE JUBAINVILLE, *Les Celtes depuis les temps les plus anciens*, Paris, 1904 . . . . . **LXXXIII**

————, *Les premiers habitants de l'Europe*, 2nd ed., Paris, 1889 . . . . **LXXXIV**

L. DE BEAUFORT, *Dissertations sur l'incertitude des cinq premiers siècles de l'histoire romaine*, new ed., Paris, 1886 . . . . **LXXXV**

J. BELLOCH, *Die Bevölkerung der griechisch-römischen Welt*, Leipzig, 1886 . . . . . **LXXXVI**

————, *Campanien*, 2nd ed., Breslau, 1890 . . **LXXXVII**

————, *(Saggi di storia antica e di archeologia a—)* Rome, 1910 . . . . . . **LXXXVIII**

————, *Der italische Bund unter Roms Hegemonie*, Leipzig, 1880 . . . . **LXXXIX**

A. BERTRAND and S. REINACH, *Les Celtes dans les vallées du Pô et du Danube*, Paris, 1894 . . . . **XC**

M. BESNIER, *L'île tibérine dans l'antiquité*, Paris, 1902 . **XCI**

————, *Lexique de géographie ancienne*, Paris, 1914 . **XCII**

————, *De Regione Pælignorum*, Paris, 1902 . . **XCIII**

E. BIANCHETTI, "I sepolcreti d'Ornavasso, scoperti e descritti," in **XXXVI**, 1895 . . . . . **XCIV**

A. BOUCHÉ-LECLERCQ, *Histoire des Lagides*, Paris, 1903-1907 **XCV**

BIBLIOGRAPHY

A. BOUCHÉ-LECLERCQ, *Histoire des Séleucides* (323-64 B.C.), Paris, 1913 XCVI

D. BRINTON, *The Ethnological Affinities of the Ancient Etruscans*, Philadelphia, 1889 XCVII

E. BRIZIO, *Epoca preistorica*, in Storia politica d'Italia scritta da una società di professori, Milan, 1898, parts 35-36 . XCVIII

C. D. BUCK, *A Grammar of Oscan and Umbrian*, Boston, 1905 XCIX

————, *Elementarbuch der oskisch-umbrischen Dialekte*, trans. E. Prokosch, Heidelberg, 1905 . . . C

FR. BUCHELER, *Populi Iguvini lustratio*, Bonn, 1876 . . CI

S. BUGGE, *Etruskisch und armenisch sprachvergleichende Forschungen*, Erste Reihe, Christiania, 1890 . . . CII

————, *Das Verhaltniss der Etrusker zu den Indogermanen und die vorgeschichtliche Bevölkerung kl. Asiens und Griechenlands*, Strasburg, 1909 CIII

R. CAGNAT, *Le portorium chez les Romains*, Paris, 1880 . CIV

————, *Étude historique sur les impôts indirects chez les Romains jusqu'aux invasions des barbares*, Paris, 1882 . CV

R. CAGNAT and V. CHAPOT, *Manuel d'archéologie romaine*, Paris, 1917-1920 CVI

J. CARCOPINO, *La loi d'Hiéron et les Romains*, Paris, 1919 . CVII

————, *Virgile et les origines d'Ostie*, Paris, 1919 . . CVIII

G. CARDINALLI, *Sulla conditione tributaria della Grecia dopo la conquista romana*, in Studi storici per l'antiquità classica, 1910, 3 CIX

A. CARNOY, *Les Indo-Européens: Préhistoire des langues, des mœurs et des croyances de l'Europe*, Brussels, 1921 . . CX

B. CARRA DE VAUX, *La langue étrusque, sa place parmi les langues, étude de quelques textes*, Paris, 1911 . . CXI

A. CERVESATO, *Latina Tellus, la campagna romana*, 2nd ed., Rome, 1922 CXII

W. CHRIST, *Geschichte der griechischen Litteratur bis auf die Zeit Justinians*, 4th ed., Munich, 1905 . . . CXIII

G. COLIN, *Rome et la Grèce, de 200 à 146 av. J.C.*, Paris, 1905 CXIV

L. A. CONSTANS, *Esquisse d'une histoire de la Basse-Provence dans l'antiquité*, Marseilles, 1923 CXV

A. S. CONWAY, *The Italic Dialects*, Cambridge, 1897 . . CXVI

W. CORSSEN, *Ueber die Sprache der Etrusker*, Leipzig, 1874-1875 CXVII

————, *Ueber Ausprache, Vokalismus und Betonung der lateinischen Sprache*, 2nd ed., Leipzig, 1868-1870 . . CXVIII

A. and M. CROISET, *Histoire de la littérature grecque*, 3rd ed., Paris, 1910-1914 CXIX

BIBLIOGRAPHY

J. Déchelette, *Manuel d'archéologie préhistorique, celtique et gallo-romaine*, Paris, 1908-1914 . . . . **CXX**

W. Deecke, *Corssen und die Sprache der Etrusker*, Stuttgart, 1875 . . . . **CXXI**

————, in *Etruskische Forschungen*, V, 1882, preface . **CXXII**

R. Delbrück, *Der Apollotempel auf dem Marsfeld in Rom*, Rome, 1903 . . . : . . . **CXXIII**

H. Delbrück, *Geschichte der Kriegskunst in Rahmen der politischen Geschichte*, I, *Altertum*, 2nd ed., Berlin, 1908 . . . . **CXXIV**

G. Dennis, *The Cities and Cemeteries of Etruria*, 3rd ed., London, 1883 . . . . . . **CXXV**

G. Dottin, *Les anciens peuples de l'Europe*, Paris, 1916 . **CXXVI**

————, *Manuel pour servir à l'histoire de l'antiquité celtique*, Paris, 1906 . . . . . **CXXVII**

P. Ducati, "Le pietre funerarie felsinee," in **LXIII**, XX, 1911, pp. 357-727 . . . . . . **CXXVIII**

J. Falchi, *Vetulonia e la sua necropoli antichissima*, Florence, 1891 . . . . . . **CXXIX**

G. Ferrero, *Grandeur et décadence de Rome*, Paris, 1904 f. **CXXX**

T. Frank, *Roman Imperialism*, New York, 1914 . . **CXXXI**

————, *An economic History of Rome, to the end of the Republic*, Baltimore, 1920 . . . . **CXXXII**

E. A. Freeman, *Geschichte Siciliens*, German edition by B. Lupus, Leipzig, 1895-1901 . . . . **CXXXIII**

Fustel de Coulanges, *Polybe ou la Grèce conquise par les Romains*, Amiens, 1858 . . . . . **CXXXIV**

E. Gabrici, "Cuma," in **LXIII**, XXII, 1913-1914, pp. 5-871 **CXXXV**

W. Gardthausen, *Mastarna oder Servius Tullius*, Leipzig, 1882 . . . . **CXXXVI**

G. Ghirardini, "La situla italica primitiva studiata specialamente in Este," in **LXIII**, II, 1893, 161-252; VII, 1897, 5-200; X, 1901, 5-222 . . . . **CXXXVII**

O. Gilbert, *Geschichte und Topographie der Stadt Rom im Altertum*, Leipzig, 1883-1890 . . . . **CXXXVIII**

G. Glotz, *Ægean Civilization*, in The History of Civilization, London, 1925 . . . . **CXXXIX**

A. Grenier, *Bologne villanovienne et étrusque*, Paris, 1912 **CXL**

————, *Les Gaulois*, Paris, 1923 . . . . **CXLI**

————, "Fouilles nouvelles à Bologne," in **LXX**, 1914,[1] 321-331 . . . . **CXLII**

BIBLIOGRAPHY

M. HAMMARSTRÖM, "Beiträge zur Geschichte des etruskischen, lateinischen und griechischen Alphabeten," *Acta Societatis Scientarum Fennicæ*, **XLIX**, No. 2, Helsingfors, 1920 . . . . . . **CXLIII**

J. HATZFELD, *Les trafiquants italiens dans l'Orient hellénique*, Paris, 1919 . . . . **CXLIV**

W. HELBIG, *Führer durch die öffentlichen Sammlungen klassischen Altertümer in Rom*, 3rd ed., Leipzig, 1912-1913 . **CXLV**

————, *Das homerische Epos*, 2nd ed., Leipzig, 1887 . **CLXVI**

————, *Die Italiker in der Poebene*, Leipzig, 1879 . . **CXLVII**

R. HEISTERBERCK, *Ueber den Namen Italien*, Friburg, 1881 . **CXLVIII**

E. HENNEBERT, *Histoire d'Hannibal*, Paris, 1870-1891 . . **CXLIX**

G. HERBIG, "Die etruskische Leinwandrolle des Agramer Nationalmuseums," in **XXVIII**, XXV, 4, 1911 . . **CL**

————, *Kleinasiatisch - etruskische Namengleichungen*, Munich, 1914 . . . . . . **CLI**

H. HIRT, *Die Indogermanen, Ihre Verbreitung, ihre Heimat und ihre Kultur*, Strasburg, 1905-1907 . . . **CLII**

M. HOLLEAUX, *Rome, la Grèce et les monarchies hellénistiques au IIIe siècle av. J.C.* (273-205), Paris, 1921 . . **CLIII**

A. HOLM, *Geschichte Siciliens im Altertum*, Leipzig, 1870-1898 **CLIV**

L. HOLZAPFEL, *Römische Chronologie*, Leipzig, 1885 . . **CLV**

L. HOMO, *Problèmes sociaux de jadis et d'à présent*, Paris, 1922 . . . . **CLVI**

————, "Flamininus et la politique romaine en Grèce," in **LXXIII**, 1916¹, 241-279; 1916², 1-32 . . . **CLVII**

C. HUELSEN, *Das Forum romanum, seine Geschichte und seine Denkmäler*, 2nd ed., Rome, 1905, and Supplement ("Die neuesten Ausgrabungen auf dem Forum romanum"), Rome, 1910 . . . . **CLVIII**

A. JARDÉ, *The Formation of the Greek People*, in the History of Civilization, London, 1926 . . . . **CLIX**

H. JORDAN, *Topographie der Stadt Rome im Altertum*, Berlin, 1871-1907 . . . . **CLX**

C. JULLIAN, *De la Gaule à la France*, Paris, 1922 . . **CLXI**

U. KAHRSTEDT, *Die Annalistik von Livius B. XXXI-XL. Vorschläge und Versuche*, Berlin, 1913 . . . **CLXII**

A. KANNENGIESSER, *Ist das Etruskische eine hettitische Sprache?* Gelsenkirchen, 1908 . . . . **CLXIII**

A. KLOTZ, "Zu den Quellen der vierten und funften Dekade des Livius," in **XLVII**, 1915, 481-536 . . . **CLXIV**

E. KORNEMANN, "Die neue Livius Epitome aus Oxyrhynchos," in **LVI**, Beiheft II, Berlin, 1904 . . . . **CLXV**

BIBLIOGRAPHY

J. KRALL, "Die etruskischen Mumienbinden des Agramer Nationalmuseums," in **XLV**, XLI, 3, 1892 . . **CLXVI**

J. KROMAYER, *Antike Schlachtfelder*, Berlin, 1903-1912 . **CLXVII**

R. LANCIANI, *The Ruins and Excavations of Ancient Rome*, London, 1897 . . . . . **CLXVIII**

———, *Storia degli scavi di Roma*, Rome, 1902 f. . **CLXIX**

E. LATTES, *Saggi e appunti intorno alla iscrizione etrusca della Mummia*, Milan, 1894 . . . . **CLXX**

K. LEHMANN, *Die Angriffe der drei Barkiden auf Italien*, Leipzig, 1905 . . . . . . **CLXXI**

J. MARTHA, *L'art étrusque*, Paris, 1889 . . . **CLXXII**

———, *La langue étrusque*, Paris, 1913 . . . **CLXXIII**

H. MATZAT, *Römische Chronologie*, Berlin, 1883-1884 . **CLXXIV**

H. MAYER, *Apulien vor und während der Hellenisierung*, Leipzig, 1914 . . . . . . **CLXXV**

A. MEILLET, *Les dialectes indo-européens*, Paris, 1908 . **CLXXVI**

———, *Introduction à l'étude comparative des langues indo-européennes*, 5th ed., Paris, 1922 . . . **CLXXVII**

———, *Mélanges Cagnat*, Paris, 1912 . . . **CLXXVIII**

O. MELTZER, *Geschichte der Karthager*, Berlin, 1879-1913 **CLXXIX**

A. MERLIN, *L'Aventin dans l'antiquité*, Paris, 1906 . **CLXXX**

A. MINTO, *Marsigliana d'Albegna; le scoperte archeologiche*, Florence, 1921 . . . . . **CLXXXI**

———, *Populonia, la necropoli archaica* (Pubblicazioni del R. Istuto di Studi superiori in Firenze, sezione di filologia e filosofia, N.S., IV) Florence, 1922 . **CLXXXII**

T. MOMMSEN, *Die römische Chronologie bis auf Cæsar*, 2nd ed., Berlin, 1859 . . . . . **CLXXXIII**

———, *Histoire de la monnaie romaine*, trans. by Blacas, Saint-Brieuc, 1865-1874 . . . **CLXXXIV**

———, *Römische Forschungen*, Berlin, 1864-1879 . **CLXXXV**

———, *Die unteritalische Dialekte*, Leipzig, 1850 . **CLXXXVI**

O. MONTELIUS, *Die vorklassische Chronologie Italiens*, Stockholm, 1912 . . . . . . **CLXXXVII**

———, "The Tyrrhenians in Greece and Italy; Preclassical Chronology in Greece and Italy," in **LII**, 1897, 254-71 . . . . . . **CLXXXVIII**

A. MOSSO, "Villaggi preistorici di Caldare e Cannatello presso Girgenti," in **LXIII**, XVIII, 1907, 573-690 . **CLXXXIX**

O. MÜLLER, *Die Etrusker*, 2nd ed. (W. Deecke), Stuttgart, 1877 . . . . . . **CXC**

BIBLIOGRAPHY

S. Müller, *L'Europe préhistorique*, trans. E. Philipot, Paris
1907 . . . . **CXCI**

K. Mullenhoff, *Deutsche Altertumskunde*, Berlin, 1870-1900 **CXCII**

K. J. Neumann, "Römische Klientelstaaten," in **XLVIII**,
1916 *f.* . . . . **CXCIII**

C. Neumann, *Das Zeitalter der punischen Kriege*, Breslau,
1883 . . . . **CXCIV**

G. Niccolini, "La Grecia provincia," in *Studi storici per
l'antichità classica*, 1910, 3, 423-44 . . . . **CXCV**

H. Nissen, *Untersuchungen über die Quellen der 4ten und
5ten Dekade des Livius*, Berlin, 1863 . . . **CXCVI**

————, *Pompeianische Studien zur Städtekunde der Altertums*, Leipzig, 1877 . . . . . . **CXCVII**

K. W. Nitzch, *Die römische Annalistik von ihren ersten An-
fängen bis auf Valerius Antias*, Berlin, 1873 . . **CXCVIII**

E. Pais, *Ancient Legends of Roman History*, New York and
London, 1906 . . . . **CXCIX**

————, *Fasti triumphales populi romani*, Rome, 1920 . **CC**

————, *Imperialismo romano e politica italiana*, Bologna,
1920 . . . . **CCI**

————, *Italia Antica*, Bologna, 1920 . . . . **CCII**

L. Paschetto, *Ostia colonia romana, storia e monumenti*,
Rome, 1912 . . . . **CCIII**

G. Patroni, "L'Origine della domus e d'un frammento var-
roniano male inteso," in **LXIX**, V, 11, 1902, pp. 467-507 . **CCIV**

C. Pauli, in *Altitalische Studien*, IV, 1885, preface . . **CCV**

————, *Eine vorgriechische Inschrift von Lemnos*, 2nd ed.,
Leipzig, 1894 . . . . **CCVI**

G. Pellegrini, "Tombe greche arcaiche e tomba grecosanni-
tica a tholos della necropoli di Cuma," in **LXIII**, XIII,
1903, 200-94 . . . . **CCVII**

C. Peter, *Zur Kritik der Quellen der älteren römischen
Geschichte*, Halle, 1879 . . . . . **CCVIII**

A. Piganiol, *Essai sur les origines de Rome*, Paris, 1917 . **CCIX**

L. Pigorini, *Le abitazioni lacustri di Peschiera nel lago di
Garda* (Atti della R. Accad. dei Lincei, Classe di scienze
morali, ser. III, i, 295 *ff.*), Rome, 1877 . . . **CCX**

————, *Terramara dell'età del bronzo situata in Castione
de'Marchesi* (in *id.*, viii), Rome, 1883 . . . **CCXI**

————, "La terramara Castellazzo di Fontanellato nella
provincia di Parma," in **LXIII**, I, 1892, 121-54 . . **CCXII**

G. Pinza, "Monumenti primitivi di Roma e del Lazio antico,"
in **LXIII**, XV, 1905, 5-844 . . . . . **CCXIII**

BIBLIOGRAPHY

R. v. Planta, *Grammatik der oskisch-umbrischen Dialekte*, Strasburg, 1892-1897 . . . . . **CCXIV**

E. Pottier, *Musée national du Louvre, Catalogue des vases antiques de terre cuite*, Paris, 1896-1906 . . **CCXV**

E. Poulsen, *Etruscan Tomb-paintings, their Subjects and Significance*, English translation by Ing. Andersen, Oxford, 1922 . . . . . **CCXVI**

W. Ridgeway, *The Early Age of Greece*, Cambridge, 1901 . **CCXVII**

L. Robin, *La pensée grecque et les origines de l'esprit scientifique*, in " L'Évolution de l'Humanité," XIII, Paris, 1923 . . . . . . **CCXVIII**

A. Rosenberg, *Einleitung und Quellenkunde zur römischen Geschichte*, Berlin, 1921 . . . . . **CCXIX**

P. Roussel, *Delos, colonie athénienne*, Paris, 1916 . . **CCXX**

R. C. Sands, *The Client Princes of the Roman Empire under the Republic*, Cambridge, 1909 . . . . **CCXX***bis*

A. Schulten, " Numantia, eine topographisch-historische untersuchung," in **XXVII**, Neue Folge, VIII, 4, 1905 . **CCXX***ter*

————, *Numantia. Die Ergebnisse der Ausgrabungen*, 1905-1912. I, *Die Keltiberer und ihre Krieg mit Rom*, Munich, 1914 . . . . . . **CCXXI**

W. Schulze, " Zur Geschichte lateinischer Eigennamen," in **XXVII**, Neue Folge, V, 1904 . . . . **CCXXII**

G. Sergi, *Origine e diffusione della stirpe mediterranea*, Rome, 1895 . . . . . . **CCXXIII**

W. Soltau, *Die Anfänge der römischen Geschichtschreibung*, Leipzig, 1909 . . . . . . **CCXXIV**

————, *Römsiche Chronologie*, Friburg-en-Brisgau, 1889 . **CCXXV**

E. Taubler, *Imperium romanum. Studien zur Entwicklungsgeschichte des römischen Reichs*, I. *Die Staatsverträge und Vertragsverhältnisse*, Leipzig-Berlin, 1914 **CCXXVI**

H. Thédenat, *Le Forum romain*, 5th ed., Paris, 1911 . **CCXXVII**

W. Thomsen, " Remarques sur la parenté de la langue étrusque " (Bulletin de l'Academie des Sciences et Lettres de Denmark, 1899, 4, 373-98), Copenhagen . **CCXXVIII**

A. Torp, *Etruskische Beiträge*, Leipzig, 1902-1903 . . **CCXXIX**

————, *Die vorgriechische Inschrift auf Lemnos*, Christiania, 1906 . . . . **CCXXX**

D. Vaglieri, *Ostia, cenni storici e guida*, Rome, 1914 . **CCXXXI**

N. des Vergers, *L'Étrurie et les Étrusques*, Paris, 1862-1864 . . . . **CCXXXII**

A. Walde, *Ueber älteste sprachliche Beziehungen zwischen Kelten und Italikern*, Innsbruck, 1917 . . . **CCXXXIII**

F. Weege, *Etruskische Malerei*, Halle, 1921 . . . **CCXXXIV**

BIBLIOGRAPHY

G. Willems, *Le Sénat de la République romaine,* Louvain,
1878-1883 . . . . . . **CCXXXV**

G. Wissowa, *Religion und Kultus der Rœmer,* 2nd. ed.,
Munich, 1912 . . . . . . **CCXXXVI**

————, " Septimontium und Subura," in *Satura Via-
drina,* Vratislavia, 1896, 1-19 (cf. *Gesammelte
Abhandlungen zur römischen Religion und Stadt-
geschichte,* Munich, 1904) . . . . **CCXXXVII**

V. MAPS AND PLANS

*Carta dei dintorni di Roma secondo le osservazione di
W. Gell et A. Nibby, et analisi storico-topografico dei
dintorni di Roma,* 2nd ed., Rome, 1849 . . **CCXXXVIII**

*Carta geologica di Roma pubblicata dal R. ufficio geologico
su rilevamento del tenente generale,* A. Verri, Novara,
1915 . . . . **CCXXXIX**

R. Lanciani, *Forma Urbis Romœ,* Milan, 1893-1901 . **CCXL**

" Rilievo planimetrico e altimetrico del Palatino, eseguito
dagli allievi della Scaola d'applicazione per gli
ingegneri " (in **LXV**, 1904, 43-46), Rome, 1903 . **CCXLI**

INDEX

Headings already included in the Contents have in general been omitted.

INDEX

INDEX

Golasecca cemetery, 167
Governor, provincial, powers of, 328 f.
Greek colonization of Italy, 24, 36, 52
Greeks, influence of, on Rome, 97

Habitations : Neolithic, 26
  Bronze Age, 30
  Latian, 70, 80, 84, 96, 109
  See also Architecture
Hannibal, 288 ff., 303, 318
Hecatæus quoted, 4
Hellanicus quoted, 5, 14, 54, 60
Hernici, distribution of, 42
  relations with Rome, 147, 172, 183, 221
Herodotus quoted, 4, 43, 50, 52, 54, 60, 161
Hesiod quoted, 4
Hiero, 155, 163, 249, 272
Himera, Battle of, 154, 210
Homer cited, 4
Hut-urns, 68-69, 84

Iapyges, 42, 52, 62, 130, 138, 161
Illyria, geography of, 246
Illyrians, 41, 52, 286, 306, 344
Immigration or influence, 38
Imperium, 327
Indo-European languages, 46, 58
Ionians, 42
Istria, campaigns in, 285, 312
Italici, 43, 48, 69, 130
Italy, origin of name, 43, 131

Jews, treaty with Rome, 309
Jus commercii and *jus connubii*, 184, 224, 228, 242
Jus honorum and *jus suffragii*, 183, 223, 226
Justinian quoted, 14, 169, 285

Languages of Italy, 42, 130
  of Roman State, 186
Latian civilization, 69
Latini, distribution of, 41, 69
Latin League : relations with Rome, 145, 172, 182
  dissolved, 184, 228
League, idea of, 73
Legion, constitution of, 231
Lemnos (?) Etruscan inscription from, 55, 59
Levy, mechanism of, 232
Lex provinciæ, 328
Ligurians, 41, 45, 47, 51, 66, 69, 100, 105, 130, 169, 282
Livy : alleged credulity of, 19
  quoted, 10, 11, 15, 18, 23, 71, 78, 94, 99, 166, 180, 197, 211, 327, 336, 343, 346
Lucanians, 41
Lusitanians, 267, 316, 318

Macedonia, 248, 253
  wars with, 258, 299
  organization of, 344
Macer, L. Licinius, 17
Magistracy, Roman conception of, 331
Malaria, influence of, 68, 71, 76, 79
Mamertines, 210, 249, 258, 260, 271
Marseilles : foundation of, 101
  relations with Rome, 319
  thalassocracy of, 210
Marsi, 70
Marzabotto ruins, 108 ff., 157
Massacres by Romans, 267, 318
Massalia. See Marseilles
Massinissa, 250, 259, 268, 296, 321
Mastarna (= Servius Tullius), 114
Mercenaries : employment of, 164, 171, 191
  forbidden, 278, 281
Metals, use of : copper, 28, 38, 68
  bronze, 30, 35, 49, 85
  iron, 34, 38, 51, 69, 85, 97
Milan : founded, 166
  captured by Romans, 285
Military pay, introduction of, 150
Military service, conditions of, 231 ff.
Milo, 215
Mines in Macedonia, 343
Mommsen, 2
Mundus of the Palatine, 16, 88
Municipium, 220, 226

Nævius quoted, 15
Nail, Capitoline, reckoning by, 7, 11
Naples : founded, 65, 101
  and Samnites, 161
  Athenians at, 163
  relations with Rome, 200, 229
National Italian feeling, growth of, 172
Navy, building of, 272, 276
Neolithic remains, 26, 68
Niebuhr cited, 2, 8, 55

Officers commanding allied troops, 234
Oppian, village on, 87
Oppida, 71, 79, 83
Orosius quoted, 211, 233
Orsi cited, 21, 27, 29, 30, 33
Oscans, territory of, 42
Ostia, colonization of, 92, 96, 225

Pæligni, 41, 53, 70
Pais cited, 2
Palæolithic remains, 25, 68
Palatine : village on, 69, 75-76, 116
  fortifications of, 134
Palatual, 79, 81, 87
Pastoral life of early Latins, 72, 81, 139
  of Gauls, 169
  of Samnites, 187

369

INDEX